Food Preparation *and* Cooking

Levels 1 and 2

Roy Hayter

Hotel & Catering Training Company

HOTEL&
CATERING
TRAINING
COMPANY

THOMSON

Australia • Canada • Mexico • Singapore • Spain • United Kingdom • United States

Acknowledgements

Industry liaison and research

Pam Frediani

Advice with the text

Clive Finch, Visiting Professor, Thames Valley University

Industry and college reviewers

Pam Rotherforth, Gardner Merchant

Peter Little, Brunel College of Arts and Technology, Bristol

Ian Davidson and Jean McNally, Edinburgh's Telford College

Graphics

Tom Lines

Line illustrations

Diana Beatty and John Woodcock

Cover photographs

Tom Stockill

Text photographs

Chris Browning, Simon Green, Richard Kirby, Christine Osborne, David Spears, Tom Stockill, Keith Turnbull

Photographic locations

The Bellhouse, Beaconsfield, De Vere Hotels

Oxford Brookes University

Shenley Church Inn, Milton Keynes, Toby Restaurants

Thames Valley University, Slough

Colour-coded chopping boards and knives kindly loaned by Staines Catering Equipment, London

Also: Butlin's South Coast World, Bognor Regis; E. Coaney & Co, Birmingham; Ealing Hospital, Southall; Gratte Brothers, Knebworth; John Layton & Co, London; Lewisham College, London; McDonald's, Wandsworth; MEL Philips, Crawley; Pizza Express, Clapham

Loan of photographs

Forte Crest, Milton Keynes; Marlow Foods; Harry Ramsden's; Pizza Hut; Toby Restaurants

Providing and reviewing new material

Pizza Hut – Section 24

Harry Ramsden's – Section 23

Sea Fish Industry Authority – Sections 9, 22 and 23

Recipes

Danny Stevenson (other recipes as acknowledged in the text)

Contributing industry procedures, recipes and other material

APV Moffat (UK Branch) Limited (for Blue Seal): Grant Emery

The Boddington Pub Company: Chris Gillespie

The British Egg Information Service

The Butter Council: Jayne Higgs

Catering & Allied Services: Sarah Banner

Caterveg: Mary Scott Morgan

The Chilled Food Association: Alison Cook

CCG Services Limited: Barbara Copland

Clementine Churchill Hospital, Harrow

Compass Retail Catering Division: Nikki Cartwright

Coppid Beech Hotel, Bracknell: Neil Thrift and Mark Morris

De Vere Hotels: Alan Makinson

Department of Health: Marcia Fryer

Everards Brewery Limited: Marshall Hodgkinson

Falcon Catering Equipment: Kara Lewis

The Flour Advisory Bureau

Forte Crest, Milton Keynes: Ronnie Clark

The Fresh Fruit and Vegetable Information Bureau: John Meagan

Frialator International Limited: Alan Flude

Garland Commercial Ranges Limited: Hazel Hudson

Gleneagles Hotel: William McGuigan

Haldane Foods for VegeMince

HCIMA library and information service: Rosemary Morrison and Kalpana Amin

Ind Coope Retail Limited: Lee Hubbucks

Jeyes Cleaning Products Limited: Keith Wishart

Joint Hospitality Industry Congress: Tom Miller

Juno UK Limited: Barbara Eldred

Lockhart Catering Equipment

Long Clawson Dairy Limited: Christine Foster

Lucas Ingredients for Wheatpro

Marlow Foods: Laura Howarth

McCain Foods (GB) Limited

McDonald's Restaurants Limited: Jeanette Row

McDougalls Catering Foods Limited: Jane Hildred

McDougalls RHM Foods Limited: Catherine Nicholls

Meat and Livestock Commission

Ministry of Agriculture, Fisheries and Food: Richard Melville and Christine Battison

Mornflake Oats

The National Dairy Council

Nestlé UK Limited for recipes by Buitoni, Crosse & Blackwell, Dufrais and Sarsons

Perfect Pizza Limited: Dulcie Briscoe

Pizza Express plc: Nick Taylor

Pizza Hut (UK) Limited: Ingrid Newbould

The Potato Marketing Board: Tony Reeve

Harry Ramsden's: Jill Hillard

The Rice Bureau: Matthew Guyer

Roadchef Motorways Limited: Marian Graveson

Robot Coupe (UK) Limited: Martin Bates

Safeway Nutrition Advice Service: Jayne Fisher

Seafish Industry Authority

The Shellfish Association of Great Britain: Dr Eric Edwards

Stakis plc: Douglas Cameron

Stott Benham Systems Limited: Mike Lang

Sutcliffe Catering Group Limited: Jan Adamson

Toby Restaurants: David Hunt

University of Sheffield: David McKown

US Quality Bean Information Bureau: Penny Clifton

The Vegetarian Society: Heather Mairs, Jane Billinge

JD Wetherspoon plc: Jane Biss

Whitbread Inns: Mike Cowan

Also helped with information and material

The British Chicken Information Service: Phillipa Browning

Convotherm Limited: Randall Webster

The Dutch Dairy Bureau: Ann Hill

Electrolux Foodservice Equipment (UK): Mike Lang

The Frozen Food Information Service: Dawn Cook

Jolly Rodgers Seafood Restaurant, Ashford: Charles Rodgers

Kraft Jacobs Suchard Foodservice: Andy Huggett

The New Zealand Lamb Advisory Service: Stewart Pope

Peerless Products: Alison Young

Quadrant: Sheila McCarty

Tartex: Vere Audrey

Van den Burgh Professional Foods: Alison Jump

Zanussi: Tim Walsh

Every effort has been made to trace all the copyright holders. If any have been inadvertently overlooked, the publishers will be pleased to make the necessary arrangements at the first opportunity.

NVQ/SVQ Food Preparation and Cooking

THOMSON

Food Preparation and Cooking

Copyright © Hotel and Catering Training Company Ltd and Thomson Learning 2000

The Thomson logo is a registered trademark used herein under licence.

For more information, contact Thomson Learning, High Holborn House; 50-51 Bedford Row, London WCIR 4LR or visit us on the World Wide Web at; http://www.thomsonlearning.co.uk

British Library Cataloguing-in-Publication Data
A catalogue record for this book is available from the British Library

ISBN 1-86152-686-5

First published 1992 by Macmillan Press Ltd
Reprinted 1993 and 1994
Revised edition 1995
Reprinted 2000, 2002 and 2004 by Thomson Learning

In association with
HOTEL & CATERING TRAINING COMPANY
International House, High Street, Ealing, London W5 5DB

Printed in China by Central Printing Press

Qualification matrix

Level 1

All these units required for the qualification:

NG1	Maintain a safe and secure working environment
1NG4	Develop effective working relationships
1ND1	Clean food production areas, equipment and utensils
1ND2	Maintain and handle knives
1ND12	Maintain hygiene in food storage, preparation and cooking

plus four of these units:

1ND3	Prepare and microwave food
1ND4	Prepare and fry food
1ND5	Prepare and bake food
1ND6	Prepare, boil, poach and steam food
1ND7	Prepare and grill food
1ND8	Prepare and finish reconstituted food
1ND9	Prepare vegetables and fruit
1ND10	Prepare cold and hot sandwiches and rolls
1ND11	Prepare, cook and assemble food for service
1ND14	Prepare and griddle food

Level 2

All these units required for the qualification:

NG1	Maintain a safe and secure working environment
2NG4	Create and maintain effective working relationships
1ND1	Clean food production areas, equipment and utensils
1ND2	Maintain and handle knives
2ND22	Maintain and promote hygiene in food storage, preparation and cooking

plus six units:

of which at least two must be from:

2ND1	Prepare and cook basic meat, poultry and offal dishes
2ND2	Prepare and cook basic fish dishes
2ND4	Prepare and cook basic sauces and soups
2ND18	Prepare and cook vegetables for basic hot dishes and salads

and the balance from:

2ND3	Prepare and cook basic cold and hot desserts
2ND5	Prepare and cook basic pulse dishes
2ND6	Prepare and cook basic rice dishes
2ND7	Prepare and cook basic dough products
2ND8	Prepare and cook basic pastry dishes
2ND9	Prepare, cook and finish basic cakes, sponges and scones
2ND10	Prepare and cook basic egg dishes
2ND12	Prepare and cook basic pasta dishes
2ND19	Prepare and cook basic vegetable protein dishes

Freestanding units (not required for qualification):

2ND11	Receive, handle and store food deliveries
2ND13	Prepare and present food for cold presentation
2ND14	Prepare and cook basic shellfish dishes
2ND15	Cook-chill food
2ND16	Cook-freeze food
2ND17	Clean and maintain cutting equipment
2ND20	Prepare and cook battered fish and chipped potatoes
2ND21	Prepare, assemble and cook pizza products

About this book

Your route to a qualification

To gain a NVQ/SVQ in food preparation and cooking, you need the five core units which deal with safety, hygiene, handling knives, cleaning tasks and working relationships. In addition, you need a certain number of units on the preparation and cooking of different types of food: four for level 1, six for level 2. You can choose these from quite a wide range (see qualification matrix on page iii), to suit the work you are doing, your interests, and your career plans.

How this book is structured

This book covers the core or mandatory units and all the food preparation and cooking units at levels 1 and 2 – some 39 in all – to meet your needs now, and in future years as your career develops. Some are grouped, some are in their own section.

To help you find your way, the NVQ/SVQ unit and element numbers are given above the main headings used within each section. These are printed in purple.

The book:

- begins with the level 1 food preparation and cooking units – **Section 1**

- works through the mandatory units for levels 1 and 2 – **Sections 2 to 7**

- continues with the level 2 food preparation and cooking units – **Sections 8 to 20**

- and concludes with the 'additional' level 2 units – **Sections 21 to 26**.

While not necessary for a Level 2 NVQ/SVQ, the additional units demonstrate that you have the skills and knowledge relevant to particular types of operation, e.g. cook-chill, shellfish, and pizza.

How to use this book

This book can be used in any way which suits your needs:

- dip into it at the pages which catch your interest – perhaps because of a photograph, an industry procedure, a recipe or a graphic

- to find information on a particular skill or technique, piece of equipment, type of food or recipe – use the index at the end of the book to find the page numbers

- concentrate on the sections which relate to the units you are preparing to be assessed in – the contents page will help you find these quickly.

As you become familiar with the book, you will notice that the section titles relate very closely to the titles of the NVQ/SVQ units.

This book and your assessment

The main text in each section helps with the three aspects which relate to your assessment:

- what you need to do – as defined in the NVQ/SVQ performance criteria for each element

- the situations, types of food, equipment, etc. which apply – as set out in the NVQ/SVQ range list. The headings within each section use the same or similar words, or you will find the range words printed in *italics* in the text

- what you need to know – as given in the NVQ/SVQ underpinning knowledge statements.

Skills checks

To help you find out what stage you are already at, to monitor progress as you work towards a unit, and to prepare for assessment, each section includes a skills check. The skills check summarises the performance criteria for the two (or sometimes, three) elements of the unit, and the range list. There is a tick box by each statement to use as you wish.

Activities

These reinforce key points from the text (through the graphics and photographs), and help you check what you have learned. Your assessor will ask similar questions to check your underpinning knowledge.

There are activity pages for each level 1 unit, for the core units and for the level 2 units on meat, fish, sauces/soups and vegetables. You need two of these four units for a level 2 qualification.

Knowledge checks

The knowledge checks for each of the level 2 units give reminders, guidance and key points for the various topics/subject areas you will be questioned on by your assessor. As you become familiar with the NVQ/SVQ structure, you will find that there are similar questions for each element on safety, hygiene and healthy eating – this is because of the importance of these aspects to your work in the catering and hospitality industry.

Introducing
food preparation
and **cooking**

Preparing vegetables and fruit

Whatever the time of year, caterers can obtain most vegetables and fruit. Produce flown in chilled conditions from the other side of the world will be quite expensive. Nevertheless, the choice ranges from the familiar to the exotic, and quality standards are very high.

The terms *vegetable* and *fruit* mean different things to different people. Vegetables are thought of as savoury in flavour, while fruits are usually sweet (with a few exceptions like the lemon).

Follow the colour-coding system in your workplace for chopping boards and knives.

Element 1
Preparing vegetables

Carefully prepared and cooked, vegetables are the highlight of a tasty, enjoyable meal. At the same time, they are a valuable source of health-giving vitamins and minerals. But vegetables are sensitive to poor treatment. Some bruise and discolour readily. Some lose their texture, others their flavour.

Bacteria of the type that cause food poisoning find their way into the kitchen via the soil on vegetables. Slugs, ants and similar creatures can work their way right into the centre of vegetables. Thorough washing removes both sorts of problem. When storing and handling vegetables which might carry bacteria and soil, keep them away from other foods.

Types of vegetable and quality points

A useful way of classifying vegetables is to think in terms of what part of the plant is eaten:

- *roots* – carrots, turnips, etc.
- *tubers* – potatoes
- *bulbs* – onions, leeks, etc.
- *leaves* – cabbage, spinach, lettuce, watercress, etc.
- *stems* – celery, fennel, asparagus, etc.
- *vegetable fruits* – tomatoes, peppers, etc.

In general, fresh vegetables should be:

- clean, no soil – some soil may be acceptable on new potatoes and on organic produce
- compact and crisp
- of good colour, shape and appearance
- free from damage – no bruising or cuts
- free from disease or pest damage.

Check that frozen and pre-prepared fresh vegetables have not passed the use-by or best-before date, and that the packaging is in good condition.

Good knife skills make tasks like this much quicker and safer.

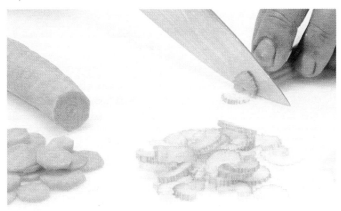

Storage

Bruising occurs and diseases are quickly passed on if vegetables are left tightly packed in bags, sacks or boxes. For fresh vegetables:

- remove from polybags, or punch holes for ventilation. Loosen or remove clingfilm
- store in a cool dry place, preferably on racks so that air can circulate freely around each vegetable
- some vegetables are best stored in a refrigerator, preferably one reserved solely for vegetables, or in salad drawers in a general-purpose refrigerator
- always separate blemished from perfect produce.

Root vegetables should stay fresh for 5 to 6 days. Green vegetables should be supplied fresh daily if possible, or at most every 2 to 3 days.

New deliveries of frozen food should be stored so that they are used after current stocks. If you rotate stocks, there is less risk of items passing their best-before date (after which they should not be used).

Preparation methods

There are some general rules, which help keep the high nutrition value of vegetables:

- prepare (and cook) vegetables as close to service as possible
- use sharp knives
- only peel vegetables when necessary, and then the minimum amount – most of the nutritional content lies close to the skin
- don't soak vegetables in cold water after you have prepared them (except for potatoes) – the vitamins dissolve out of the vegetable, into the water.

Washing is done to remove any remnants of soil from the vegetable. Even when there is no soil or dirt visible, thorough washing is recommended. This is because you do not know what the vegetable has been exposed to, during its growth, harvesting and the various stages before it reaches your workplace. The exception is when the supplier states READY TO EAT, PRE-WASHED (or words like this) on the label.

Peeling is done to remove the outer skin of certain vegetables – because it is inedible (e.g. onion skin), or because it is not required for the dish (e.g. for roast potatoes). For large-scale catering, vegetables may come pre-peeled, or large machines are used to do the job. In other situations, a hand-held peeler is the quickest way, or you may find it easier with a very sharp trimming knife.

Some vegetables are too large to hold in your hand to peel, e.g. swedes. Put the vegetable on a chopping board and, using a large cook's knife, cut down the sides (the orange on the previous page is being peeled like this).

Trimming gets rid of small blemishes, outer leaves and inedible parts of the vegetable. It is also a way of giving the vegetable a more uniform shape.

When washing, peeling and trimming vegetables:

- begin with a clean sink – if you have a sink which is used at other times for washing pots and pans, etc., clean the bottom and sides thoroughly before starting work on the vegetables
- work tidily – don't make more clearing up for yourself by scattering peelings all over the wall and floor
- be well organised – if using a double sink unit, or a sink and a bowl, use one for the washing, peeling and trimming, the other for the prepared vegetables, and a second washing
- watch for hidden dirt – with lettuce and cabbage of the loose-leaf varieties, celery and leeks, soil gets between the leaves or stems, sometimes right to the centre
- avoid damaging the vegetable – lettuce leaves will bruise if roughly handled
- find out what the vegetable is being used for – the root has to remain on onions which are to be chopped, and leeks which are to be cooked whole, otherwise these vegetables fall apart
- peel and trim carefully so as not to waste good parts of the vegetable – the shape you want can usually be achieved by trimming a little at a time, while taking too much off makes the situation worse.

Slicing and *chopping* are two similar ways of preparing vegetables. Which is used depends on what the vegetable is required for, and to some extent on its shape. The terms slicing and chopping can even be used in different ways by different people. So before starting, check you are doing what is required for the final dish. Take the example of an onion. When it is for a:

- salad – quite thin slices are easy to chew and look attractive
- thick soup or sauce, used alongside other vegetables such as leek, carrot and celery – rough cubes, not particularly small, will give their flavour to the dish. They are then strained out and discarded, or puréed if both flavour and body are required
- stew, soup or sauce, when the vegetables are part of the dish, contribute to its flavour but should not dominate the final appearance – fine chopping to produce small, evenly sized cubes will deliver the right result.

Preparing fruit

Fruit offers an unlimited range of colours, shapes, flavours and textures. The pleasing appearance of fruit is a large part of the enjoyment people get from eating it. But many varieties are at their best for one or two days only, and easily get damaged. So to serve fruit at its best, you need to know what quality points to look for, and how to handle and prepare it properly.

Bacteria that cause food poisoning are not usually present in fruit. But fruit does attract bacteria of the type that cause moulds. It is also possible that the fruit has soil on its skin, and that bacteria are present in the soil.

Types of fruit and quality points

There are a great many varieties of fruit available, but the main ones can be put into three groups:

- *soft* fruits – strawberries, raspberries, etc.
- *hard* fruits – apples and pears
- *citrus* fruits – grow only in warm or hot countries, e.g. oranges, grapefruit, lemons and limes.

In general, fresh fruit should be:

- good size and shape – no wide variation in size and shape in any one box
- good colour, with no signs of bruising
- fresh appearance with no sign of wilting, ageing or insect damage
- clean, although with freshly picked local farm produce or organically grown items, the presence of a little soil is acceptable.

Packages of pre-prepared and frozen fruit should be in good condition. Discard the fruit if it has passed its use-by or best-before date.

Storage

Remove any fruit which is bruised, damaged or overripe. Depending on the variety, it may be possible to trim off the damaged parts, and use the remainder sliced or chopped in a fruit salad or puréed for a fruit sauce.

No fruit should be stored packed tightly together, or in multiple layers. The exception is when the fruit can be kept in the special packaging in which it was shipped – e.g. a box of apples will have moulded cardboard trays for each layer, and each apple may be individually wrapped in paper.

With strawberries, raspberries and other soft fruits, remove any plastic wrapping, and keep the fruit in the refrigerator.

Apples are usually kept chilled to retain their crispness. Pears are ripened in a warm place. Most varieties can be kept in their unripe, hard condition in a refrigerator for a week or longer. Once ripe, they should be used within a day or so.

Oranges, lemons, grapefruit and other citrus fruit should be kept cool, but not refrigerated.

Never put bananas in the refrigerator – they go black rapidly and loose flavour.

Frozen fruit should not be kept beyond the best-before date on the packaging. Do not over-stack or roughly handle packets of frozen fruit, as the contents are quite delicate.

Preparation methods

Washing should be done just before the fruit is required, and carefully to avoid damage to the fruit. Place soft fruits in a large colander, and hold under a gentle stream of cold water running from the tap.

Even if you will be peeling the fruit (e.g. an apple or orange for a fruit salad), you should wash it first. Small pieces of dirt or traces of insecticides may remain on the fruit from when it was grown and harvested. If so, you will pick these up on your fingers.

Allow the fruit to drain fully after washing. If necessary, carefully dry with kitchen paper.

Peeling to remove the outer skin of fruit is necessary when the skin tastes unpleasant, or is rather coarse for the intended use. Strawberries and raspberries are never peeled. Apples are peeled sometimes, e.g. for an apple sauce or the filling of a pie, but not when the apple is being baked whole, or the peel will add colour and texture to a fruit salad. Grapes are sometimes peeled for a fruit salad, oranges always are.

Take care during peeling not to remove too much fruit. With citrus fruit, the white pith that lies just under the skin should also be removed. Sometimes this can be quite thick.

After peeling fruit, some *trimming* may be needed to remove remaining pieces of pith, small areas of damage, or pips.

Slicing or *chopping* is done when small pieces of the fruit are needed in a salad, to make a sauce, or as garnish for a meat or fish dish, for example. Check what shape and size are wanted beforehand. If the fruit is being puréed, rough chopping or slicing will be sufficient. For a fruit salad, apples and oranges are usually sliced, while melon will be cut or chopped into small squares.

1 What can vegetables and fruit bring into your kitchen that you don't want to spread to other food?

2 Why should you keep unwashed vegetables and fruit away from other food?

3 If the sink is used for washing pots, pans, etc., what must you do before washing vegetables or fruit in it?

4 Why must you clean your preparation area and equipment thoroughly after washing and preparing vegetables and fruit?

5 What can happen if care is not taken with knives used for preparation?

6 For the two vegetables illustrated here, and two others used in your workplace, how can you tell they are the right quality for their intended use?

7 What vegetables and fruit would you peel like this? What is the name of the knife used?

8 Pick two of these vegetables. Where and how they should be stored?

9 Choose two of these fruits. Where and how they should be stored?

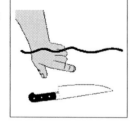

10 This peach was blanched (i.e. dipped in boiling water for 30 seconds, then rinsed cold). What other items can you blanch to make them easier to peel?

11 When you put a delivery of frozen vegetables or fruit in the freezer, what should you do with the stock that is already there? Why?

12 State two points you should look for to check the quality of a packet of frozen vegetables or fruit

NVQ
SVQ
Skills check
Prepare vegetables and fruit
Unit 1ND9
leve **1**

Use this to check your progress against the performance criteria (e.g. PC1 to PC6 below) for each element.

You must demonstrate competence in different situations to which the element applies (the range). The words with grey triangles by them will remind you of these situations.

Element 1

Prepare vegetables

Get your preparation area and equipment ready for use ☐ PC1

Prepare vegetables of the correct type, quality and quantity ☐ PC2

▲ Types: roots, tubers, bulbs, leaves, stems, vegetable fruits (tomato)

Use appropriate preparation methods ☐ PC3

▲ Washing, peeling, slicing, chopping, trimming

Store correctly vegetables not for immediate use ☐ PC4

Deal effectively with problems relating to food and equipment ☐ PC5

Do your work in an organised, efficient and safe manner ☐ PC6

Element 2

Prepare fruit

Get your preparation area and equipment ready for use ☐ PC1

Prepare fruit of the correct type, quality and quantity ☐ PC2

▲ Types of fruit: hard, soft, citrus

Use appropriate preparation methods ☐ PC3

▲ Washing, peeling, slicing, chopping, trimming

Store correctly fruit not for immediate use ☐ PC4

Deal effectively with problems relating to food and equipment ☐ PC5

Do your work in an organised, efficient and safe manner ☐ PC6

Preparing cold and hot sandwiches and rolls

There is almost no limit to the imaginative ways you can prepare sandwiches and rolls.

The bread comes in different shapes – from cottage and bloomer, to cob and plait, and is made with different types of flour – from wheatgerm and wholemeal, to soft-grain or stoneground. In addition there are rye breads, pittas and baguettes adopted from other countries, or novelty breads flavoured with herbs and spices.

To complement these, an even bigger choice of fillings is available, from cold meats of various sorts, and classic favourites like smoked salmon, to more exotic combinations such as fried onion and pepper slices and cooked spicy sausage. Your aim is to produce something appropriate to the occasion:

- fresh and appetising with a good flavour – most sandwiches do not keep well (unless wrapped very carefully). The bread dries and curls up at the edges, or if it has a soft, moist filling, becomes soggy
- easy to handle and eat – a chunky sandwich is acceptable for a pub lunch, but not for an elegant tea
- satisfying – to stimulate the appetite if it is served at a cocktail party, to satisfy the appetite if it is a lunchtime snack.

It helps to sell sandwiches and rolls when customers can see the filling.

Preparing cold sandwiches and rolls

The very highest standards of hygiene are essential when preparing sandwiches and rolls. There is no final cooking to kill any harmful bacteria. If the products are prepared in advance, and not adequately chilled, bacteria have the ideal conditions to multiply to dangerous numbers.

Organise your work area before you start, so that you have everything to hand that you will need. For example:

- *on the left of your chopping board*: stack of sliced bread
- *at the top*: containers of spreadings, fillings and garnishes, arranged in the order in which they will be used
- *to the right*: palette knife for spreading, sharp knives for cutting, spoons for fillings like mayonnaise, a damp cloth (or supply of disposable sanitising wipes) for cleaning the board down between operations
- *nearby*: dustbin, refrigerator, washing facilities, any cooking equipment you will need to use.

Work in a logical sequence. For example:

1 Cream spreadings and prepare all your fillings.

2 Slice the bread.

3 Spread all the bread.

4 Place the filling on to each bottom slice.

5 Cover with the top slice.

6 Stack into piles, about 4 rounds deep, and cut into halves or quarters as required.

Types of bread

There are three main groups of bread which are filled to make sandwiches, etc.:

- loaves of bread, which may be *sliced* or *unsliced*. If your workplace makes many sandwiches regularly, the bread may come sliced to a specific thickness or shape by the baker (e.g. along the length of a loaf). Alternatively this can be done on the premises using bread-slicing machines. Hand-sliced bread is ideal for the chunkier sandwich, made to order
- *rolls, baps* and *baguettes*, which are usually single-portion size, although larger varieties can be cut into two or three pieces for smaller portions. Rolls may have soft or hard/cripsy crusts. Baps are usually soft, baguettes (narrow French sticks) crispy. Baguettes can be sliced in half lengthwise, leaving a hinge. Alternatively, make two parallel cuts running the length of the baguette. Rolls and baps can be treated similarly, or have their tops sliced off and replaced as a 'hat' on the filling
- *pitta*, which is a thin, flat bread, oval in shape. By slitting along one side, you can open out the centre cavity to take a suitable filling.

Fillings and preparation methods

Before fillings are put in sandwiches, the bread needs to be *spread* with butter, margarine, low-fat spread, mayonnaise, or a combination of these. The spread provides flavour and stops the bread from soaking up moisture from the filling. With some fillings like cucumber and tomato slices, the spread has limited effect, so these are best made to order.

Butter can be salted or unsalted and flavoured, for example, with mustard, horseradish, lemon, garlic, parsley or tarragon. Sweet flavourings (use with unsalted butter) include cinnamon, honey and orange.

Spreadings should be used soft so that they coat the bread smoothly and do not damage its surface. In most kitchens, butter will not take long to become soft. For reasons of hygiene, avoid leaving butter out overnight, or even for a few hours. A few seconds in the microwave on the defrost program will soften butter quickly.

When spreading by hand, use a round-bladed or palette knife. With a smooth, sweeping movement, spread right to the edge. A short dabbing motion takes longer, and can damage the slices of bread.

Fillings can be:

- *sliced* – e.g. cucumber, cold meats and poultry
- *chopped* – e.g. raw onion, lettuce, hard-boiled egg
- *grated* – e.g. Cheddar cheese, apple
- *mixed* – e.g. flaked tuna fish with mayonnaise
- *mashed* or *puréed* – e.g. smoked salmon trimmings with cream cheese.

Some may first need to be:

- *peeled* – e.g. banana or freshly-cooked beetroot
- or *shelled* – e.g. hard-boiled egg.

Making healthy sandwiches

Bread is low in fat. It is a good source of fibre-rich starch, protein, vitamins and minerals essential to good health.

For healthier sandwiches, reduce the amount of fat in spreadings and fillings by using:
- low fat spreads and spread thinly
- lower fat cheeses
- lean meats, fish or skinless chicken

increase the fibre by using:
- thickly sliced bread
- wholegrain or wholewheat bread
- vegetables such as lettuce, carrots, celery and sweetcorn
- pulses, nuts, dried fruits

reduce the salt by using
- other flavourings such as fresh herbs, lemon juice, low-fat yogurt, low fat/low salt dressings

---

Preparing hot sandwiches and rolls

The range of hot sandwiches and rolls and their fillings is very wide:

- a *roll, bap* or *baguette* with a hot filling, e.g. freshly grilled sausage, or bacon, cheese or a fried egg. Sometimes the bread is also warmed – in an oven or hot plate – or toasted

- *pitta bread* with a warm filling, e.g. sliced lamb for a Doner kebab

- *toasted sandwiches* – two or more slices of freshly toasted bread with a cold filling, e.g. prawns and cream cheese. The filling (depending on the type) can be hot, e.g. minute steak, or if it is ham and cheese, grilled on one of the pieces of toast, and the sandwich then completed

- *sealed toasted sandwiches,* so that the filling (e.g. chopped, cooked chicken and sweetcorn relish) is trapped inside. The filling and bread are cooked at the same time in a special contact grill.

Sometimes fillings are a combination of hot and cold items, e.g. hot bacon and a cold salad garnish (lettuce, sliced tomatoes, onion rings).

Finishing and presenting the sandwich

Hot sandwiches and rolls are at their best made to order. The ingredients can be prepared in advance. In a busy place, some of the ingredients may be pre-cooked and kept warm. But the final assembly or cooking should be done while the customer is waiting, and the sandwich served immediately.

When fillings are kept hot, the temperature should be not less than 63°C. Cold ingredients must be kept chilled, at 5°C or below. This is to prevent the growth of harmful bacteria.

Be careful to keep ingredients which might carry harmful bacteria separate from other foods. For example, salad items which have not been washed (and therefore might carry bacteria) should be stored apart from prepared salads and any cooked foods.

To avoid bacteria spreading via equipment, clean down your work area regularly. Use one set of knives, chopping boards, etc. for preparing cooked foods, and another for uncooked foods. Colour coding of utensils will help you recognise which is which.

1 When lifting a large, heavy tray (e.g. of bread), what precautions do you take to prevent back injury?

2 What might happen if sandwiches or rolls are kept unrefrigerated for some time?

3 If you are not careful, what harmful things might get into sandwiches during preparation?

4 Why is it dangerous to leave butter standing around in a warm kitchen? How should you soften it?

5 What are the minimum and the maximum temperatures at which food not required immediately for service must be kept?

6 Describe two attractive ways of presenting sandwiches.

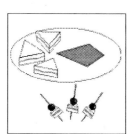

7 Describe four ways in which sandwiches and rolls can be made healthier.

8 How would you change this roll to appeal to the health-conscious customer?

9 Name three different styles or types of hot sandwich and roll.

10 Name four types of food which are suitable as hot sandwich and roll fillings.

11 When presenting a sandwich, why does it help sales if the customer can see immediately what the filling is?

12 What are your workplace rules for keeping sandwiches that have been prepared in advance?

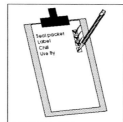

Use this to check your progress against the performance criteria (see page 4).

Element 1

Prepare cold sandwiches and rolls

Get your preparation area and equipment ready for use — PC1

Use bread and fillings of the right type, quality and quantity — PC2

▲ Bread: sliced and unsliced bread, rolls/baps/baguettes, pitta bread

▲ Fillings: fats/pastes/spreads, cooked meat/poultry, fish, eggs. salad/vegetables/fruit, cheeses, sauces/dressings/relishes

Use appropriate preparation methods — PC3

▲ Spreading, slicing/chopping, grating, mixing, mashing, shelling, peeling

Store correctly cold sandwiches and rolls not for immediate use — PC4

Clean preparation areas and equipment after use — PC5

Deal effectively with problems relating to food and equipment — PC6

Do your work in an organised, efficient and safe manner — PC7

Element 2

Prepare hot sandwiches and rolls

Get your preparation area and equipment ready for use — PC1

Use bread and fillings of the right type, quality and quantity — PC2

▲ Bread: filled roll/bap/filled baguette, toasted sandwich, filled pitta bread

▲ Fillings: hot meat/poultry/fish products, salads/vegetables/fruits, hot egg filling, cheese, sauces/relishes/dressing

Use appropriate preparation and cooking methods — PC3

Finish and present hot sandwiches and rolls — PC4

Clean preparation areas and equipment after use — PC5

Deal effectively with problems relating to food and equipment — PC6

Do your work in an organised efficient and safe manner — PC7

Unit 1ND11

Preparing, cooking and assembling food for service

In small operations, which offer a limited range of dishes, there may only be one member of staff on duty, or perhaps two or three at very busy periods. That means each person has a much wider range of tasks to do, from preparing, cooking and serving the food to washing up and removing the waste.

Element 1

Preparing food and kitchen areas for service

Good organisation will make your job easier. Don't clutter yourself up with things that you won't be needing for the task in hand. You might think, for example, that it will save time to take everything you want out of the freezer or storeroom on one trip. But if this means food is exposed to warm kitchen temperatures for some time, the practice is dangerous.

Hygiene and safe working practices are vital in all types of catering establishment. If your customers are watching you handle the food they are about to eat, they want to see only the highest standards.

Getting food ready for use

With pre-prepared and convenience foods, there is little or no preparation to do. But the quality of the product will suffer, and this can lead to expensive waste, if you do not follow instructions about storage and handling. Points to look out for include:

- *how to check the quality*

  What points to look for – e.g. packaging in good condition, cans not dented or blown, not beyond the best-before or use-by date?

- *how to store food ready for use*

  When should packaging be removed? Are there any special things to do when disposing of packaging (e.g. keep paper and cardboard separate for recycling)? What temperature should the food be kept at?

- *how to handle frozen items*

  Do you defrost the food before cooking? If so, do you remove the packaging? How long will defrosting take? Where should the food be kept during this time?

- *how to store the food when all the contents of a package have not been used*

  Is this acceptable? If so, what type of covering is required? At what temperature should it be kept?

Element 2

Cooking and assembling food for service

Remember customers eat at your place because they know what to expect. That's not just the look and taste of the food, but also how much they get – and this must be same as everyone else gets, and not different from what they got yesterday, or last week.

Use any written or pictorial aids to keep to the company's quality standards and portion control.

Pay attention to timings. You have to strike a balance – and it's not always easy – between cooking enough food for people not to be kept waiting, and cooking too much, when food will spoil because it has been kept hot for a long time.

The amount you cook at one time should not be more than the equipment can cope with:

- attempting to deep fry too many pieces of fish at once will result in an unpleasant tasting, fat-saturated product

- overloading the grill will make it difficult to turn the food over

- turning the fryer or grill temperature up won't cook the food much faster either – and it's very likely to lead to burning on the outside while the inside is undercooked.

Carefully follow instructions on how long food can be kept hot for, and how to dispose of food that has passed its time limit. Tell your manager of any difficulties.

Cooking or reheating food

Points of detail which you should check, include:

- *how to cook or reheat*

  Do you remove the cover? Do you pierce the wrapping? What oven temperature or microwave setting do you use? How long do you cook/reheat for?

- *how to check food is adequately cooked or reheated*

  What temperature should it reach at the centre? Do you check the temperature at several places with large items?

- *how to measure portion sizes*

  Is this a certain number per packet, by weight, by size, by using a particular size spoon?

- *how to present the finished dish*

  Is the dish garnished in a particular way? What sauces or accompaniments are provided or offered?

1 What can go wrong if your work area is not kept hygienic?

2 How do harmful bacteria spread from one food to another in a kitchen?

3 What other things might get into food and make it harmful to eat?

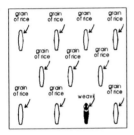

4 What rules should you follow when disposing of waste food and other rubbish?

5 Over what temperature range do bacteria most readily multiply? What is the safe temperature for keeping: a) hot food and b) cold food?

6 What should you do if you find the refrigerator or cold room is not operating at the right temperature?

7 Describe a safe way for defrosting frozen food. What can you do if you need to defrost food quickly?

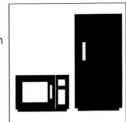

8 For dishes which are served hot, what is the temperature to which the food should be cooked/ reheated?

9 How long can food which is hot be held ready for service? What is the time limit for cold foods on display?

10 What should you do with food which has been held for service for longer than the stated period? Why is this important?

11 Whom should you inform if a customer complains about the food? What information should you make note of?

12 Describe some ways in which you can make food look attractive.

Use this to check your progress against the performance criteria (see page 4).

Element 1

Prepare food and kitchen areas for service

Get your preparation, cooking and storage areas, equipment and utensils ready for use — ☐ PC1+PC2

Use pre-prepared and convenience foods of right type, quality and quantity — ☐ PC3

Defrost frozen foods correctly, remove and dispose of packaging — ☐ PC4

Hold food stocks ready for use at correct temperature — ☐ PC5

Dispose of waste correctly — ☐ PC6

Deal effectively with problems relating to food and equipment — ☐ PC7

Do your work in an organised, efficient and safe manner — ☐ PC8

Element 2

Cook and assemble food products for service

Get your preparation, cooking and storage areas ready for use — ☐ PC1

Portion and prepare pre-prepared and convenience foods ready for cooking — ☐ PC2

Cook or reheat foods to specified temperature — ☐ PC3

Assemble cooked foods and other ingredients — ☐ PC4

Hold foods at correct temperature ready for service — ☐ PC5

Dispose of foods not served in specified time — ☐ PC6

Deal effectively with problems relating to food and equipment — ☐ PC7

Do your work in an organised, efficient and safe manner — ☐ PC8

Preparing and microwaving food

Meals and snacks can be provided in a few minutes with very little effort using microwave cooking. Besides being fast, energy-saving and versatile, microwave ovens are easy to operate. Many have a range of preset programs. Press the program button, or select the program number, and the machine does the rest.

With these advantages it is not surprising that microwave ovens are used in many catering kitchens. These ovens are of a more robust nature than their domestic counterpart. A commercial microwave oven has to be. In a household, the microwave might be used three or four times a day. In a busy catering outlet, the pattern could easily be 2000 uses a day.

How microwaves work

In microwave cooking, energy (not heat in the ordinary sense of the word) is transferred to the food by electromagnetic radiation. Microwaves pass into the food and make the water molecules vibrate, causing them to heat up very quickly.

The microwaves do not brown the surface of the food, nor make it crispy, as happens in grilling, roasting and frying. The effect they achieve is nearer to boiling or steaming, but a lot faster, and there is no need to put the food in water. It is similar to warming food in a low oven, and far quicker.

Microwave energy has another use: it can defrost food without cooking it. A special program (which most but not all ovens have) turns the energy on and off rapidly.

Preparing food for microwave cooking

The ease and convenience of using microwaves to reheat, cook and defrost food can lead people to pay less attention to good hygiene. This is a mistaken view. The need is as great as ever for careful temperature control, high standards of personal hygiene, and precautions to prevent cross contamination.

What food products are suitable

Because of the way microwaves work, not all food products are suitable. With convenience and pre-prepared items, always read the instructions printed on the packaging (or refer to workplace guidelines).

If there is no reference to microwaving on a food label, check with your manager. Dishes which require browning or crisping are not suitable for microwaving. Eggs in their shells cannot be 'boiled' in a microwave: they will explode. It is also very dangerous to attempt to fry food in a microwave.

Preparing the food

Prick or pierce food which has a skin or shell (e.g. tomatoes, potatoes, apples, egg yolks). Unless this is done the build-up of pressure as the water molecules turn to steam will cause the skin or shell to explode, and the food will splatter all over the inside of the oven.

Spread solid foods out over the container, do not pile them up. Irregular shapes heat unevenly. A large shallow dish is better than a small deep dish for solid foods.

Brush off any visible ice crystals from food which is to be defrosted. Microwaves are reflected away from ice.

Do not sprinkle sugar on the surface of pastries or other foods. The sugar will caramelise and may even burn.

Deciding on the container

Containers made of, or containing metal, are unsuitable. The metal reflects the microwaves, which means cooking or reheating takes longer, and is uneven. If you hear a crackling sound and see a sort of sparking effect inside the oven, the container is unsuitable. Transfer the food to a glass or ceramic container, otherwise you risk causing permanent damage to the workings of the oven.

Covering the food

Most foods are covered to trap the steam and encourage even heating. Use microwave-quality clingfilm, a lid or an upturned plate.

Do not cover breads, croissants or pastries, or they will go soggy. Instead, place a piece of kitchen paper under the product to help absorb excess moisture.

Food to be defrosted should be kept in its original packaging if possible, or else covered. Remove metal twist ties and pierce plastic pouches and boil-in-the-bag type products (unless instructions state otherwise).

Microwaving food

Four aspects of the way microwaves work have an impact on the use of microwave ovens for defrosting, cooking and reheating food:

1 The microwaves rapidly penetrate the outer surfaces of the food (top, bottom and sides) to a depth of about 5 to 20 mm (the exact value depends on complex factors, including the water, fat, carbohydrate, protein and mineral contents of the food). With food thicker than this, the rest of the cooking (towards the centre) occurs by conduction of heat from the outer layer, a slower process.

2 The water molecules take a while to stop vibrating after the microwave energy is switched off. This means the food continues to get hot for a few minutes after it has been removed from the oven. This is known as *carry-over cooking*.

3 The inside of the microwave oven does not get hot, nor does the plate or container used to hold the food. This means the food will not keep warm if you leave it in the oven after the program has finished. Nor is there much point in reheating food on the plate on which you will serve it – customers prefer hot food on hot plates. You need to heat the service plate in a hot cupboard or some other way, and transfer the microwaved food to it.

4 Microwave ovens come in different designs, like any other piece of kitchen equipment. Some work faster than others.

Microwave times

Always follow instructions for the equipment you are using, and the task. Timing depends on the:

- power of the oven – called the *output wattage* (e.g. 1500 watts) – and the setting you are using (full, half power, etc.)

- design of the oven: position of the fan and magnetron (and there may be more than one of these), also size of oven cavity

- type of container used

- amount and location of the food within the oven – two jacket potatoes may take up to 50% longer to microwave than one

- and on the food itself. Foods which are dense, such as meat, will take longer to microwave. On the other hand, a beef burger will cook in a shorter time and more successfully than a piece of steak of the same size. This is because the meat in the burger has been minced up. For the steak, the microwave heating pattern is complex. The result may be over-hot, shrunk gristle, less hot fat, and the lean meat undercooked.

Checking temperature when cooking and reheating

Impressions can be misleading. The food might look and feel very hot on the surface – because of the speed at which microwaves penetrate the outer layer, but be quite cold at the middle – because the conduction of heat towards the centre is slower.

Use a temperature probe to be sure. Check every corner, and several points in the centre of large dishes. The reading should be 70°C to 75°C.

Cooking and reheating liquids

Stir sauces, soups, stews and other thick liquids regularly to prevent them over-thickening at the outer edges, and to allow the heat to penetrate to the middle of the container. Remember to turn the microwave energy on again, once you have returned the food to the oven (if there is a pause setting, you will not need to do this).

Liquids should be heated in a tall container (e.g. a jug) – not a low, shallow dish such as a soup plate. This makes handling easy and the liquid is less likely to spill over the top if it begins to boil.

Defrosting

The defrost program of a microwave oven switches the microwave energy on and off in rapid bursts. Do not use a cooking or reheating program. Vegetables are best cooked straight from the freezer.

Allow the food to rest after or between bursts of defrosting so the heat can equalise throughout.

Thoroughly stir liquids and dishes like stews after they have begun to defrost.

Do not attempt to defrost the food completely. Otherwise, there is a risk it will start to cook and dry out, while the centre remains frozen.

Microwaving is not recommended for defrosting large joints, or for large quantities of food. For these use a refrigerator or rapid-thawing cabinet.

1 Why can't you hold food hot in a microwave, as you might in a ordinary oven?

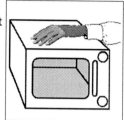

2 Tick those types of food container that are safe to use in a microwave.

3 Which of these two containers is better for heating a liquid in a microwave? Why?

4 How should food be arranged on a plate for microwaving? Say what is wrong about the other illustration.

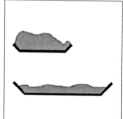

5 Which of these shaped containers should you use for microwaving a stew or similar dish? Mark the other illustration to show what could go wrong.

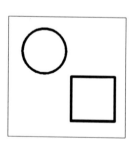

6 Mark which part of the fish would be cooked by the action of the microwaves, and which part by conduction.

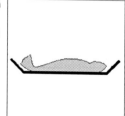

7 Tick the types of food that are suitable for microwaving.

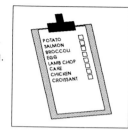

8 What precautions should you take when microwaving these foods?

9 What foods should be covered before microwaving? What sort of covering can you use?

10 What sort of dishes should be stirred during microwaving and why?

11 How do you tell when a microwaved dish is ready for service? Base your answer on some of the dishes you prepare and serve at work.

12 Describe how you defrost food by microwave. What happens if you continue the process for too long?

Use this to check your progress against the performance criteria (see page 4)

Element 1

Prepare food for microwave cooking

Get your preparation areas and equipment ready for use — PC1

Use pre-prepared and convenience foods of right type, quality and quantity — PC2

Prepare foods for defrosting/cooking/reheating by microwave — PC3

Store food stocks not for immediate use — PC4

Clean preparation areas and equipment after use — PC5

Deal effectively with problems relating to food and equipment — PC6

Do your work in an organised, efficient and safe manner — PC7

Element 2

Microwave food

Get your cooking areas and equipment ready for use — PC1

Defrost/cook/reheat pre-prepared and convenience foods by microwave — PC2

Cook or reheat foods to specified temperature — PC3

Finish and present foods cooked by microwave — PC4

Clean cooking areas and equipment after use — PC5

Deal effectively with problems relating to food and equipment — PC6

Do your work in an organised, efficient and safe manner — PC7

Preparing and frying food

There are three basic methods of frying food:

- *deep frying* – cooked in a deep fat fryer, fully covered by very hot oil. Popular for breadcrumbed or battered fish portions, small whole fish (also coated), chicken pieces, chips, onion rings, possibly other vegetables, eggs, fruit fritters and doughnuts

- *stir frying* – small pieces of tender meat, poultry, fish and vegetables, cooked quickly (not more than a few minutes) in a wok (bowl-shaped pan) or deep sided frying pan, with a small amount of oil

- *shallow frying* – cooked in a frying pan, usually with a small amount of oil or fat. Popular for fried eggs, tender cuts of meat and poultry, fish portions and small whole fish (coated in breadcrumbs, etc.).

Element 1
Preparing food for frying

Check that the food to be cooked, and any ingredients, coatings or sauces, are in the proper place, and that your working surfaces and equipment are clean and ready for use.

Fried foods are best served immediately. You should not have to keep the food standing, while you prepare the salad garnish or look for the accompanying sauce.

Follow instructions on which foods can be cooked from frozen or defrosted in advance. When defrosting is required, you need to plan your requirements carefully, so that enough food is available, but not too much.

For stir frying, all food should be in tiny pieces. Never attempt to fry large pieces of food which are still frozen, such as chicken portions. The food will end up overcooked on the outside, but undercooked inside. This will lead to customer complaints and is dangerous from a hygiene point of view (harmful bacteria will survive).

Chips can be deep fried straight from the freezer, but shake off excess ice crystals. Do this away from the fryer – water and oil get along badly! The oil will froth dangerously.

Excess moisture shortens the deep frying life of oil. Do make sure the food is dry before frying. Other enemies of oil are:

- salt and sugar – season foods after frying, not before, and do so well away from the oil

- small bits of food and coating which fall into the oil during cooking – always shake off excess breadcrumbs and drain battered food carefully before frying.

The satisfying crunchy texture and distinctive taste of fried food result from good control of cooking times and temperatures, and proper care of the oil.

Oils start to spoil from the moment they are heated up, and as soon as they are exposed to air – or, to be more precise, the oxygen in air. Deep frying oils are expensive commodities, so it makes sense to look after them.

CHECKlist
Looking after the oil

✔ filter oil daily

✔ wipe the inside of the fryer thoroughly with kitchen paper before replacing the oil

✔ once a week (or more often, depending on use), wash the fryer (see page 72)

✔ turn the thermostat down, or put the fryer on stand-by during slack periods – the recommended stand-by temperature is 93°C

✔ switch fryers off when you know they won't be used again

✔ use the correct utensils for handling food and filtering oil – the wrong ones, if they use iron or copper in their construction, will set up a chemical reaction which harms the oil

Reducing oxidation (from contact with air)

✔ put the lid on fryers as soon as you have finished using them

✔ avoid pouring from a great height when you are filling or topping up a fryer

✔ keep the container as close to the tap as possible, when you drain oil for filtering

Element 2
Frying food

To get good results, you must pay close attention to the food for the (short) time it is cooking. Is the food browning properly, while at the same time cooking through to the centre?

Deep frying

Check that you are using the right temperature (or program) for the food you are frying. The temperature for blanching chips, for example, is lower than that used for the final browning.

Do not place too much food in the oil at one time. This will cause the temperature of the oil to drop, which means the food will absorb more oil, spoiling its eating quality. The correct ratio is *one part food to six parts oil*.

Allow time for the heat to recover when you are frying frozen food. Temperature falls of 18°C to 28°C can occur when frozen pieces of food are immersed in hot oil.

Small bubbles as the food cooks, and being able to see the food quite clearly in the oil are good signs. Excessive bubbling and smoke rising from the surface are bad signs. When you first put the food in the oil, there may be some steam given off. This is nothing to worry about.

While the food is cooking:

- skim food particles from the surface regularly – this reduces the risk of them burning, spoiling the appearance of the food and the quality of the oil

- keep an eye on the food so that it does not brown too much – if you are using a fryer with a timer, make sure the setting is correct for the particular task

- turn over food which floats on the surface, so that both sides get browned

- handle fragile foods and foods with loose coatings carefully – to avoid bits falling off in the oil

- even if the food is not browning, never set the thermostat above 205°C – very high temperatures are dangerous, and cause the oil to spoil rapidly.

Drain food well after frying.

Stir frying

Note the order in which the ingredients are to be cooked, and for how long. In some dishes, everything is added to the pan together. In others, items which need longer to cook go into the pan first.

Many stir fried recipes state a particular type of oil, e.g. sesame. The flavour of the oil is part of the dish.

Keep the food moving around the pan while it is cooking.

Shallow frying

For health reasons, and to give a better tasting dish, use as little oil as possible, and the right oil or fat. The oil should just coat the base of the pan. Ideally, it should be high in polyunsaturates, and the type that will not smoke at normal frying temperatures.

Let the oil heat up before you add the food. You have got the temperature right when the food immediately starts to sizzle gently. If there is no sound or sign of activity, the oil is cold. Fierce sizzling and smoke mean the fat is too hot.

You may need to lower or raise the heat under the pan during cooking. Most foods need turning once during cooking. Do this with care so you do not splash oil, nor damage the appearance of the food. Some customers prefer their fried eggs turned, so the yolk is well cooked.

CHECK list
Safety in deep frying

✔ check the fryer is filled to the correct level before turning on

✔ remain at the fryer while food is cooking

✔ keep the lid off the fryer when it is in use (unless it is a pressure fryer)

✔ allow oil to cool before draining and filtering

✔ tell your manager if you think the thermostat is not working accurately

✔ turn the fryer off if you suspect it has a fault, and call your manager

✔ recognise the danger signs of oil overheating: an unpleasant smoke that irritates the eyes, ears, nose and throat. If heating continues, the oil will burst into flames – the 'flashpoint'

✔ know what to do in the event of a fire – how to sound the alarm, when it is safe to fight the fire and how you should do this

Activities
Prepare and fry food

1 Describe the safe way to handle a heavy container (e.g. of oil), so that you avoid injury to your back.

2 What should you do when this happens?

3 And when this happens?

4 Which of these would you use to put out a fire in the fryer? Explain how you would use it.

5 Which of these foods can be cooked from frozen?

Tom's Cafe
MENU
Scampi
Chicken leg
Plaice fillet
Vegetable burger
All served with chips or potato croquettes

6 Why should food (e.g. freshly prepared chips) be dried before frying?

7 Which of these oils should you use for frying?

SUNCRISP
high in polyunsaturates
low in saturates

LARDOLENE
high in saturates

8 How do you tell when
a) deep fried,
b) stir fried,
c) shallow fried
food is cooked?

9 Describe how food which is ready for frying should be stored. Why is the temperature so important?

10 When
a) deep fried,
b) shallow fried
food is cooked a little in advance of service, how should it be stored?

Phew! This cover is making me go all soggy!

11 Why must stir fried food be served immediately?

I wish they wouldn't keep us hanging around - we only took a minute to cook!

Illustrations for questions 6 and 9 with thanks to McCain Foods.

NVQ SVQ

Skills check
Prepare and fry food
Unit 1ND4

level **1**

Use this to check your progress against the performance criteria (see page 4).

Element 1

Prepare food for frying

Get your preparation area and equipment ready for use ☐ PC1

Use pre-prepared and convenience foods of right type, quality and quantity ☐ PC2

Prepare foods for frying ☐ PC3

Store correctly prepared foods not for immediate use ☐ PC4

Clean preparation areas and equipment after use ☐ PC5

Deal effectively with problems relating to food and equipment ☐ PC6

Do your work in an organised, efficient and safe manner ☐ PC7

Element 2

Fry food

Get your cooking area and equipment ready for use ☐ PC1

Use appropriate frying method for pre-prepared and convenience foods: deep frying/stir frying/shallow frying ☐ PC2

Deep fry/stir fry/shallow fry food ☐ PC3

Finish and present fried foods ☐ PC4

Store food not for immediate consumption ☐ PC5

Clean cooking areas and equipment after use ☐ PC6

Deal effectively with problems relating to food and equipment ☐ PC7

Do your work in an organised, efficient and safe manner ☐ PC8

15

Unit 1ND5

Preparing and baking food

Bread, cakes and pastries are what most people think of in connection with baking.

In addition, there are many baked dishes made with eggs, meat, fish, vegetables, pasta, rice and fruit. These include old favourites, such as steak and kidney pie and baked apple, modern variations of traditional dishes, such as baked jacket potato with chilli con carne, and dishes inspired by the cuisine and culture of other countries, such as chicken tikka. There is also a whole range of convenience dishes which are finally cooked in the oven, e.g. cannelloni, chicken and ham pie.

Element 1

Preparing food for baking

Success in baking requires accurate measurement of ingredients, and careful control of cooking temperatures and times. Some baked products must stand before cooking so that the yeast can do its work, or the pastry can rest. Others have to go in the oven at once so they will rise properly.

Points to look out for include:

- *whether to defrost frozen products*

    If defrosting is required, should the product be taken out of the packaging? How long will defrosting take? Where should the product be kept in the meantime?

- *whether to remove the lid / pierce the covering*

    For made-up dishes, this depends on if the food should be browned, and on the type of packaging.

- *what quantities to use*

    Do you have to adjust the instructions for the amount you are making? Are the items you need to hand: added liquid (water, milk, etc.) and optional extras (e.g. dried fruit, chopped parsley)?

- *what temperature added ingredients should be at*

    Should milk and water, for example, be 'warm'?

- *what further preparation steps are required*

    This might involving mixing, portioning, decorating.

- *how long, and in what conditions, the food needs to be kept before cooking*

    Do pastries need to rest? Do doughs need to prove? If so, for how long? Should they be covered? Should they be put in a cool or warm place?

- *what preparation of the baking container is required*

    Should the container be greased, and if so with what? Sometimes greasing and flouring are required, or lining with paper (e.g. for a cake), or a sprinkling of coarse salt (e.g. for potatoes).

Element 2

Baking food

Ovens need time to reach the right temperature, but turning them on too soon is wasteful. Check that colleagues do not want to use the oven at the same time.

Where you place the food in the oven depends on the type of oven you are using, and what is recommended for the product. Forced-air convection ovens give an even heat distribution. Most pastry ovens can be set to give more heat at the bottom or the top, or an even heat. General-purpose ovens are hotter at the top.

Getting the correct consistency and appearance

Products baked very fast do not usually need temperature adjustments. With longer cooking times, look to see how the food is cooking and turn the heat up or down a little, as necessary.

Be careful when opening the oven to check cooking. Many breads and cakes are fragile until cooking is almost complete. The quality will suffer if the door is opened too widely (letting in cool air). Rough handling of cooking containers can also cause harm.

Test the food before you remove it from the oven:

- tapped on the base, bread should make a hollow sound

- cakes should be firm and springy when the centre of the top crust is lightly pressed

- a skewer pushed into the centre of a cake should be clean when drawn out – if any mixture sticks to it, the cake needs further cooking

- made-up dishes should be tested with a temperature probe, to ensure that the centre has reached 70°C or higher.

Always remove items carefully from the oven – fully loaded trays can be very heavy. Handle baked items, especially when hot, with great care. Cakes can easily be damaged. Bread can dent and distort.

Finishing the dish

If the baked food is to be eaten hot, transfer it carefully to a warm serving dish and serve immediately.

If it is served cold, requires decoration or is forming part of another dish (e.g. trifle), allow it to cool in a suitable area of the kitchen (dust-free, away from the main cooking areas):

- transfer to a cooling rack (tray made from wire-mesh), so that air can circulate round the base

- remove any lining paper

- leave delicate cakes to cool in the cooking container for about 15 minutes before turning out.

1 What might happen if you pick up a hot tray with an oven cloth that is damp or greasy?

2 Why is it important to stand well back when opening the door of a hot oven?

3 If you spill or drop something (e.g. fat or a liquid) on the floor, why must it be wiped up quickly?

4 What temperature should a) hot food and b) cold food which is not required immediately be kept at?

5 Why is accurate measurement of baking ingredients essential?

6 What points should you look for when deciding about the quality of baked products?

7 For customers who want healthy foods, what are some of the attractions of baked foods?

Healthier Eating Menu

Stuffed tomato

Baked Potato

Lasagne

Baked cod

Baked apple

8 How do you prevent non-food items getting into baked food while it is being prepared, cooked or stored?

8 What are your workplace rules for how long you can keep baked products ready for service? Why is the time limit important?

Use this to check your progress against the performance criteria (see page 4).

Element 1

Prepare food for baking

Get your preparation area and equipment (cooling racks, ovens, display units) ready for use — ☐ PC1

Use pre-prepared and convenience foods of right type, quality and quantity — ☐ PC2

Prepare foods for baking — ☐ PC3

Store correctly prepared foods not for immediate use — ☐ PC4

Clean preparation areas and equipment after use — ☐ PC5

Deal effectively with problems relating to food and equipment — ☐ PC6

Do your work in an organised, efficient and safe manner — ☐ PC7

Element 2

Bake food

Get your cooking area and equipment (cooling racks, ovens, display units) ready for use — ☐ PC1

Bake pre-prepared and convenience foods for the right time and at the right temperature, to the correct consistency and appearance — ☐ PC2

Finish baked foods — ☐ PC3

Cool baked foods before use, when appropriate — ☐ PC4

Clean cooking areas and equipment after use — ☐ PC5

Deal effectively with problems relating to food and equipment — ☐ PC6

Do your work in an organised, efficient and safe manner — ☐ PC7

Preparing, boiling, poaching and steaming food

These methods use a hot liquid (usually water or stock) or steam to cook the food in a moist environment. The temperature during cooking is at boiling point (100°C), slightly lower for poaching and possibly a few degrees higher for steaming (depending on the pressure in the steamer):

- in boiling, the food is covered by the liquid, and kept on the boil, often in a saucepan on top of the stove

- in poaching, the food is partially or fully covered, and the liquid kept a few degrees below boiling point to provide a gentler cooking action. Cooking can be on top of the stove, or in the oven

- in steaming, the food is surrounded by steam, usually in a steamer (a special type of oven, or a combination oven which can be operated as a steamer). Or the food can be placed in a saucepan, partially filled with water at boiling point. The lid is kept on, so the steam stays around the food.

Boiling

Poaching fully covered

Steaming

Poaching partially covered

Element 1

Preparing food for boiling, poaching or steaming

Recipes and workplace instructions will tell you what cooking container to use, where to place the food, at what temperature and for how long. Don't worry too much whether the process is called boiling, poaching or steaming, or if you find these terms used differently.

The main foods cooked by these methods are:

- *boiling* – vegetables, pulses, pasta, rice, eggs cooked in their shells, the less tender cuts of meat, shellfish, and for making soups and sauces

- *poaching* – fish, poached eggs and fruit

- *steaming* – vegetables, sometimes fish, and for certain dishes which include meat (e.g. steak and kidney pudding) and fruit (e.g. Christmas pudding).

Points you should check before cooking pre-prepared or convenience foods by these methods are:

- *what, if any, additional preparation is required*

  Should rice be washed? Do pulses need to be soaked, and if so for how long? Eggs are best taken out of the refrigerator about 30 minutes before cooking. Do fresh pre-prepared vegetables require washing? To keep the vitamin content, do not soak vegetables in water before cooking, except for potatoes.

- *should frozen food be defrosted*

  Most made-up dishes (e.g. boil-in-the-bag) are cooked from frozen. So are vegetables. Raw, frozen meat and fish should be defrosted first.

- *what protection is required*

  How should steamed puddings be covered, e.g. with kitchen foil, a cloth, or paper? How should poached foods be covered, e.g. with greased paper and/or a lid? Does the base of the pan need to be oiled or greased to prevent the food sticking (e.g. when poaching in a small amount of liquid)?

Element 2

Boiling, poaching and steaming food

Food is cooked to make it tender, enjoyable and safe to eat. The changes which take place during cooking are complex, and depend on the food. In meat, poultry and fish, the muscle structure softens. In vegetables and fruit, it is the fibre which softens. Overcooking takes this process too far. Vegetables, fruit and fish turn to pulp. Meat, on the other hand, shrinks and toughens.

The presence of moisture – a common feature of boiling, poaching and steaming – helps the balance between softening and toughening. There is no risk of the food burning: the temperatures are not high enough.

Some flavour transfer can take place between the food and the water or cooking liquid. In poaching, this is encouraged, so the cooking liquid may include wine or herbs, for example. These give flavour to the food, and in turn the food gives flavour to the cooking liquid. This is why the cooking liquid is usually incorporated into the sauce which accompanies poached food.

Reducing nutritional loss when cooking vegetables

Unfortunately, vitamins can be lost to the cooking liquid. As vegetables are one of the principal sources of vitamins in people's diets, it is important to reduce this loss to the minimum. That is why you are recommended when boiling vegetables to:

- use the minimum amount of water
- bring the water to the boil before adding the vegetables – you should do this even for potatoes
- keep the lid on the pot during cooking
- lift the lid from time to time during cooking to allow volatile acids created during the cooking of cauliflower, broccoli or Brussels sprouts to escape
- keep liquid movement to a gentle simmering action, to avoid damaging the vegetables
- take particular care with leaf vegetables (e.g. Brussels sprouts, spinach). These are easily overcooked, losing colour and nutritional value. Flower vegetables (e.g. cauliflower, broccoli) are quite difficult to cook because the stalk takes longer to cook than the flower. If the stalk is tough it should be trimmed off, or the vegetable divided into florets. It is a common mistake to cook the stalk until it is edible and end up overcooking the delicate flower.

Steaming vegetables: the advantages

Steaming has several advantages over boiling as a cooking method for vegetables:

- cooking is very fast, particularly in pressureless convection steamers and high pressure steamers. This means the vegetables can be cooked immediately before they are served
- two or more vegetables can be cooked at the same time, without transfer of flavours
- the food remains still and does not roll around, as it does in a boiling liquid, so it is less likely to break up
- fewer vitamins are lost
- cooking times can be calculated precisely, so the food is less likely to be overcooked. Many steamers can be set to stop cooking at the required time.

Cooking and finishing

Points you should check are:

- *when to turn cooking equipment on*

  What temperature does the oven need to be for poaching? When should the steamer be turned on? Does the internal water bath need filling?

- *what container to use*

  Will the food expand during cooking? Spaghetti does. Will the food require stirring during cooking? Pasta will need to be, and rice might, depending on the cooking method you are following. With boiling, the pan should be sufficiently large for the water or food not to boil over the sides. For steaming, should the tray be perforated (with holes so the excess moisture runs off), or does the food need to have some moisture around it? For poaching, will some or all the cooking be in the oven? In this case, the lid and handles of the poaching pan must be heatproof.

- *how much liquid to use (for boiling and poaching)*

  Use the minimum amount of water for boiling vegetables, to cut down on vitamin loss. Use plenty of water for pasta and eggs. With rice, it depends on the type of rice and cooking method you are following.

- *for boiling, what temperature the water should be at the start of cooking*

  Some rice recipes start with cold water. Pasta, pulses and vegetables go into boiling water.

- *for boiling, how vigorous should the water movement be*

  In most cases, the bubbling action of the water should be quite gentle. Rapid boiling does not cook the food any faster, and there is a risk it will cause the food to break up. An exception is pulses. These should be boiled vigorously for the first 15 minutes to get rid of poisonous compounds.

- *for poaching, where to cook the food*

  This will depend on what you are poaching, and what container you are using. Eggs are always poached in a pan on top of the stove.

- *what attention does the food need during cooking*

  Pasta should be stirred from time to time, so that it does not stick together. Rice may need to be stirred, depending on the type of rice and the cooking method you are following. Vegetables are not usually stirred, since this will damage them. The poaching liquid should not be allowed to boil. Check from time to time, and turn the heat up or down as necessary.

- *how to check the food is cooked*

  Use the tip of the knife blade, or a cocktail stick – but avoid damaging the food – to determine when the texture has reached the degree of tenderness required. For rice, take a few grains out of the water with a perforated spoon and press them between your thumb and forefinger to test the texture (and then discard them)

- *how is the dish finished*

  Drain poached and boiled foods carefully, so you do not damage the food nor end up with a pool of liquid on the serving dish. The cooking liquid may form part of the sauce.

1 Describe some of the accidents which could occur if you do not take care when handling hot liquids and hot equipment.

2 What colour board should you use for a) preparing meat for cooking, b) cutting cooked meat? What is the reason for using different boards?

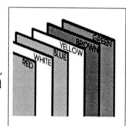

3 What changes occur in meat when it is boiled, poached or steamed? What happens if the meat is over-cooked?

4 And what changes occur with vegetables? What happens if they are over-cooked?

5 State some of the advantages of steaming, compared with boiling, for reducing the loss of vitamins.

6 When you are boiling vegetables, what steps can you take to reduce vitamin loss?

7 How do you prevent vegetables getting discoloured and limp like these?

8 Why do some customers not like their food salted during cooking?

Salt?
No thanks
My doctor
won't allow it!

9 How would you improve the presentation of these potatoes? How can you test the potatoes are cooked?

10 Steamed fish is a very plain dish. For health reasons, why might some customers prefer this to poached fish with a rich sauce?

NVQ
SVQ
Skills check
Prepare, boil, poach and steam food
Unit 1ND6
leve
1

Use this to check your progress against the performance criteria (see page 4).

Element 1

Prepare food for boiling, poaching and steaming

Get your preparation area and equipment ready for use ☐ PC1

Use pre-prepared and convenience foods of right type, quality and quantity ☐ PC2

Prepare foods for boiling/ poaching/steaming ☐ PC3

Store correctly prepared foods not for immediate use ☐ PC4

Clean preparation areas and equipment after use ☐ PC5

Deal effectively with problems relating to food and equipment ☐ PC6

Do your work in an organised, efficient and safe manner ☐ PC7

Element 2

Boil, poach and steam food

Get your cooking area and equipment ready for use ☐ PC1

Boil/poach/steam pre-prepared and convenience foods ☐ PC2

Finish boiled/poached/steamed foods ☐ PC3

Store correctly cooked foods not for immediate use ☐ PC4

Clean cooking areas and equipment after use ☐ PC5

Deal effectively with problems relating to food and equipment ☐ PC6

Do your work in an organised, efficient and safe manner ☐ PC7

Preparing and grilling food

Grilling is one of the quickest and most straightforward ways of cooking food. It produces an attractive brown colour and crisp texture. Little or no additional fat is required, and many foods lose fat during cooking. This means grilled food is popular with customers who are trying to reduce the amount of fat they eat for health reasons.

Grilling is best for food which is tender and has a reasonable moisture content. The pieces of food should not be too large or too thick, otherwise it is difficult to control the cooking evenly. The risk is that the outside burns or dries out before the centre is cooked.

Element 1

Preparing food for grilling

The main points you should check before grilling pre-prepared or convenience foods are:

- *what seasoning to use and when*

  Can you use herbs and other flavourings in place of salt (because of the health risks from eating too much salt)? Salt added to red meat before grilling may delay the browning.

- *any final preparation to be done*

  Will tomatoes be grilled in halves or whole, and if whole, should the top be cut (e.g. in a criss-cross shape)? Do mushrooms need washing and the stalk removing? Do sausages need pricking (necessary with some types to prevent them from bursting)?

- *whether the food needs brushing with oil or butter or a coating of flour*

  The oil or butter stops food which has little or none of its own fat from drying out too much. Fish is often lightly coated with flour just before grilling, to help the surface brown attractively.

- *what garnishes and sauces will be accompanying the dish*

  Grilled food is at its best served immediately it has been cooked. Cooking is very fast, so get accompaniments ready before you start.

Element 2

Grilling food

If the grill is not already on, it will need a little time to get hot (around 30 minutes on full power for a simulated charcoal grill). The grilling elements or charcoals should be glowing red. At this stage, you should turn a simulated charcoal grill down slightly.

Grills use a lot of energy, so it is wasteful to leave them on unnecessarily.

You should also check that serving dishes are in the hot cupboard or wherever they are warmed, ready to take the food. The top of an overhead grill gets extremely hot during use. Do not place dishes there to get warm.

Before use, brush the grill bars lightly with oil. This will help stop the food sticking. A general-purpose cooking oil will be fine, preferably one that is high in polyunsaturated fats, for health reasons. Do not be tempted to use old cooking oil from the fryer. This will pass on flavours from the frying.

Develop your own system for keeping track of different orders when you are busy, e.g.:

- well-done steaks in the centre of the grill
- medium steaks on the left
- rare steaks on the right.

Remember that it takes three or four times as long to cook a well-done steak as a rare one. If the orders in the example above are from the same table, you would put the well-done steaks under the grill first, the medium ones about five minutes later, and the rare ones a few minutes later (depending on the size and thickness).

Halfway through grilling, turn the food over carefully with grilling tongs. Piercing it with a fork is not recommended, as this lets the juices escape.

For cooking a whole fish, you may find it easier to place it between grilling wires, or to put the fish on a shallow, heatproof tray. A tray is also easier for small items like sausages and mushrooms.

Using a brander

It is usually not necessary to turn the food when your grill has a brander. This is a solid, quite heavy grilling surface available with some overhead grills. The brander has to be fully heated first.

Testing when the food is cooked

With experience, and when you have got to know the grill you are using, you will know how long it takes to cook the different food items. Points to check include:

- *appearance* – some browning is a good sign, but too much is a warning the food is overcooking
- *feel* – pressed with grilling tongs, a steak changes from feeling flabby when rare to quite firm when well done. A tomato feels soft when cooked, fish is firm
- *colour of juices* – pressed with grilling tongs, the juices will be red for a rare steak, have traces of blood for medium, and be clear for well-done.

1 Why is it dangerous to put plates and other things on top of a grill?

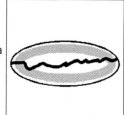

2 Why must you empty the fat/oil from the drip trough on the grill regularly?

3 What should you do if food catches alight under the grill?

4 How should you keep food which is ready for cooking, but not required immediately?

Yes, Chef. It's all ready and in the fridge.

5 Describe two bad practices which would lead to the presence of harmful bacteria on grilled food.

6 Why would the risks be much greater if this food was then left in the warm kitchen for a few hours, before being reheated and served?

7 Why are grilled dishes popular with customers who want to reduce the amount of fat they eat?

8 What steps can you take to reduce even further the amount of fat on grilled dishes?

9 With the brander in a sloping position, some food is nearer the heat. Mark where to put steaks A (rare), B (medium) and C (well-done).

10 When the brander is flat, all the food will cook at the same speed. If you want the food to cook slowly, what shelf position would you use?

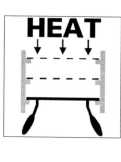

11 How can you judge when grilled dishes are properly cooked? Choose a range of dishes for your answer.

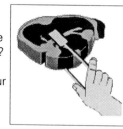

12 For the dishes used in your previous answer, how do you keep those that cannot be served immediately?

NVQ SVQ

Skills check
Prepare and grill food
Unit 1ND7

level 1

Use this to check your progress against the performance criteria (see page 4).

Element 1

Prepare food for grilling

Get your preparation area and equipment ready for use ☐ PC1

Use pre-prepared and convenience foods of right type, quality and quantity ☐ PC2

Prepare foods for grilling ☐ PC3

Store correctly prepared foods not for immediate use ☐ PC4

Clean preparation areas and equipment after use ☐ PC5

Deal effectively with problems relating to food and equipment ☐ PC6

Do your work in an organised, efficient and safe manner ☐ PC7

Element 2

Grill food

Get your cooking area and equipment ready for use ☐ PC1

Grill pre-prepared and convenience foods ☐ PC2

Finish grilled foods ☐ PC3

Store correctly cooked foods not for immediate use ☐ PC4

Clean cooking areas and equipment after use ☐ PC5

Deal effectively with problems relating to food and equipment ☐ PC6

Do your work in an organised, efficient and safe manner ☐ PC7

Preparing and griddling food

This method takes its name from the type of equipment used: basically, a quite large, heavy piece of metal, usually flat, which is heated from underneath by gas or electricity. The food is placed directly on the very hot surface, which is kept lightly oiled or greased to prevent sticking. For cooking meat, a griddle with a ridged surface is sometimes preferred, as it gives the food an attractive marking and allows the fat to drain away.

Although the word 'griddle' sounds like grilling, the type of heat used is different from that in grilling. Grilling uses radiant heat which reaches the food from a heat source above or below, or both. Griddling uses conducted heat, which travels into the food from direct contact with the cooking surface. It is very similar to shallow frying, but:

- there are no sides, so you cannot use a griddle for those dishes where cream, wine, lemon juice, stock, etc. is added to the cooking juices left in the pan to make a sauce. Nor is it suitable for very small pieces of food, e.g. button mushrooms, as you would have to spend most of your time stopping them from rolling to the floor

- you can't pick up a griddle, so it is not an effective way of cooking food that has to be moved around a lot during cooking, or tossed in the pan.

Preparing food for griddling

Griddling is used for burgers, steaks, cutlets, bacon, sausages and similar, small, tender pieces of meat which do not need long cooking, or the presence of a liquid or steam. It is also used for tomatoes and for fried eggs, although these are usually placed in a small ring to prevent the white running everywhere.

Fish can be griddled (small pieces, or small whole fish of the types that are also suitable for frying or grilling). But you should not try to griddle fish and meat at the same time, or without thoroughly cleaning the griddle first. Otherwise, the flavours will get transferred from meat to fish, or fish to meat via the cooking surface and the oil.

Frozen food should be defrosted before griddling. Eggs should be removed from the refrigerator 20 to 30 minutes before you will be cooking them. Other foods should be kept chilled until you are ready to cook them.

Griddling food

Allow the griddle to warm up before you start cooking. The setting you choose will depend on what you are cooking. If you are using a griddle with two or more plates, these can be set at different temperatures:

- a lower one for fried eggs, pork chops, chicken pieces and thick steaks, etc. which have to cook more slowly

- a higher setting for burgers, thinner steaks, lamb cutlets, bacon, tomatoes, etc., where you want an attractive brown colour to develop in the fairly short cooking time.

When you are cooking large quantities of food, you may need to turn the griddle to a higher setting. Each piece of food absorbs heat from the plate, so with many pieces the plate may be giving out more heat than it is getting from the electric or gas element, and the temperature drops.

In between periods of cooking, the griddle should be turned off, or at least turned down to a low setting. To prevent overheating of the plate, which can damage it, never leave the griddle plate on a high setting for long periods when no food is being cooked on it.

The container which collects fat running off the griddle surface may require emptying from time to time when you are doing a lot of cooking. Once a day it should be thoroughly cleaned.

Put the old oil in an empty can or container reserved for collecting waste oil. Do not pour hot oil into a plastic container, or it will melt. Nor should you pour old oil down the sink, as it is likely to cause a blockage.

1 Why is it dangerous to store equipment or food on the griddle surface?

Before / After

7 Why do you need to lightly oil the surface of the griddle before – and if necessary during – cooking?

Who glued this burger to the griddle again?

2 What can happen if a griddle is left on a high setting, while it is not being used?

MIN MAX — OUT OF ORDER

8 Where should you keep food which has been prepared in advance for griddling? Why is the temperature at which food is stored so important?

It's too cold for me in the fridge!

3 What should you do if the food on a griddle catches alight?

FIRE BLANKET

9 For five items that can be griddled, say how you judge when they are sufficiently cooked?

You can see and feel we're done!

Hey! Don't forget us!

4 Why is it wrong to pour or spray lots of water over a griddle to clean it?

Hello! Bridge Street cafe here. Our griddle's shorted again.

10 How can you reduce the amount of fat in the finished dish?

5 How often should you clean the container that collects fat/oil which runs off the food during griddling?

Cleaning schedule
Griddle fat trough daily
Griddle surface every use

11 What should you do if the griddle goes cold during cooking, even though it is still turned on?

Hello! Manager of Bridge Street again. Can I speak to the griddle service engineer?

6 How do you remove heavy deposits of burnt food that form on the griddle surface?

12 What should you do if, part-way through a busy period, you run low on some of the food?

HEAD Clive Finch CHEF

Use this to check your progress against the performance criteria (see page 4).

Element 1

Prepare food for griddling

Get your preparation area and equipment ready for use — PC1

Use pre-prepared and convenience foods of right type, quality and quantity — PC2

Prepare foods for griddling — PC3

Store correctly prepared foods not for immediate use — PC4

Clean preparation areas and equipment after use — PC5

Deal effectively with problems relating to food and equipment — PC6

Do your work in an organised, efficient and safe manner — PC7

Element 2

Griddle food

Get your cooking area and equipment ready for use — PC1

Griddle pre-prepared and convenience foods — PC2

Finish griddled foods — PC3

Store correctly cooked foods not for immediate use — PC4

Clean cooking areas and equipment after use — PC5

Deal effectively with problems relating to food and equipment — PC6

Do your work in an organised, efficient and safe manner — PC7

Preparing and finishing reconstituted food

The range of reconstituted foods available to caterers is vast. They come as powders, cubes, pastes, jellies and liquids. With the addition of one or two readily-available ingredients (e.g. water, milk, butter) and the minimum of preparation they turn into creamed potato, jellies, custards, cream-substitutes, chocolate mousses, lemon meringue pies, cheesecakes, biscuits, etc.

Reconstituted foods are not the same as convenience products like pastry and cake mixes. These involve more complex preparation like rolling and shaping and usually have to be cooked for some time.

Reconstituted foods are simple to use, saving a lot of preparation work and much time. Another advantage is ease of storage. They take up less space than the product they become. They also have a longer shelf-life, and many can be stored at room temperatures.

Element 1
Preparation methods

There are four main methods:

- *diluting* – adding water or another liquid to give the product the right volume
- *combining* – making two or more substances into one
- *mixing* – stirring, shaking or combining in some other way two or more substances so that they become one
- *whisking* – stirring the product very fast to get air into it, usually done with a whisk, or an electric mixing machine with a suitable attachment.

When following product instructions, pay particular attention to:

- *how much you need to make*

  How many portions will the packet/container make? Alternatively, what weight or volume of the product do you need per portion and how many portions are you making?

- *what other ingredients you need*

  Before you start, collect all these: water, milk, instant chocolate, etc.

- *what quantities of ingredients you need to add*

  Be accurate, using a scale and measuring jug as appropriate. If the recipe gives both metric (e.g. 100 g) and imperial measurements (e.g. 4 oz), follow one system or the other for all ingredients.

- *whether added liquid should be cold, warm, hot or boiling*

  You may need a saucepan to heat the liquid up, and to allow extra preparation time for this step.

- *how to combine ingredients*

  Should a little liquid be added to the powder, then the rest, or the powder sprinkled over the liquid, then stirred together? Is a resting period required, e.g. stir to combine, leave for a minute, then whisk.

- *how long to whisk or mix*

  And what result this should achieve, e.g. smooth texture, soft peaks, thick and creamy. If you are using a machine to mix, what speed should you use, and what mixing tool, e.g. balloon whisk?

- *the setting time, and the temperature*

  Should the product be chilled or frozen? How long will it take to set? Having been made, is there a limit to the time the product can be kept?

Element 2
Finishing dishes

There are many ways to make the finished dish look attractive and appetising. Some guidelines are:

- use the garnish to say something about the dish – a pecan nut to decorate a pecan cheesecake, a slice of apricot on an apricot mousse
- don't mix savoury with sweet – chopped parsley or grated nutmeg on creamed potatoes is acceptable, depending on your customers, grated chocolate would never be
- choose something which suits the type of dish, complementing or contrasting with the flavours and colour – a crystallised lemon slice will complement a lemon mousse, an orange slice will provide a contrast. On the other hand, a slice of fresh pineapple would introduce too much of a contrast
- avoid clash of colours – sometimes a contrast is successful, e.g. red cherry with chocolate mousse, sometimes a deeper or lighter shade of the same colour, e.g. a chocolate flake on a chocolate mousse
- restrict the number of colours – more than three colours tend to look messy
- add variety – people get bored with a glacé cherry on trifle. Try flaked chocolate, fresh strawberry, or a whirl of cream sprinkled with instant coffee
- texture – another way of adding variety, e.g. chopped fruit with a jelly.

Remember, the simplest ideas work best.

1 How can you check that the quality of reconstituted food is right?

2 What signs would warn you that a packet of food has been attacked by pests? What should you do about the situation?

3 If you only use some of the contents of a newly opened packet of food (e.g. custard powder), how should you store the remainder?

RICE

4 If you do not fully understand the instructions for reconstituting food, what should you do?

Instructions

Open the packet
Put it in a saucepan
Serve immediately
Boil for 5 seconds
Do not allow to boil

5 For each of the four main preparation methods, give at least one example of a food product that is reconstituted in this way.

6 What do you think has gone wrong if you get lumps in a reconstituted food dish that should have a smooth consistency?

Instructions
αμφφγφφγ δγγ ουγ
ασφδγφ φδη
αδγφβ γφφ   σγφν
Add liquid a little at a time
ηκ κ ημηκ φλζλ
σηδφ δφγ δλλλδφφ

7 What sort of containers can you use if you have to whisk a product? What can go wrong if you use a container which is too small?

8 Once you have made up a food, how should it be kept until service time? If you use several reconstituted foods, answer this question for the main ones.

Instructions
αμφφγφφγ δγγ ουγ
ασφδγφ φδη
αδγφβ γφφ σγφν
Chill after mixing

9 Describe some of the ways in which reconstituted food might become unsafe to eat. Say what should be done to avoid each danger.

10 Why should the finished dish look attractive and appetising to your customers? Describe some ideas for improving the presentation of various dishes.

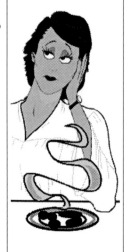

Element 1

Prepare reconstituted food

Get your preparation area and equipment ready for use — PC

Use reconstituted foods of right type, quality and quantity — PC

Dilute/combine/mix/whisk reconstituted food — PC

Store correctly prepared foods not for immediate use — PC

Clean preparation areas and equipment after use — PC

Deal effectively with problems relating to food and equipment — PC

Do your work in an organised, efficient and safe manner — PC

Element 2

Finish reconstituted food

Get your preparation area and equipment ready for use — PC

Dilute/combine/mix/whisk reconstituted foods — PC

Finish reconstituted foods — PC

Store correctly prepared foods not for immediate use — PC

Clean preparation areas and equipment after use — PC

Deal effectively with problems relating to food and equipment — PC

Do your work in an organised, efficient and safe manner — PC

Safety, security and personal hygiene
in food preparation and cooking

Personal health and hygiene

Handling food and working in a kitchen gives you particular responsibilities:

- for food safety – poor standards of personal hygiene, or an illness or infection, can lead to the food being contaminated with harmful bacteria. The person who eats that food may become ill, possibly seriously, perhaps fatally

- for kitchen safety – if you are not feeling well, or are overtired and so loose concentration, you can easily have an accident. Perhaps you drop a pan of boiling water, or knock a knife off the table, injuring yourself or a colleague.

To keep these risks to the minimum, your employer expects you to follow certain rules and procedures. Some of these will be linked to legal requirements – for example, on the types of illnesses and infections which have to be reported. Some will be part of your employer's duty to maintain a safe workplace, and to serve safe food.

What you wear at work

You spend much or all of your working time standing. Wear comfortable shoes that won't slip, and which protect your feet against spills and dropped objects. Wash your feet every day, and keep your toe nails trimmed. Change socks daily.

Leave your outdoor clothing and footwear in the changing area or locker. Don't take it with you into the kitchen.

Respect your uniform. The traditional double-breasted chef's jacket keeps away some of the heat of the kitchen, and the long sleeves protect your arms from accidental contact with hot equipment.

Remove rings, bracelets, necklaces and earrings before going on duty. If you wear a plain wedding ring, this may be left on. Although it is important to know the time in a kitchen, it is best to rely on a clock rather than your watch which will trap food and dirt. There is also a risk that you will damage your watch by getting it wet.

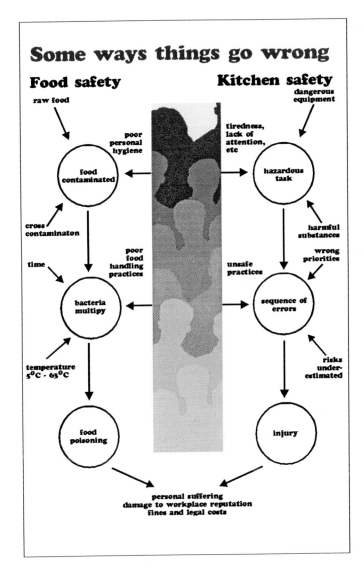

Some ways things go wrong

Food safety — Kitchen safety

raw food

poor personal hygiene

food contaminated

cross contaminaton

time

poor food handling practices

bacteria multipy

temperature 5°C - 63°C

food poisoning

dangerous equipment

tiredness, lack of attention, etc

hazardous task

harmful substances

wrong priorities

unsafe practices

sequence of errors

risks under-estimated

injury

personal suffering
damage to workplace reputation
fines and legal costs

How you look

Keep yourself healthy. A clear skin and complexion depend largely on adequate sleep, exercise and a balanced diet. You will enjoy your work more, and do a better job, if you are not overtired.

For work in food preparation areas, perfumes and aftershave are not appropriate. Your colleagues want to smell the food, not you.

Long flowing hair is not acceptable. It might get trapped in machinery and pieces of hair are likely to fall into food. There is usually a strict rule that hair must be kept in a net or covered by a hat. Whether or not this is the case, you will find that your hair (and this applies to beards and moustaches as well) absorbs smoke and food smells. Daily washing will keep it clean and in healthy condition.

Some people at work in food preparation and service

Personal hygiene

Keep yourself clean and fresh. The body produces moisture constantly through sweat glands located all over. You will perspire more when working under pressure in a hot environment. Sweat itself is virtually odourless and normally evaporates quickly. The smell comes from bacteria which live on the perspiration, especially in areas such as the underarms where it cannot evaporate freely. A daily bath or shower is the best protection.

Pay special attention to your hands. Unless you look after them well and wear gloves when you are meant to, they will get very dry and rough. Keep your fingernails clean, trimmed and definitely no varnish for work time!

Wash your hands often (see checklist) and thoroughly, in the wash hand basin (never a food sink). Use plenty of hot water, soap and the scrubbing brush. Then dry your hands well with the paper towels, roller towel, etc. (never a tea towel or kitchen cloth).

If you feel a sneeze coming, or you need to cough, turn away from any food. Hold a disposable paper tissue over your nose and mouth, and wash your hands afterwards.

Use a clean spoon for tasting food and wash it after use. Never taste food with your fingers.

Do not lick your fingers or touch your nose, mouth or hair.

Never smoke or spit in food handling areas.

Do not sit on work tables.

CHECK list
When to wash your hands

✔ when coming on duty or entering the kitchen

✔ after changing into uniform

✔ after going to the toilet

✔ after handling raw food

✔ between one task and another

✔ after leaving the kitchen

✔ after meal and rest breaks when you have been eating, drinking or smoking

✔ after handling money

✔ after handling waste or putting food in the waste bin

✔ after handling cleaning materials

Kitchen standard of dress and personal hygiene

Capri Beach Hotel

All staff to have clean:
- chef's jacket, neck tie, checked trousers, tall chef's hat
- apron to be worn below the knees
- kitchen safety footwear, black/navy socks
- oven cloths.

Personal appearance:
- hair well groomed, kept off the collar
- finger nails short, clean, no varnish
- no jewellery (wedding ring allowed), no watch
- each individual responsible for personal hygiene and daily bathing.

Reporting illness and infection

Report *any* illness or infection. Your supervisor will judge if it is safe for you to work with food. Don't put other people's health at risk, because you don't want to admit to feeling ill.

Covering cuts, grazes and wounds

Cover cuts, grazes, open sores and wounds with a waterproof dressing. Dressings for kitchen staff (from the first-aid box) are usually coloured blue so that if they do drop off they will be easily spotted.

If the wound or sore is infected, or you think it might be, report this to your manager.

Legal requirements

You have a duty under the Food Safety (General Food Hygiene) Regulations 1995 to tell your manager if:

- you know or suspect you are suffering from, or may be a carrier of, any disease likely to be transmitted through food
- you have an infected wound, a skin infection, sores, diarrhoea or any similar medical condition.

Until you have been cleared of the condition, you will not be permitted to handle food, or work in any capacity where you might put at risk the safety of the food.

Your employer has a responsibility to ensure that every person working in a food handling area:

- maintains a high degree of personal cleanliness
- wears suitable, clean and, where appropriate, protective clothing.

The Regulations also require the provision of adequate hand washing and toilet facilities, and somewhere to change into uniform, and store personal and work clothing.

Reporting illness and infections

If you are suffering from any of the following you must report it to your manager:

- diarrhoea
- vomiting
- cuts or sores
- boils
- skin infection
- discharge from ears/ nose/ eyes

If your doctor has diagnosed any of the following you must report it to your manager:

- food poisoning
- typhoid or paratyphoid
- any infectious disease

Food handlers' induction training checklist – *extract*

Personal hygiene/safety

- need to wash hands in warm soapy water **after** visiting WC – blowing nose – smoking – handling raw foods – handling refuse
- storage of outdoor clothing
- location of first-aid facilities – name of first-aider – recording accidents
- reporting illnesses
- covering cuts and wounds
- securing hair – general cleanliness
- not smoking or spitting in food areas
- not washing food in a wash hand basin
- hands and nails – jewellery – perfume

Kitchen hygiene

- dispose of refuse properly
- clean as you go (surfaces, utensils, cloths)
- how to clean properly
- keeping food containers clean and free from contamination
- use of equipment

Look after your hands. You need them to do your job.

Fire procedures

Many of the fires which occur in restaurants, hotels, pubs, etc. start in the kitchen. Kitchens have a good supply of the three things a fire needs: heat, fuel and oxygen (in other words, air).

Some foods start burning not many degrees higher than their normal cooking temperature. Fats and oils are a special danger: left unattended on the stove, the oil for frying food can quickly reach the temperature where it starts to smoke. Left for a few more minutes, it can burst into flames. If the oil in a deep fat fryer has not been properly filtered or replaced, it can reach this danger point at its normal setting for frying chips, for example.

Raising the alarm

Speed is vital. It is the alarm which warns other people and gives them time to get to safety. It is the alarm which brings help from those who have been trained to fight the fire and to rescue anyone trapped by the smoke, heat or flames.

This means you need to know what to do. Your employer will provide training, and there will be fire notices and other reminders around your workplace telling you what to do. But you are putting a lot of people at risk if you wait until there is a real emergency before trying to get to grips with what has to be done.

Safety and emergency signs and notices

Many fires cause terrible damage and suffering because they start in an area (e.g. the storeroom) or at a time (e.g. late at night) when there is no one present. Automatic fire detection equipment will quickly alert those on duty. But often the smoke and perhaps the fire itself spreads to other parts of the building because people have not closed fire doors. You've seen the signs – do you always obey them?

And what about those signs that say FIRE EXIT KEEP CLEAR? If fire exits are used to store furniture or equipment, people will find their escape route blocked. Also, the fire can spread rapidly down the escape route, as the furniture fuels its progress.

Safety signs and notices are there to make your workplace safer for everyone. Respect this.

Evacuation procedures and the assembly point

The rules are on the fire notices around your workplace. From time to time, there will be a chance to practise an evacuation. If you find any problems during such a fire drill (e.g. a door which is hard to open, or uncertainty about your assembly point), tell your manager.

Be quite clear about any specific responsibilities you have been given, such as turning off the gas or electricity in the kitchen.

Using fire fighting equipment

Around your workplace is a range of fire extinguishers and other appliances for fighting small fires. Get to know their positions, how they should be used and what fires they are suitable for.

Remember, using the wrong extinguisher can make the fire worse. So can a few moments' delay, if you have to fumble around to get the extinguisher to work.

Never put yourself at risk by attempting to fight a fire. This judgement may be difficult to make, and you might be tempted to play the hero. The rule is, if in doubt, don't. Concentrate on raising the alarm and helping with the evacuation.

Fire notices: what they will say

What to do if the fire alarm sounds:
- how to leave the building
- where to assemble

What not to do:
- do not stop to collect personal belongings
- do not run
- do not use the lift
- do not open a door if you suspect there is a fire on the other side
- do not re-enter the building until advised to do so by the manager/officer in charge

What to do if you discover a fire
- raise the alarm by breaking the glass of the nearest fire alarm point [location will be stated]

Extinguishers in use: water (above); *carbon dioxide* (right).

Extinguishers in use: foam (above); *powder* (right).

Fire blanket in use.

Water extinguishers

Coloured red, these are suitable for fires involving wood, paper and cloth:

- direct the jet at the base of the flames
- keep it moving across the area of the fire
- after the main fire is out, respray any remaining hot spot
- if the fire is spreading vertically, attack it at the lowest point, then follow upwards.

Do not use on live electrical equipment, burning fats or oils.

Carbon dioxide extinguishers

Coloured black, these are for fires involving flammable liquids or liquefiable solids, e.g. oil, fat, paint, petrol, paraffin, grease. They are safe and clean to use on live electrical equipment:

- direct the discharge horn at the base of the flames
- keep the jet moving across the area of the fire
- do not touch the discharge horn – this gets extremely cold.

The fumes can be harmful – ventilate the area as soon as fire has been extinguished.

Carbon dioxide cuts off the oxygen supply to the fire, but whatever was on fire remains very hot. Watch that it does not re-ignite.

Foam extinguishers

Use for fires involving paper, wood, etc. AFFF (aqueous film-forming foam) extinguishers, also cream-coloured, are suitable for fires involving flammable liquids. To use:

- stand well back and sweep jet from side to side
- for fires in a container, direct the jet at the inside edge.

Do not aim the foam directly into a burning liquid in case it splashes the fire further.

Some types of foam extinquisher are not suitable for live electrical equipment.

Powder extinguishers

Coloured blue, this type will put out fires involving flammable liquids or liquefiable solids, e.g. oil, fat, grease, etc. It is safe for fires involving electrical equipment, but does not readily penetrate spaces inside equipment, so the fire may re-ignite. To use:

- direct the nozzle at the base of the flames
- with a rapid sweeping motion drive the flame towards the far edge until the flames are out
- repeat as necessary (some extinguishers can be shut off).

For electrical equipment:

- disconnect the equipment from the mains
- direct the jet straight at the fire if possible, so that the powder can penetrate right inside the equipment.

Powder extinquishers have a limited cooling effect, so take care the fire does not re-ignite.

The powder makes a great mess. It can take several hours to clean up after quite a small fire.

Fire blanket

Use for small fires involving burning liquids and burning clothing. You will find one by the deep fat fryer.

Hold the blanket carefully so that it protects your body and hands from the fire, and place it over the flames. Take care not to waft the flames in your direction, or towards bystanders. You may need to put something across a large fryer, e.g. a metal tray, to stop the blanket falling in to the oil.

For a fire involving clothing, wrap the blanket around the burning area, but not over the victim's nose and mouth. Roll the patient on the ground.

Fire hose

For fires involving wood, paper and cloth. To use:

- release the locking mechanism on the reel
- open the valve (to allow water into the hose)
- unreel the length of hose required to reach the fire
- aim the jet of water at the base of the flames and move across the area of the fire.

Maintaining a safe environment

Everyone at work, from the most junior member of staff, to the most senior director, has a duty to protect the health and safety of those around them. This is a moral responsibility and a matter of law.

For your employer, serious breaches of health and safety law can lead to thousands of pounds in fines and legal costs, or even a prison sentence. For you, it can mean the loss of your job.

In fact most workplace accidents are not caused by serious breaches of the law. They happen because of inattention, carelessness, forgetfulness, or gradually falling into bad habits. Put these with an unlucky chain of events and the results can be fatal.

When there are so many other pressures on you and your colleagues, it is not easy to maintain the highest safety standards. No one underestimates the effort involved, but safety must have top priority.

Besides the risk of burning yourself, lifting heavy trays of food from the oven can cause back injury unless you follow the safe lifting techniques.

Identifying hazards

It's unlikely your working area will be free from hazards. Many are unavoidable – electrical equipment has the potential to cause harm (which is what 'hazard' means). Knives can cut you as well as the food. Many slicing and food mixing machines are officially 'prescribed dangerous machines'. Some cleaning agents cause serious burns or poisoning.

For these items, the real dangers arise from their misuse, or through poor maintenance, or because safety guards have been removed.

You will get training or instruction on how to use and clean the various items of kitchen equipment you are expected to operate, and the safety precautions. Don't be afraid to ask questions. Don't put yourself and others in danger (and perhaps risk damaging the equipment) by using equipment you are unfamiliar with, or saying you have already had training, or acting the expert when colleagues can't get it to work.

If you find or suspect the equipment is not working properly, or a safety guard is missing, or there are visual signs of damage (e.g. a frayed electrical cable):

- stop using it immediately

- tell your manager

- label the machine OUT OF ORDER so that no one else attempts to use it.

There is more information throughout this book on the safety measures necessary when using cleaning agents, knives, grills, cooking ranges, deep fryers, microwaves, slicing machines and other types of equipment. What of the other hazards you are likely to encounter?

Over one-third of accidents in the catering and hospitality industry are the result of *slips, trips and falls*. Other common types of accident are *burns and scalds*, *cuts* and *injuries to your back*. Typical hazards to look out for are:

- grease or a spill on the floor – to avoid slips, trips or falls

- pan handles sticking over the edge of the stove – to avoid burns and scalds

- cracked or chipped china and glassware – to avoid cuts

- saucepans or packages of food which are too heavy or awkward to lift without assistance – to avoid injuries to your back, etc.

Warning others and reporting hazards

The hazards you put right, cease to be a danger for you or anyone else. What happens though, when you can't mop up that spill because you are carrying a tray of hot food to the restaurant? Or having found that a shelf in the storeroom is coming away from the wall, you clear the things off it but forget to leave a notice warning others not to restack the shelf?

Don't assume that because you have seen a danger, other people will. It may not be enough to tell your colleagues. In a busy hotel and catering establishment, it's impossible to be sure that customers won't enter even those areas reserved for staff, or that someone else will, who is not as familiar with that part of the building as you are.

Depending on the problem, position a hazard warning sign, rope off the entrance, put a safety barrier in place, attach a label, or remove the dangerous equipment to a safe area.

Then see that the right people in your workplace know of the problem. This may be your manager, one of the other managers, or the maintenance department.

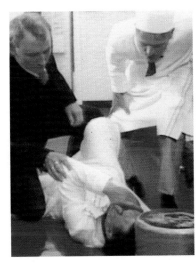

An unfortunate chain of events led to this accident (reconstructed for The Human Factor, *an HCTC training video). People were rushing because of a crisis, some equipment had been mislaid, the arrival of a delivery distracted the person who had gone to get a mop....*

Dealing with an accident

If you are a trained first-aider, you will know what to do to help the casualty. Otherwise, immediately inform the first-aider in your workplace, or in the absence of a first-aider, the person who has been appointed to take charge if a serious injury or illness occurs.

When you started work, you should have been told how to contact the first-aider (or appointed person), and the location of the first-aid box. A notice or poster in the workplace will remind you of this information.

In the first-aid box you will find a supply of dressings and bandages for minor injuries. There will also be a card with general first-aid guidance (an example is given opposite).

(an example is given opposite)

CHECK list
Preventing burns and scalds

✔ properly buttoned up, the double-fronted jacket of a chef's jacket will protect you from burns

✔ keep the sleeves down to protect your arms

✔ take metal spoons out of boiling liquids not left to get dangerously hot while you do something else

✔ keep pan handles away from gas flames and electric radiants, and not sticking out from the edge of the stove, where they may be knocked

✔ turn off unused burning gas flames or electric elements before stretching over them, keep pans where you can best reach them

✔ avoid standing in the path of the steam when removing lids from hot pans

✔ use the oven door to protect yourself from the heat when opening ovens or steamers

✔ always use dry oven cloths when lifting hot items

✔ when filling pans, allow for the boiling action – too full, and the pan will boil over

✔ take great care when moving large pans of hot food. If the pan is too heavy to handle safely, ask someone else to do it or to help you (e.g. if there are two handles). With a liquid, you may be able to ladle some of the contents to another pan

---

Calling an ambulance, the fire brigade or police

1 Use the nearest telephone.
2 Dial 999. No money is required.
3 Ask for the necessary service: ambulance, fire brigade or police.
4 When you get through, give the number of the telephone you are calling from so that the operator can call you back if necessary. Speak clearly.
5 Give the location of the accident.
6 State the nature of the accident or illness, the number of casualties, and as much detail of the injuries as you know.
7 Remain on the phone until the emergency service operator rings off – to be sure that you have given sufficient information.

While help is on its way, stay calm.

Reassure the casualty kindly and confidently. Keep the casualty protected from the cold, but do not cover major burns.

Do not move the casualty unless absolutely necessary.

If the accident has been caused by an electric shock, break the contact by switching off the current at the plug or mains. Do not touch the casualty until the current has been switched off, or you will become a second victim.

Reporting accidents

There should be an accident book (or an appropriate form) available in your workplace, kept where you can easily have access to it. By law you must tell your manager as soon as you have had an accident, but you can do this by writing about the accident in the accident book, or asking someone else to do this on your behalf.

Legal requirements

The main law on health and safety at work is the Health and Safety at Work Act, 1974. Your employer must:

- provide safe equipment and safe ways of carrying out jobs

- ensure that the use, handling, storage and transport of articles and substances are safe and without health risks

- provide information, instruction, training and supervision to ensure health and safety

- maintain the workplace in a safe condition, provide and maintain safe ways of getting into and out of the workplace

- provide a working environment which is safe, without risks to health and has adequate facilities and arrangements for the welfare of employees

- prepare, and as often as necessary, revise the written statement of general health and safety policy, which should also describe the organisation and arrangements for carrying out that policy, and bring the statement and any revisions to the notice of all employees.

Regulations have been made under the Act. These include first-aid and the reporting of accidents (see below), the control and use and hazardous substances (including cleaning agents), gas and electrical equipment, noise and safety signs. Regulations have also been made to bring the UK law into line the EC directives on workplace safety, wearing of protective clothing, manual handling and work equipment.

You have a responsibility towards the safety of others, under the Health and Safety at Work Act (see *Knowledge Check*, page 41). You also have a duty under The Management of Health and Safety at Work Regulations 1992, to use correctly all work items provided by your employer in accordance with the training and instructions you have received to enable you to use the items safely.

Responsibilities of employees

Whilst management has a prime responsibility for ensuring the effectiveness of the company's health and safety policy and procedures, their successful implementation requires the cooperation of all employees and the acceptance by each individual of their responsibility in law.

Each employee has responsibility therefore to:

- take reasonable care for their own health and safety

- ensure that other persons are not endangered by their acts or omissions

- comply with safety rules and practices applicable to the job they are doing

- report all fire and safety hazards to their immediate superior/unit manager

- cooperate with the company to enable it to comply with its legal obligations

- wear as instructed, any protective clothing and safety appliances or equipment which is supplied by the company in the interests of health and safety practice and legislation

- report all injuries or dangerous incidents in accordance with the company procedures

- attend training sessions and safety meetings as required.

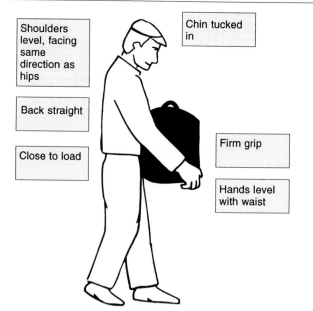

When carrying an object

1 Examine the object.
2 Plan the task and route.
3 Get close to the load, feet slightly apart to give a stable base.
4 Adopt a good posture (see diagram): don't bend your knees fully as this will leave little power to lift, keep your back straight, keep shoulders level and facing in the same direction as the hips.
5 Move smoothly, keeping control of the load. Use your feet if you need to turn, don't twist your body.
6 Place the load down. If necessary adjust its position – check it won't fall, roll over, etc.

First-aid provision

Your employer must make adequate first-aid provision for anyone who is injured or falls ill while at work. There should be at least one first-aid box, kept in a easy reach, and someone appointed to take charge in the event of a serious illness or accident. In larger workplaces, and especially those regarded as high risk, this person must be a qualified first-aider. Other first-aiders may be required to cover days off, or the late shift.

Recording and reporting accidents

By law, even minor accidents in the workplace have to be recorded. More serious incidents also have to be reported to the enforcing authority (usually your local environmental health department). Normally the person in charge of the workplace has to do this, but you may find it helpful for the future to know that:

- a major injury, acute illness, death, or a dangerous occurrence (e.g. a boiler which explodes and might have caused fatal injury) must be reported by the quickest practicable means (i.e. by telephone)

- this must be followed up within seven days by a written report on the official form (code number F2508). The form has a full list of the reportable injuries, illnesses, and dangerous occurrences)

- injuries which result in more than three consecutive days off work following the day of the accident, also have to be reported on the official form.

If you make a claim to the Department of Social Security for benefits in respect of personal injury, or work-related illness, your employer will have to provide detailed information on the accident. This includes where and what you were doing at the time, whether you were authorised to be in that place and to do what you were doing.

Information for the accident record

- date and time of incident
- your full name, address and occupation
- nature of the injury (e.g. cut finger) or illness (e.g. if you have been in contact with a harmful cleaning agent, you may not suffer any pain until some hours later)
- place where the incident happened and description of the circumstances
- names of any witnesses, and their addresses if they are not usually based at your workplace
- details of the person making the report, and date the report was made.

Example adapted from the form used by Catering & Allied Services, with thanks.

Suspicious items and packages

People who leave bombs and similar devices usually make it difficult to find them. But there are few rules in their business, and an increasingly wide range of extremist groups (and individuals with grudges) seek to create fear and destruction.

If you work in a place where high-profile conferences are held, or politicians, royalty, celebrities and leading business people are guests, you will be used to strict security procedures. These will probably include restrictions on when deliveries come from suppliers, and regular searches of the entire building. You will be expected to report any suspicious looking item you see, and trained to recognise anything that is out of the normal. You may be asked to help search your area of the workplace if a bomb threat has been received.

In these and other situations, there are two general rules that you should follow:

- if you see a suspicious-looking item, do not touch it yourself or let colleagues or customers put themselves in possible danger

- call for help, from management and security officers. Tell them calmly and accurately where the item is located, and why you think it is suspicious. They will get in touch with the emergency services.

Incident report form

In the event of any accident or dangerous incident, please complete and return this form to your Operations Manager. A separate form must be completed for each person injured.

UNIT NAME ....

Date of incident .... Time ....

Area in which incident occurred ....

Full name of person involved ....

Address ....

Age ....Sex ❏ Male ❏ Female

Status: ❏ Employee ❏ Contractor ❏Customer

Details of injury/condition (if applicable) and part of body affected ....

....

Details of treatment (if applicable) ....

....

Describe how incident occurred.........................

....

Describe any action taken ....

....

Is the client aware of the incident: ❏ Yes ❏ No

Form completed by ....

Signature ....

Position ....Date ....

Maintaining a secure environment

You may think that security is a subject more appropriate for front of house staff, and those handling cash.

This is far from being the case. Substantial sums of money are tied up in food stocks. Then there's the question of your own belongings, and those of your colleagues. And if you are working in a quick service or fast food operation, you will have contact with customers, and may be expected to deal with lost property.

Thieves are often opportunist. That is, they do not plan a burglary, but seize the opportunity when it arises: a window left slightly open, a key carelessly dropped by a member of staff, deliveries left unattended, money left lying around.

CHECK list
Protecting property

✔ keep keys on you, never left in locks, nor lying around or in supposedly safe places such as the top drawer of the storekeeper's desk

✔ be responsible for your own keys, never lend them to others

✔ leave your personal valuables at home. If you have to bring some to work, keep them safe in your locker while you are on duty

✔ keep personal lockers locked and the key with you

✔ put equipment and materials in the correct place after use. Storage areas must always be kept locked when unattended

✔ report anything belonging to you, colleagues, customers or the your employer, which appears to be missing. This means taking the trouble to notice what is going on around you

✔ respect workplace rules regarding, for example, taking personal handbags, shopping bags or baskets into work areas. Since these are a favourite way of removing stolen property from the premises, you will put yourself under suspicion.

Identifying and reporting security risks

Many of the improvements to security require management action. For example, there is little you can do about an entrance which allows people to enter or leave the building unobserved.

But even when all weaknesses have been corrected, and the best systems installed, their success depends on:

- your vigilance – being alert to anything which is out-of-place, or unusual

- your detailed knowledge of the physical layout of your work area, the normal work routines, and who has regular access to the area – so that you are more likely to notice anything unusual

- your prompt action in reporting the unusual or out-of-place

- your diligence – it is not always easy to challenge someone you think is acting suspiciously, or convenient to stop what you are doing to report a storeroom you find unlocked.

If there is an opportunity, make a tour of your workplace with the person in charge of security or a crime prevention officer from the local police (your manager might arrange this as part of a security training session for you and your colleagues). They can point out security risks you might never think of.

Preventing unauthorised access

When you have reason to enter a room or area which is kept locked, it is your responsibility to see that it is locked again after you have finished. If you have to leave the room temporarily, relock it. Unless you are sure of the person's identity and reason for entering the room, do not to let anyone else in while you are there. Keep the key with you, not left in the door or some other place where it might be removed unnoticed by you.

Good key control is essential. You may be asked to sign for keys, and to get your manager or the security officer's signature when you return them. Don't pass keys on to a colleague. If they go missing, it could be rather awkward proving that you were not responsible.

There may be a cash box in your workplace for buying emergency supplies, or small value purchases in local shops. If you have access to this, you will be expected to produce receipts or some other record to account for what has been spent. Be quite sure you return the cash box to its proper place, and that it is locked.

In some top luxury hotels and restaurants, silverware for presenting and serving food is kept in a strong room or large safe. Some items may be worth thousands of pounds, so make sure that anything you have used is put back at the end of service.

Reporting lost property

When a customer's or colleague's property (e.g. coats, bags and umbrellas) is left behind, hand it in immediately to a manager. Put a note on it giving details of where it was found, and the date and time. This will help identify the true owner.

When a claim is made for lost property, ask for a description of the item. If there is any doubt that the claim is genuine, or the lost property is a particularly valuable item, ask a manager to deal with the matter.

Dealing with suspicious individuals

Check the identity of contractors, sales representatives, tradespeople, local authority officials, meter readers, etc. before you let them into the building. In a large establishment, there will probably be a security officer who does this. All visitors and staff will be issued with an identity badge. In this case you should report anyone you see in the building who is not wearing a badge. Where appropriate, ask politely if you can help the person.

In a small workplace, you are likely to be much more aware of the comings and goings, and more trusting. But there are people who take advantage of this, pretending to be an engineer calling to collect the microwave for repair, or a supplier to take back cases of wine delivered to the wrong address. They are relying on you not checking their story.

Legal requirements

You have a duty to protect the property of your employer and of others in your workplace (e.g. hotel or restaurant customers). You also have a duty to protect the safety and welfare of customers, staff and visitors by preventing unauthorised access to the premises.

The law is also there to support your action. For example, someone destroying or damaging property which is not theirs, stealing or attempting to steal, is committing a criminal offence.

Tackling the problem

There is no definitive description of what a bomb looks like. They vary in size, shape, colour and design as well as make-up. They can be disguised in many ways – in briefcases, handbags, carrier bags, holdalls, radio cassettes and even 'cigarette' packets are just a few examples.

Receiving a bomb threat

Most threats are delivered by telephone because the caller:

- knows or believes an explosive device has been placed and wants to minimise injury
- wants to disrupt normal activities by creating anxiety and panic: this caller may simply be a disgruntled employee or customer.

If you take a telephone call which turns out to be a bomb threat, try to find out from the caller, and make note of:

- where the bomb is located
- what it looks like
- when it will go off
- what will make it go off
- why the bomb was planted.

Also note any details about the caller: accent, male/female, background noises, etc.

After taking the call, immediately tell a manager.

With thanks to The Boddington Pub Company.

Security

- keep all non-public access doors locked when not attended

Suspicious items

- keep a look out for any unattended bags or packages of any description
- an unaccountable smell of petrol or marzipan could mean a bomb
- report any suspicious packages to your manager
- if the unit is to be evacuated, lead all customers to the nearest safe fire exit, calmly

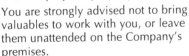

- when customers have been evacuated, leave the bulding yourself and assemble at the fire point and await the roll call
- remember: do not use a fire extinguisher on any suspect bomb
- never attempt to move suspicious objects

Personal property

The security of personal property is the responsibility of the individual employee, and the Company does not accept liability for loss and/or damage to an employee's property.

You are strongly advised not to bring valuables to work with you, or leave them unattended on the Company's premises.

Lost property

All lost property found in or about the Company premises should be handed to management of the branch who will examine the contents in front of you.

Should a customer enquire as to an item of lost property, ask him or her to take a seat and inform management.

1 Why should you wear a hat when handling food?

2 Describe the purpose of
(a) the necktie,
(b) the double breasted jacket,
(c) the long sleeves,
(d) the apron,
of the traditional chef's uniform?

3 Describe the standards of personal hygiene required at your workplace.

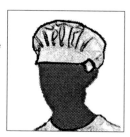

4 By having these high standards, how does it benefit you?

5 After taking the customer's money, what should you do before handling food, and why?

6 Why must you use hot water and soap when washing your hands?

Questions 3 to 6 are adapted from the training manual of Compass Retail Catering Division.

38

7 Why is food hygiene so important to our business?

Questions 7 to 12 are from the food hygiene induction test at McDonald's.

8 Give four common sense guidelines you should follow concerning your appearance.

9 Give six examples of when you should wash your hands.

10 How should cuts, burns, abrasions, etc. on your hands be protected?

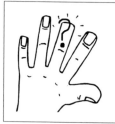

11 What must you do if you lose a plaster while working?

12 What should you do if you are ill with sickness or diarrhoea?

Illustrations with thanks to McDonald's Restaurants Limited

Bacteria, you and food poisoning

The bacteria *Staphylococcus aureus* can be:

- in your nose – do not sneeze over food or food surfaces
- on cuts and grazes – keep them covered with a plaster
- on spots, boils, and styes (red swelling on the eye lid) – tell your manager if you are suffering from any of these
- on your mouth – avoid touching your mouth when you are handling food
- on your hands – because you have touched your nose or your mouth.

From your hands, or because you have sneezed, the bacteria can get on to food. If the food has already been cooked, or is of the type that will not be cooked (e.g. a salad), the bacteria will soon multiply to harmful numbers.

You also have to be careful with food that will be cooked. Although the bacteria are killed at temperatures above 100°C, they produce poisons which can survive high temperature for 30 minutes or longer.

Within a few hours of eating food contaminated with *Staphylococcus*, the unfortunate person can be vomiting severely, and in great pain from stomach cramps and diarrhoea.

13 Where is your nearest fire call point? How do you operate it?

14 What is the escape route from your work area? How do you escape if this route is blocked by fire?

15 For each of the extinguishers in your work area, say how it is to be used.

Cartoons from J D Wetherspoon's training manual.

16 What do you do if you believe there is a gas leak in your work area?

17 What sort of fire should this extinguisher be used to fight? What precautions should you take? (You can recognise the extinguisher from its distinctive cone-shaped nozzle.)

18 If equipment you are using develops a fault, what must you do?

19 How can you prevent trips and falls in your workplace?

20 What could happen if you wear loose items of clothing when using equipment?

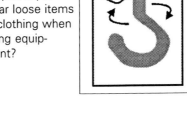

21 Why is it important that your hands are dry when touching electrical equipment?

22 Describe how you should dispose of a broken piece of china or glass.

23 Why is it dangerous to store cleaning agents in unmarked containers?

FIRE PREVENTION is everybody's business

Fire exits and routes – are for your safety. Keep them free from obstruction at all times.

Extinguishers – are provided to tackle fires. Do you know where they are and how to operate them? Find out today – tomorrow may be too late. Never use them to prop open fire doors.

No smoking areas – are for your safety and comfort. Never try to beat the ban – that secret smoke could become embarrassingly public.

Security – protects against people who start fires for kicks.

Waste – is fuel for fire. Do not allow it to accumulate on the floor. Clear it away regularly.

Stock (of food, cleaning materials, etc.) – is always on the move. Keep it away from heaters and lights.

Storage areas – kept tidy help prevent fire and allow any outbreak to be tackled more easily.

Equipment servicing – and repair are jobs for the experts. Report suspected faults, damaged cables, etc. to your manager at once.

Shut-down check

Power	off at mains.
Appliances	switched off and unplugged.
Keep tidy	get waste outside to a safe place.
Lock up	you don't know who your next visitor might be.

If you detect leaking gas

1 Avoid doing anything that might cause the gas to ignite – e.g. using a naked light, or striking a match, or turning a light or other electrical equipment on or off (which can create sparks).

2 Turn off any gas appliances which are still on, and check that all others are properly turned off.

3 Open windows (and exterior doors) to get rid of the gas and leave open until the leak has been stopped and any build-up of gas has dispersed.

4 Call your manager.

24 What precautions must you take when opening a can of food?

25 Say what you must do if a work colleague has a serious accident, and you are the only other person in the kitchen.

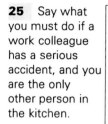

In case of Emergency
Dfggkfg hgghig
Gh hdhg gh gd
Efg'rf 'er ghkig .xcj
Og hdf hdigeei34i ei f
Gr fregii igtg
Hy GGG hjlfr o jd

Kgfghh hdafkh
Igh e943jh5 irly
Jjgb elge
Kjg 936jk dg
Kfu84f
Rg igflie frieigf gigc figfler

26 If you have a minor accident at work, what is the procedure for reporting it?

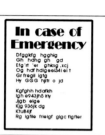

Accident Report

27 Where is the first-aid box kept? Who do you contact for first-aid assistance?

First Aid

28 Why is it important to report anyone you see behaving suspiciously?

29 What details should you make a note of if you find lost property?

30 What rules should you follow when lifting a box of food or item of equipment from the floor?

With thanks to Whitbread, reproduced from the Manual Handling and Lifting Staff Training Package, Backbreakers.

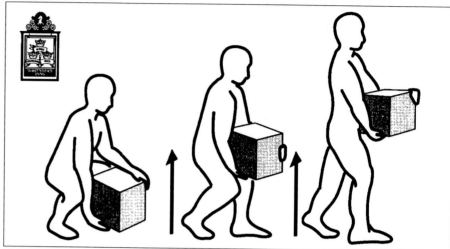

31 Study the before and after pictures below. What hazards can you spot in the first scene? Mark safety hazards in one colour, hygiene hazards in another.

32 Imagine yourself working in the second kitchen when it is in the midst of a busy meal preparation. What hazards might there be?

With thanks to Jeyes

JEYES

For help to answer questions
relating to:

Health and safety

complying with safety legislation

The fire safety legislation requires
your employer to provide instruction
on what you should do in the event of
a fire, and an opportunity to
familiarise yourself with the
evacuation procedure.

You have a responsibility under the
Health and Safety at Work Act 1974:

- not to interfere with or misuse
  anything provided in the interests
  of health, safety or welfare
- take reasonable care for the
  health and safety of yourself and
  of other persons who may be
  affected by what you do, or do not
  do, at work
- perform health and safety-related
  duties and comply with health
  and safety requirements imposed
  by your employer or any other
  person with health and safety
  responsibilities.

obtaining information on legislation

The Health and Safety Executive
(HSE) poster *Health and safety law:
what you should know* should be on
display in your workplace. On it are
details of those who enforce the law
in your area.

Alternatively you may have been
given a copy of the leaflet published
by the HSE (code number HSC5),
and a separate note of the useful
addresses.

Many employers have in-house
health and safety material. Others
provide employees with leaflets or
books published for general industry
use, and to meet special needs, e.g. of
those whose first language is not
English.

potential hazards in your workplace

Think of what you and your
colleagues do, the equipment in your
workplace, what cleaning agents you
use, what lifting and moving of
heavy items are required, any
features of the building which might
cause a hazard (e.g. a narrow, steep
staircase, a concealed entrance to the
delivery area). Ask your colleagues
what hazards they have noted. It's
also worth while asking about the
accidents there have been in the
workplace, and getting your
manager's permission to look
through the accident book. What
hazards led to the accident?

measures you can take to warn others

Your answer should reflect the types
of hazards you have just mentioned,
and the procedure in your workplace
for labelling faulty equipment,
indicating wet floors, or stopping
people from entering an unsafe area.

possible causes of fire

Look around you. Could oil or fat
used in frying or roasting catch fire?
Could food left unattended under the
grill start a fire? Is the rubbish
stored safely? What about the
storage areas? If smoking is allowed
in staff changing rooms, etc. or
customer areas, what about
discarded matches and cigarette
ends? Where are flammable cleaning
materials stored?

minimising the risk of fire

Much of this will follow on from the
analysis you have just done of the
possible causes of fire. You will get
some further ideas from the industry
advice on fire prevention given on
these pages.

procedures in the event of a fire

If you can't remember, have another
look at the fire notice on display in
your workplace. Remind yourself
why it is so important to know *in
advance* what has to be done.

where to find/how to use fire alarms

There's likely to be one very close to
you, so check now.

dangers of approaching a fire

Too many people have
underestimated the danger of trying
to fight a fire. The lucky ones have
had some minor injuries and rather a
fright. Others have lost their lives.
Sounding the fire alarm and calling
the fire brigade (if this is your
responsibility) will bring help from
the experts. They have the clothing
and equipment which offers some
protection from the intense heat and
suffocating smoke, and the training
and experience to use rescue and fire
fighting equipment.

suspicious items and packages

Unfortunately, items or packages
apparently mislaid by their owners
could be a bomb. If it is, it is
probably set to go off immediately
anyone touches or moves it. Making
the device harmless is strictly a job
for the bomb disposal experts.

Terrorists use unpredictable ways to
achieve their aims. The actions of
terrorist copycats – members of
extremist pressure groups or even
disgruntled ex-employees – can be
even more difficult to anticipate. You
must leave decisions to those who
have experience at dealing with
these situations.

location of first aid box and accident book

Ask your manager if you are not
sure.

your workplace first aider

As above, ask if you do not know.
Also find out who to contact if you
need first-aid while on weekend or
late night duty.

correct lifting techniques

Around one in five accidents in the
catering and hospitality industry
result from handling, lifting or
carrying. Sometimes injury to your
back does not become apparent for
days or weeks.

It is not just the weight of the item.
Many factors make lifting or moving
an object difficult, or even
dangerous. Your employer has a duty
to minimise the risk of injury from
manual handling, or preferably to
eliminate it – by ordering smaller
packages from suppliers, providing
trolleys, etc.

security from unauthorised access

Examples of keys, property and
areas should be secured from
unauthorised access at all times are:
your personal locker, the food
storerooms, freezers and cold rooms
which are not in immediate sight of
the kitchen. After service, you may
be expected to lock the kitchen, or
parts of it such as the chef's office
and refrigerators.

If you have to work in a mobile
kitchen for an outdoor event, or in a
service kitchen to the banqueting
room for example, these may have to
be locked when unattended.

Overnight, cleaners may require
access to the kitchen and there will
be an arrangement over where the
keys are left (e.g. at the security
office).

security awareness

Effective security depends on all
those in the workplace noticing the
unusual or suspicious. With
experience and training, you will
become aware of risks that
previously you had not recognised.
This will be a continual learning
process.

lost property procedures

Unless you do so, it will be difficult
to return the property to its owner.
Accusations could be made that the
property was stolen – and in the
absence of a proper procedure for lost
property, it would be hard to
disprove these.

security of information

Robberies and terrorist actions are
often successful because information
on the security systems has been
skilfully extracted from employees.
This information is carefully
analysed to spot weaknesses in the
system.

Maintain a safe and secure working environment

? reporting unusual/non-routine incidents

The people in charge of security in your workplace can only act on the information they receive. You are a key part of the network. Leave to them the judgement whether the information is useful or not. Often a series of events, each insignificant on its own, add up to give warning of a major problem.

Hygiene

? complying with hygiene legislation

Consider what might happen if you handle raw food, then cooked food, without washing your hands. If (and this is quite possible) there were salmonella bacteria on the raw chicken, these would be transferred to the cold ham you have arranged for the buffet lunch. Customers subsequently get ill, and visit their doctor. The doctor diagnoses food poisoning and informs the environmental health department. This leads to a visit to your premises from the environmental health officer (EHO). Lots of questions are asked. Samples of food are taken away. A prosecution may follow, leading to a large fine and bad publicity in the local papers. The business might be ordered to carry out improvements, or in serious cases be closed.

? general hygiene practices

The main text and industry examples give many examples of good practice. Have a look at the training aids you are given at work, including reminder notices.

? correct work clothing

There are four reasons: hygiene, safety, appearance and comfort.

? reporting illness and infections

To whom? Usually the manager, but check your workplace procedures.

Why? It's a requirement under the public health and the food safety regulations. There is a great risk that you will pass on the harmful infection through the food you handle. The bacteria get on to your hands when you use the toilet, or through touching your mouth, nose or ears, for example. From your hands they get on to food, or to surfaces that later come into contact with food.

Some bacteria are not easily removed from your hands by washing.

? importance of good personal hygiene

Think of the close contact you have with food. Think of your employer's legal responsibilities to serve food which is safe to eat. Think of what could happen to your employer's business and to your job if unsafe food is served, and the people who suffer seek financial compensation.

NVQ SVQ

Use this to check your progress against the performance criteria.

Element 1
Maintain personal health and hygiene

Wear clean, smart and appropriate work clothing ☐ PC1

Keep your hair neat and tidy ☐ PC2

Comply with workplace rules on jewellery, perfume, cosmetics ☐ PC3

Have cuts, grazes and wounds treated by the appropriate person ☐ PC4

Correctly report illness and infections ☐ PC5

Follow good hygiene practices ☐ PC6

Clean preparation areas and equipment after use ☐ PC7

Carry out your work in an organised, efficient and safe manner ☐ PC8

Element 2
Carry out procedures in the event of a fire

In the event of a fire, immediately raise the alarm ☐ PC1

Use fire fighting equipment correctly ☐ PC2

▲ Fire hose, fire blanket, foam extinguisher, powder extinguisher, water extinguisher, carbon dioxide extinguisher

Conform to instructions on safety and emergency signs and notices ☐ PC3

Follow evacuation procedures ☐ PC4

Reach assembly point in a calm and orderly manner ☐ PC5

Identify problems with the quality of the dish and report these promptly ☐ PC6

Carry out your work in an organised, efficient and safe manner ☐ PC7

Element 3
Maintain a safe environment for customers, staff and visitors

Identify and where possible rectify hazards and potential hazards ☐ PC1

Follow procedures for making people aware of hazards ☐ PC2

Follow procedures for giving warning of hazards ☐ PC3

Correctly report accidents, damage and hazards you cannot rectify ☐ PC4

Carry out your work in an organised, efficient and safe manner ☐ PC5

Element 4
Maintain a secure environment for customers, staff and visitors

Identify and report potential security risks ☐ PC1

▲ Risks: prohibited areas, suspicious items unauthorised open entrances/exits, missing keys

Secure customer and staff areas against unauthorised access ☐ PC2

▲ Public facilities, public areas, work areas, staff facilities

Secure storage and security facilities against unauthorised access ☐ PC3

▲ Storerooms, safes, cash boxes

Follow procedures for reporting lost property ☐ PC4

Challenge (politely) or report suspicious individuals ☐ PC5

Carry out your work in an organised, efficient and safe manner ☐ PC6

Hygiene
in food storage, preparation and cooking

Units 1ND12 and 2ND22 – Element 1

Hygiene in food storage

Good hygiene practice starts here. Delivery checks help establish that the food is safe when it comes into your workplace. Careful storage ensures that the food remains safe until it is ready to prepare, cook and serve.

Working safely

You can injure yourself by attempting a manual handling task that you have not been trained to do (see Section 2). Remember this when you help with a delivery, or move food into or out of stores, freezers, etc.

The weight is only one factor. Some things are not easy to grasp properly because of the wrapping or the shape. If the store is on another floor and there is no lift, or the delivery is a very large one, this will add to the difficulties.

Safe storage also means neatness and good organisation. Consider where best to put things: heavy items near the floor, passageways kept clear, etc. (More detail is given in Section 5.)

Working hygienically

Food will normally come well wrapped when it is delivered. When the consignment consists of large drums of cooking oil, boxes of canned products, bags of flour, etc., your hands will get dirty from the packaging. This won't harm the food, but you must wash your hands thoroughly before resuming your other duties.

Take special care with deliveries that include unprotected food, e.g. loaves of fresh bread on open trays. The tray itself, and even the paperwork that you have to check, is likely to soil your hands. You should not then pick up individual loaves of bread to examine their quality – unless you have washed your hands.

Checking a delivery of lettuces, for example, will involve touching some of them. Although the lettuces will be washed before use, you still need to be careful that your hands are clean. This is particularly so if you have just been moving containers of a cleaning fluid. And of course, you should wash your hands again after you have finished with the lettuces, since they may have dirt, slugs or other forms of insect life on them!

Spills which occur during a delivery should be cleared up as soon as possible. This will help keep the area clean and safe. Remove packaging no longer required.

Flow chart of the catering operation
with thanks to Catering & Allied Services

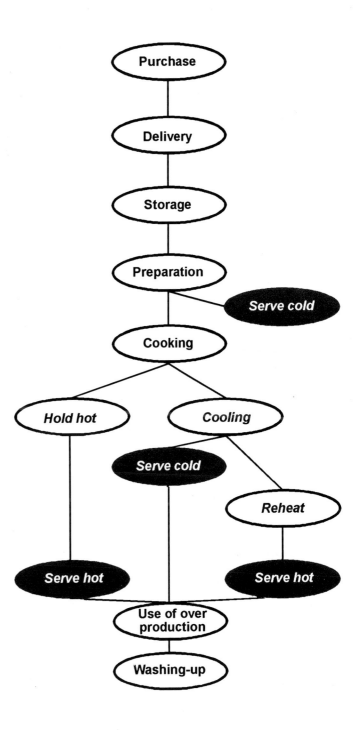

Your employer will look at the whole process of storing, handling, preparing, cooking and serving food, and develop a control system for the critical points.

Reporting deliveries

When it is not your responsibility to accept a delivery, call the appropriate person without delay. Be firm, but polite, if the delivery person claims to be in too much of a rush to wait, or uses arguments like 'it really doesn't need to be checked', or 'no one bothers to normally'.

Goods must be checked at the time of delivery, so that problems over the quality or quantity can be noted on the delivery paperwork. Otherwise, there is a risk that a claim will be disputed. How can you prove, several days later, that some jars of mayonnaise were broken?

Checking deliveries

Here are the general points likely to be reflected in your own workplace procedure:

- *appearance of the food* – is this appropriate for the type of food, e.g. no green on the skin of potatoes? Guidelines on quality can be found in Sections 8 to 24, which deal with the preparation and cooking of different foods

- *packaging* – is this sound? Broken packets may indicate that the contents have been crushed, or damaged by pests, or that food has spilled out (e.g. liquids, frozen peas)

- *temperature* – chilled and frozen foods and many uncooked foods, such as meat, fish and dairy products, should be at a safe temperature at the time of delivery. Most workplaces set their own level; for chilled foods this will be between 5°C and 8°C, for frozen foods around –10°C

- *date indicating the maximum period for which the food can be stored* – foods which have to be stored at low temperatures, and have a relatively short product life after manufacture, carry a *use-by* date. Frozen, canned, vacuum packed foods and virtually all other prepacked foods carry a *best-before* date (before which the food will retain its optimum condition). Items which have already reached their use-by or best-before date should not be accepted and, if the date is very close, you should check the acceptability with your manager or whoever placed the order

- *general cleanliness* – delivery vehicles which are not clean, dirty outer packaging on food, signs of spillages over food or contamination from dust, etc. are indications of poor hygiene standards of the supplier. Certainly these should be reported to your manager, and if there is evidence that the safety of the food has been affected, you should reject that part of the delivery.

Checking food deliveries

IND COOPE RETAIL

1 Examine canned and bottled products and reject any that are dented, rusted or swollen. Also return bottled products with an abnormal colour. Vacuum packed products should not show loss of volume.

2 Return any frozen foods that are thawing or where ice has formed in the bottom of the packaging.

3 Reject refrigerated foods if the temperature on delivery is warmer than 8°C.

4 Joints of meat and meat products are to be examined for quality and colour. Fresh meat deliveries should arrive below 8°C. No raw and cooked foods should be transported together.

5 Reject dry goods of unusual colours or with punctured or torn packaging.

6 Any product, the odour or appearance of which is unusual or causes concern, should not be accepted, nor will any product delivered in an unhygienic manner.

7 Examine use-by and best-before dates to ensure the product has sufficient life for your needs, and taking into account stock levels.

8 Immediately place foods in a designated storage area. Keep raw and cooked foods separate. Place new deliveries in date sequence, to ensure adequate rotation.

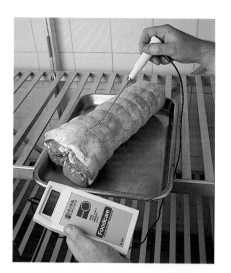

Don't take shortcuts when you accept deliveries, or place new stock on shelves. Good temperature control is one of the main defences against harmful bacteria. Good stock rotation prevents wastage and ensures the quality of the food you prepare is high.

Rotating stock

Older stock should be used before the more recent deliveries. Say there are two cartons of cream in the refrigerator or cold room, with the use-by dates of 5 March and 8 March. Unless the 5 March carton is used first, there is a danger that the cream will pass its use-by date before it is required. On 6 March any of that cream remaining would have to be thrown away.

Careful organisation of storage space makes it easier to use older stock first. This may be as simple as moving the older stock to the right of the shelf. If storage space is limited, you may have to clear a whole shelf, so that the new stock can be put at the back.

Food storage conditions

The aim of storing food is to keep it in the best possible condition until the time it is required. This means protecting it from:

- *harmful bacteria* – uncooked food should be stored well apart from cooked food

- *harmful substances* – cleaning agents should be kept in a separate room and in the original or clearly marked containers. Poisoned baits for pests should only be moved by the pest control contractor

- *physical contamination* – food should be kept in its original packaging or transferred to a container which will keep out dirt, dust, pieces of packaging, loose flakes of paint and plaster, etc. If the original packaging does not sufficiently protect the food once it has been opened (often the case with vacuum-wrapped food), the food should be wrapped well with clingfilm, or transferred to a suitable container

- *pests* – keep the food covered, away from walls, windows and ventilators which attract pests, and above floor level (see below)

- *unsuitable temperatures* – keep frozen food in the freezer, and foods which require chilled temperatures in the cold room or refrigerator. Check the best storage place for fruit and vegetables if you are unsure (e.g. bananas will discolour if refrigerated, see page 3 and Section 11)

- *excessive humidity or dryness* – your workplace instructions will take account of this. Too humid or damp conditions will, for example, cause sugar to become lumpy, bread mouldy, and breakfast cereals soft and flabby; too dry will cause sultanas and raisins to shrivel excessively.

Preventing pest infestation

Kitchen stores offer unlimited supplies of food to pests. But good hygiene practices discourage them: checking goods at the time of delivery, keeping the store clean and tidy, rotating stock, removing waste promptly, keeping food in closed containers, etc.

Report any signs of pests (see checklist) promptly. This also applies to damage to fixtures and fittings, which might allow pests entry to the stores: windows or external doors not closing tightly, gaps in the boxing around pipes or ventilation ducts, etc.

Legal requirements

The Food Safety (General Food Hygiene) Regulations 1995 require food to be protected from the risk of contamination at all stages including transportation, handling and storage. Specific points include:

- raw materials or ingredients should not be accepted if you know or suspect they are contaminated – unless the normal preparation or cooking processes will make them safe to eat

- food must be placed and/or protected so as to minimise any risk of contamination

- adequate procedures must exist to control pests

- hazardous and/or inedible substances must be kept in separate or secure containers, adequately labelled.

Temperature controls will be the subject of separate regulations.

CHECK list
Pests: signs to look for

✔ droppings – the droppings of mice and rodents are black, small and oval shaped

✔ damage – holes in bags and sacks, gnaw marks on the food itself, packaging, food containers, stored equipment (e.g. plastic trays), electric cables, shelves, etc.

✔ footprints, tail marks – in dust or on food

✔ dark, greasy marks on walls or pipes – suggests mice and rodents frequently use that route, the stains coming from the animals' coats

✔ the pest itself – dead or alive

✔ the pest's habitat – holes and nesting sites

✔ offensive odours – often noticeable when you move a piece of equipment, or clean a corner or cupboard which is not often disturbed

Hygiene in food preparation and cooking

Studies of food poisoning incidents by food safety experts show that the most frequent causes are:

1 food prepared too far in advance

2 food stored or held at room temperature for too long

3 inadequate cooling/refrigeration

4 inadequate reheating

5 insufficient cooking

6 holding food too long in hot cupboards

7 cross contamination

8 inadequate thawing.

All these can occur when food handlers are not sufficiently aware of the standard good practices, and the reasons for them. Or, in a kitchen which is not well organised and where staff have few or no guidelines.

Problems often follow a combination of circumstances. What might normally be safe becomes dangerous when a previous step in the storage or preparation process has been overlooked.

Hygienic work practices

Never use utensils which have been in contact with raw food – including chopping boards, knives and slicing machines – for cooked food, unless they have been thoroughly washed and sanitised. This is to prevent cross contamination.

Wherever possible, keep knives and chopping boards for specific uses. This is much easier if your workplace has a system of colour-coding (see page 233), or the purpose of the equipment is etched on to the surface.

Temperatures are a key control point in food safety. Don't rely on appearances: a portion of food may look very hot on the surface, but in the centre it could be many degrees lower. Use a temperature probe for accuracy, and if the dish or piece of food is a large one, probe it in two or three places. Always clean the probe before and after use, with a wipe of sanitising solution.

Clean as you go. This applies to your hands, to work surfaces and to the equipment you are using. Clear up any spills on the floor without delay. Remove waste quickly.

Requirements for various food types

Follow the cooking temperatures and times stated on food labels or in recipes carefully. A general rule is that the temperature at the centre of the food must reach 70°C or higher depending on the food, for a minimum of two minutes. Make sure the oven/grill/fryer etc. is at the right temperature before you start cooking the food.

Ambient

There are no special requirements for ambient foods. In other words, items like flour, pulses, rice, dried pasta which can be safely kept at room temperature. Once the item has been cooked, or it has been used as an ingredient in a particular dish, the normal rules for prepared foods apply.

Canned foods should be treated as prepared food once the can has been opened. Any unused contents should be transferred to a suitable, clean bowl or food storage container, covered and placed in the refrigerator.

Chilled

Chilled foods should spend the minimum time in kitchen temperatures. Arrange your work routine so that such foods are not taken out of the refrigerator or cold room until required for preparation or cooking. For best cooking results, remove eggs from chilled storage about an hour before required.

Frozen

Frozen foods like chickens, turkey, joints and cuts of lamb, beef, pork, etc., must thaw completely before cooking (see page 48 and 94). This can take up to two days for a large joint of meat or a big turkey.

Frozen vegetables are normally cooked from frozen. This also applies to items like scampi and other frozen pre-prepared dishes like chicken kiev and moussaka.

Ice-cream is sometimes kept in an ice-cream conservator before service (this operates at higher temperatures than a deep freeze, so the ice-cream is not rock-hard). The temperature of the ice-cream should not exceed –2°C, or it will start to melt and must be discarded. By law, it must never be refrozen.

If you are reheating (or reconstituting) chilled or frozen food this should be done quickly and thoroughly, so that the temperature at the centre reaches at least 70°C. In some establishments a minimum core temperature of 75°C is laid down.

STAKIS

Receipt, storage and use of frozen foods

1 Delivery of frozen foods must be checked to ensure that: temperature is no higher than –10°C: use a probe thermometer, but do not pierce packaging; product specifications and quantities accord with what were ordered; packaging is in good condition: damaged packaging may lead to 'freezer burn'.

2 New supplies of frozen food must be placed into deep freeze storage (at –18°C) at once, unless intended for immediate use.

3 Deliveries must be date marked and used in rotation. Goods must be placed on shelves with sufficient gap to allow easy circulation of cold air. In chest freezers, new stock must be placed underneath existing stock. In walk-in units, food must be placed on shelves.

4 There is no provision for freezing foods on the premises, and this practice is therefore strictly prohibited.

5 Deep freeze cabinets may not be used for rapid chilling of food. Neither may hot food be placed into the freezer as this will raise the temperature of the unit and adversely affect other foods.

6 Frozen raw meat joints and poultry should be thawed out slowly and thoroughly in refrigerators or using rapid thaw equipment. Crash thawing by immersion in sinks of water (e.g. poultry) is **not** permitted. Crash thawing of foods using the defrost cycle of a microwave oven is permitted, provided the product is used or processed immediately afterwards, or held in a chill cabinet for not longer than 24 hours before consumption.

7 Thawed or partially thawed food must be stored in refrigerators, and should be used within 24 hours.

8 It is permissible to partially use the contents of a frozen food package (e.g. peas), provided that the remainder is returned unthawed to the freezer immediately, and that the package is completely resealed.

Cooked

Cooked foods should be served as soon as possible. Follow your workplace instructions on the temperatures at which food should be kept if there is a delay before service (generally this must be above 63°C) and how long the food can be kept.

The answer to how long depends on the type of food. A soufflé has to be served at once to prevent it collapsing, but most soups, casseroles, etc. can be kept hot throughout service without the quality suffering. In burger and other fast food restaurants, the holding time for cooked food may be as short as ten minutes.

Cooked food which is intended to be served much later should be chilled as quickly as possible (within 90 minutes) and should then be kept refrigerated.

Keep raw meat and poultry, fresh vegetables, fruit and similar *uncooked foods* separate from cooked foods to prevent cross contamination. To preserve quality, do not remove from storage ahead of time.

Main contamination threats

One of the reasons for cooking food, apart from making it more digestible and palatable, is to kill harmful microorganisms which may be present in the food.

The greatest danger is *food-poisoning bacteria*. There might be literally millions of these present on the food, yet they will be completely invisible. The food looks, smells and tastes perfectly normal.

The symptoms of food poisoning can start within an hour of eating harmful food, or as many as five days later. The commonest symptoms are stomach aches, vomiting and diarrhoea.

The bacteria responsible may have been:

- present on the food when it entered the kitchen – *salmonella* and *campylobacter*, for example, are found widely in the environment, in water, soil and sometimes therefore in raw foods such as poultry, meat and eggs

- spread from another food already contaminated – through poor food handling and storage – this is known as *cross contamination*

- carried by pets or pests, or by dust – through poor cleaning practices, inadequate supervision of the premises, badly designed premises or equipment, lack of maintenance, etc.

- introduced by those handling the food – through poor personal hygiene practices.

Other dangers to food arise from:

- *physical objects* – finding their way into the food as a result of bad practice, lack of cleanliness or poor maintenance: pieces of jewellery, food packaging, plasters which have fallen off fingers, loose pieces of paintwork or bits of equipment, etc.

- *chemical contaminants* – from using inappropriate cooking equipment, e.g. copper or aluminium pans for cooking fruits, vinegar or other acidic foods

- *cleaning agents* – confused for food items because they have been stored in the wrong place, or in unlabelled containers, e.g. bleach in a lemonade bottle

- *poisons in the food itself* – not removed because of inadequate preparation, e.g. not boiling kidney beans vigorously to get rid of poisonous toxins, not trimming off the (poisonous) leaves of rhubarb.

Time and temperature

Bacteria which cause food poisoning prefer a warm, moist environment which is not too acid, nor too alkaline. They like foods rich in protein, such as meat, milk or eggs.

Growth does not begin immediately but, once the bacteria have adapted to their environment, the number will increase very rapidly. In ideal conditions, some bacteria will double in number every 10 minutes.

Most food-poisoning bacteria prefer a temperature range of 20°C to 40°C – so kitchens are perfect for them! Some types will grow anywhere in the range 5°C to 63°C. This is known as the *temperature danger zone*.

Above 63°C most bacteria are rapidly killed. Below 5°C most types do not feed or multiply, but stay inactive.

There are exceptions. *Listeria monocytogenes* can grow to dangerous numbers in chilled foods. Certain bacteria form spores at high temperatures. Like the seeds of plants, these can withstand difficult conditions, then, as soon as the environment is favourable, they germinate.

The spores formed by *Bacillus cereus* (occurs in rice, cereals and vegetables) reactivate during long moist storage at warm temperatures.

Clostridium perfringens will also form spores. It occurs in the intestines of animals and many humans, also in raw meat and poultry, in water and in the soil.

Staphylococcus (various strains) produces a toxin (poisonous chemical) if allowed to multiply. Although the bacteria are destroyed by normal cooking, the toxins can survive. Staphylococcus occurs in infected cuts, sores, boils and inflamed throat conditions, on normal healthy skin, especially on the face and hands, and in the nasal passages.

Great care is needed with dishes that have already been cooked, and with dishes that are not cooked. If these are contaminated with bacteria, a delay in service and failure to keep them at safe temperatures could lead to food poisoning.

Defrosting foods

Defrosting is best done in a thawing cabinet. The temperature is kept in the range 0°C to 5°C, allowing the ice cystals to melt slowly, causing minimum damage to the structure of the food. There is also no risk of thawing juices running on to other foods.

To avoid this happening when the food is defrosted in a refrigerator or cold room, use a deep tray or suitable container. Place the food on the lowest shelf.

Defrosting takes about 24 hours for a small cut of meat or a chicken, and double this time for a medium-sized turkey. Check the recommended time on the packaging or with workplace instructions. Defrosting of small items of food can be done quickly in a microwave with the appropriate program (see page 11).

Food which has not completely defrosted before cooking creates a serious hygiene risk. The centre of the food is unlikely to reach a safe temperature (to kill bacteria) by the time the outside of the food is cooked. It is even possible that ice crystals will remain.

Dealing with waste

Don't let waste clutter up your work area, or risk contaminating food which is to be eaten. Put it in the bin or waste disposal machine without delay.

If you have to open the lid of a waste bin with your hands (many models are foot-operated), wash them well afterwards.

Legal requirements

The Food Safety (General Food Hygiene) Regulations 1995 require food to be protected against contamination during all stages of handling, preparation, cooking and service. All articles, fittings and equipment with which food comes into contact must be kept clean, and food waste must not be allowed to accumulate in food rooms.

Separate regulations will deal with temperature controls. These are expected to state one minimum temperature for foods likely to support the growth of harmful bacteria (but not food which will be cooked) – replacing the current regulations which have two minimum temperatures, 5°C and 8°C. Hot food held for service must be kept at 63°C or higher.

These temperatures do not apply during preparation of the food, nor if the food is being kept for service, or on display for sale (subject to time limits). There are various other (quite complex) exceptions which your workplace instructions will take account of.

In Scotland, a minimum temperature is not specified – the food must be kept refrigerated or in a cool, ventilated place. For food which is reheated before service, the temperature must reach 82°C.

1 Give three safety rules you should follow when storing food.

2 What injury can you suffer if you handle something heavy or awkward or beyond your strength?

3 Give three signs which indicate a pest control problem.

4 Describe four ways in which food can be unsafe to eat because of poor personal hygiene during handling and storage.

House Rules

NO spitting
NO smoking
NO sneezing
NO coughing

5 Give another four examples, this time relating to storage areas and equipment which are not hygienic.

More House Rules

Clean as you go
Cover food
Report pests
Remove waste

6 Identify two foods which are 'high risk' (i.e. those which harmful bacteria grow on very quickly). How these foods can be kept safe?

7 What are the safe temperatures for storing food so that bacteria do not grow?

Here is the weather forecast. It will be fine for Bacteria today, with temperatures ranging from 5° C to 63° C. There will be a sharp frost in the fridge and serious burning in the oven.

8 When the temperature is suitable, 20 bacteria become 40 in 10 minutes or so, 80 after another 10 minutes, then 160, and so on. What temperature range is suitable?

20, 40, 80, 160, 320,...

What are you doing?

...multiplying!

?

9 On each type of food in the illustration, mark what storage is required:
A – ambient
C – chilled
F – frozen

Flour

CREAM

BULLETS FROZEN PEAS

10 Why is it important to store cooked food separate from uncooked food?

It looks lovely next door. Can we move over?

Some questions and answers

Why is it vital our dairy products are kept refrigerated at between 1°C and 5°C?

- they will 'go off' very quickly if not kept cool
- failure to do so may result in high levels of bacteria and may cause food poisoning.

When receiving dairy products what must you check?

- containers/wrappings have not been tampered with
- the use-by/best-before date has not passed
- goods are in top quality condition
- as with all ingredients, if the quality is not to our standard, we must not use them: either waste or return to the supplier.

Once the packaging is opened on dairy products, what must you ensure?

- the remaining ingredients are re-sealed and kept in 'fridge
- that any special instructions on the packaging as to when they must be used by when opened are followed.

How can you ensure you avoid cross contamination when dealing with our dairy ingredients?

- keep hands clean, hot water and soap and nail brush
- store in the 'fridge with lids on/sealed
- wash equipment after use – never use the same equipment for different food types.

Adapted with thanks from the training manual of Compass Retail Catering Division.

1 Say when you should wash your hands (when your duties involve handling food).

2 Thorough hand washing is essential. Describe the routine.

3 Besides regular hand washing, what other aspects of personal hygiene are important for food handlers?

> **Diary**
> **Tuesday**
> **15th July**
>
> 7.00 alarm
> 7.15 shower
> ....
> 18.30 hair cut
> ....

4 What might happen if a customer eats food you have not properly cooked?

5 Why must you cover any cut or graze on your hands before handling food?

6 What should you do if you find some of the food you are preparing or cooking has an unusual smell or appearance?

7 Cleaning equipment not often used, you find small black pellets. What should you do?

8 If the waste bag starts leaking liquid out the bottom, what should you do?

9 What has been done wrong if the juices from a joint of meat which is defrosting spill on to a trifle?

10 Some of the food you are about to prepare has passed its use-by date. What must you do?

> **Wastage Report**
>
> **Date:**
> **Food:**
> **Reason:**
> **Action:**
> **Signed:**

11 Where should raw fish be stored in your workplace? Why is this important?

12 If you only use part of the contents of a packet of food, what is it important to remember when storing the rest?

Use this to check your progress against the performance criteria for each element.

Element 1

Maintain hygiene in food storage

Keep your hands clean and washed after carrying out unhygienic activities **PC1** ☐

Maintain storage areas in a clean and hygienic condition **PC2** ☐

Report deliveries to the appropriate person **PC3** ☐

△ Deliveries: meat/poultry/fish, dairy products, vegetable/fruit, eggs, dry goods

Store food under correct conditions **PC4** ☐

△ Conditions for food types: ambient, chilled, frozen, cooked, uncooked

Deal effectively with problems relating to deliveries and equipment **PC5** ☐

Do your work in an organised, efficient and safe manner **PC6** ☐

Element 2

Maintain hygiene in food preparation and cooking

Keep your hands clean during food preparation and cooking **PC1** ☐

Keep your work area and equipment clean and hygienic **PC2** ☐

Prepare and cook food under correct hygiene conditions **PC3** ☐

△ Conditions for food types: as above

Deal with waste (including food waste) safely **PC4+PC5** ☐

Deal effectively with problems relating to food and equipment **PC6** ☐

Do your work in an organised, efficient and safe manner **PC7** ☐

For help to answer questions relating to:

Knowing the enemy

There are two types of bacteria which are common in raw meat and poultry: *Salmonella* and *Clostridium perfringens*. Both cause food poisoning if the food is not cooked sufficiently, or if the bacteria spread to other foods through unhygienic equipment or handling.

The temperature at the centre of meat and poultry during cooking needs to reach 70°C or preferably 75°C to kill *Salmonella*. This would normally happen during cookng, but problems are likely to occur if a roast joint has been boned or stuffed, or the centre of a frozen piece of meat has not properly defrosted. The safest way of checking is to use a temperature probe.

Clostridium perfringens occur in the soil, in dust and water and are carried in the intestines of animals and people. The bacteria grow rapidly when there is no oxygen present – in the centre of a rolled piece of meat, for example. They can survive in a stew or braised piece of meat which is cooked for a few hours. And when conditions get uncomfortable, the bacteria form what are called spores.

Spores are hardy. They can withstand several hours of boiling temperatures. As soon as the temperature falls, they turn back into bacteria. These will multiply rapidly at temperatures between 5°C and 63°C. To reduce the risks:

- plan cooking times so there is minimum delay between finish of cooking and service
- when stews, braised, boiled and steamed dishes have to be kept hot before or during service, keep the temperature above 63°C, and check regularly with a temperature probe
- for dishes which have to be chilled, do this as quickly as possible
- reheat dishes thoroughly so that the temperature at the centre of the food reaches at least 75°C – in Scotland, the minimum temperature (by law) is 82°C
- never reheat dishes more than once.

Health and safety

safe working practices

Think of the manual handling tasks required to move food items to and from storage, during cleaning of storage areas and when rearranging stock. Think of what might make each task less difficult and hazardous, e.g. placing heavier items on the lower shelves, breaking large packages down to manageable sizes, keeping the floor areas between shelves uncluttered, not staking shelves too tightly. Section 5 will also help you answer this question.

heavy/bulky items

What is safe to lift is a complex subject. Some of the circumstances which make the task hazardous have just been mentioned. The difficulty of the task also depends on your physical fitness and strength. Your trainer or tutor can explain these factors in the context of your workplace, and what equipment and methods are available to make various tasks easier.

pest infestation

The checklist (page 45) will help you spot signs of pest infestation. If your premises get a visit from a pest control firm, ask if you can be taken along for the inspection to get a better understanding of what to look out for.

Food hygiene

good personal hygiene

One of the difficulties when moving food into or out of storage areas is that the outer packaging on many items will be dirty. This transfers to your hands and possibly to your uniform. From there it can easily be transferred to food which is not protected by packaging – unless you make the effort to wash your hands thoroughly.

hygienic storage/cooking areas

The reasons for good hygiene are similar to those you have just thought of. So are the problems. For example, it takes time and may be quite hard work to remove everything from the store shelves so they can be cleaned thoroughly. Large bins used to store flour, sugar and similar items are usually topped up before they get empty. Nevertheless, they do have to be cleaned inside and out from time to time – find a temporary container to keep the contents.

In kitchens, good hygiene is also necessary to remove and control harmful bacteria – present in dust, on some food, on food handlers, etc.

main contamination threats

Anything which might make the food unsafe to eat is a contamination threat. Do a hazard spotting exercise in your storerooms, cold rooms, food preparation and cooking areas, etc. Look at how the food is stored, and the processes of moving it to and from stores. Note anything which might harm the food (including possible threats, e.g. if the area is not kept clean). Then organise your list under headings, e.g. not washing hands under POOR PERSONAL HYGIENE PRACTICES.

time and temperature

At the right temperature, bacteria can double in number in minutes. This is one reason why different types of food have to be stored at a safe temperature, below –18°C for frozen foods, and below 5°C for chilled foods.

Some foods do not support the growth of dangerous bacteria, but have to be kept chilled or they spoil in quality or appearance (e.g. fresh fruit juice). Others are safe from bacteria, and keep best in a cool room, e.g. fresh bread, most types of fresh fruit and vegetables. Others (e.g. dried spices) withstand most temperatures.

The other aspect of time is the use-by or best-before dates which appear on most foods. Food should not be kept beyond these dates, and one way to reduce the risk of this happening is to ensure that older stocks are used first through proper stock rotation. If you transfer food which carries such a date to another container, e.g. a bulk storage bin, do make sure the container is labelled properly, including the best-before/use-by date.

checks of food deliveries for hygiene

If you are not sure what checks you have to do (e.g. cleanliness, condition of packaging, temperature, etc.), re-read your workplace instructions.

checks for pest infestation

If the standards of pest control at one of your suppliers are unsatisfactory, pests could gain access to your premises with a delivery of food, and quickly spread to other foods.

Flour attracts the flour beetle. Small holes in the packaging might be noticeable on delivery.

Fresh vegetables, especially if they are from a local farm or similar supplier, might have the occasional slug, ant or worm. This is not normally a problem provided the vegetables are thoroughly washed before use and can be stored so there is little risk of the pests harming other food.

Maintain and promote hygiene in food storage, preparation and cooking

storing raw and cooked food

To reduce the risk of bacteria, which is often present on raw food, from spreading to cooked food.

cross contamination and its prevention

Cross contamination is when bacteria are spread from raw to cooked food. This can happen if the two types of food are stored next to each other, when knives, chopping boards and other preparation equipment are used for both types of food, and via food handlers (not washing hands after each task).

defrosting food

Use a defrosting cabinet. If this is not available, place the food in the refrigerator or cold room in a deep tray so the defrosting juices will not spill on to other foods or the floor. A microwave can be used for defrosting small pieces of food.

covering cuts and grazes

Harmful bacteria, *Staphylococcus aureus*, are present on cuts and grazes, sores, etc.

keeping waste bins covered

Keeping the waste covered looks tidier and discourages flies, etc. In the kitchen, this advantage is outweighed by the fact that lids are frequently touched by food handlers and so become a serious source of contamination. Therefore containers used for temporary storage of waste in food preparation areas do not have to have lids, but if they do the lid should be of the type that can be opened without using your hands.

identifying unfit food

Some of the ways you can tell that food is unfit for its purpose are: *appearance* (e.g. mould on the surface), *age* (e.g. beyond the use-by or best-before date), *conditions of use* (e.g. never refreeze ice-cream which has melted); *workplace instruction* (e.g. discard food which has been in the hot holding cabinet for more than 20 minutes).

Any food which is unfit for use must be thrown away. Put the details on a wastage report, or tell your manager.

handling food as little as possible

Each time food is handled, there is a risk of transferring harmful bacteria from your hands or from equipment you are using. If the food is at room temperature, this presents ideal conditions for bacteria to multiply.

sources of food poisoning

Food handlers (e.g. hands not washed), raw food (e.g. eggs which carry salmonella), food which has not been stored correctly, dirty equipment or food surfaces, pests, waste.

legal responsibilities of food handlers

You have a responsibility to tell your manager if you have an infected wound or sore, or you are suffering from, or likely to be carrying any disease which can be transmitted through food (see page 29).

You also have a responsibility to maintain a high degree of personal cleanliness and to wear suitable, clean and, where appropriate, protective clothing.

FOOD TEMPERATURES

Week commencing 7 FEB

Day	Food	Temp.
MON	Chilli con carne (microwave)	78°C
	Tuna pie	74°C
TUE	Tagliatelle (- microwave)	82°C
WED	Coleslaw (in fridge)	5°C
	Chilled chilli mix	4°C
	Chilled steak & kidney mix	3°C
THUR	Sausage hot pot	88°C
	Vegetable chilli	77°C
FRI	Chicken & leek pie	88°C
	Coleslaw	4°C
SAT	Coleslaw (in fridge)	
	Chopped ham	
	Defrosted chicken casserole	
SUN		

Comments: All food temperatures satisfactory. air temp. high for part of day. A = All food thrown away. Equipment...

The system for recording food and refrigerator temperatures at pubs in the J D Wetherspoon organisation.

AIR TEMPERATURES

Week commencing 7 FEB Equipment Type Large fridge

	Temp.	Int.	Temp.	Int.	Temp.	Int.
MON	3 / 8.30am	JP	4 / 1.20pm	JP	3 / 8.00pm	JP
TUE	2 / 8.45am	JP	5 / 1.45pm	JP	3 / 9.00pm	JP
WED	8°C / 8.30am	TW	8°C / 12.00pm	TW	4°C / 8.30pm	
THUR	2°C / 8.30am	JP	4°C / 1.00pm	JP	2°C / 8.00pm	TW
FRI	2°C / 8.30am	JP	3°C / 12.40pm	JP	3°C / 8.15pm	JP
SAT	15°C / 8.30am	JP	Equipment out J		action until repaired	
SUN	2°C	TW	3°C	JP	3°C	JP

Comments: Food temperatures taken - see next page. Engineer called. Food temps. taken.

Use this to check your progress against the performance criteria.

Element 1

Maintain and promote food hygiene in food storage

Keep your hands clean and washed after carrying out unhygienic activities ☐ PC1

Keep your work area in a clean and hygienic condition ☐ PC2

Check that deliveries are in good hygienic condition ☐ PC3

▲ Deliveries: meat/poultry/fish, dairy products, vegetable/fruit, eggs, dry goods

Store food under correct conditions ☐ PC4

▲ Conditions for food types: ambient, chilled, frozen, cooked, uncooked

Rotate stock ☐ PC5

Minimise risk of pest infestation ☐ PC6

Identify and promptly report problems relating to deliveries and equipment ☐ PC7

Prioritise and carry out your work in an organised, efficient and safe manner ☐ PC8

Element 2

Maintain hygiene in food preparation and cooking

Keep your hands clean during food preparation and cooking ☐ PC1

Keep your work area and equipment clean and hygienic ☐ PC2

Prepare raw and high risk food separately, using separate equipment ☐ PC3

Remove promptly unfit or waste food, and store waste safely ☐ PC4+PC5

Maintain food items at a safe temperature during all stages ☐ PC6

Identify and promptly report problems relating to deliveries and equipment ☐ PC7

Prioritise and carry out your work in an organised, efficient and safe manner ☐ PC8

Unit 1ND2, Element 1
Maintaining knives

You use knives for a great many tasks in the kitchen. Well looked after and carefully handled, they make your job easier. Poorly used, they can cause accidents. Not properly cleaned, they can spread harmful bacteria.

Types of knives

There are three main groups. Those with *straight blades* include:

- *cook's knives* – of varying sizes, with firm blades, sharp points and a large heel, so that they can be held during use without your hand hitting the chopping board. They are suitable for slicing, shredding and chopping vegetables, trimming and cutting, etc. The largest, fairly heavy knife is good for tasks like chopping parsley, where a rocking motion is used (see page 132). The wide blade is also useful for crushing garlic cloves

- *filleting knife* – with a thin, very flexible blade that makes it ideal for following the bones closely, as in filleting fish. The blade and point should form one of the sharpest knives in your set

- *paring knife* – with a thin, sharp and slightly flexible blade, useful for hand-held work, for example cutting an apple into segments, or trimming potatoes

- *carving knife* – the long, thin, flexible blade makes it possible to slice meat thinly. Some chefs prefer a knife with a *scalloped* or *fluted* edge for carving cold meats, poultry, ham and smoked salmon. The hollows stop a vacuum forming, so there is less risk of the food sticking to the blade, and you get a cleaner cut

- *boning knife* – with a strong, very firm blade and sharp, pointed tip. The knife is held like a dagger. The blade will not bend or break under the considerable force that may have to be used. But this means that great care must be taken, because if the knife slips it could cause serious injury

- *palette knives* – one type has no cutting edge, and the blade is flexible, with a rounded end instead of a point. It is used to shape smooth mixtures, or lift firm foods such as a burger. The other type, used for cutting and lifting portions of cakes and gâteaux, has a serrated edge on one side.

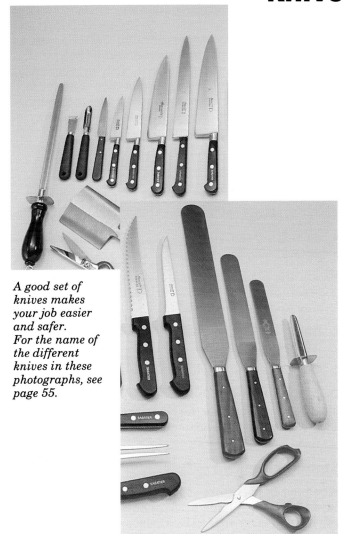

A good set of knives makes your job easier and safer. For the name of the different knives in these photographs, see page 55.

Knives with *serrated blades* are good for cutting crusty loaves of bread, etc. Use a sawing action, pulling the knife blade back and forth. Do not push it down into the bread.

Some people working in food and drink service like to use a paring knife with a saw-edged blade for slicing lemons, oranges, tomatoes, etc. It has the advantage of never going blunt. The fine indentations along the cutting edge quickly penetrate the tough skin of the fruit.

Some chefs do not use a knife for certain tasks, instead they prefer:

- *scissors* – to trim the fins and tails of fish, and for more general tasks like cutting the string or the paper for a steamed pudding

- *poultry secateurs* – to cut through the softer bone joints of chicken (e.g. the wing).

Keeping knives clean

Knives must be absolutely clean before you use them. Otherwise, the knife will pass on to the food flavours of other foods it has been in contact with.

The second danger is that harmful bacteria will be spread by the knife. This is very serious if the knife has been in contact with raw meat, fish or vegetables (which often carry bacteria), and is then used for food which has already been cooked, or does not require cooking before service. (Cooking is the usual way of making food safe from harmful bacteria.)

How to clean knives

Once you have finished using the knife for a particular task, e.g. slicing onions, wash it thoroughly:

- do this at the sink, in lots of hot water with a general-purpose detergent
- rub the blade and handle all over, using a nylon brush or cloth – keep your fingers away from the sharp edge of the blade
- rinse in very hot water (to kill any remaining bacteria)
- dry with paper towelling.

Do not put knives in dishwashers. The jostling movement can damage the blade and cutting edge. The chemicals may cause pitting of the blade.

Storing knives

When not in use, store your knives in a purpose-made case, wallet, box, knife block or on a magnetic rack. If you have to carry your knives from one area to another, first put them back in their case. Do not keep knives in a drawer, where they will knock together and get damaged edges.

CHECK list
Buying your own knives

- ✔ knife feels comfortable and balanced to hold
- ✔ blade made of high carbon stainless steel (will not rust or stain, nor colour foods)
- ✔ blade forged from one piece of steel, which runs right through the handle
- ✔ blade held in the handle with a minimum of three retaining rivets, or a moulded handle
- ✔ waterproof handle that will not be damaged when washed at very high temperatures
- ✔ colour-coded handle, or blade permanently etched with the intended use of the knife, e.g. FRUIT/VEG

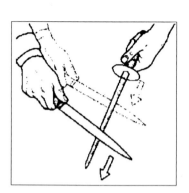

Using a steel to sharpen a carving knife.

Keeping knives sharp

A sharp knife means a job done better, faster and with less effort. It is safer, being less likely to slip than a blunt one.

Only knives with straight edges can be sharpened.

Some chefs use a *grinder*. This is made from carborundum stone. Move the blade in a direction away from you, holding the blade at an angle of about 25° to the stone.

The other way of sharpening knives is with a *steel*. To get a really sharp edge on the blade, you need to have the blade at the right angle to the sharpening surface, and get the right arm movement. Watch how your colleagues do it, and practise for yourself:

- hold the steel firmly in one hand, pointing away from the body and downwards at a slight angle
- hold the knife with the sharp edge of the blade pointing away from you
- put the edge of the blade nearest the knife handle on the steel with the blade at an angle of 20° to 25° to the steel
- sweep the knife down the length of the steel, moving the blade across the steel as you do so, to finish with the tip of the knife in contact with the tip of the steel
- repeat this sweeping movement several times, using alternate sides of the steel.

You may find it easier to hold the steel upwards at an angle, and to pull the knife towards you.

Wash the blade after sharpening, to remove any loose steel particles. Then test the blade is sharp, by cutting a soft tomato.

A knife should be sharpened little and often. The blade will wear away gradually and, after a lot of use and sharpening, become too thick to get a good edge. It is then time to have the blade reground: suppliers of professional chefs' knives may be able to do this themselves, or recommend suitable alternatives. Don't risk having your knives reground by someone you are not confident can do the job properly.

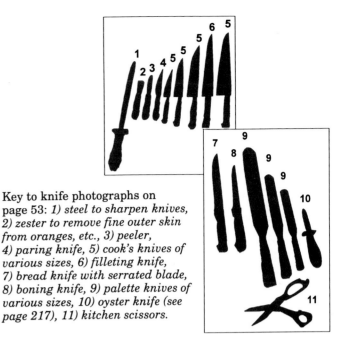

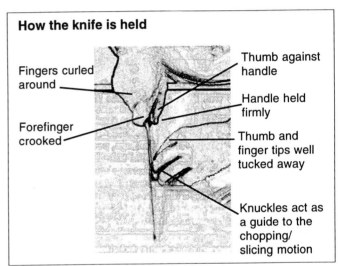

Key to knife photographs on page 53: *1) steel to sharpen knives, 2) zester to remove fine outer skin from oranges, etc., 3) peeler, 4) paring knife, 5) cook's knives of various sizes, 6) filleting knife, 7) bread knife with serrated blade, 8) boning knife, 9) palette knives of various sizes, 10) oyster knife (see page 217), 11) kitchen scissors.*

How the knife is held

Fingers curled around

Forefinger crooked

Thumb against handle

Handle held firmly

Thumb and finger tips well tucked away

Knuckles act as a guide to the chopping/ slicing motion

Handling knives

Much of your work as a chef requires good knife skills. But this means more than being able to chop at high speed or slice very thinly. For good knife skills to be really useful, your approach to each task must be organised and efficient:

- before starting on a new task, set out only the tools and equipment you will need

- keep the rest of your work area uncluttered

- always pay full attention to the job you are doing

- keep unprepared and prepared food separate

- establish a logical sequence, so that food is processed from left to right, or right to left.

Selecting the right knife

Use the right knife for the right job, with the correct chopping board. The best practice is to use different sets of knives and boards for preparing raw and cooked food, for meat, fish, vegetables, etc.

Using knives safely

Many of the accidents which occur in kitchens are caused by knives. It only takes a moment's lack of concentration, and you can find yourself with a nasty cut. Sometimes it is a colleague who suffers through your carelessness, or a light-hearted moment which goes terribly wrong.

To protect your safety and that of others, there are some things you should do:

- always cut or chop on a board – never on a stainless steel table or in the hand

- cut against the firm surface of a cutting board wherever practical. The board should not be in danger of slipping. It may help to put a damp cloth between the table and the board

- as necessary, clean knives from time to time during use, in the sink or using a sanitised wipe

- wash knives immediately after use

- when wiping a knife, keep the blade facing away from your hands and body. Wipe from the blunt to the sharp edge

- put the knife down so the blade lies flat against the work surface, chopping board, etc. If you put a cook's knife down quickly, without being careful, it will often stand on its edge, with the blade uppermost

- when passing knives to others, keep the handle towards them.

And there are some practices you should avoid:

- do not attempt to cut frozen food – not only would you need a lot of pressure, which is dangerous, but the cut is likely to be ragged. And your hands may get so cold that you can't feel what you are doing

- don't let the handle get greasy when you are cutting a lot of meat, otherwise the knife might slip

- never leave knives hidden in a pile of partly prepared food, or in a bowl or sink of water

- never fool around with knives or use them as screwdrivers or can openers

- never attempt to catch a falling knife – let it fall to the floor, and then pick it up by the handle

- never leave knives near or hanging over the edge of a work surface – the safest position is where they cannot be knocked by someone passing by

- never walk around carrying a knife – if this is unavoidable, hold it close to the body with the point facing downwards, and the blunt edge facing in the same direction as where you are walking

- do not use a knife which is damaged (e.g. loose blade, or the tip of the blade bent).

For help to answer questions
relating to:

Health and safety

? keeping knives sharp

There are at least three reasons:
a) efficiency – sharp knives do a
neater job, and require less effort;
b) safety – blunt knives can slip;
c) cost – a knife kept sharp will do its
job well for years, blunt knives
eventually lose their edge to such an
extent that they can't be
resharpened.

? storing knives safely

If a knife is left or put away in the
wrong place, e.g. among other pieces
of equipment in a drawer, or on a
high shelf, there is a great risk that
it will not be seen. You or a colleague
could get a nasty cut from the blade,
while searching through the drawer
for something, or be stabbed in the
foot as the knife falls to the floor
from the shelf.

? using the appropriate knife

There are two aspects to this:
• *for the task* – as you will know
from your own experience and the
text, certain knives are intended
for specific tasks
• *for the type of food* – to make this
easier, many professional knives
have differently coloured handles
or their use etched on the blade.

? keeping knife handles free of grease

Safety is the reason. Have you ever
had a problem with a knife slipping
because of grease on the handle?
What sort of food were you preparing
at the time? What should you do to
avoid such problems?

? handling knives correctly

Safety is not the only reason: watch
a skilled chef at work with a knife
and note the speed with which the
task is completed, and the quality of
the job. With practice you will get as
fast, provided you learn the right
techniques from the start.

? having a secure cutting surface

Safety is the main reason. You can
loose control of the knife if the board
slips away, or wobbles as you cut.
This is why heavy, large chopping
boards are better for the jobs which
involve vigorous use of the knife (e.g.
chopping parsley). Butchers, when
they chop bones, prefer to use what
is in effect a heavy wooden table,
with a very thick top that forms the
chopping surface.

? reporting accidents

One of the common causes of
accidents in kitchens is poor knife
techniques, so it's relevant to remind
yourself of what was said in
Section 2 about reporting accidents
(page 35).

Food hygiene

? cleaning knives between tasks

Think why you wash your hands
between tasks, and why you clean
the chopping board (see Section 3).
Knives can also spread bacteria, and
carry flavours from one food to
another.

? risks of infection from handling knives

Tetanus, a very unpleasant disease,
can occur when bacteria get into a
cut or wound. The blade of a knife
which has not been properly cleaned,
or is being used to prepare food, may
carry bacteria.

Knives can also transfer bacteria
that cause food poisoning, e.g.:
• *Salmonella* – found on raw meat
and poultry, and carried by people
• *Clostridium perfringens* – found
in soil, dust and water, from
which it can transfer to raw meat
and vegetables and on to exposed
food. It is also carried by people
• *Staphylococcus* – carried by
people, from which it gets on to
food.

? cross contamination risks from knives

A knife not properly cleaned after
cutting raw meat, fish or vegetables
will harbour bacteria. The next time
the knife is used – and it may look
perfectly clean, so the user won't
know of the dangers – the bacteria
will contaminate other food. To
reduce this risk, different knives
should be kept for particular tasks
(in the same way that chopping
boards are, see pages 46 and 233).

? importance of clean cutting surfaces

It is just as important to use a clean
cutting surface as it is to use a clean
knife.

The reason wooden chopping boards
are not much used in professional
kitchens is because they are difficult
to keep clean. Plastic boards are
more satisfactory, but with heavy
use the surface becomes deeply cut.
The boards must be replaced at this
stage, otherwise bacteria trapped in
the cuts will form a hygiene risk.

? not using damaged knives

Any cracked and heavily cut surface
(e.g. knife handle) can harbour
bacteria. Damaged blades will not
cut well, spoiling the appearance of
the food, and probably reducing the
number of portions that can be
obtained from a joint of roast meat,
for example. The extra force you use
trying to cut with a damaged knife,
may lead to an accident: the knife
slips, or perhaps the blade snaps.

NVQ SVQ
Skills check
Maintain and handle
knives
Unit 1ND2

levels
1+2

Use this to check your progress against
the performance criteria.

Element 1
Maintain knives

Keep knives clean, complying with the food safety regulations	☐ PC1
Keep knives sharp, using safe sharpening methods	☐ PC2
Store knives correctly after use	☐ PC3
Deal effectively with problems and inform appropriate people	☐ PC4
Carry out your work in an organised, efficient and safe manner	☐ PC5

Element 2
Handle knives

Select knives appropriate to the task and type of food	☐ PC1
Use cutting surfaces which are safe, clean and ready to use	☐ PC2
Handle knives safely	☐ PC3
Deal effectively with problems and inform appropriate people	☐ PC4
Carry out your work in an organised, efficient and safe manner	☐ PC5

Self-check questions

1 Give uses for: a) small cook's knife,
b) filleting knife, c) secateurs.

2 What can happen if you use a knife which
is blunt?

3 After sharpening a knife, how do you test
that the blade is sharp?

4 Why must you wash a knife after
sharpening?

5 Describe how knives should be stored
when not in use. Give three ways.

6 To reduce the risk of an accident with a
knife, describe three things you should do,
and three you should not do.

7 Give the procedure you must follow for
reporting an accident at work.

8 Explain why it is good practice to use a
different set of knives for preparing raw
food and cooked food.

9 Suppose you are filleting fish and one of
the restaurant staff asks you to cut a
lemon for a drink, how can you best help?

Unit 2ND11, Element 1

Receiving and handling deliveries

Kitchens run better when the stores are organised and clean, food deliveries are properly checked, and no food is allowed to reach its use-by or best-before date.

Preparing for deliveries

Some deliveries are made at regular times and require no special advance preparation, e.g. fresh vegetables and bread which arrive early each morning and are taken straight into the kitchen to be used.

But for most deliveries, especially those for the dry stores or the freezer, you should check beforehand that:

- a copy of the original order is available for checking
- sufficient storage space has been cleared
- old stock is moved to a position where it will be used before the new delivery (to help stock rotation)
- access to the storage area is clear
- trolleys are available to help move large loads and heavy items
- any returns (including faulty goods) have been put ready for collection, and counted.

Checking deliveries

There are three reasons for checking deliveries:

- is the quantity (number, weight, size, etc.) what was ordered?
- is the quality (grade, appearance, temperature, condition of packaging, etc.) what was ordered, and acceptable?
- is the paperwork (delivery note, etc.) correct?

Good suppliers want to avoid claims some time after a delivery that items were missing or not in acceptable condition. After checking the delivery, both parties should initial or sign the appropriate piece of paper to say they are satisfied.

Knowing what is in stock, taking note when stocks run low, preparing for deliveries, checking deliveries carefully no matter how busy you are, and storing deliveries properly – these all form part of an efficient catering operation.

Checking quantity

Count numbers of cans, bottles, boxes, cartons, etc. Check that the contents of boxes or cartons agree with what is stated on the outside of the packaging (e.g. contents: 20 x A10 cans – A10 is one of the standard sizes of can).

If the seal appears to have been opened, or the packaging is damaged, you should not accept the delivery. Even if everything seems to be present, individual items may have been damaged.

Weigh fresh meat, fish, vegetables and other items sold by weight.

Checking quality

If a particular quality has been ordered, e.g. *Extra class* (the top quality) for fruit, then this is what should be delivered. Your company may have formal requirements set out in a *purchase specification*, e.g. the size and weight of steaks, amount of visible fat, etc.

Besides meeting specific requirements of these types, there are three more general quality checks:

- *appearance and aroma*: experience and knowledge of what to look for (see checklist) are the best guides
- *date mark*: the use-by or best-before date on the label should not have passed, but allow for reasonable time in storage
- *temperature on delivery*: pre-prepared and convenience chilled foods, fresh meat, poultry and offal, fresh fish and shellfish, dairy produce (milk, cream, cheese, yogurt, etc.), cooked and smoked meat and fish products should be a minimum of 8°C. Many workplaces state 5°C or lower for specific products. The outer layer of frozen food should be below −12°C.

When using a temperature probe on chilled foods, take care not to damage the food by piercing it or the packaging. Because frozen food is solid, you can only check the temperature of the outer layer, or between packets (e.g. of frozen peas).

Checking paperwork

Check against your record of the order, and against the supplier's delivery note. Have you received all the items that were ordered? Does the quantity and quality agree with that specified?

CHECK list
Delivery checks

✔ quantity and weight as ordered

✔ quantity and weight agrees with the delivery note/invoice

✔ quality as ordered

✔ packaging in good condition

✔ cans in good condition: not blown, no damage to seams or rust

✔ within use-by or best-before date

✔ information on label matches content

✔ temperature correct for product

✔ frozen food feels solid, with no sign of thawing

✔ meat smells fresh, and good colour (more details on pages 93 and 94)

✔ fresh fish well iced, good appearance and fresh smell (see page 111)

✔ fresh shellfish alive (see page 215)

✔ vegetables and fruit good colour and shape, no signs of bruising, decay or insect damage (see pages 1 and 131–4)

SUPPLIERS COMPLAINT FORM

CCG

TO: _____

DATE: _____

FROM: _____

SUPPLIER: _____

DATE OF DELIVERY: _____

INVOICE/DELIVERY NO: _____

COMPLAINT: *(Please give as much detail as possible.)*

_____
_____
_____
_____
_____

WHAT ACTION HAVE YOU TAKEN ALREADY:

_____

NAME & ADDRESS OF UNIT:

_____
_____

Left: *this form is sent to the head office of CCG Services Limited, if the unit manager has a complaint about a delivery.*

Below: *at Catering & Allied Services, the delivery record sheet provides a means of quickly checking any detail about a delivery, and identifying problems.*

Delivery record sheet

Date	Time	Supplier	Item	Invoice number	Temp °C	Condition of package	Accept/ reject	Signed

With thanks to Catering & Allied Services

Rejecting goods

Any goods which do not correspond with the order will usually have to be returned. This is best done at the time of delivery, but suppliers normally accept returned goods provided they are told of the reason without delay.

Make sure that both you and the delivery person have a record of returned goods. This may be on both copies of the delivery note, on the order copy, or by asking the delivery person to make out a returns form. There has to be some means of making sure that returned goods are not subsequently paid for.

Handling deliveries

Move goods into their proper storage area immediately after delivery.

If this hasn't already been done, transfer old stock to a position where it will be used before the new stock.

Check what, if any, packaging should be removed from chilled and frozen convenience foods before storage. Some packaging is necessary to protect the food from damage and problems such as freezer burn.

At what stage cartons, boxes and bags of bulk items like flour are emptied, will depend on the space available, and stock levels. Do not leave boxes:

- stacked on the floor where they might get in someone's way. Food should be kept well above floor level

- part-filled – boxes that are not full take up unnecessary space. Also, someone might assume that there is more of the item in stock than is actually the case.

Once a bag has been opened (e.g. of bulk granulated sugar), the remaining contents should be transferred to a bin or some other container that can be properly closed.

Collapse and dispose of empty boxes and cartons. There may be a special place for keeping waste which can be recycled.

Receipt, storage and use of refrigerated foods

1 All deliveries must be taken directly to the kitchen where they must be checked for:
- quality/weight (against the order)
- grade (unit size, weight)
- damage (freshness, bruising, smell, packaging)
- price (against quoted/order price
- temperature on delivery (meat and poultry 5°C or lower; fish 5°C or lower; cook-chill 0°C to 2°C; dairy/cheese 4°C or lower).

2 Food which fails to meet the required control standards MUST be rejected and a credit note obtained.

3 A probe thermometer must be used to check delivery temperature. Insert the probe between sealed packages. Do not puncture the package.

4 Fresh and chilled foods delivered must be stored in the appropriate refrigerator as quickly as possible after delivery, if not intended for immediate use.

5 Chilled and fresh foods stored in refrigerators/cold rooms must be used in strict rotation. New supplies must be placed at the back of existing stock.

6 Newly delivered stock must be date marked on the package where possible (if not already marked on packs), to ensure products are used in the correct sequence, and by the intended date.

7 Where the use-by dates are given, strict adherence must be observed. Fresh meat, fish and other perishable produce not labelled with use-by dates should be cooked and used within 48 hours.

8 Fresh shellfish must be used within 24 hours of delivery.

9 Cooked products must be completely segregated from raw. If both types are stored in the same refrigeration equipment, separate zoning is to be observed. Where cooked and raw products are stored in the same equipment, then cooked items must be stored above raw materials (not the other way round).

10 All foods stored must be covered/sealed. Cling film is not to be used for wrapping high fat content foods, e.g. cheese. Containers for the storage of foods must be scrupulously clean/sanitised before use.

11 Opened cans of food may not be used for storage. Any remaining food must be placed in a suitable plastic or stainless steel container and either lidded or covered with clingfilm. Put a label on the container stating the contents and the date. The use of glass and china containers is not recommended because of possible breakage or chipping.

12 Boxes and cartons may not be used as containers for storing fresh meat and fish in refrigeration equipment. The meat/fish must be transferred to suitable leak-proof containers.

13 Food containers must not be double stacked. It is essential to allow proper circulation of air between shelves.

14 It is very important to keep fish, meat and dairy produce separate, so that taste and smell are not transferred.

15 Temperature tests of cabinets/cold rooms must be taken and recorded TWICE each day to monitor the efficient and safe working of the equipment. Staff must be fully familiar with the prescribed temperature for the storage of difference types of food, the use of thermometers, the checking of accuracy of temperature readings and the actions to be taken in the event of plant failure.

Safe manual handling

Back injuries account for a high percentage of the accidents which occur in kitchens. Many result from lifting, moving or carrying objects the wrong way, or handling something which is too heavy.

Employers are required by the Manual Handling Operations Regulations 1992 to make sure that employees do not need to undertake manual handling operations at work that might injure them. Where this is not reasonably practicable, the level of risk must be kept to the minimum, e.g. through training and workplace procedures.

What you can safely carry depends on the weight of the object. But even if you have a good idea of what you can manage, you must consider other, equally important factors:

- *your physical strength* – this will be less if you have done a lot of carrying already, are tired or unwell or pregnant, for example

- *the shape of the object* – a bulky item is often difficult to hold and control, and it might therefore be less easy to see where you are going

- *how the object can be held* – smooth sides, round surfaces, greasy hands, wearing gloves, these all make your grip less sure

- *how far the object has to be moved* – to get it into a carrying position (something on a shelf at waist level is generally easier to pick up than it would be from the floor), and to take it to its destination

- *in what conditions you are working* – outdoor delivery areas on a frosty morning, narrow, steep flights of stairs, low ceilings, and uneven surfaces are typical hazards.

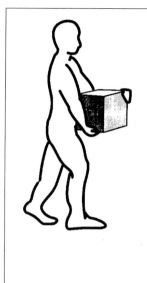

Lifting an object
- keep a firm grip
- keep close to the load
- if you need to turn, for example to place the object down on your left, turn your whole body by using your feet
- place the object down, then if necessary adjust its position.

With thanks to Whitbread

Pushing a trolley
- check your route is clear
- face in the direction you are moving
- keep close to the trolley
- keep control of the trolley
- keep your back straight
- push the trolley

How you can help

To reduce the risk of injury when you are handling something:

- use a trolley and the goods lift where possible

- if the object is unfamiliar, test its weight first, for example by raising one end. Don't make assumptions: an old oil container may not be empty, the rubbish bin could be much heavier than usual

- divide the load down into smaller/less bulky loads, but if this means making many journeys you may need to have a break

- if you can't make the load easier to handle, get the assistance of a colleague

- if you are lifting something from a shelf or table, first move anything that is in the way, so that you can get right up to the object

- plan in advance how to lift the item, and where it is to be placed

- if you have to carry the item a distance, check that your route is clear first, if necessary give people warning, prop open doors, etc.

- to avoid confusion when lifting something with another person, agree in advance who should give the instructions, and who will take the load.

Storing food deliveries

The storage areas, refrigerators and freezers in your kitchen will reflect its size and style of operation. Here are some general rules which apply to food storage.

Security

In most workplaces, the contents of the food stores represent a lot of money. This means that they must be kept locked when there is no one in attendance, and the keys returned to the proper place. Often there will be specific times when food can be drawn from the stores, e.g. between 8 a.m. and 10 a.m.

General organisation

It should be easy to find items which are required, and to spot items which are running short. Keep similar things together.

Safety

Put heavier items on the lower shelves. Stack shelves so there is no danger of items falling off. Use safety steps for reaching high shelves.

Storage conditions

Cleanliness – store food on shelves (not the floor), or in bins. Follow the cleaning schedule for your workplace. This is written so that each area gets the necessary attention, e.g. floors in stores are washed weekly, shelves every two months, refrigerators every week, etc. Defrost refrigerators and freezers regularly (for equipment which does not do this automatically). Report any signs of pests (see checklist on page 45).

Temperature – refrigerators and freezers will generally have an external display so that the temperature can be checked with a quick glance. Some models monitor the temperature and provide a printout. There may be an alarm system to warn if the temperature varies too much. Whatever sort of equipment there is in your workplace, you must tell your manager at once about any problem, or if you suspect a fault. Keeping food at the correct temperature is one of the main ways of ensuring it is safe to eat.

Ventilation – good air circulation and the right conditions of humidity help keep the good condition of food. Fridges and freezers should not be so tightly packed with food that the cold air is unable to circulate. Dried foods like sugar and salt, which readily absorb moisture and become lumpy, should be kept away from steam. Fresh fruit and vegetables will develop mould if there is inadequate air circulation (which is why they should not be kept in plastic bags).

Tidy, well organised stores make it is easier to find what you want...

...and the food is kept in hygienic conditions.

Storage of different food types

There are six main groups of food for storage purposes.

Frozen

The freezer should keep frozen food at a temperature of not higher than –18°C. Some caterers specify –22°C. These temperatures are colder than most domestic freezers. The best-before date on catering packs of frozen food assumes the food is kept at these low temperatures.

Chilled

This category covers any food on which harmful bacteria will multiply, unless the food is kept at a safe temperature. Some foods, e.g. butter and fruit juices, do not support the growth of harmful bacteria, but suffer in quality if they are not kept chilled. Most pre-prepared and convenience foods need to be kept chilled (the label will give storage instructions). The industry accepted safe storage temperature for chilled foods is 5°C, but many workplaces operate a lower standard, e.g. between 0°C and 1°C for fresh meat and fish.

Ambient

Ambient or room temperature is satisfactory for canned and dried foods, for items like loaves of bread, bread rolls, cakes (unless they are filled with cream), breakfast cereals, potatoes, bananas and many other types of fresh vegetable and fruit, and for foods which have been processed so that they are safe at room temperature.

Preserved

Before the days of refrigerators, preserving was the main method for keeping food. Jams, marmalade, chutney, various types of pickle, smoked and cured meats and fish, salted beef, etc. are examples of products which have been preserved. Many preserved products are made to different recipes now (as refrigerators are commonplace), and the makers recommend that they are kept chilled after opening. Some have to be kept chilled all the time – follow the instructions on the label.

Cooked

This category includes food which has been cooked on the premises, or bought in already cooked, to be served cold or reheated at the time of service. The cooking process has made the food safe from bacteria. During storage, the food has to be kept at a temperature (below 5°C) where any bacteria which have survived the cooking process do not multiply, and separate from any food which might be carrying bacteria (uncooked food).

Uncooked

The distinction between uncooked food and other food which has to be kept chilled or at ambient temperatures is made because uncooked food is one of the main sources of harmful bacteria in a kitchen (poor personal hygiene practices being another). The fact that there is often bacteria on uncooked food is not a problem because the cooking process kills most of the bacteria. But things go seriously wrong if the bacteria are able to get on to any food which will not be cooked before service. This can easily happen when uncooked food is stored next to cooked food.

Stock-taking is easier when the stores are well organised, with similar products grouped together.

STOCK SHEET   PAGE 3

PRODUCT	SIZE	WK1	WK2	WK3	WK4	WK5	STOCK	TOTAL
POLIPETTI	815g	12.41					7	86.87
SEPPIOLINE	815g	13.22					2+1	39.66
VONGOLE GUSCIO	105g	12.24					8	97.92
SALSA FOGUA	83cg	8.93					1	8.93
CIPOLLINE	830g	8.40						
BOLETUS BADIUS	82cg	8.93					4	35.72
FUNGHI PORCINI	72c	8						

Stock rotation

You may come across this referred to as FIFO, which stands for First In First Out. The principle of stock rotation is that older stock – *first in* – is used before any more recent stock – *first out*. There are three main reasons:

- *for safety* – foods which have passed their use-by or best-before date are not considered safe to eat and must be thrown away. This is the law

- *for economy* – it is expensive and wasteful to have to throw food away because the quality has spoiled, or it has passed its date

- *for quality* – most foods spoil in quality with time. Changes start from the time vegetables and fruit are harvested, milk is taken from the cow, fish are caught, animals slaughtered, etc. These changes damage the appearance, flavour, texture and smell.

Food is less likely to have to be wasted when the older stock is always used first. But if items with different dates are kept together, in no particular order, then there is a good chance that some will sit there until beyond the date of expiry.

There are some foods which do need to be kept to be at their best. Meat improves for the first few days, but normally this happens before it reaches the caterer. Some fruits (e.g. avocados and pears) are usually sold under-ripe, to prevent bruising. They need a day or longer to ripen fully. Once ripened, they soon become too soft, go black, etc. Some cheeses (e.g. brie and camembert) require a few days to mature, then are at their peak condition for a short time (this may be hours or days).

Some of the paperwork used at Gleneagles Hotel. Requests for stock are made on the Store requisition, details of orders are sent to the supplier on the Purchasing schedule, and when goods arrive, details including cost, are recorded on the Receiving sheet.

Stock control systems and the paperwork

Management has two main reasons for stock control:

- to encourage people to be careful about the stock they use – one way of doing this is a system of written *requisitions* (the name for stock orders from the kitchen and other departments, which go to the storekeeper to fulfil). The requisition has to be authorised by a supervisor or manager, and there is a system for tracking who has used what

- to know when it is time to re-order, and how much to order. A balance has to be struck between obtaining quantity discounts, the risk of stock spoiling, and the amount of money tied up in stocks.

In smaller establishments the emphasis is on ensuring that suppliers are paid for the goods accepted and no more. If at the end of a particular trading period (a week or month, typically) the results are unsatisfactory, then stock usage is one of the areas that will be looked into by management.

In bigger establishments, there is often a computerised system to monitor all aspects of stock control. This produces information at the touch of a button on such details as:

- what has been received, by type of commodity and by supplier

- the cost of all foods issued to the kitchen, by department

- what is left in stock, and its value

- the pattern of usage, so that minimum and maximum stock levels can be established, and adjusted as necessary.

Some systems will work out for the day's menu, and from information on the number of meals which are expected to be served, exactly what has to be ordered. The computer has details of each recipe.

1 What problems can occur if delivery and storage areas are untidy and dirty?

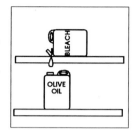

7 What do you do if some items you are checking, are slightly damaged? The delivery person says it will make no difference to the quality.

11 Study this advice from Whitbread Inns on handling goods and materials. For each point, say why things could go wrong.

You run the risk of injury if:
- you bend down wrongly
- you lift badly
- you are overweight
- you are p64 pregnant
- you wear high heeled shoes

With thanks to Whitbread

2 State the rules in your workplace for getting items from the store.

8 If you find that stocks of an item that is ordered irregularly are running low, what do you do?

3 What do you do if you need something urgently from stores, and it is not the usual time for getting stocks?

9 What are the rules for safekeeping keys to the stores, kitchen, etc. in your workplace.

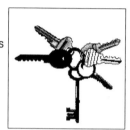

12 Complete the caption to these two cartoons. One shows the right way, the other the wrong way.

4 Say what checks you must make when accepting a delivery. Why is it important that you make these checks carefully?

10 Comment on the stores in the photograph below. Some points you might mention are: a) two types of weighing machine and their uses, b) bulk storage bins, c) stacking and organisation of shelves, d) reason items might be on table in foreground, e) tray of eggs on centre table.

5 What must you do if, when checking a delivery, you find an item which has today's date as the use-by date?

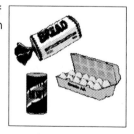

6 For each of the food items in the illustration, give the quality points you must look for when accepting a delivery.

Use this to check your progress against the performance criteria.

13 Why is it important that the delivery area doesn't look like this?

'16 Say what you would do if you find someone in the stores who shouldn't be there?

14 Identify the wrong practices in this illustration. What should be done?

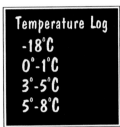

17 What should the temperature be of the various refrigerators/cold rooms and freezers in your workplace.

Temperature Log
-18°C
0°-1°C
3°-5°C
5°-8°C

18 What must you do if you find the temperature is several degrees higher?

15 Study the two photographs carefully. What should management note about the condition of the shelves? Say what you would do about:
a) covering/no covering,
b) mixture of things on the shelves (e.g. china and empty glass bowl).

19 Mark the shelf in this refrigerator on which you would store a) cooked meats, b) uncooked meats, c) salads, d) other prepared foods.

20 If you are the first to come to work one morning and find a delivery of frozen food has been left outside the door, what should you do?

21 In a dark corner of the stores, you see what you think are mouse droppings. What actions do you take?

PEST SIGHTING REPORT
Evidence:
Date:
Signed:

Element 1
Receive and handle food deliveries

Prepare receiving and storage areas ready for delivery ☐ PC1

Ensure food deliveries are of good quality and within expiry date ☐ PC2

⚠ Food items: meat/poultry, fish, fruit/vegetables, eggs, bread items, cakes and biscuits, dairy items, dry goods
Quality: aroma and appearance

Handle food items with appropriate care, so as not to damage packaging ☐ PC3

⚠ Packaging: cans, bottles/jars, packets/boxes, bags/sacks

Keep receiving areas clean, tidy and secure ☐ PC4

Identify and promptly report problems relating to equipment, food, packaging ☐ PC5

Prioritise and carry out your work in an organised, efficient and safe manner ☐ PC6

Element 2
Store food deliveries

Store food items under correct conditions for their type ☐ PC1

⚠ Conditions: ventilation, temperature, cleanliness
Food items (as PC2 above), type: ambient, chilled, frozen, cooked, uncooked, preserved

Follow stock rotation procedures, and use stock in date order ☐ PC2

Keep accurate records of foods received, stored and issued ☐ PC3

Ensure food items are not used beyond their expiry date ☐ PC4

Report low stock levels to the appropriate person ☐ PC5

Maintain storage areas under correct conditions ☐ PC6

Identify and promptly report problems relating to equipment, food, packaging ☐ PC7

Prioritise and carry out your work in an organised, efficient and safe manner ☐ PC8

Illustrations for questions 11, 12, 13 and 19, with thanks to Whitbread

For help to answer questions
relating to:

Health and safety

tidy/secure delivery and storage areas

Rubbish is a safety hazard: people might trip over it, and it provides fuel for a fire. It is also a hygiene hazard, being dirty and encouraging pests.

When there is rubbish everywhere, it takes longer to find things, and to do anything, because you have to find a way around empty boxes, piles of old packaging, etc.

The financial value of food and other items in the stores will amount to several hundred or several thousand pounds, depending on the size of the establishment. Good security is essential to protect these items.

food storage areas clean, well lit, etc

There is clearly a need for high standards of *hygiene* in any area where food is kept. But standards can drop when people are very busy, or careless, or feel that it is someone else's job to clean. You must be prepared to play your part.

Good *lighting* makes it easier to find where everything is, to read labels, to notice dirt which has accumulated in corners, and to see pest damage or signs of their presence.

Good *ventilation* and the correct *temperature* do much to keep the quality of the food at its best. When the air can circulate easily, there is less risk of food becoming mouldy.

Correct temperature is essential for those foods which support the growth of harmful bacteria – above 5°C and bacteria quickly multiply to dangerous numbers. Frozen foods will spoil in quality and therefore not last as long as they should, if the temperature is higher than –18°C.

approved safe methods for lifting

Unless you use the right method, you will injure yourself. Your back is particularly at risk.

Almost one-third of reported accidents in catering establishments (and a great many more go unreported) are caused by:

- lifting heavy objects such as pans, trays, packs, tables
- handling sharp objects such as exposed blades during cleaning
- awkward lifts such as out of low ovens, or off high positions.

Approved safe methods are those you are trained to use. They help you:

- judge what you can safely handle, taking into account not only the weight, shape, wrapping, etc., but also the distance to be moved, the conditions you are working in, and your physical strength
- use trolleys, lifts, team lifting, etc. to make the task easier
- adopt the correct position as you lift and move objects.

Food hygiene

date mark on food deliveries

Good suppliers will ensure that the food they deliver is well within its date. But mistakes do occur, so it is always better to check at the time of delivery. Reject any food which has passed its date.

You will find two types of date marking:

- the *use-by* date is the date up to and including which the food may be used safely, e.g. cooked and consumed
- the *best-before* date is the date up until which the food will retain its optimum condition, e.g. it will not be stale.

The food producer/supplier is responsible for deciding which type of marking to use, following government guidelines. Foods which have to be stored at a low temperature to protect them from harmful bacteria need use-by dates.

storing cooked and raw food separately

Many raw foods carry harmful bacteria. This is not usually a problem because the cooking process kills most or all of the bacteria. But a really dangerous situation is caused when the bacteria move from raw food to cooked food – and they have lots of opportunity to do so if both types of food are stored together. These bacteria will start increasing in numbers, very rapidly during any time the cooked food is at room temperature (e.g. on the buffet table). This can lead to serious food poisoning.

storing chilled/frozen foods immediately

The quality and safety of chilled and frozen foods depend on their being stored at the correct temperature. Any delay in moving the food from the delivery point to the cold room, refrigerator or freezer will cause the temperature to rise. The increase will be rapid on a hot day, or if the food is in the kitchen during the delay. When suppliers have invested large sums of money in delivery vehicles that keep food at low temperatures during transport, it makes even less sense for you to leave the food waiting around for no good reason.

dangers of pest infestation

Pests carry bacteria and disease. They cause physical damage to food and to equipment and fittings (e.g. chewing through electric cables). When pests find food and suitable conditions (i.e. undisturbed), they quickly get established, start breeding, and become more difficult to deal with.

Product knowledge

quality points in food deliveries

There are two aspects of quality, the appearance and the smell or aroma. Both have to be right for the product – but this does not necessarily mean you personally will find the appearance or smell pleasant.

Answer the question for the products you most frequently deal with, e.g.:

- frozen vegetables – packaging in good condition, no smell
- canned foods – can in good condition, no signs of rust or damage which might let air into the contents, or blowing
- fresh vegetables – good colour and shape, fresh appearance and smell.

Stock control

reporting damaged deliveries

Unless you tell the right person (ask your manager if you don't know who this should be), the damaged items might be paid for, instead of being returned to the supplier. It is also possible that they get used by someone who fails to notice the problem.

maintaining constant flow of stock

You know what problems it causes if you run out of something: the recipe may have to be adapted, the menu changed, or customers disappointed. On the other hand, if very large stocks are kept of everything (ignoring the fact that this does not make financial sense, and puts a great strain on storage space), there is a risk that food will have to be thrown away because it has passed its expiry date.

Most managers aim to keep a steady flow of stock, sufficient but not too much to meet immediate demands.

importance of stock control

Stock represents money in the business. If too much is used – because of wastage, or misuse, or lack of security – costs go up and profits go down. Keeping proper control of stocks discourages these problems. It means management can find out at any time exactly what should be in stock, and account for all stock movement. Any differences, e.g. between what is actually on the shelves and what the record says there should be, can then be investigated and appropriate action taken.

Stock control also helps purchasing. When records show what has been used over a week or month, and how much is left, then a better decision can be made about the quantity to re-order, and when to re-order.

Cleaning
food production areas, equipment and utensils

Cleaning food production areas

Your kitchen is likely to have a cleaning schedule. This sets out what should be cleaned and when. It may say who should do each task, and give details of the equipment and method to be used.

The cleaning schedule is a sort of master plan. It makes sure that every area gets the attention it needs, e.g. floors washed daily, walls and shelves monthly.

Types of surface and their cleaning

Hygiene standards in food preparation areas must be the highest. This is why the floors and walls must be made of materials that can be easily and effectively cleaned. Damaged surfaces are difficult or impossible to clean. Cracks get filled up with grease and dirt. Flaking paint comes away, possibly falling into the food.

Check that the cleaning agent is suitable for its use. The wrong one, or the wrong method, can permanently damage surfaces. However, you may not notice the harm, especially if the effect builds up over time.

Here are the main surfaces you will come across in professional kitchens:

- *metal* – mostly stainless steel, but ventilation ducting may be made of galvanised steel, and other metal work may have painted surfaces

- *wall tiles* – ceramic, resistant to chipping, cracking and scratching. The grouting should be of a type that does not encourage mould

- *floor tiles* – ceramic or quarry tiles, non-porous, very strong and slip resistant

- *vinyl* – used for the floor covering, as sheets or tiles. Less expensive than ceramic floor tiles, but wears less well, and can absorb moisture and dirt

- *painted* – ceilings, doors and walls (where it is not cost effective to tile the whole wall area). The paint must be of a type that does not absorb moisture. Sometimes you will find painted wooden shelves and cupboards in storage areas

- *laminated surfaces* – made with very strong plastics which do not absorb dirt and moisture, and are scratch-resistant

- *glass* – windows and vision panels in doors (so you can see when someone is on the other side and open the door more carefully).

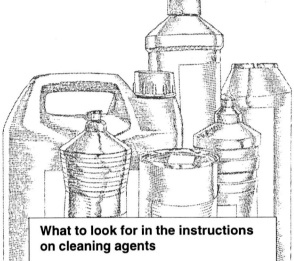

What to look for in the instructions on cleaning agents

any safety warning such as to wear protective clothing

dilution rates: too strong will damage surfaces and is wasteful; too weak will not do the job properly

how much time must be allowed for the cleaning agent to work

how to rinse dirt and cleaning agent from the surface

at what temperature the agent works best

how to store cleaning agents when not in use

how often to use the cleaning agent

how to dispose of used cleaning agents

CHECK list
Storing cleaning agents

✔ keep well away from foodstuffs

✔ close all containers firmly after use

✔ store containers upright

✔ use in the original container where possible

✔ if transfer to another container is necessary (e.g. because the product is bought in bulk), label the new container

✔ store in a well-ventilated cupboard or room, away from fire risks

Types of cleaning agent

Workplace instructions usually refer to cleaning agents by the maker's name. However equipment suppliers (and books like this one) refer to types of agent, leaving the choice of product to the workplace. These are the main types you will come across:

- *general-purpose (or neutral) detergents* – able to penetrate moderately greasy and/or dirty surfaces. Suitable for cleaning floors and walls, and similar routine tasks

- *sanitisers* – for 'clean-as-you-go' use, both cleaning and disinfecting surfaces. But sanitisers do not replace the need for thorough washing with a detergent. Powder sanitisers, dissolved in hot water, require a final rinse and are not suitable for use on certain metals. Liquid sanitisers are diluted before use. They must be left to dry, not rinsed off

- *sanitiser wipes* – a quick and convenient way of cleaning food temperature probes and small utensils, and for wiping food preparation surfaces on a 'clean-as-you-go' basis. Use once only, then discard

- *hard surface cleaners* – for heavier or more specialised tasks, although they are corrosive and damage surfaces if not used with care

- *solvents* – dissolve heavy grease and oil which water-based cleaners cannot cope with

- *abrasives* – or scouring cleaners. Mostly used for cleaning enamel and ceramic surfaces, including tiles. Abrasive powders are much coarser than liquids, creams and pastes, but all of them can damage surfaces.

Water is the simplest cleaner of all. Applied under pressure, it cleans hard surfaces such as the floors and walls in delivery and waste disposal areas. Water also rinses out dirt removed from a surface by other cleaning agents.

Soap is not suitable for cleaning equipment and surfaces because it leaves a scum. Disinfectants are added to some liquid soaps for washing hands.

Chemical disinfectants are not recommended for kitchen use, as their effectiveness can be destroyed by waste food materials, by the fabric of cleaning cloths, and by the materials of some surfaces. Bleach, for example, attacks cloths, some plastics and metal fittings. There is also a risk that the disinfectants will leave a strong smell or taste.

Cleaning safely and effectively

There are many cleaning products or agents on the market, and a variety of equipment. Your managers will have decided what is best for your workplace, and you will be trained and instructed in how to use such products safely and effectively. Just as your employer has a duty to establish safe working methods, so you have a duty to follow the methods set out by your employer.

Here are some points to support your workplace training:

- *different cleaning tasks require different methods* – getting things wrong can cause damage to surfaces, harm to yourself, and spread bacteria and dirt to surfaces which were previously clean

- *many cleaning agents are harmful* – contact with your skin or eyes, or breathing in the fumes, can cause serious illness. Always follow instructions about the wearing of gloves (a particular type may be required), eye protection (i.e. goggles), an apron or other protective clothing

- *many cleaning agents are sold in concentrated form* – usually they must be mixed with water. Follow instructions carefully, e.g. should the water be hot or cold? Measure amounts accurately

- *mixing one agent with another can be very dangerous* – a chemical reaction can be set up, and in some cases this produces poisonous fumes

- *cleaning solutions need to be changed if you are doing a lot of cleaning* – they will not do a proper job if you try to economise or, perhaps, to save yourself time. Do not top up the old solution, but begin again with a completely fresh one

- *rinsing water requires frequent changing* – otherwise you will not be rinsing the surface properly. Rinsing water should normally be hot

- *the good done by cleaning can be easily undone* – if, for example, the cloth you use has become contaminated with bacteria from wiping a surface on which raw meat was prepared. To reduce this risk, many workplaces use colour-coded cleaning equipment (in a similar way as chopping boards are colour-coded)

- *clean in a logical order* – so you do not make surfaces which have just been washed dirty. For example, walls should be cleaned before floors, as some dirty water will run down the walls on to the floor. Doing the floor after other cleaning is complete, gives it a chance to dry before anyone walks over it

- *give yourself space to work in* – before cleaning, move the contents of shelves, cupboards and drawers to a safe place. Be sure to rinse the surfaces well, and leave them to air-dry before reloading

- *standing on chairs or tables to reach high surfaces is dangerous* – use safety steps

Where possible, close off areas where you are cleaning.

- *wet floors are a safety hazard* – close off the area you are cleaning. If this is not possible, put warning signs to catch the attention of anyone entering the area. Do not remove them until the floor is dry

- *water and electricity are a dangerous combination* – movable electrical equipment should be put elsewhere while you clean that area. Before washing walls, cover plugs with insulation tape, so the water will not get inside. Never spray water or steam into or near electrical appliances.

Disposing of rubbish and waste food

Before you start cleaning, remove any rubbish to the waste collection area. You may need to use a dustpan and brush, or sweep some or all of the floor if there are bits of food and other waste around.

The disadvantage of brushing or sweeping is that it sends dust into the air, which will settle on other surfaces. This is not a problem if all those surfaces are going to be washed – so sweeping, when necessary, should be done before any other cleaning.

CHECK list
Safety with cleaning agents

✔ always wear protective gloves – cleaning agents irritate and burn the skin

✔ always wash hands after doing any cleaning

✔ dilute the product according to instructions

✔ use the right amount for the task

✔ prepare a fresh solution as necessary and dispose of the old – do not top up a cleaning solution

✔ use the weaker agent first – use a stronger agent only if the dirt proves stubborn

✔ never mix different cleaning agents, because this may produce harmful gases

✔ do not pierce an aerosol can, even if it appears to be empty – it may explode

Cleaning floors, drainage channels, etc.

Damp-mopping is the usual method for the routine cleaning of floors:

- use a push-and-pull action – avoid stretching too far, or trying to cover too large an area at once, as this can put a strain on your back

- regularly rinse out the mop head in the detergent, and squeeze out excess solution so you do not flood the floor

- pay special attention to areas in front of and around cooking equipment, under tables and racks, and in corners

- pull out equipment which is on castors, so that you can clean the floor underneath properly. Unlock the castors first, and if you find any difficulty in moving the equipment, get the help of a colleague. Take care not to damage connections to the gas, water or electricity supply. If it is necessary to disconnect the safety chain (this stops the equipment moving beyond the reach of flexible connections), reconnect when you have completed cleaning.

Drainage channels and grid housings may require a strong detergent, and perhaps scrubbing. Gratings should be removed and scrubbed outside the kitchen.

Cleaning walls

Work only over small areas at a time, rubbing over the surface with a cloth well rung out in detergent. Rinse with another cloth, and very hot water. You may need to polish tiled surfaces with a dry cloth.

Dirty water running over a dirty surface can leave marks which are difficult to remove. If this happens, start cleaning at the bottom of the wall and work upwards. Work downwards when rinsing.

Cleaning sinks

Rinse away any food debris using cold water.

Half fill the basin with warm water. Wet a cleaning cloth, and apply general-purpose detergent, or if necessary a scouring cream. Clean the draining board, taps, splashback, overflow, underneath including the pipes, and the top half of the basin. Change the water as necessary.

Drain the basin, and clean the remaining part.

Rinse all areas with warm water. Polish taps with dry disposable towelling or kitchen paper.

Cleaning handbasins

Follow the method for cleaning sinks. Put the scrubbing brush to one side while you are working. You will also need to clean the overflow, the plug and the chain.

Cleaning food production equipment

Never attempt to clean equipment unless you are confident you know what to do – from workplace training or instruction, or from following the supplier's manual. If you are under the age of 18, you are not allowed by law to clean any machine, if doing so exposes you to risk of injury.

You are at risk from contact with sharp blades, hot surfaces, etc., as you clean the machine. Others who use the equipment, after you have cleaned it, are at risk if you have not done the job properly, e.g. re-assembling it incorrectly.

Turning the equipment off

Equipment should be turned off before you start cleaning. Electrical equipment must be isolated from the supply: pull out the plug if there is one, otherwise turn off the main electrical switch to the machine.

Check with your manager about how to turn off the gas supply to stoves, grills, hot cupboards, etc.

Dismantling equipment

Remove the shelves and shelf supports (if they are the removable type) from ovens, steamers and hot cupboards. Remove the fat drawer or trough from grills and hobs. Also the crumb tray, splash guards, side racks and stainless steel grilling bars, and the wire frying baskets from fryers.

Equipment can be cleaned more thoroughly in a large sink, and you can get at food which has accumulated on shelf supports or under trays.

Using suitable cleaning equipment and materials

A general-purpose detergent is suitable for equipment or any parts which are not heavily engrained with burnt food, dirt and grease:

- remove loose particles of food
- rub exterior and interior surfaces with a cloth
- pay particular attention to runners and sliding door channels
- be careful not to flood the equipment and surrounding area
- rinse with clean, hot water.

Wash removable shelves, fat troughs, etc. in a sink filled with hot water and detergent. Rinse thoroughly.

In some workplaces, equipment is wiped with a sanitiser after rinsing.

Usually the kitchen is hot enough for equipment to air-dry quickly after rinsing (wet objects attract bacteria). Otherwise use disposable paper towels, but take care not to leave torn pieces of paper in the equipment.

For heavy deposits, you may have to use a degreasing agent and a nylon scouring pad. Check first with the instructions for the particular piece of equipment. Do not use a knife to scrape surfaces clean. Be careful not to damage surfaces with excessive rubbing. Deep scratches may cause rusting.

Use a spray-on glass cleaner for glass panels on oven and steamer doors. Never apply cold water to a hot glass panel, or the glass will almost certainly crack.

Aerosol cleaners are not suitable for microwaves and similar equipment where the spray can get into (and damage) the internal parts of the oven.

Wear goggles, apron and any other protective clothing stated in workplace instructions and on the cleaning material. Gloves should always be worn:

- insulated gloves for equipment which has to be cleaned while still hot
- long gloves that protect your forearms for cleaning ovens and other equipment which you have to stretch into.

Re-assembling equipment

Pilot lights on gas equipment will have to be re-ignited when you have completed the cleaning. This may be your supervisor's responsibility – it is essential that the equipment is not used by someone who is not aware that the pilot light is out.

Dealing with problems

Some faults with equipment are easy to spot, e.g. a damaged blade, or a missing piece. Or you may find the machine does not work after re-assembling. If you think you have put everything together properly, this suggests a fault.

Never attempt to investigate or repair the fault yourself:

- report the problem to your manager immediately
- label the equipment OUT OF ORDER (see page 33)
- if it is movable, take it somewhere it cannot be used, e.g. to the manager's office, or to the maintenance department.

Types of equipment and their cleaning

Always consult your workplace instructions, or those which came with the equipment.

Don't forget to clean the equipment legs, connecting gas and water supply pipes, and, if necessary, the surrounding walls or floor.

More on cleaning steamers

If you are using a bucket to drain the water tank (or cistern), keep an eye on the bucket while it is filling. The steamer may hold more than one bucket-full.

After cleaning, don't forget to close the drain tap. Usually the water tank is left empty in readiness for the next day's work. But do make sure that the tank is refilled before lighting the burner/turning on.

More on cleaning ovens

It is better to remove staining and spillages on a very regular basis, rather than leaving them to build up. Wipe with a slightly damp cloth using general-purpose detergent. Then wipe the surfaces with a soft cloth rinsed in fresh water.

How you clean the oven interior depends on the type of finish. Sometimes the oven needs to be warm during cleaning. Follow instructions carefully and do not neglect to rinse the oven interior.

More on cleaning microwave ovens

Wipe up spills when they occur – with a soft cloth dampened in warm, general-purpose detergent solution. Rinse with a clean cloth (well wrung out) and polish with a soft, dry cloth. Loosen baked-on splashes by boiling an open jug of water inside the oven.

Keep door seals spotlessly clean. A build-up of spilt food prevents a tight seal being formed. The oven does not work as well, and may become dangerous (letting out microwave energy).

Check the instructions for removing and washing the air filter – which is usually at the back or bottom front of the oven. Shields, which protect parts such as the stirrer, also require cleaning.

More on cleaning hobs and ranges

Clean regularly to avoid a build-up of grease and burnt food deposits. Do not neglect the sides and back, including taps and gas pipes.

Check for specific instructions on cleaning drip trays, burners, open and solid tops. Some metals become permanently stained and discoloured if wrongly cleaned.

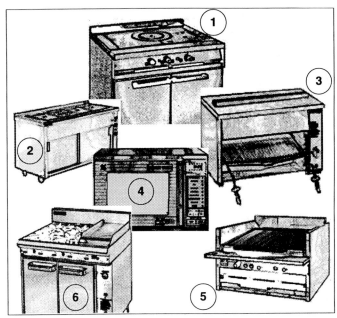

1) Solid top oven, 2) Closed top bain-marie with hot cupboard 3) salamander, 4) microwave/convection oven, 5) simulated charcoal grill, 6) gas range with griddle.

More on cleaning griddles, grills and salamanders

To clean the aluminium branders on overhead/steakhouse grills/salamanders, leave under the full heat of the grill until the spillages carbonise. Remove the carbon with a wire brush.

For simulated charcoal grills:

- lift out the brander bars daily and clean with a wire brush – this prevents carbonising and keeps the channels clear

- clean the burners regularly – once a week is recommended to stop the burner holes from getting blocked. You will have to remove the lava rock and burner grates first. Use a wire brush, taking care to remove all deposits of lava dust and grease. Ensure the burners are dry and free from any cleaning material before replacing.

For griddles:

- when cool, wipe clean with a dry cloth

- use a broad metal scraper to remove heavy deposits (also do this from time to time when cooking for long periods)

- if the griddle is not to be used for a few days, brush the surface lightly with oil to prevent rusting.

Cleaning the salamander

Copid Beech Hotel

1 Turn off gas supply and allow to cool.
2 Remove shelf. Soak and clean separately.
3 Spray with salamander cleaner and leave for 15 minutes.
4 Use scouring pad to remove any spillages.
5 Rinse all surfaces with clean, hot water.
6 Dry throughout with a cloth.
7 Replace grill tray.

A range of fryers and the baskets used to hold the food.

More on cleaning fryers

Drain the oil, using the tap at the bottom of the fryer. Pour the oil through the special filter, taking care not to let it splash. You should never try to save time by filtering the oil while it is still hot. If some spills on you, you could get a nasty burn. If you drain hot oil into a plastic bucket, the bucket will melt and the oil will spill everywhere, burning your feet.

Remove all debris from the empty fryer. Hinged electric elements can be moved so that the bottom of the compartment can be cleaned.

A typical sequence for cleaning a fryer goes like this:

- close the drain valve, fill the fryer with hot water and detergent, and turn the fryer on

- once the water has started to boil gently, turn the fryer off. Do not allow to boil vigorously, or the water may spill over the sides of the fryer

- when the cleaning solution is cool enough to work with safely, remove any build-up of oil in the fryer, using a long-handled brush or soft abrasive pad

- if deposits remain, bring the cleaning solution to a gentle boil for a second time, allow to cool, then brush the sides again

- drain the fryer, rinse well with clean hot water – three times is usual (any trace of detergent will make the fresh oil spoil very rapidly)

- wash the exterior of the fryer with warm water and a general-purpose detergent

- thoroughly dry interior and exterior with a soft cloth

- close the outlet tap and refill with oil (fresh if necessary).

This sequence is not suitable for a fryer filled with lard (which is solid at room temperature).

More on cleaning bain-maries and hotplates

When removing containers which have been sitting in a water bath, hold them over the water for a few moments, then wipe the base with a cloth.

If you are using a bucket to drain the bain-marie, take care not to overfill it.

Avoid touching the electric elements when you clean the bottom of the heating compartment.

More on cleaning food processors

Use a well rung-out cloth for washing and rinsing, so you don't flood the interior mechanism.

Take care not to cut yourself when handling or washing the sharp blades. Always wipe the blades well after washing, to prevent rusting.

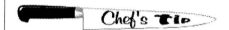

Chef's Tip

On steamers – *with thanks to Juno*

After each use, remove any food residues.

When steamer is not in use, leave door slightly open so that the air inside remains clean.

On grills – *with thanks to Stott Benham*

When cleaning the inside of a gas-operated grill, take care not to damage the burner plaques. Do not attempt to clean these – any deposits will burn off.

On griddles – *with thanks to Blue Seal*

To remove accumulated carbon, use a scraper and fine grit griddle brick. Occasionally, to bleach the plate, wipe vinegar over the cold surface.

On vegetable preparation machines – *with thanks to Robot-Coupe*

Rinse the bowl by filling with hot water and switching on for a few moments.

Whatever the attachment, clean it by hand using washing-up liquid rather than in a dishwasher. This will help the machine last longer.

The blades on the slicing discs, the plates on the julienne discs and the graters wear out with use. Change them every so often to ensure high-quality cutting. Sharpen smooth blades daily using a sharpening stone.

On stainless steel – *with thanks to Falcon*

To keep the attractive, shiny finish of stainless steel, clean regularly and often by rubbing over with a damp cloth and mild detergent. Rinse and dry.

If there is a build-up of grease or stubborn deposits on the surface, use a soft cleaning pad. Rub in the direction of the grain.

On enamel finishes – *with thanks to Falcon*

You find these on the facia panels of some grills and ovens.

Clean with a general-purpose detergent solution. Never use oven-cleaners, aerosol cleaners or other products, especially those which may have a high caustic content. They can cause serious damage or discolouration to the enamel finish, particularly when the appliance is hot.

On aluminium – *with thanks to Robot Coupe*

Do not use a dishwasher to clean aluminium fittings from equipment. The aluminium will get tarnished.

Cleaning food production utensils

As you will see from suppliers' catalogues and catering equipment shops, and from your own workplace, there is a wide range of utensils.

Using suitable cleaning methods

Some types of utensil require special treatment because of the material they are made from – examples are given below. If you are washing something for the first time, ask how it should be done.

Rinse (or lightly scrape) utensils free of food debris before hand or machine washing. Avoid using pot scourers or metal wool as they damage surfaces.

For hand-washing:

- fill the sink with hot water (at about 60°C) and the correct concentration of general-purpose detergent
- use a disposable washing-up cloth or nylon brush/scouring pad to clean all surfaces of the utensil
- put in very hot water (80°C to 85°C) for two minutes to rinse and kill any remaining bacteria. Use baskets to hold the utensils, as these temperatures are too hot for hands
- air dry – if this is not possible, use disposable paper towelling.

Change detergent and rinsing water frequently. In some workplaces, a sanitiser is added to the rinsing water, or this is a separate stage after rinsing.

After use, thoroughly wash nylon brushes and scouring pads. Leave to dry.

For machine-washing:

- heavily encrusted items may have to be pre-washed in the sink, using a nylon scouring pad
- stack the dishwasher baskets carefully, so that utensils will not crash around in the machine, possibly getting damaged.

Commercial dishwashers wash at around 60°C, and rinse at around 85°C. The utensils will air dry within a short time of coming out of the machine. If hand drying or polishing is necessary, use disposable towelling.

Saucepans and frying pans should not be cleaned in a dishwasher.

Types of utensil

Food production utensils can be grouped according to what they are made from:

- *stainless steel* – very durable and easy to clean, but not a good conductor of heat (unless the pan has a heavy copper base)
- *coated metal* – non-stick pans are coated in a special way but only the very best quality ones are suitable for the heavy use they get in a catering kitchen. Follow the label instructions for cleaning. *Copper* pans have a tin coating (except those used for boiling sugar, as the tin would melt in the high temperatures). They need re-tinning from time to time. Coated iron cookware (e.g. with enamelled paint) is sometimes used for presenting food on hot buffets, but not usually for cooking because of the weight and the risk of the coating being chipped from heavy use
- *wooden* – never leave soaking in water, as this will cause the wood to split or warp (when it becomes a serious hygiene risk). Rub over with a cloth sanitising wipe and leave to dry. If food remains stuck on, scrape this off, wash briefly in hot soapy water, rinse and leave to dry away from direct heat
- *plastic* – durable when well looked after, and no risk of shattered pieces getting into food (as there is with glass and china utensils). Do not soak in water for long periods. Withdraw from use if the surface becomes badly scratched and/or stained
- *porcelain, earthenware* and *glass* – required for cooking and serving various dishes. Handle carefully. Even if there is no visible damage, internal weaknesses can develop which may cause the utensil to break in normal use
- *cast iron* – used mostly for frying pans. Do not wash cast iron utensils, but wipe firmly with a dry cloth or absorbent kitchen paper. Use salt as a scouring agent where necessary, or a little detergent and hot water. If an iron pan is washed by accident, warm it slightly, then give it a coating of oil and rub with salt before use
- *aluminium* – inexpensive and hard-wearing, but light coloured sauces cooked in them can become grey. Some foods (e.g. eggs when boiled) leave a stain. To remove stains, boil a weak solution of vinegar and water in the pan.

More on utensils

These are some of the utensils you will find in your workplace:

- *chopping boards* – for any food preparation task which involves cutting, slicing, chopping, carving, etc. Plastic boards are considered the easiest to keep clean, but with heavy use the surface becomes scratched and may stain – they should not be used in this state. A system of colour-coding reduces the risk of cross contamination (see page 46)

- *pots and pans* – of many different shapes and sizes, some for specific uses, e.g. milk pans (with a pouring lip). Made from aluminium, stainless steel, copper and iron

- *bowls, dishes and moulds* – used for mixing ingredients, for storing, for moulding cold dishes (e.g. a fruit jelly), and for cooking. Stainless steel is the most durable type. Egg whites do not whisk properly in plastic bowls

- *whisks* – for beating or whisking cream, eggs, etc., and blending thickeners into sauces and soups. Check food is not trapped at the base, or between the strands of the whisk

- *sieves, colanders and strainers* – size of hole and shape depend on their use. Colanders (used for draining vegetables and salads) have the largest hole and are fairly easy to clean. Sieves made with fine wire mesh need special care when cleaning – use the force of water from the tap to dislodge food caught in the sieve. If badly treated, the sieve will get mis-shapen and become detached from the rim. A conical strainer is also called a *chinois*. Food tends to get caught in the holes, especially at the narrow bottom

- *spoons, ladles and slices* – for stirring, handling food, measuring, pouring and portioning. Made from stainless steel, coated steel and plastic (plastic utensils are best for dishes which require a lot of stirring, as they do not conduct heat). Some have perforations for draining food: check that food is not caught in the holes

- *graters* – for grating cheese, carrots, etc. Check that no food is caught in the holes. This is less likely to happen if the grater is washed soon after use

- *peelers, zesters and corers* – these are the hand-held type. Peelers are used to remove the hard skin of vegetables and hard fruits like pears. Zesters are used to remove the thin outer skin (not pith) of oranges, lemons, etc. Corers are used for removing the centre, including the pips, from apples and similar fruit. Clean well, so food does not remain caught in the blade

- *tin openers* – these may be bench-mounted or hand held. Wash after use, as food will be in contact with the cutting blade and possibly the turning mechanism – openers not kept clean are a serious hygiene hazard.

Storing utensils

When utensils are absolutely dry, return them to their usual place. Store pots and pans upside-down on racks or shelves (racks are best because they allow air to circulate inside the pot).

Do not leave plastic utensils in very hot places (e.g. on the rack above the cooking range).

Chopping boards are best stored in a rack, so the air can circulate freely. If stacked or put away in a drawer, moisture may be trapped and mould will develop.

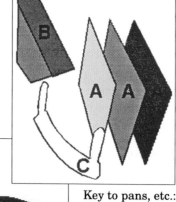

Key to pans, etc.: *1) tin-lined copper sauteuse, 2) non-stick frying pan, 3) tin-lined copper flambé pan (for use in the restaurant), 4) aluminium frying pan, 5) omelette pan, 6) sauté pan, 7) cast iron frying pan.*

Key to boards etc.: *A) colour-coded chopping board holder and boards, B) mandolin (see page 76), C) two-blade* hachoir *(for chopping parsley, use with a rocking motion).*

For help to answer questions relating to:

Health and safety

? protective clothing

Gloves should always be worn. The type and whether you need to wear eye protection, apron, etc. depend on the task and the cleaning agents being used.

? marking areas being cleaned

Other people who enter the area when the floor is wet may not be aware of the need for caution. They could slip and injure themselves.

? reporting faulty equipment

By not reporting a fault, you are risking your own and your colleagues' safety. Label faulty equipment, so that no one else uses it. Where possible, remove the equipment to a place where it cannot be used.

? following manufacturers' instructions

Cleaning materials and equipment are safe when used in the way intended by the maker, but many are hazardous if used wrongly. What is right for one product may be wrong for another.

? storing in labelled containers

Think about the appearance of each of the cleaning substances used in your workplace. If put in what was normally a food container, would you and others in your workplace know what they were? And what might happen if the instructions for safe use of the substance were not there on the container to remind you?

? turning equipment off before cleaning

Safety is the over-riding concern. What would happen if the switch to a slicing machine was accidentally knocked to the ON position after you had removed the blade cover?

Be quite clear that you know what has to be turned off or disconnected, and how. What do you have to do after cleaning to leave the machine ready for its next use?

? dismantling and re-assembling

Most equipment has parts which cannot be cleaned effectively without dismantling. It is hard to clean the interior of an oven unless the shelves are first removed. A food slicer might look clean and shiny, but there could be a heavy build up of food debris under the slicing blade, apparent only when it is removed.

Some equipment does not require dismantling to clean or should only be dismantled when it is serviced and cleaned by the engineer, e.g. induction cookers, bratt pans and bulk boiling pans.

? equipment and material for cleaning

This depends on the equipment and the cleaning products used in your workplace. There should be minimum risk of spreading bacteria or harmful substances to surfaces which come into direct contact with food, or damaging equipment by using over-abrasive cleaning methods, or cleaning agents which chemically react with metals, plastics and other substances used in the construction of the equipment.

? cleaning/drying/storing utensils

The points which apply to most types of utensil are: 1) pre-rinsing to remove food debris; 2) washing in detergent solution; 3) avoiding damage when scraping off stubborn deposits; 4) rinsing in very hot water; 5) air-drying; 6) returning to storage. Some utensils, because of what they are made of, or how they are made, need special methods.

Hygiene

? separate cleaning equipment for floors/work surfaces

Floors get dirtier than work surfaces. If a cloth which has been used to wipe a spill on the floor, for example, is used on a work surface, bacteria and dirt will be transferred.

? cleaning after use

The sooner cleaning takes place, the sooner bacteria are prevented from multiplying and spreading. The risk of food being contaminated by dirt is reduced. Clean kitchens are less attractive to pests. It's also easier for you – if just left, grease builds up and dirt bakes hard.

? handling and disposing of waste

Waste attracts bacteria and pests, so the sooner it is removed from food preparation areas the better. When you touch waste and the lids of waste containers, your hands are likely to become contaminated with bacteria and dirt.

? risks of not keeping utensils clean

Any equipment not cleaned is a safety risk. Bacteria will multiply and contaminate food.

? storing cleaning equipment separately

In doing its job, cleaning equipment comes into contact with dirt, bacteria, grease, etc. Even when the equipment is well rinsed and dried after use, there is a danger that some harmful substances remain. Separate storage reduces the risk of these substances getting on to food.

? use of disinfectants

Some chemical disinfectants do not have a long staying power. Some are inactivated by food. Others attack metal and/or plastic surfaces.

Use this to check your progress against the performance criteria.

Element 1

Clean food production areas

Keep sinks and handbasins thoroughly clean and free-flowing	☐ PC1
Clean floors and walls in line with service operations	☐ PC2
Keep drains, gullies, traps and overflows clean and free-flowing	☐ PC3
Keep surfaces, shelving, cupboards and drawers hygienic, ready for use	☐ PC4
Use suitable cleaning equipment and materials and store correctly after use	☐ PC5
Dispose of rubbish and waste food and keep waste containers hygienic	☐ PC6
Deal with unexpected situations and inform appropriate people	☐ PC7
Carry out your work in an organised, efficient and safe manner	☐ PC8

Element 2

Clean food production equipment

Turn off and dismantle food production equipment for cleaning	☐ PC1
Clean and correctly re-assemble equipment	☐ PC2
Use suitable cleaning equipment and materials and store correctly after use	☐ PC3
Deal with unexpected situations and inform appropriate people	☐ PC4
Carry out your work in an organised, efficient and safe manner	☐ PC5

Element 3

Clean food production utensils

Use suitable cleaning equipment for the type of utensil	☐ PC1
Clean utensils correctly	☐ PC2
Ensure that finished utensils are clean, dry and free from damage	☐ PC3
Identify damaged utensils and report them to the appropriate person	☐ PC4
Handle and store finished utensils correctly	☐ PC5
Dispose of waste and food debris correctly	☐ PC6
Leave cleaning areas and equipment hygienic and ready for use	☐ PC7
Deal with unexpected situations and inform appropriate people	☐ PC8
Carry out your work in an organised, efficient and safe manner	☐ PC9

Cleaning cutting equipment

The methods you follow, and cleaning agents, are similar to those used for cleaning food production equipment (see pages 67 to 69). With cutting equipment, particular care must be taken because of the risk of injury from the sharp blades. Never attempt to clean such equipment on your own, unless you have been trained and feel confident you know what to do.

If you are under the age of 18, do not clean cutting equipment. It is against the law.

Here is a reminder of the main points from earlier in this section:

- *turning the equipment off* – turn off at the mains switch or pull out the plug. Do not rely on the machine's control switch: you might accidentally knock it on during the cleaning

- *dismantling equipment* – follow instructions for removing safety guards and other parts of the equipment, so that cleaning can be thorough. Keep everything together, so you do not lose some of the parts

- *re-assembling equipment* – usually the reverse of the method you followed for dismantling the equipment. Safety guards must be put back in place before the equipment is tested or used

- *dealing with problems* – report any difficulty directly to your manager. Label and/or remove the equipment so you do not put others in danger.

Using suitable cleaning equipment and materials

Wash loose parts and attachments in a sink filled with hot water and detergent. Rinse in clean, very hot water and allow to air dry.

To clean the body of the equipment:

- fill a cleaning bowl with hot water and general-purpose detergent

- apply to all surfaces with a well wrung-out cloth

- use a nylon brush to dislodge food particles, and a nylon scouring pad for ingrained dirt

- rinse with clean, hot water (using a well wrung-out cloth)

- air dry, or use a paper towel.

Do not allow water to get into the electrical fittings. Never immerse the motor unit in water.

Always remove the blade of a slicing machine using the special carrier provided.

Types of equipment and their cleaning

Cutting equipment includes the following:

- *mincing machines* – may be an attachment on a mixer or a separate item of equipment. Usually the mincing mechanism consists of several parts (the worm, cutting disc, etc.), so that pieces of gristle and food can be easily removed during cleaning

- *chipping machines* – wash with generous quantities of water to remove the starch from the potatoes

- *slicing machines* – set the slice thickness control at zero to prevent access to the blade edge. If the blade is intended to be removed for cleaning, do not separate it from the special carrier

- *rotary knife chopping machines* – be sure to clean all the recesses and areas which food comes into contact with

- *mandolins* – these can be fully submerged in the washing and rinsing water, as there are no mechanical parts. Use a nylon brush to clean around the (very sharp) blades. The force of water from the tap will also help dislodge food trapped in the blades

- *food processors* – see page 72.

Maintaining cutting equipment

Cutting equipment varies in size from hand-operated mandolins, which are usually stored in a cupboard or on a shelf, to large floor-mounted machines that never get moved. Because cutting equipment can be so dangerous, it should be in a place where there is:

- adequate room for you to work the machine

- minimum risk of your being bumped or distracted

- good lighting, so you can see clearly

- a secure base for the machine, so it will not move or rock when in use

- a suitable floor surface, so you can stand comfortably, with minimum risk of slipping.

Some cutting machines require basic maintenance on a regular basis, e.g. lubricating some of the moving parts (there are special food-safe products for doing this). The instructions which come with the machine will tell you what to do.

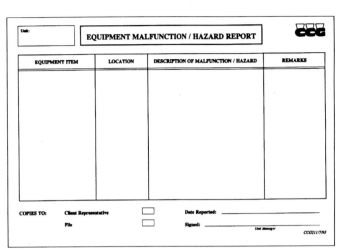

At CCG Services Limited this form is completed by the unit manager when a piece of equipment is not working properly.

Storing and handling cutting equipment

Large machines are usually left in one position. Some models are bolted to the floor or table to provide stability during operation.

When you do have to move a machine to clean under the base, or because it is a small model and shortage of space means that it must be put away after use:

- plan the move, so that space is available at the machine's destination, and your route is clear

- unplug the machine, and wind the cable up carefully so it will not become tangled with your feet or other objects

- get help from a colleague if you cannot safely move the machine on your own – a trolley will also make the task easier (see general guidelines for manual handling, page 60)

- carry attachments (push sticks for mincers, mixing bowls, cutting plates for specific uses, etc.) on a second journey – to lighten the load, and to reduce the risk of them dropping to the floor part-way through your journey. Or else put them on the lower shelf of the trolley.

Dealing with faults and problems

You have two responsibilities if you find any fault or problem in operating cutting equipment:

- report the matter promptly to your manager, so that steps can be taken to get the machine checked and repaired by an engineer

- attach a label or sign to the machine to warn others that it is faulty.

Your manager will normally ensure the faulty machine is moved from the kitchen, e.g. to the maintenance department, if this can be done safely.

The law on equipment safety

Under the Provision and Use of Work Equipment Regulations 1992 your employer has a duty to ensure that equipment is:

- suitable for the purpose(s) for which, and the place in which, it will be used
- used in accordance with the maker's specifications and instructions
- in efficient working order and good repair, inspecting, testing and maintaining it as necessary.

Where a specific health and safety risk is involved, use of the equipment must be restricted to those who have had training.

Health and safety information, instructions and training must be provided to all those who use work equipment, and to their supervisors or managers.

For help to answer questions relating to:

Health and safety

? **turning off and dismantling**

Turning equipment off at the power source is an essential safety precaution. The on–off switch might be knocked during cleaning. Dismantling is necessary to get access to all the parts which come into contact with food.

? **dangers when cleaning**

The main danger is from the blade itself. Take the greatest care not to touch the razor-sharp cutting edge.

? **precautions when dismantling**

The razor-sharp blade has been mentioned. Carry out the steps for dismantling the equipment in the right order, otherwise you may cause damage. If a particular step proves difficult, check with the instructions that you have done everything else correctly.

? **following makers' instructions**

The makers have to meet rigorous safety standards in the design and construction of their equipment. But these depend on the equipment being used in the intended way, properly cleaned and maintained.

Besides the risk of an accident, or damage to the machine if you do not follow instructions, you may invalidate guarantee or warranty terms against which your employer can claim the costs of repair.

You will also be failing in your general duty to protect the safety of everyone in your workplace.

? **inspecting cutting equipment regularly**

The safety of equipment depends on regular checks. Are safety guards in place and operating effectively? Are cutting blades, and other parts of the equipment which can be seen when the equipment is dismantled for cleaning, in good condition?

? **storing cutting equipment**

Check your workplace instructions on how to turn the machine off at the main power supply, what attachments need to be fitted before use (e.g. the food processor left unassembled so the next operator can fit the blade he or she needs), and how to move or cover the machine for long-term storage.

? **safe handling methods**

Serious injury can follow from trying to move or lift equipment that is heavy or bulky. See page 60.

? **security of storage areas**

Safety will be the main concern when cutting equipment is stored in a place other than the kitchen. An untrained person might attempt to use it, or someone might damage it by placing other equipment on top of, or against it.

Hygiene

? **risks of cross contamination**

While it is not too costly to equip a kitchen with separate sets of chopping boards, knives, etc. for different types of food, this is not often practical for expensive equipment like cutting machines, food processors and mincers. That puts a great responsibility on you to make sure that cutting equipment has been thoroughly cleaned between jobs. Otherwise bacteria will be spread from raw to cooked food.

Use this to check your progress against the performance criteria.

Element 1

Clean cutting equipment

Switch off and dismantle cleaning equipment before and during cleaning PC

Use appropriate materials and equipment to clean cutting equipment PC

Store cutting equipment correctly after cleaning, dry and ready for use PC

Identify and promptly report problems PC

Prioritise and carry out your work in an organised, efficient and safe manner PC

Element 2

Maintain cutting equipment

Get your cooking areas and equipment ready for use PC

Store cutting equipment clean and in good working order PC

Handle and lift cutting equipment using approved safe methods PC

Label faulty cutting equipment, isolate to prevent use, and report PC

Maintain equipment storage areas in a clean, tidy state, no rubbish, secure PC

Identify and promptly report problems PC

Prioritise and carry out your work in an organised, efficient and safe manner PC

Operating a mixing machine

Extracts from the training plan

Step 1 Switch off and unplug machine.

Question Why is this important?

Answer No chance of the machine starting while being cleaned.

Step 2 Approach machine with attachment (e.g. whisk) inside the bowl. The bowl to be fitted with collar guard.

Question Why is the machine attachment inside the bowl?

Answer More efficient and effective. It's also safer.

Step 3 Fit bowl clamps.

Question Why is this done?

Answer To avoid the bowl becoming dislodged in action.

Step 4 Fit attachment to spindle.

Question Why must it click in place?

Answer To avoid it becoming dislodged when in operation.

Step 5 Explain speeds/gears.

Question Why must we always start the machine up in low gear?

Answer To avoid food being thrown out.

Step 6 Demonstration of mixer.

Question Why must our hands be dry?

Answer To avoid any electrical shocks when starting the machine.

Question What could happen if we had loose items of clothing?

Answer They could get caught up in the machine while it is running.

Question Why do we switch off the machine before adding more ingredients?

Answer To avoid splashes.

Question Why do we never leave the machine running unsupervised?

Answer To reduce the risk of accidents.

Question Why would you never reach into the bowl whilst the machine is running?

Answer It could result in a very serious injury.

Always switch off at the isolating switch prior to putting your hand into the bowl.

With thanks to
The University of Sheffield

Removing waste to collection points

Waste is material your workplace does not want, but waste may be attractive to others. Dogs and cats will soon rip into plastic bags, scattering the contents in their search for titbits. Birds, pests and vermin are determined to get at waste.

Waste not properly secured is a hygiene and a safety risk. The sight of it offends neighbours, members of the public and customers.

Creators of waste (i.e. your workplace) have a legal duty to look after it, and to see that it is disposed of safely. Any waste handed on to someone else must be secured in a suitable container. Loose material loaded in a vehicle or skip should be covered.

The collectors of waste require a written description of the waste. For day-to-day items, this requirement is covered by a general transfer note, issued yearly. But specialist waste has to be dealt with as a one-off.

The types of waste

These are the different types of waste you need to know about, with some examples:

- *food waste* – trimmings from preparing the food, left-overs returned on the service dishes and customers' plates, and food which has to be discarded for some reason

- *commercial waste* – waste created by the business: packaging, empty cans, bottles and other disposable containers from the kitchen, restaurant and other departments in your workplace

- *domestic waste* – waste from a private household.

Private householders pay for the disposal of their waste through the council tax. It is collected by the council, or a contractor on the council's behalf.

Businesses have to pay the council or a licensed contractor to remove food waste and commercial waste. The charge depends on the amount of waste handled.

CHECK list
Safe storage of waste

✔ container not worn or damaged and (for hygiene reasons) cleaned regularly

✔ liquids not liable to leak out

✔ not liable to be knocked or blown over

✔ lid will not blow open in a strong wind

✔ secure against animals, vandals, children, etc.

✔ contents will not chemically react with each other

✔ minimum fire risk

Unidentifiable and hazardous waste

The waste from your workplace could include items that are dangerous if handled in the wrong way by people who collect and dispose of the waste, and anyone else who gets access to it (e.g. scavengers):

- hazardous cleaning agents – cause burns, may chemically react with other waste items

- used oil from the fryers – a fire hazard

- cigarette ends and waste paper – a fire hazard

- sharp objects – could cause severe cuts

- syringes, hypodermic needles, used condoms, sanitary towels, nappies, used razor blades, etc. – health risk (including Aids).

Each type of waste must be kept separate from general waste, securely contained to minimise the risk of accident or contamination:

- hazardous liquids including used oils in a suitable and clearly labelled container

- glass in its own container or bin

- syringes and needles in a *sharps* box (of the type used in hospitals, etc.). Or, if only found occasionally, put in an empty drinks can or similar container that won't be pierced by the needle.

Handling waste

When collecting waste from the various departments and areas of the workplace, find out what sort of materials you are dealing with. You may already know from your knowledge of the work done in that area, or be able to tell from the appearance of the waste and its weight.

If you find something unusual, check with the person responsible for putting the waste there. A new member of staff, or someone not aware of the risks of handling waste, may have placed unwrapped broken glass in the disposable waste bag, for example.

Cleaning waste containers and areas

Waste containers are heavily used. So is the waste collection area. Both have to be regularly cleaned, and kept in a tidy, orderly state.

Preparation routine

Decide what you need, and collect the various items of equipment and cleaning agents required for the task. You will need strong gloves, and usually waterproof outer clothing and over-shoes (or Wellington boots). Eye protection should be worn when using some cleaning agents.

Selecting cleaning equipment and cleaning agents

Your workplace instructions or cleaning schedule will list the equipment and cleaning agents required for each task, and special safety precautions to be followed. Here is an introduction to the equipment you might be using:

- *brooms* – used for sweeping floors of rubbish and debris

- *hosepipes* – connected to the mains, these provide quite a strong force of water, sufficient to dislodge some of the dirt and debris that collect in corners of bins, and around the waste collection area; a plentiful supply of water helps in the rinsing of bins

- *deck scrubbers* – help release stubborn soiling, and useful for cleaning the bottom of bins

- *pressure washers* – provide a powerful jet of water, so that it is not usually necessary also to scrub.

There are three main groups of cleaning agents (sometimes called cleaning chemicals):

- *detergents* – general-purpose detergents remove light soiling, and the washing and rinsing process removes most bacteria. They are suitable for cleaning waste bins in the bars, restaurant, plate wash and other work areas. Stronger detergents may be required for heavily soiled bins

- *sanitisers* – combine the action of detergents with disinfection (to kill bacteria) – sometimes used for cleaning waste bins in food preparation areas

- *disinfectants* – have a more powerful bacteria-killing action, and will normally be used for cleaning heavy duty bins kept in the waste collection area, as well as floor (and perhaps wall) surfaces.

Your workplace cleaning schedules will take account of the advantages and disadvantages of each of these, and such factors as:

- *nature of the surface* – e.g. disinfectants harm some surfaces

- *nature and degree of soilage* – e.g. sanitisers will deal with light soiling in food preparation areas

- *environmental constraints* – e.g. the noise of a pressure washer very early in the morning would disturb guests in the hotel, or neighbours

- *location* – e.g. a broom sends light dust into the air, so is not suitable in food preparation areas

- *availability of water and power* – e.g. a pressure washer requires a supply of electricity and water

- *drainage* – e.g. a mop and bucket will have to be used for washing floors where there is no means for the water to run off.

Cleaning safely

Safety rules are there to protect you and others affected by the work you do. Here are some reasons why they are necessary:

- many cleaning agents cause harm if they come into contact with your skin or your eyes, or if you swallow even a few drops. Some give off fumes which are harmful if breathed in

- while floors are being cleaned, there is a risk that you and other people will slip on the wet surface

- water and electricity are a dangerous combination – this can happen if pressure washers are used near unprotected electrical equipment

- hazardous waste will be a safety risk if the container or packaging is damaged during cleaning, exposing the contents or causing them to spill out.

Disposing of slurry and waste

Slurry and waste block drains if not washed away with liberal quantities of water. Where drains feed into private sewerage systems, additional rules may exist to prevent pollution.

Completing the task

After cleaning, replace disposable bags where used. Check that lids on bins are secure, and that all equipment is in place. Clean cleaning equipment and put away:

- wash brooms and scrubbers in general-purpose detergent solution, rinse in fresh water, then hang by the handle (if left to rest on its bristles, the head of the broom will become mis-shapen)

- role up hosepipes and secure. If necessary, clean the hose by wiping the full length with a cloth and detergent solution, as you reel it up

- wipe over the outside of pressure washers with a cleaning cloth and general-purpose detergent, rinse with clean water, and allow to air dry

- wipe over or wash gloves, aprons, boots, etc., and hang to dry.

Leave the store for your cleaning equipment tidy. Air should be able to circulate freely, so the equipment dries. Lock the store when not in use.

Report any damage or faults to equipment promptly. If you see signs of pest infestation or the pests themselves, your manager should be told.

CHECK list
Waste left for collection

✔ strong containers/bags to resist wind and rain

✔ containers/bags secure against disturbance by animals, vandals, etc.

✔ old packaging/cardboard cartons collapsed and securely bundled

✔ not likely to be blown away by wind

✔ not likely to be knocked over by passing vehicles or pedestrians

✔ drums (e.g. of old cooking oil) and similar containers labelled clearly and firmly closed

✔ items left outside for collection no longer than necessary

✔ skips covered

For help to answer questions
relating to:

Health and safety

? **following regulations and instructions**

Waste can attract pests, animals and human scavengers – spreading bacteria, and causing a safety risk. Some waste is a fire risk. Some contains hazardous chemicals. Some has sharp edges. Some may be contaminated with disease or bacteria. Your workplace has a legal duty to look after waste, and see that it is disposed of safely.

? **types of waste**

If you work for a small business which is also the home of your employer, it is possible that some of the waste will be accepted as *domestic waste*, collected and disposed of without charge as for any other private householder.

The collection of *commercial waste* and *food waste* has to be arranged by the business, and paid for directly. A written description of the waste has to be given, and a transfer note completed.

? **reporting doubt about waste**

If you don't know what sort of waste you are handling, you could be risking your own safety. Nor will you know whether the waste has to be stored or labelled in a special way, because it is hazardous. Your manager will tell you who should be informed.

? **own responsibilities**

Everyone at work has a duty towards the safety of themselves and everyone else in the workplace. Think of the different people you come into contact with in the course of your work. What might happen if people don't warn you when some of the waste is hazardous, or fail to keep such waste apart from general refuse? What might happen if you don't pass on this information to those who come to collect the refuse?

Your duties will take you into various areas of the workplace. In the kitchen and food stores, you will know of the strict hygiene requirements. High standards will also be expected in the restaurant, bars and housekeeping departments.

? **wrongly disposing of slurry and waste**

The drains may block, especially if the waste solidifies at low temperatures (e.g. fat). Some types of waste could set up a chemical reaction with other waste, leading to an explosion in the drainage system. Pollution of water sources or the soil might occur.

? **not preparing properly for your work**

Your tasks will probably take longer to complete, as you find you have to stop to fetch equipment, and then again because of something else you have forgotten.

From the safety point of view, you will be exposing yourself to danger by not wearing protective clothing, gloves, etc., and not checking carefully what precautions you should follow when using cleaning agents.

? **dangers of contamination**

Waste not in its proper place is a contamination risk. Suppose a piece of broken china escapes from the rubbish and gets into food, the food is then no longer safe to eat.

Bacteria can grow rapidly on food waste and is easily spread to food and food surfaces, e.g. if hands are not washed after disposing of waste.

Pests are attracted to waste – they crawl all over it, then move on to food and food surfaces, carrying bacteria with them.

The virus that causes Aids can be spread by handling or cleaning anything that might have had contact with another person's blood or semen, e.g. hypodermic needles, sanitary towels, or used razor blades.

? **infestation**

The occasional fly, wasp, mosquito or ant, especially on a hot day, is inevitable around waste collection areas. But if they are present in large numbers, or birds are causing a nuisance, tell your manager.

Other pests are not easily spotted. Cockroaches, for example, emerge from their hiding places when it is dark. Rats and mice are generally very timid, scuttling away at the slightest sound. A sighting of even one of these creatures could indicate a serious problem, and you should report the matter without delay.

? **lids on refuse containers**

Lids help keep pests and animals out of the waste. They prevent the waste from being blown or spilled over the surrounding area. They keep rain, leaves, etc. out of the waste.

? **recording and reporting procedures**

To whom do you report faults, damage and signs of pest infestation in your workplace? How are you expected to report such matters: verbally, using company forms, etc.?

NVQ
SVQ

Skills check

Maintain hygienic waste removal
and storage conditions
Unit 1ND15

lev
1

Use this to check your progress again
the performance criteria.

Element 1

Remove accumulated wastes from specified disposal containers to collection points

Identify (and, if necessary, verify) waste materials to be collected and removed ☐ PC

If not sure about the nature of wastes, report or refer the matter ☐ PC

Handle, collect and segregate waste materials in the correct containers ☐ PC

Safely remove and secure waste materials in the waste area ☐ PC

Element 2

Clean non-disposable refuse containers and refuse holding areas

Prepare your work area and yourself to operational requirements ☐ PC

Select and use appropriate cleaning chemicals and equipment ☐ PC

Carry out the cleaning process systematically and safely ☐ PC

Dispose of all slurry and wastes in the prescribed manner ☐ PC

Record and report evidence of infestation, faults or damage ☐ PC

At the conclusion of operations, replace refuse containers in the correct position, dry, replenished, lidded ☐ PC

At the conclusion of operations, ensure refuse holding areas are free from debris and slurry ☐ PC

Return cleaning equipment and chemicals to storage in a clean and safe condition ☐ PC

Working

in food preparation and cooking

Working relationships with other staff

Your time at work is more enjoyable when you get on well with the people there. You do your job better.

Good working relationships require effort to develop. What greatly helps the process is a respect for others' points of view, a willingness to sort out problems before they become major difficulties, and a polite, good tempered attitude to everyone, even under pressure.

Doing what's asked of you

At work you're part of a team. The standards of service and food your customers get depend on the contribution of different people. Standards are highest when:

- the efforts of everyone in the team is coordinated – this is the job of your supervisors and managers, but they can't do it without your cooperation

- everyone is clear about their role and responsibilities – this depends on being given information, but also on taking notice of it.

When you first start a new job, you get guidance on your role and responsibilities. Your job description will be up-to-date, and questions will be encouraged as you settle into your job.

In a busy place, and especially if other members of the team change, or there are staff shortages, you find yourself doing a wider range of tasks. Perhaps some of these involve more responsibility. There is nothing unusual in this, it is a valuable way of getting experience, developing your skills and opening up opportunities for promotion.

Where do you fit into the team?

Good teamwork depends on people knowing their individual contribution, and on thinking of the needs of others. Where does your work tie in with that of other people? How can you make the job of your colleagues easier? Do you do what is asked of you by your manager? Do you meet your commitments to others within the agreed time?

Do you know what are acceptable working practices to your employer?

Get to know your workplace rules on uniform, safekeeping of personal property, checking deliveries of goods, dealing with customer complaints, etc. When you undertake a new task, or deal with a situation for the first time, check what is the right way to do it: from written procedures or instructions, or by asking your supervisor.

Don't rely on your own sense of what is right and wrong. In a hygiene or health and safety prosecution, your employer's main defence may be that procedures are in place to prevent safety problems – if so, why have you not followed them? In handling a customer complaint, if you serve a free drink or do not charge for the meal, and this is not your employer's policy, you have made the situation worse, not better.

Do you know what to do if you have a grievance?

A grievance is an employment-related matter that troubles you, e.g. hours of work, overtime payments, training opportunities, promotion prospects, or holiday entitlement. If you are doing or not doing something that gives your employer dissatisfaction, that is a disciplinary matter.

Unless you work for a very small operation, your employer will have a formal procedure for handling grievances. This is usually set out in your employment contract or the staff handbook, stating who you should approach, and what you can do if the outcome is still not satisfactory.

Do you know your rights in a disciplinary situation?

If you deliberately ignore a workplace instruction that relates to licensing laws, health and safety or hygiene, this is likely to be a serious disciplinary matter. Your action puts the business at risk, and endangers the well-being of all those in your workplace.

Similarly, being drunk on duty or under the influence of drugs, violent or abusive behaviour and theft are serious disciplinary matters. If your guilt is established beyond reasonable doubt, you can expect to be dismissed without notice. Your employer will have a procedure (set out in your contract of employment or the staff handbook) covering such matters, as well as the sequence of verbal and written warnings which follow timekeeping offences, poor standards of work, or other problems that do not justify immediate termination of your employment.

The disciplinary procedure exists to protect your rights, as well as establishing what your employer can do.

Passing on information

You like to be told by serving staff that customers have enjoyed their meal – and not just hear about the complaints. In the same way, restaurant staff can do their jobs better when you give them good warning that a dish is running low.

Other examples of how you can help others by passing on information are:

- making a note on the 'to order' board when you see stocks are almost out
- telling the chef that many cans of a soup not much used are near their best-before date.

Requesting assistance

If in doubt, ask. You don't help yourself or anyone else by struggling on, wondering if there is an easier way.

When everyone is under a lot of pressure, it may be difficult to find the opportunity to ask. But people know you are learning, and realise they have a duty to help you. When your request is politely made, and quite clearly a genuine one, you should not be rebuffed.

Building better working relationships

There will be occasions when:

- you can help a colleague contribute more fully to the team, e.g. by being friendly and supportive
- your influence has to be directed to the whole team, e.g. saying things at department or team meetings, which make the work easier for everyone
- you want to persuade your boss, e.g. to let you try out some new recipes.

In deciding the best way to do this, you can learn from the effect other people's actions (at work and outside work) have on you. In your mind, run through your friends, tutors and trainers, bosses, etc. How do they make you feel more significant, more confident, more positive – in other words, encouraged? Perhaps by:

- asking your opinion and taking your ideas seriously?
- letting you take the lead?
- trusting you to make decisions?
- encouraging you to try new skills and techniques?
- telling you what you have done well?
- supporting you in front of other people?

Now practise some of these things on work colleagues.

 The Clementine Churchill Hospital

How we care for each other

Work as a team dedicated to meet our customers' needs

- flexibility in work areas
- show respect to each other
- listen to each other
- share ideas and discuss constructive comments and ideas
- communicate at all times
- help each other where possible
- discuss internal matters with each other
- no recriminations
- compliment, when in order
- be polite, cheerful and helpful to all customers.

Contributing ideas and making proposals for change

As you would like your idea listened to, give some thought to the best occasion to explain it. This may be at a team meeting, in a training session, during an appraisal interview, in the course of conversation, responding to a questionnaire, putting a note in the suggestion box, or writing a memo.

Doing so face-to-face may require more courage, especially if you are shy. But it does give you a chance to explain yourself more fully, and to answer questions.

It helps if you have anticipated what questions you will be asked. Plan your answers from the point of view of your audience. Your boss will like ideas that are going to increase sales, or reduce costs. Your colleagues may focus on the impact it will have on their jobs. Will it save them time? How will their customers benefit?

If your ideas and proposals are rejected

Rejection of your proposals can be a disappointment. Knowing the reasons helps, and a personal presentation will give you the chance to ask. If the general view is going against you, try and be reasonably detached, presenting your responses calmly but firmly. Getting angry will not help. Nor will it if you appear weak, giving way without protest.

Your proposals may have to be taken to others in the organisation, perhaps by your boss. If rejection follows, your boss will give you some feedback. When this is not possible, or the reasons seem weak to you, try to:

- understand the pressures that management is under

- accept that management is paid to make decisions

- not take rejection of your ideas personally, or to dwell on it.

Dealing with difficulties

There are two aspects: doing your best to play a positive and full role in the team yourself, and doing what you can to help colleagues overcome difficulties.

Calm discussion may help clear the air, and enable each person to express points of view. Often the team leader or manager can provide the necessary authority.

Understanding how difficulties can arise, willingness to listen, and sensitivity are strong healing forces. It does no good to dwell on disagreements, or build up grudges.

Telling your manager about your problems

Not all managers are easy to approach with a problem, and you might be afraid to waste their time. But your manager is human. He or she will also have experienced problems and recognise the help an outsider can give.

You also have to weigh up the consequences of keeping silent. Someone else may say things which are not true, or only part of the story. You don't want to lose the trust of your manager, nor leave the problem to develop to the stage where the manager can't do much to help.

When problems affect your timekeeping, concentration at work, or your relationship with your colleagues, your manager will soon notice. You deserve help. You are more likely to have this when your manager knows the reason is not laziness, or some such failing.

If you become aware of a work colleague's problem, think first what you can do to help as a friend or fellow team-member. Try and get the person concerned to take the lead.

Using suitable methods of communication

Good teamwork and getting a clear understanding of your job role depend to a large extent on effective communications. In the sort of work you do, the spoken word will be the most used method of communication. But there may be forms and documents to complete (e.g. requisitions for stock) and written messages to leave for colleagues on duty at a different time from you.

Choosing the best methods

If you need to ask your manager for a day off to go to a friend's wedding, would you do so in the middle of a busy meal service, or when the person is engaged in another conversation? Almost certainly not. Instead, you might decide it is necessary to write a note.

In this example, you would be choosing the timing and method of your communication to increase the prospect of a 'yes' answer. You want to be heard clearly. You want to avoid any distractions which conflict with your message. In deciding whether to speak or write to your manager, you will balance the advantages of each:

- speaking gives you the opportunity to answer questions and add further explanation

- writing gives your manager more time to think about the reply

as well as the disadvantages:

- speaking carries the risk that your manager will tell you off for being late recently, an incident you do not intend to repeat and would prefer not to discuss

- a written message could get lost among the other papers on your manager's desk.

This process of choosing the best method of communication can be extended to all areas of your work. Mentioning that one of the outdoor waste bin lids is missing, as the manager rushes out to a meeting, is not helpful. A scruffy note for the person on the next shift 'Don't use the deep fryer' is not an adequate explanation. Is it because the oil needs changing (which would spoil the food, but the later shift might have time to change it), or because the thermostat is faulty (a potentially dangerous situation)?

Communicating to colleagues with special needs

Some of your colleagues – if not now, then in a future job – may have difficulties hearing, a speech impediment, sight problems or a combination. Similarly, colleagues whose first language is not English may find it hard to communicate with you. These situations demand patience and understanding, and the use of some simple skills (see checklist).

Respecting the confidentiality of information

You will get quite a lot of information during the course of your work which could cause problems if passed on during a conversation, or by being too helpful answering the questions of a visitor. For example:

- knowing the number of meals your place served, or what discount has been given to attract a large conference, helps a competitor undermine your employer's business

- a freelance journalist overhearing what you told your friends in the pub about the environmental health officer's recent inspection (exaggerating somewhat to make the story more interesting) leads to bad publicity in the local newspaper

- in a similar way, unwelcome publicity might appear about a well-known personality who had arranged with management to stay incognito at your hotel, or be treated as a patient in your hospital.

Greeting and assisting visitors

Visitors get a good impression of your workplace when they are greeted promptly and courteously. Just as you do when you take your purchases to the shop counter to pay for them. You appreciate a friendly greeting, not being kept waiting and a thank you for your custom. You expect to be charged the right price, and to be given the correct change. What might really impress you, is an offer to exchange your purchase if later you find it is not the size you need.

There is another aspect to visitor and customer care: safety and security. If a stranger comes into your kitchen, one of your first thoughts will be: what's this person doing here? There are the risks of an accident, e.g. the visitor could get in the way of a colleague carrying a heavy tray of hot food.

For hygiene reasons, there may be rules regarding overclothing and head covering for everyone entering the kitchen. There is a possibility that the visitor is not who she or he claims to be: e.g. a trickster, posing as a health inspector, with plans to blackmail your employer, or a thief, watching for a chance to take something valuable – a case of wine, a wallet left in a hanging jacket, even a valuable piece of furniture – such things regularly get stolen because of lack of attention to security.

Greeting styles

From time to time you will be the first person in your workplace to greet a visitor or customer, whether on the telephone or face-to-face:

- overcome any shyness you feel: rushing away without saying anything does not help anyone

- remember that you represent your employer and your colleagues: those first few moments of contact with a member of staff generally form a powerful impression on the visitor – when it's a good one, that helps everyone

- follow any company or house rules

- politely greet the person – this has as much to do with your tone of voice and the expression on your face as it does with the words you use: a warm smile and 'hullo' is more effective than a long form of words said without meaning

- don't be afraid to say who you are – it would waste a lot of time if the visitor proceeded on the assumption you were the head chef or catering manager

- don't shorten the name of your organisation or company, or drop part of it, unless you have been told how to do this. A lot of thought goes into business names, and the messages they give to customers.

Your role in customer care

The next step is to establish how you can help the visitor. This should be done without exceeding the limitations of your own role and responsibilities. Your manager may not want to be called away from a meeting to find the 'important visitor' is a sales representative who 'happened to be in the area'. But a visit from the environmental health officer (who is unlikely to have made an appointment) is something your manager expects to be told about immediately.

Obtain, politely, the information you need to get the appropriate person to take the matter over. At the minimum, this will be the name of the visitor, the company or organisation he or she represents, the reason for the visit and whom the person wants to see.

It helps when you are offered a business card. Most representatives from suppliers will do this, while government or local authority officials, engineering contractors, etc. will be happy to show their identity card. This is a widely accepted security precaution.

You may find yourself being asked questions. Be wary when you answer these that you are not giving away information which is no business of the visitor, or saying things which might cause difficulties for your employer. For example, someone anxious to get the contract for pest control on your premises might try and find out who currently did the work.

Knowing your workplace

If visitors don't know who can help them, or the person they want is unavailable, offer alternatives. In a small place, the proprietor may be the only person who can help. If he or she is absent, you might offer to take a message. But should you suggest another time for the visitor to call? Do you know when the proprietor will be back, and if so can you tell the visitor? These decisions, which have to be taken quite quickly, are much easier when you take an interest in what goes on around you at work, and have a good grasp of who does what.

In many premises, there are special security procedures. Visitors are required to sign in at the security officer's desk, and to wear an identity badge while they are on the premises. Your own responsibilities will be clear, e.g. to call security immediately if you see anyone not wearing a badge.

It might also be part of such a procedure, that visitors are met at reception by the person they are seeing, or escorted to the catering area by you or one of your colleagues. In other situations, you will need to decide on a waiting place, where the visitor will be comfortable, not in the way of people who have work to do, and safe.

Explaining delays

Visitors will have a poor impression of your workplace if they are kept waiting for a long time without explanation or apology. Ask for an indication from your manager, or the person the visitor has come to see, how long the delay might be. The visitor will appreciate being offered suitable refreshment (e.g. tea or coffee).

When, at the end of this time, the visitor is still waiting, try and get an update from your manager and pass the information on, with renewed apologies. At some stage, the visitor may decide not to wait any longer, and you could find yourself acting as a go-between. Potentially awkward situations like this, and a visitor who gets cross with even a five minute wait, can usually be overcome by apologising, and offering to do what you can to help.

Special mobility needs

When a person depends on a wheelchair to get around, or uses crutches or walking sticks, the things most other people take for granted become potential obstacles. Stairs can be difficult or impossible to manage. Doors which are on a strong spring – as many fire doors are, so they close firmly after the person has passed through – can be very hard to negotiate.

You can help by being aware of these difficulties. Some businesses which make a point of providing for those with special mobility needs, get their staff to use a wheelchair and experience for themselves the journeys customers and visitors might make.

Don't make assumptions about the help the person needs: some wheelchair users do not want to be pushed. Ask how you can best help. Treat the person with respect, talking directly to them if possible, not through their companion.

Communicating with visitors

On the occasions you found visitors difficult to deal with, what do you think went wrong? What led you to misjudge some aspect of their visit, which caused problems?

Verbal and non-verbal communication

Communicating with visitors inevitably has an element of uncertainty. You won't know the visitor as well as you do your work colleagues. This means you have to rely much more on what they say. But you can also pick up valuable clues from how they say it, their facial expressions and what they are doing with their arms, or how they are standing. For example:

- someone bright red in the face might be angry – perhaps after a bad journey and thus not your fault, but you know this is not a person to keep waiting

- fidgeting with a briefcase – could indicate nervousness, in which case you can help put the person at ease.

These non-verbal forms of communication, which can be very powerful, are described as body language. The activity overleaf will help you recognise and react appropriately to the most common forms of body language.

Special communication needs

Visitors who have special communication needs should, like any of your colleagues in a similar situation (see page 86), receive your patience and understanding. Because they have difficulty expressing what they want to say, do not make assumptions about their intelligence. Gently try and find out what the best method is of reaching an understanding. Speaking very loudly and slowly is rarely effective, as you will know if you've had someone shouting at you in an unfamiliar language. What can help is a combination of very simple words and gestures: pointing to show a direction, nodding to indicate 'yes', shaking your head for 'no', shrugging for 'don't know', etc.

CHECK **list**
Communicating to those with special needs

✔ move away from loud noises

✔ speak slowly and clearly

✔ use plain language

✔ look directly at the person

✔ keep your hands away from your mouth

✔ avoid standing with your back to a window or bright light (which make it difficult for the person to see your face)

With speech difficulties

✔ avoid correcting the person or trying to take over what the person is saying

✔ ask short questions that can be quickly answered or only require a nod of the head or other gesture

✔ be honest when you don't understand something

✔ repeat what you do understand, checking from the other person's reactions whether or not you are right

1 Why is it wrong for you to tease or bully a work mate because he or she has another skin colour, culture, etc.?

7 What are the rules you must follow at work?

2 Give three sorts of information that you pass on to colleagues/ supervisors/ managers, and state the method you would choose.

8 What do you do if you have a grievance about a work-related matter?

3 How would you communicate differently if you had to pass the information on to someone who had a severe hearing difficulty?

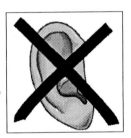

9 If you are in trouble with your employer, e.g. for failing to come on duty, what is the procedure for warning you/ possible dismissal?

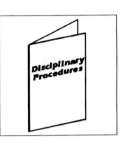

The law on equal opportunities

Your employer will be mostly concerned with this at the recruitment stage and in the subsequent career of individuals (e.g. in promotion or training opportunities, or in rates of pay). There should be no discrimination on grounds of sex, race or marital status.

Direct discrimination has become rare, e.g. employing only male staff. Indirect discrimination is also illegal, although more difficult to prove. It occurs if, for example, unreason-able and unnecessary job requirements make it impossible for women to do the work.

It is at this level that you and fellow employees may make the situation worse. For example, if:

- a woman joins a previously male-only team, making her life unbearable by foul language, taunting and giving her the most unpleasant work duties
- a colleague from a minority ethnic group is bullied or constantly teased about skin colour/race/personal hygiene standards/culture/appearance.

4 Explaining something to a colleague who does not speak or understand English well, how can you help communication?

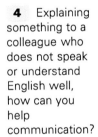

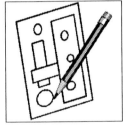

10 Give some reasons why good working relationships help everyone.

5 Say what your main job roles and responsibilities are.

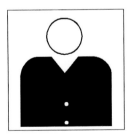

11 Describe some of the things that make working relationships good.

6 What are the job roles and responsibilities of your colleagues?

12 What things can harm working relationships?

1 List all the people who visit your workplace.

Management and staff from other departments — Maintenance engineers — Environmental health officers — Trading standards inspectors — Sales representatives — Suppliers — Head office personnel

2 What are your responsibilities with regard to visitors?

3 Why do you need to be aware of security when dealing with visitors? What are the procedures for your workplace?

4 What sort of information should you be careful not to give visitors?

Apparently, Joan Collins is staying here incognito!

In what?

5 Why is it so important to speak clearly when dealing with visitors?

Now, was it four candles or fork handles you were after?

6 What is the greeting style used in your workplace for visitors (e.g. by the telephonist/ receptionist)?

Thank you for calling International Adventurers Hospitality Inn Invertrossachs. This is Eugene speaking, how may I help you?

'7 Who are the people that visitors to your workplace might wish to see? What do they do, and how would you find them if a visitor called?

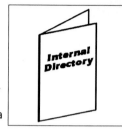

Internal Directory

8 How can you best help someone in a wheelchair? What should you be careful not to do?

9 Some people have special communication needs. What are these? How can you best communicate with such people?

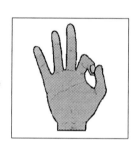

10 Identify the main forms of verbal and non-verbal communication. How can you recognise them?

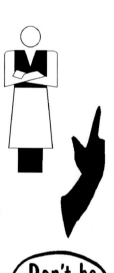

11 How should you react to each type of communication (e.g. if it is used by a visitor)?

Don't be stupid!

NVQ
SVQ
Skills check
Develop effective working relationships
Unit 1NG4
level
1

Use this to check your progress against the performance criteria.

Element 1

Create and maintain effective working relationships with other members of staff

Promptly and cooperatively action requests from colleagues ☐ PC1

Pass on information to colleagues promptly and accurately ☐ PC2

Politely request assistance when required ☐ PC3

Discuss or resolve difficulties, or report them to the appropriate person ☐ PC4

Use methods of communication and support suited to needs of colleagues ☐ PC5

Element 2

Greet and assist visitors

Promptly and courteously greet visitors and identify their needs ☐ PC1

Give visitors only disclosable information ☐ PC2

Direct or escort visitors to destination as required ☐ PC3

Explain politely reasons for delay or unavailability of information ☐ PC4

Refer situations outside your responsibility to appropriate person ☐ PC5

Use methods of communication and support suited to needs of visitors ☐ PC6

For help to answer questions relating to:

Health and safety

? security systems

If you work for a contract catering firm, or in any sort of business where the main activity is not catering (e.g. hospital, school, factory, the armed forces, commercial office such as a bank or insurance company), there will probably be a reception area that all visitors report to. In some of these places, for security reasons, visitors have to be escorted to the person they are going to see, and back to reception at the conclusion of the visit. It may also be a requirement that you notify reception in advance of the visitors you are expecting. This might be by telephone, or involve completing a form.

Some hotels and large catering firms have an office at what doubles as a goods entrance and staff entrance. Visitors for the catering department may have to report and sign in there, including anyone making a delivery, and engineers calling to repair or service equipment.

? dealing with aggressive visitors

Try and contain the situation while you get help from a manager or security officer:

- keep calm, or at least give that impression to the visitor – inwardly you might be very angry or very nervous. Becoming awkward or aggressive yourself merely raises the temperature higher still. Try and control your body language so you appear relaxed. Maintain a careful distance. Avoid prolonged eye-contact

- gently encourage the visitor to move away from any other people who might be disturbed or provide an audience, preferably to a room where he or she can be comfortable and from which you can phone for help. Stress it's their comfort and convenience you are considering

- when the matter is related to security (e.g. a stranger you have accosted in the corridor, who probably shouldn't be in the building at all), try and get him or her to an area where other people can keep a watchful eye, or remain with the person yourself until help arrives. But don't put yourself in danger.

? dealing with emergencies

If there's a fire, you know how to leave the building. So in an emergency, you have the advantage over visitors – you know what to do. Re-check your workplace procedures specifically on how you can help visitors, e.g. escorting them out of the building, helping to calm them, helping those with vision or hearing difficulties, or special mobility needs.

Legislation

? employee's responsibilities

The law makes it illegal to discriminate in work-related matters on the grounds of sex, race or marital status. Your behaviour towards a colleague could contribute towards a charge of discrimination, e.g. by harassing someone of a different ethnic group.

Communication

? constructive work relationships

To answer why this is important, think of all those occasions and activities which involve a work colleague, e.g. collecting from the store supervisor, the different items of food you need for the day's menu. Then consider what makes the relationship a good one, and what difference this makes to the task concerned, e.g. *being polite* (please and thank you's, apologising when you make an error), *being organised* (list prepared, quantities given for all items), *being timely* (going to stores at the regular time), being helpful (offering to lift heavy items), *providing information* (giving news of a large event next week, commenting on the excellent quality of the canned asparagus spears).

? exchange information/get advice

Where and when you do this depends on the sort of information you are exchanging, or what advice you need. In catering, much information has to be passed on quickly if it is to be of any value, e.g. telling the serving staff that there are not many portions of the dish of the day left. If the sauce you are making has become lumpy, it is best to get help straight away.

There is other information that can and should wait until the people you are telling have time to consider it properly. The text gave the examples of the missing waste bin lid, and the request for a day off.

? handling disagreement or conflict

When this is with colleagues, try the tactics that help in any disagreement with friends, and avoid those that worsen the situation. This list is a mixture of both types: as you work through it, think why the tactic would help, or not help:

- shout the person down
- give up and walk away
- ask the other person to explain the objections, point by point
- angrily accuse the other person of not listening
- say the other person's a fool and stupid
- interrupt constantly as the other person tries to make a point
- say you can understand their objection, but ... and proceed to explain your point of view

- say you regret raising the matter, and you will now take it to someone higher up, who will understand
- start crying or being obviously upset
- make a joke, or introduce another subject to lighten the atmosphere, before returning to tackle the argument from a different angle
- go for points where you can get agreement, restate what these are, then move on to the other areas, one step at a time
- suggest another person (who you think will see both points of view) is brought into the discussion.

If the disagreement or conflict is with your supervisor or manager, and discussions cannot resolve the matter, you will have to consider the grievance procedure.

? procedures for confidential information

Confidential means that the information is only for the people to whom it has been directly given. You would be wrong to read a memo or letter to your manager addressed CONFIDENTIAL, unless your manager actually gave it to you to read. Similarly, if you and all the other members of staff get a letter from your employer explaining various changes to the business which is marked CONFIDENTIAL, you should not let anyone outside the business read it, or discuss the contents with them.

Your employer may also have rules to protect the confidentiality of general information on the business, and all documents you have access to in the course of your work.

? need for discretion

The text gave three examples of how information in the wrong hands could cause a problem for your employer: helping competitors, leading to bad publicity for the business, and for customers.

? informing and consulting

The strongest and most successful teams are those where everyone shares similar values and attitudes. Everyone puts similar importance on delivering a quality product and quality service. Everyone pulls their weight.

This process of coming together is greatly helped when problems and good ideas are shared and discussed.

As for the best time to do so, this will depend on your work routine. Team or department meetings present a useful forum, free from the various pressures and distractions that otherwise occur. Meal breaks can provide a more informal setting, and a chance to share ideas with those closest to the problem.

Times you should definitely avoid are when customers are waiting to be served.

?

Knowledge check continued
Create and maintain
effective working relationships

NVQ SVQ

Skills check
Create and maintain effective
working relationships
Unit 2NG4

level 2

? proposals for change

The methods you choose should reflect the way your workplace is organised, and the number of people involved. In a small business, the most effective time can be during a quiet moment in the day, when your boss is in a relaxed mood. In larger organisations, there are usually a mixture of informal and formal channels of communication.

? approaches for different situations

If you want to communicate successfully, you have to take account of the situation. Make a list of the various occasions during your work when you need to pass on or get information from a colleague, supervisor, manager or customer. Then make a note of the characteristics of each:

- *method of communication* – e.g. spoken, written
- *style of communication* – e.g. formal (at a meeting), informal (by way of conversation), indirect (via a staff representative or supervisor)
- *style of approach* – e.g. suggesting, questioning, proposing, humorous, combative.

Job role

? your role and responsibilities

Your job description will help, if you need a reminder. Also refer to cleaning and production schedules and duty rotas, which break down tasks among members of the team.

Equipment

? paging systems

Some people move around quite a lot during their job, e.g. the head chef has several catering areas spread around the building. In these situations you may find yourself using a paging system:

- sending a signal to a bleep which the person carries (the unit to do this is usually located centrally)
- broadcasting a message through public rooms or offices and work areas over the loudspeaker system.

Product knowledge

? reception activities

The overall aim is to help the visitor and to give a good impression. This has to be achieved cost-effectively, so it is not usually the only job the person has to do.

Think of the many tasks a hotel receptionist performs, besides greeting guests and visitors: taking bookings, registering guests, allocating rooms, answering the telephone, dealing with enquiries, preparing bills and taking payment, typing letters of confirmation, liaising with housekeeping, and passing on bookings to the restaurant. The list depends on the size of the hotel, and the organisation of reception activities. In a large place, for example, there may be separate reservations and billing offices.

? routing procedures

There are usually places where visitors should not go – for safety and security reasons, or because it might give them a wrong impression. Find out where suppliers should be taken, e.g. to the chef's office or to a public area? Some visitors have a right to go to many areas, e.g. an environmental health officer, but usually they should be accompanied by a manager or the proprietor.

? receiving and assisting visitors

Draw an outline plan of your building, marking the entrances which visitors might use, and where they will find someone to help them. Then note who these people are, and what they do to assist the visitor.

Finally, consider what could go wrong if the visitor used another entrance, or was met by someone who didn't know how to help.

? services available to customers

If you are working in a small restaurant, sandwich bar, etc., you will find this question easy to answer. If you work in a large place with a variety of services and products, you might find it helpful to collect some brochures, or look at the information customers get.

If your unit is part of a large company, which has many activities (e.g. leisure centres, brewing), or you work in the kitchen of a bank, hospital or school, where the main activity is not catering, you may need to do some research for the second part of the question. Check with the notes from your induction. Ask at reception for brochures. Look at advertisements and promotion panels aimed at customers.

? your organisation's structure

There may be an organisation chart in your staff handbook, or on the noticeboard. If not, your manager will be able to help.

Use this to check your progress against the performance criteria.

Element 1

Establish and maintain working relationships with other members of staff

Take appropriate opportunities to discuss work-related matters with staff ☐ PC

⚠ Staff: line managers, immediate colleagues, other members of staff with related work activities

Promptly and accurately pass on essential information ☐ PC2

Maintain effective working relationships with individuals/teams ☐ PC3

Meet commitments to others within agreed time-scales ☐ PC4

Use methods of communication and support suited to needs of other staff ☐ PC5

Element 2

Receive and assist visitors

Greet visitors promptly and courteously ☐ PC1

Identify the nature of the visit and match visitors' needs to products, personnel or services ☐ PC2

Receive and direct visitors in accordance with procedures ☐ PC3

Describe and promote services, etc. to visitors ☐ PC4

Use suitable methods of communication and support ☐ PC5

Openly acknowledge communication difficulties and seek help ☐ PC6

Acknowledge difficulties in providing support to visitors and seek help ☐ PC7

Make complete, legible and accurate records ☐ PC8

Follow procedures for dealing with awkward/aggressive visitors ☐ PC9

Preparing and cooking basic
meat, poultry
and **offal** dishes

Preparing meat, poultry and offal for cooking

For many people, the meat or poultry dish is the highlight of a meal. Whether they want it roasted, grilled, stewed or fried depends on personal taste, the occasion of the meal, or even the weather. The dishes offered by your workplace will aim to give customers what they want.

Meat, poultry and offal are high-cost items, so there is not much room for error. Poor preparation will reduce the number of portions you can serve from a particular piece of meat. The same problem occurs if temperatures and times are not carefully controlled during cooking, and so the meat shrinks excessively. If a customer gets a well-done steak instead of the rare one he or she ordered, you might have to cook another. These all mean higher costs, and less profit.

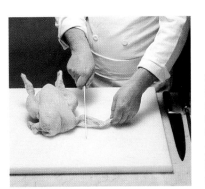

Chopping boards and knives for preparing raw meat and poultry should be reserved for this use only.

Below: *coating with breadcrumbs the organised way!*

Quality points

Purchase specifications, where these are used, state in detail the quality required. For meat, poultry and offal, points which might be covered include – the examples are for leg of lamb:

- *country of origin and carcase type* – e.g. British lamb caracases, slaughtered within one year of birth

- *cut removal* – e.g. to be removed from the chump at a point no more than 25 mm below the round of the aitch bone

- *trim level* – e.g. remove aitch bone, trim off ragged edges, discoloured tissues and fat

- *fat level* – e.g. external fat thickness not to exceed 10 mm at any point

- *preparation* – e.g. to be tied securely with 5 strings at even intervals

- *weight* – e.g. 2 kg to 2½ kg.

Checking that the delivery meets these requirements provides a valuable form of quality control. More general points to look out for are:

- *temperature* – between 0°C and 8°C is acceptable for meat, poultry and offal (check with a temperature probe, see page 97)

- *appearance of the packaging* – if it is dirty or damaged, the food may have been harmed

- *appearance and smell* – detailed points are given below for different types of meat and poultry. Danger signs are a noticeable, unpleasant smell, discolouring of the flesh, and slimy or mouldy surface

- *date stamp* – indicating when the food must be used by. Food which has passed this date should not be on the premises: check with your manager before throwing it away.

Beef

- smells fresh, not stale or sour (rancid), nor unpleasantly strong (high)

- outer fat layer even, smooth in texture, firm to the touch and creamy-white in colour (creamy-yellow for Scotch beef)

- outer surface of lean meat is purple/brown, with a smooth texture

- meat itself is bright red, without excessive fat or gristle

- fat flecks (called *marbling*) are visible in the prime cuts such as fillet or sirloin

Lamb

- lean flesh firm, dull red, with fine texture or grain
- bones porous, with slight bluish tinge
- fat evenly distributed, hard, brittle, flaky and clear white in colour

Pork

- rind or skin smooth
- flesh lean, pale pink, firm, with little gristle
- fat white, firm, smooth and not excessive

Bacon

- no sign of stickiness
- thin, smooth, wrinkle-free rind
- white, smooth fat and not too much in proportion to the lean
- meat deep pink colour and firm

Chicken

- white skin (yellowish for corn-fed chickens)
- flesh firm to the touch, no stickiness on the skin
- legs and breast well fleshed
- breastbone flexible

Turkey

- white skin, free from blemishes
- flesh firm to the touch, no stickiness on the skin
- breast and thighs well fleshed

Kidney

- deep red colour
- fresh smell
- surface moist and shiny, but not sticky

Liver

- little, if any, smell
- attractive colour, without tubes or dryness
- surface moist and shiny, but not sticky

Basic preparation methods

The meat, poultry and offal used at your workplace may be bought ready prepared. Nevertheless, there are some steps that are best done just before cooking, and other steps that your manager may prefer to control directly.

Defrosting

Meat, poultry and offal must be completely defrosted before it is cooked. The only exceptions are pre-prepared foods like burgers, which are sometimes cooked from frozen (follow package or workplace instructions).

In good time before it is required – up to 48 hours for a large joint – transfer the joint or bird to the refrigerator. Alternatively use a thawing cabinet. Fast defrosting can damage the food and increase fluid loss.

If chickens or turkeys come with their giblets packed in the cavity of the bird, remove these as soon as you can (probably about half-way through the thawing process).

When defrosting is complete, the limbs of chickens and turkey should move easily. There should be no signs of ice crystals in the cavity.

Washing

Generally, the only occasion on which you will have to wash meat or poultry is when it has come into contact with blood during preparation.

Offal usually requires washing if you are having to prepare it yourself.

After washing, dry the food thoroughly with absorbent kitchen paper.

Skinning

Most of the meat you deal with will already have been skinned by the supplier.

For chicken breast and legs, gently pull the skin away, using the fingers. It should part quite easily from the flesh.

If you are dealing with a whole liver from a calf, lamb, pig or ox, the thin skin or membrane (if present) will need to be removed before slicing. Gently pull it away using the fingers and the tip of a small sharp knife. Take care not to cut the liver.

For lamb kidneys, remove the outer skin or membrane (if present) before cooking. Nick the membrane on the rounded side with the tip of a small sharp knife. Draw the skin back until it is only attached at the core. Cut a deep V-shape with scissors on either side of the core, so that you can remove the core and the skin together.

Dicing

Meat and poultry are diced – that is, cut into cubes – for various types of casseroles, stews and curries, and dishes such as steak and kidney pie and pudding. The size of the finished piece will depend on the type of dish you are making and sometimes on the quality of the meat. For the sake of illustration, the following steps are based on cutting 25 mm cubes:

- trim off any visible fat or gristle
- cut the meat into slices of the required thickness (e.g. 25 mm). With chicken breast and other small pieces of meat, this step is not necessary
- cut these slices into strips (25 mm wide)
- cut these strips into pieces of the required size cube (25 x 25 x 25 mm).

Any fat or gristle which appears during slicing and cubing, should be trimmed off or at least avoided.

Trimming

Do this carefully so that you:

- improve the appearance of the cut or joint
- leave as much of the meat intact as possible
- remove as much gristle and sinew as possible
- leave an even thickness of fat (where fat is to be left). How much fat you trim off will depend on the type of meat, customer preference, and the cooking process to be used.

Slicing

Trim off any visible fat or gristle.

For beef, pork, lamb and bacon, slice across the grain of the meat (the same rule is followed when carving).

For liver, kidney and chicken or turkey breast, you can get larger slices (if this is required) by cutting at an angle of about 30°.

Seasoning

Seasoning – the addition of salt and white or black pepper – is considered to improve the flavour of food:

- use white pepper or cayenne pepper on foods which you want to keep an attractive white colour
- add salt to roasts and grills after the meat has browned – adding salt before cooking will attract the juices of the meat to the surface, and so slow down the browning reactions (which need high temperatures and dry heat)
- use freshly ground black pepper – it is more aromatic and flavourful than pre-ground.

Coating

The two basic coatings are:

- *flour* – e.g. for liver which is shallow fried. Coat the meat just before cooking, otherwise the flour becomes sticky and unpleasant
- *breadcrumbs* – e.g. for chicken breasts which are baked or shallow fried. Coat the meat in flour, then *eggwash* (lightly beaten whole egg, sometimes with a little water or milk), then breadcrumbs.

Make sure all surfaces of the food are coated evenly. Shake off excess flour and breadcrumbs, let excess eggwash run off.

If you are doing a breadcrumb coating on your own, split the task into three steps and use deep trays so that you can do a few pieces of food at one time (see photograph on page 93):

- *step one* – dip each piece in the flour and place in the eggwash
- *step two* – coat each piece with eggwash, and place in the breadcrumbs. Wipe the eggwash off your fingers
- *step three* – cover each piece in breadcrumbs and place on a tray, ready for use.

If you have the help of a colleague, one person can do steps two and three.

Food can be coated with breadcrumbs in advance. Lay the coated pieces of food spaced slightly apart on a tray, cover and refrigerate.

Storing food prepared in advance

Once you have prepared the meat, it should be cooked immediately, or stored so it will be safe from harmful bacteria and not put other food at risk. Cover the meat, and place in the cold room or refrigerator, well separated from any cooked foods (ideally, these should be in a separate refrigerator).

Follow your workplace system for labelling the container, e.g. description, number of portions/weight, date of preparation.

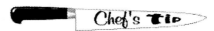

Healthy options to salt

With beef – horseradish, ginger, tomato, bay leaf, beer, black pepper, mustard

With chicken – lemon juice, garlic, paprika, parsley, orange juice, almonds

With pork – ginger, garlic, thyme, sage, apple, pineapple, cider

With lamb – mint, rosemary, basil, redcurrant, apricot, kidney beans, chilli powder, onion, tomato, vinaigrette

Element 2

Cooking basic meat, poultry and offal dishes

Begin with a careful read of the recipe or your workplace instructions. Take note of:

- the equipment and ingredients you need
- what you will be doing and when
- how many portions you need to cook
- at what time the dish should be ready for service.

Use the checklists in this book to help prepare yourself.

Dry cooking methods

Dry cooking describes cooking in which dry heat plays the main role. The meat is exposed to the heat of the oven, grill or frying surface. In practice, the food has to be protected from the direct heat, otherwise it will burn or dry out too much. A small amount of fat or oil and perhaps a coating of flour or breadcrumbs provide this.

Cooking by the dry methods is quick and high temperatures are used. A small piece of food takes a few minutes to fry or grill. But the meat has to be tender – that means the more expensive cuts: beef and lamb steaks, lamb cutlets, pork chops, escalopes of turkey and chicken breast, etc. Liver and kidney from young animals (i.e. calves and lamb) are sufficiently tender to be fried or grilled.

Larger pieces of food take more time to cook and require lower temperatures. They also have to be tender: sirloin and topside of beef, leg of lamb or pork, whole (young) chickens and turkeys, etc.

Success depends on careful control of temperatures and cooking times.

Cooking healthier meals

1 Where you have the choice, use lean cuts of meat (e.g. beef rump, topside for roasting or braising).
2 Trim off all visible fat before cooking.
3 Keep meat out of fat and cooking juices. When roasting or braising, raise the meat off the base of the pan with chopped vegetables, a trivet (metal stand made for this purpose) or bones (e.g. if the joint was boned before cooking).
4 Use oils high in polyunsaturated fats and low in saturated fats. Do not baste during cooking.
5 Before serving, remove the skin from chicken and turkey.
6 Make sure every bit of fat has been skimmed off the juices in the pan before you use them to make gravy or sauce.

Roasting

Roasting is cooking the meat or poultry in an oven. It is a popular way of cooking the best quality joints and poultry.

Set the oven at the temperature stated in the recipe. Place the meat in a suitable roasting tray – large and deep enough to hold the meat, and catch the juices produced during cooking. Before putting the meat in the oven, spoon a small amount of oil or fat over it (e.g. sunflower oil or lard, but not margarine and butter which would burn at roasting temperatures).

From time to time during cooking (every 20 to 30 minutes, or so), spoon oil or melted fat over the joint. This is called *basting*.

Basting is not usually necessary when thin strips of fat have been tied over the surface of the meat (done for top quality joints, e.g. whole fillet of beef). Basting may be done only once or twice during roasting, or not at all, for health reasons. In this case, the joint can be covered with a piece of kitchen foil once the surface has browned. The foil stops burning, reflecting the heat away from the surface.

The fat:

- prevents the surface of the food from drying out and becoming hard, so the roast looks and tastes good
- spreads through the food, helping to make it more tender
- flavours the food.

Most roasting joints have some fat of their own:

- at the surface (e.g. on a leg of pork) – as this fat melts, it runs over the sides of the joint
- running through the meat – blended in with the muscle fibres and hard to see, or readily visible as *marbling* (white specks against the more red colour of meat). It melts during cooking, helping to keep the meat moist.

This type of temperature probe is left in the meat throughout cooking. The oven sounds an alarm when the preset temperature has been reached, signalling that the food can be removed.

To take advantage of the external fat under the skin of their legs, place chickens and turkeys in the roasting tray on their side. Mid-way through cooking, turn the bird over, to allow the other side to brown. If the breast has not coloured, sit the bird upright for the final stage. Avoid puncturing the skin when you turn the bird – this leads to excessive fluid loss and toughens the meat.

High temperatures and dry heat give roasts their golden brown, flavourful crust. The higher the temperature, the quicker the meat colours. But high temperatures increase shrinkage and loss of juices.

One way of getting a balance is to begin with a high temperature (e.g. 225°C). This is called *searing*. After 20 minutes or so, turn the oven down (e.g. to 165°C for a joint which is stuffed).

For large turkeys and large joints where a light surface colouring is acceptable, use a low temperature (around 150°C) for the entire cooking time. This reduces weight loss, and means the joint can be cooked through to the centre without burning on the outside.

Roasting time depends on the temperatures used and, in general-purpose ovens, where the meat is placed in the oven (the top is hotter). Other factors are: the size and shape of the joint (not just its weight), how the joint has been prepared (a joint with a large bone through its centre will cook faster than one which has been boned and rolled), and for beef and lamb, whether the meat is to be served well done, medium or rare (for beef).

To be sure that the meat is cooked, use a temperature probe:

- dip the point of the probe in a sanitising solution, or wipe with a sanitising cloth.

- insert the probe into the centre of the joint – away from bones or layers of fat (which retain far more heat than the meat), otherwise it will give a false reading. With a chicken or turkey, insert the probe into the fleshy part of the thigh, not the breast. This is because the thigh takes longer to cook.

Grilling

Grilling uses the intense heat radiated by an electrical element, gas flame, or glowing charcoal. The heat source can be above or below the food, or both.

The high temperatures produce the attractive surface browning and delicious flavours characteristic of grilled meat. But the heat needs longer to reach the centre of the food. To get the balance right:

- select small cuts, preferably of an even shape and not too thick

- move the food away from the hottest part of the grill if you find it is cooking too quickly – or turn the grill down.

Before you start cooking the meat, get the ingredients, garnishes and serving dishes prepared. Grilled food is at its best served immediately.

Lightly brush the grill bars with oil before use. This prevents the food sticking. Place small items which might fall through the grill bars (e.g. cocktail sausages) on a lightly oiled tray.

Use tongs to turn the food – spearing them with a fork lets juices escape. For the same reason, try to turn the meat once only (experience helps you judge how cooking is going).

Rare or blue – feels flabby when pressed.

Underdone – when pressed the flesh springs back and there are signs of red juices.

Medium – feels firm and there are slight traces of blood.

Well-done – feels firm with no sign of blood. Note how the texture of the meat has altered in comparison with the rare steak.

Baking

Baked meat is cooked in the oven without fat or oil (the main difference from roasting). To protect the meat from the oven heat, it is covered with pastry or a breadcrumb coating, for example.

For many types of pie, the contents are cooked first, e.g. the chicken for a chicken and leek pie has been roasted, boiled or steamed. The baking stage – to cook the pastry covering and reheat the contents of the pie – is quite quick, and the oven temperature moderate to high.

Steak and kidney pies are usually cooked in this way. If you are following the traditional method, using raw steak and kidney, cook the pie for 2½ to 3 hours in a moderate to low oven.

Small, tender pieces of turkey, chicken and pork (the fillet) are often baked in a coating of breadcrumbs.

Use a flat tray for baking breadcrumbed food, so the heat can reach all sides. Put pie dishes on a baking tray. This makes it easier to lift the pie in and out of the oven without damaging the pastry top. Another advantage is that the tray catches any liquid spilling out of the pie.

If pie ingredients take a long time to cook, cover the pastry top with kitchen foil once it has browned.

As you can't see what is happening below the pastry lid, use a temperature probe to find out what the temperature is at the centre of the pie. Take great care not to insert probes too deeply in coated foods that have been stuffed (e.g. chicken Kiev with garlic and parsley butter), otherwise you let all the juices escape.

Frying

In this method of cooking, the food is placed on a very hot surface, usually a frying pan, in which has been heated a little fat or oil. Some workplaces use a griddle (effectively a large, flat frying surface) to achieve a similar result.

This sort of frying is called *shallow frying*, to distinguish it from *deep frying* – where the food is submerged in very hot oil, usually in a deep fat fryer. This method is popular for fish dishes (see Sections 9 and 23), but not much used for meat and poultry as the end-product can be greasy. Without specialist equipment (e.g. the pressure fryers used in some fast food restaurants to cook chicken pieces) it is difficult to control the speed of cooking, so there is a risk that the centre of the food is still raw, while the outside is overcooked.

Two other methods of frying are:

* *stir frying* – the food, very tender and cut into tiny pieces, is cooked quickly in the minimum amount of oil, over a high heat (one to two minutes for meat and poultry), and stirred constantly, usually in a deep, bowl-shaped pan called a *wok*

* *sautéing* – tossing the food in the pan during cooking so that it browns on all sides. The name comes from the French for 'to jump'.

Some foods will not brown and crisp satisfactorily unless they are first coated with flour, or a mixture of flour and beaten raw egg (called *eggwash*) which is then covered with dried breadcrumbs.

Very little oil is needed for shallow frying, just enough to:

* enable the food to be moved during cooking, so that all its surfaces cook properly and there is no burning or sticking

* ensure that heat is conducted to all parts of the food's surface even when an uneven shape means that some of it is not in direct contact with the cooking surface.

When a good quality non-stick surface is being used and quite fatty foods such as streaky bacon, pork and lamb chops are being shallow fried, no oil is necessary. The food will release sufficient fat of its own to prevent sticking.

Getting the best from frying

✔ **fresh oil (or fat) used**

follow workplace or recipe instruction for the type of oil. Some dishes are best cooked with a particular oil, e.g. sesame oil provides a nutty flavour that complements certain Chinese dishes. Some fats and oils have good flavour but are too expensive for general use (e.g. olive oil) or burn too readily (e.g. butter)

✔ **ingredients, garnishes and serving dishes prepared**

fried food is at its best served immediately

✔ **minimum amount of oil used**

some griddle chefs use a spray oil to give the lightest coating

✔ **oil at correct temperature before adding food**

this is largely a matter of experience. Watch what happens when the food first comes into contact with the oil. If the oil is too cold, almost nothing will happen, while the right temperature usually produces a sizzling sound. If the oil is too hot, it will smoke

✔ **food lowered in gently**

so that the hot oil does not spit or splash

✔ **frying time staggered**

when frying differently sized pieces of food, begin with the pieces that require the longest cooking time – with a chicken, this would mean the thighs and drumsticks, adding the breast pieces later

✔ **food moved around**

so that it cooks evenly without burning or sticking. Use a palette knife or fish slice for handling the food. Do not pierce the food with a fork, as the juices will be lost

✔ **better-looking side cooked first**

it is easier to turn the food over without damage when it is only partly cooked, so the side cooked first tends to look better

✔ **heat controlled**

to ensure the right degree of cooking through to the centre of the food. Do not turn the heat down too much or the food will absorb excessive fat

✔ **fat drained off when removing food from pan**

placing it on kitchen paper briefly after cooking helps remove any excess oil

✔ **food served with minimum delay**

if delay is unavoidable, do not cover crisply finished items (e.g. chicken breast in breadcrumbs) or they will become soggy

Frying for large numbers

✔ **fried in batches to suit pan size**

if you overfill the pan, the temperature of the fat drops too low. It is also difficult to turn the food

✔ **pan cleaned after each batch**

drain off the juices and remaining fat – the juices can be used later if a sauce is being made. Wipe the pan clean – kitchen paper is ideal – add fresh oil, and reheat ready for the next batch

Wet cooking methods

Water, steam or a liquid such as stock plays the main role. The moisture softens the effect of the heat, making the wet cooking methods suitable for the less tender (but flavourful) cuts of meat, poultry and offal.

Braising

In braising, whole joints or large cuts of meat are cooked in the oven, partially covered with a thickened, flavoured liquid which forms part of the finished dish. It is a cross between stewing – with the sauce and slow cooking – and roasting. The longer, gentler cooking makes it ideal for meat which is not the top roasting quality (e.g. beef topside, shoulder of lamb).

Use an ovenproof container with a tight-fitting lid. The container should be high enough for the meat to fit in without touching the lid, and not so wide that a lot of sauce is needed in relation to the size of the meat.

Braised dishes rely for part of their taste on the flavours caused by browning. Shallow fry the meat in hot fat, or roast larger joints for a short time in a very hot oven (about 250°C). Many recipes include chopped vegetables (e.g. carrots, onions, leek and garlic). These are also shallow fried, and placed in the cooking container as a base for the meat.

Add the cooking liquid next. Bring to the boil on top of the stove, cover with the lid and place in the oven.

From time to time during cooking, skim off fat and impurities. Turn the heat down if the liquid boils too vigorously: it should simmer gently.

The finished sauce should flow easily over the food, coating it evenly.

Sometimes the meat is glazed to give an attractive, shiny sheen or gloss to the outer crust. For the final 30 minutes or so of cooking, transfer the meat to a deep tray with some of the cooking liquid, return to the oven and baste every 10 minutes.

Boiling

Boiling is cooking in liquid at boiling point. Although the movement of the liquid (usually water or stock) can range from a rapid and vigorous bubbling action to a gentle simmering, the temperature remains constant at 100°C.

For meat and poultry, boiling is used to:

- remove impurities from, and cook joints which have been pickled or salted, e.g. silverside and brisket
- cook meat and poultry which has good flavour, but needs long cooking in a moist environment, e.g. boiling fowls (old laying hens)
- remove impurities from meat and offal before braising or stewing. This is called *blanching*.

Use a saucepan big enough for the food to be fully covered by liquid, and for any vegetable garnish or dumplings added later in the recipe. Start with cold water, to draw the impurities out of the meat, and leave the pan uncovered (a lid tends to trap impurities).

Skim off fat and impurities frequently, otherwise they make the liquid cloudy and unpleasantly flavoured.

To test the meat is cooked, pierce it with a skewer or trussing needle. Hardly any pressure will be needed when the food is cooked.

For long, slow cooking of large items:

- keep the heat down so the liquid bubbles gently – if boiling is very vigorous, the liquid will boil away and the food can start to break up
- top up with boiling water as necessary. A lid can be used once all the impurities have been removed (about half-way through cooking). This reduces the liquid loss.

Steaming

The meat or poultry is cooked in a steamer. A saucepan with a tightly fitting lid can also be used, partly filled with boiling water.

The steam provides a moist heat at about 100°C, cooking the food gently. There is no flavour transfer between the food and the steam.

Steaming is used for steak and kidney pudding and similar dishes where the flavour is deliberately trapped in. Put the raw meat, cut into small pieces, in a basin lined with pastry (normally suet). Add a little stock and other flavouring ingredients (e.g. chopped onion, parsley). Place a circle of pastry on the top, to seal the contents of the pudding. Cover with greaseproof paper and a cloth (see page 185) and place in the steamer for around three hours.

Before using the steamer, always check the internal water bath has been refilled after the steamer was cleaned. The water in a saucepan should be boiling.

If you are cooking several puddings in a steamer, put them on a perforated tray. This allows the steam to circulate around the basins, and makes it easier for you to lift them in and out. If using a saucepan, choose one large enough for the pudding to rest off the bottom of the pan, on a suitable rack (otherwise there is a risk that the base of the pudding will burn).

You should be able to see steam coming out of the vent at the top of the steamer, or from under the saucepan lid. Check the water level in the saucepan every 30 to 45 minutes, and top up as necessary with boiling water.

As you cannot open a steamed meat pudding, you must be guided by the recipe timing and experience. If in doubt, it is better to extend the cooking time slightly – there is little risk of overcooking the food by doing this.

How to blanch meat

1 Cover with cold water. Bring to the boil and simmer for a few minutes. You will see a scum form on the surface (as shown in the photograph).
2 Take the pan off the heat and carry carefully to a sink. Get help with a large pan.
3 Place the pan under the cold water tap. Run the tap until the cooking liquid has been replaced by cold, clear water. This stage is known as *refreshing*.
4 When there is a danger that the food will spill out into the sink (e.g. with cubed meat), use a conical strainer to break the force of the water from the tap.
5 If the next stage is to boil the meat or offal to cook it, wash the pan or exchange for a clean one. Put the food back, cover with fresh cold water, add recipe ingredients and return to the heat.

Stewing

In stewing, small pieces of food are gently cooked in a small amount of liquid. This can be done on top of the stove, in a saucepan, or in the oven in a suitable lidded container. The liquid should not boil vigorously. A gentle bubbling action is best – known as *simmering*.

The slow, gentle cooking is ideal for cooking the less tender cuts of meat and poultry. The liquid forms part of the finished dish and, with the help of other ingredients, contributes to the overall flavour.

There are several variations on stewing, which determine how the cooking is started:

- frying over a high heat to brown the meat and vegetables
- frying the food over a low heat so that it does not brown – known as *sweating*
- blanching to remove the impurities (see box opposite)

and at what stage the liquid is thickened:

- at the start of cooking, when a sauce is used, or a roux (see page 123) made to thicken the liquid as it is added
- during cooking, by using ingredients such as potatoes which break down and thicken the liquid
- after the food has finished cooking (see box).

Stews are usually begun on top of the stove. Once the cooking liquid has come to the boil, cover with a tight fitting lid and transfer to the oven. The more even, gentle heat of the oven produces a better (slower) speed of cooking, and reduces the risk of burning.

How to thicken the cooking liquid

1 Place a little of the thickening agent in a small bowl:
   - *cornflour, arrowroot or waxy maize starch* – use with cold water or cold stock
   - *beurre manié* – use equal quantities of flour and butter (no liquid)
   - *fromage frais and flour* – as beurre manié: the cheese gives a pleasant tangy flavour to the cooking liquid, and has a much lower fat content than butter
   - *jaysee* – use equal quantities of the cooking liquid and flour.
2 Blend thoroughly so that you have a smooth paste.
3 Add the paste to the cooking liquid, a little at a time, and bring to the boil for a few minutes, stirring vigorously.
4 If the sauce is still too thin, repeat the process.

If using *egg yolk and cream* – called a *liaison* – to lighten the colour and add richness and flavour to a white stew, do so at the last minute. Allow the stew to reheat briefly, but not boil, otherwise the sauce will curdle.

Thick yogurt, added at the last moment, will thicken a stew and provide a tangy flavour.

Getting the best from stewing

✔ **oven at right temperature**
check recipe, otherwise around 180°C is a general guide

✔ **saucepan or container of suitable size**
big enough for the contents not to spill over during cooking or stirring, and with room for any ingredients added at a later stage

✔ **saucepan or container of suitable type**
with ovenproof handles, and a close-fitting, ovenproof lid

✔ **meat and vegetables browned (if required)**
when making a large stew, it is best to shallow fry the vegetables separately from the meat. Otherwise the juices released by the meat will make it difficult to brown the vegetables

✔ **impurities and fat removed**
every 20 to 30 minutes, skim off any impurities and fat which have risen to the surface, then stir the stew gently

✔ **heat controlled carefully**
if the stew is cooking too fast (i.e. burning at the edges, rapid boiling which continues for a time after it has been removed from the oven), turn the oven temperature down 10°C or so

✔ **no burning at bottom of pan**
if cooking is continued on top of the stove, the stew needs to be stirred more frequently to make sure that food does not catch on the bottom of the pan and burn. The disadvantage of stirring is that you may cause the food to break up (which is another reason why the oven is better)

✔ **cooking time staggered**
when vegetables contribute to the presentation (as well as the flavour) of the finished dish, add them to the stew in stages, so that they retain their shape and do not overcook

✔ **food cooked sufficiently**
when cooked, meat should be easy to penetrate with a cocktail stick. The flesh on chicken joints or lamb cutlets should come away from the bone easily

✔ **sauce not too thin, or too thick**
if the final sauce is too thin, strain off into a second, clean saucepan. It can then be thickened without damaging or overcooking the main food item. Either boil rapidly to reduce, or add a thickening agent (see box). Strain the corrected sauce back over the food (which should have been kept hot)

Combination cooking

Combination cookery has been made possible by advances in the technology of catering equipment. There are two types of combination oven. Both use the all-round heat of a normal oven and a second heat source. Both can be used with either heat source on its own or in combination mode. Where they differ is in the nature of this second heat source:

- *combi-ovens* (and there are other, similar names) use steam. For roasting large joints of meat and turkey, the combination of high temperatures (from the heating elements in the oven) and a moist atmosphere (from the steam injected into the oven) reduces weight loss and prevents drying out

- *combination microwave ovens* use microwave energy. On its own, microwave energy does not brown or crisp the outer surface of meat. Used in combination with oven heat (from electric elements or gas burners), a result similar to a conventional roast is produced in far less time (because of the rapid cooking ability of microwaves).

Paprika beef with wholemeal dumplings

by McDougalls (RHM Foods)

SERVES 4

450 g	stewing steak, cubed	1 lb
30 ml	oil	2 tbsp
1	red pepper, sliced	1
1	onion, chopped	1
15 ml	paprika	1 tbsp
275 ml	stock	½ pt
	salt	

Dumplings

175 g	wholemeal flour	6 oz
15 ml	baking powder	1 tbsp
75 g	suet	3 oz
	salt	
	cold water to mix	

> This recipe involves frying the meat (to colour it), and stewing, but the cooking liquid is not thickened (which is usual with a stew).
>
> The use of wholemeal flour increases the fibre content.

1 Fry beef in oil until browned. Add peppers and onion, frying until soft. Stir in paprika, stock and salt. Bring to the boil.

2 Turn into an ovenproof casserole dish. Cover and place in oven for 1½ to 2 hours at 180°C, or until almost cooked.

← Use a dish which is sufficiently large for the dumplings (step 3).

3 Mix all the dumpling ingredients together with sufficient cold water to make a firm dough. Shape into 8 balls and place in the casserole. Simmer for a further 20 minutes. Serve.

Finishing methods

Each dish you prepare should be at its very best when it goes to the customer – cooked as the customer requires, pleasing to look at and appetising.

What customers expect and enjoy depends on many factors. Often, restaurants use photographs of the finished dishes to promote sales, either in the menu or on display panels. Others rely on words, but use photographs and detailed instructions to help staff achieve the same standard of presentation and appearance each time.

Garnishing

Garnishing is adding something to the dish to improve the look of the food. It's like decorating the restaurant table with napkins, flowers, etc.

Garnishes may provide contrast – of colour, flavour or texture – or reflect a particular theme. They do not have to be edible (e.g. a paper frill to hide the end of bone on a cutlet), but should never be unsafe to eat.

Many garnishes are determined by tradition – what is usually done and what works well. Watercress with roast meat is a well known combination.

In expensive restaurants featuring classical dishes, the aim is to serve the dish in the style laid down by its creator, maybe hundreds of years ago. When the restaurant is offering its own unique dishes, the choice is wide open.

Glazing

Glazing is giving the surface of the food a shiny, attractive appearance. This is done with some braised dishes, by frequently basting the meat with sauce during the final stage of cooking. The effect is partly created by gelatin (which comes from the bones used to make the base of the sauce, a good stock).

Coating

Coating is lightly covering the cooked meat, poultry or offal with a sauce. The aim is to make the food look attractive, so the sauce must neither be:

- too thin or it will all run straight off the meat, nor

- too thick or it will completely hide what's under it; the customers might then be rather suspicious as to what they are getting!

Quality points of finished dish

The finished dish should look and taste good, something you are proud to have helped prepare. Some workplaces give their staff detailed guidance on what the standard should be. Here are some general points:

- *texture* – the way the food feels in the mouth: chewy, tender, crunchy, soft, hard, etc.

- *aroma* – the smell of the food: roast meats have a characteristic, strong aroma, as do many of the herbs and spices used in sauces for meat and poultry dishes

- *flavour* – the taste of the meat, poultry or offal – this will depend on how it has been cooked, and the ingredients used in the dish

- *appearance* – the way the dish looks, the colours (a lot of the appeal of grilled food is the attractive brown colouring it gives the food), the different textures (e.g. smooth sauce, a slice of tender meat), and the shapes.

Experience will help you know what to look for, and to recognise signs that things are not right. Remember, your own reaction to a dish may be different from that of the customer. If you are in a situation where you can get feedback from customers, this is a great bonus. You can learn a lot from what colleagues and friends tell you when they taste your dishes. And from their and your reaction to dishes of similar style that you eat at home and elsewhere.

There are two, more measurable, aspects of quality:

- *freshness* – the length of time dishes are at their best depends on how they have been cooked. Most stews keep well, provided they are covered. Roasts can and should stand a short time after coming out of the oven before carving but, once carved, roast beef is best served quickly. Fried food loses its crispness if it has to be kept hot for a long time. There is a second aspect to freshness – food safety: bacteria multiply rapidly in warm temperatures

- *quantity* – careful control of portion sizes is essential to keep the customers happy and for money reasons. It's a balance between the price customers are willing to pay, what they expect, and what will cover costs and generate a financial return for the business. Your employer will make the decisions on pricing and portion sizes. It's your job to follow instructions, and to tell your manager about any difficulty in doing this, for instance, if you are running low on servings of a dish.

Compare this recipe, which involves boiling, with that for paprika beef (opposite page).

Instead of soaking the beef, you could blanch it to remove the excess salt. →

Standing the beef for a short time helps it carve better. →

Boiled silverside of beef and dumplings

SERVES 4

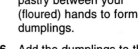

600 g	cured silverside	1 lb 5 oz
4 each	small carrots and small onions	4 each
	cold white stock or water to cover	
	bouquet garni	
	chopped parsley (optional)	
100 g	suet pastry (see page 187)	4 oz

1. Soak the beef in cold water for 24 hours to remove excess salt.

2. Discard the soaking water and place the beef into a suitably sized saucepan. Cover with cold stock or water and bring to the boil. Skim if a scum forms.

3. Add the bouquet garni and allow the liquid to simmer until almost cooked (about 1½ hours).

4. Add the carrots and onions and simmer for another 10 to 15 minutes.

5. Roll the pieces of suet pastry between your (floured) hands to form dumplings.

6. Add the dumplings to the cooking liquor and simmer until cooked: a further 15 to 20 minutes.

7. Remove the beef from the pan, allow to stand in a warm place for about 10 minutes, then carve.

8. Garnish with the carrots, onions and dumplings, and coat with a little of the cooking liquor. Sprinkle some parsley over the dumplings or onions if desired. Serve a sauceboat of the cooking liquor separately if required.

Note this recipe is for 20 portions. Half the quantites to make 10 portions, or divide by four to make 5 portions.

In place of demi-glace, you can use a good stock and a little cornflour to thicken.

Liver and onions

SERVES 20

2½ kg	thinly sliced lamb's or calf's liver	5½ lb
225 g	flour, seasoned	8 oz
125 ml	oil for frying	4 fl oz
	chopped parsley (garnish)	

Lyonnaise sauce

100 g	oil or butter	4 oz
550 g	onions, sliced	1 lb 4 oz
125 ml	vinegar	4 fl oz
125 ml	white wine	4 fl oz
1¼ litre	demi-glace or jus lié	2½ pt

1   Melt the oil in a saucepan or sauté pan. Add the onions and shallow fry until light brown.

2   Add the vinegar and wine. Boil rapidly until the liquid has reduced by two-thirds.

3   Add the demi-glace and simmer for 2 to 3 minutes until the sauce is well blended. If it seems too thin to coat the liver evenly, reduce further. Skim if required and check seasoning.

4   Coat the liver with the ◄ seasoned flour, shake off any excess flour, then fry quickly on each side.

> Add the flour coating at the last moment.

5   Remove the liver from the pan and place on absorbent paper to drain thoroughly. Transfer to warm serving dish(es). Coat with the hot sauce. Sprinkle with parsley and serve.

Sautéed kidneys with peppers
by Dufrais

SERVES 4

10–12	lambs' kidneys, skinned, cored and quartered or halved	10–12
25 g	flour, seasoned	1 oz
45 ml	olive oil	3 tbsp
1	large onion, finely chopped	1
1	clove garlic, crushed and peeled	1
200 ml	red Bistro Chef or red wine	7 fl oz
50 ml	beef stock	2 fl oz
1	bay leaf	1
100 g	red pepper, deseeded and sliced	4 oz
45 ml	fresh parsley, chopped	3 tbsp

1   Heat the oil in a large frying pan. Fry the onion and garlic until golden. Add the kidneys which you have coated in seasoned flour.

2   Cook, stirring, for 1 to 2 minutes. Gradually stir in the Bistro Chef and stock. Add the red pepper and bay leaf. Simmer, uncovered, for about 10 minutes.

> The flour coating on the kidneys thickens the sauce slightly.

3   Remove the bay leaf, stir in the parsley and serve.

You can use veal or pork escalopes for this recipe.

Shallow frying is the method of cooking.

Veal escalopes in cider sauce with Viennese cabbage
by Dufrais

SERVES 4

60 ml	grapeseed oil	4 tbsp
2	medium onions, 1 sliced, 1 chopped	2
450 g	red cabbage, shredded	1 lb
50 g	brown sugar	2 oz
75 ml	cider vinegar	5 tbsp
4	veal or pork escalopes	4
1	eating apple, peeled and sliced (optional)	1
15 ml	wholegrain mustard	1 tbsp
150 ml	double or single cream	5 fl oz
	seasoning to taste	

1   In a large saucepan, heat 30 ml (2 tbsp) oil and soften sliced onion. Add cabbage, sugar, 30 ml vinegar and 60 ml water. Stir well, cover and gently simmer for 35 to 40 minutes.

2   Meanwhile, heat 15 ml (1 tbsp) oil in a large frying pan. Fry the escalopes. When cooked, remove from pan and keep hot. Add remaining oil and chopped onion to the pan and cook for 3 to 4 minutes. Add apple, remaining vinegar and mustard. Cook for 5 minutes or until the apple is soft.

> For veal, 2 to 3 minutes on each side, pork 4 to 6 minutes.

3   Stir in cream and season well. Replace escalopes, heat through and serve with the cabbage.

> Do not boil once you have added the cream.

Lower the liver into the pan gently, otherwise you will splash yourself with hot fat.

Healthy choices – put the parsley butter on a grilled steak after the customer has said 'Yes, I would like some please.'

Finishing touches to the grilled steak, cooked here on a charcoal grill.

Rump steak maître d'hôtel

SERVES 1

1 x 225 g	rump steak	1 x 8 oz
	seasoning to taste	
	oil	
	few sprigs watercress (garnish)	

Parsley butter makes 50 g (2 oz)

50 g	butter	2 oz
	squeeze of lemon juice	
	chopped parsley, good pinch	
	cayenne pepper, pinch	

1   Lightly brush each side of the steak with oil. Season with pepper. ← Oil the grill bars to prevent the steak sticking.

2   Grill the steak until it has developed a good colour on both sides. If the meat is drying out, brush with a little oil. When cooked, season with salt (if required). ← If salt is added before grilling, the steak does not brown properly.

3   Place on a warm serving dish and decorate with watercress. Accompany by a slice of parsley butter placed in a sauceboat with iced water so that it remains firm.

Parsley butter

1   Mix together the butter, lemon juice, parsley and cayenne pepper. ← This is easier if the butter is soft.

2   Place the mixture on a sheet of dampened greaseproof paper. Roll to form a neat sausage shape about 25 mm in diameter. Chill.

3   For service, remove the paper and cut the roll into rounds about 3 mm thick.

An example of how traditional methods can be adjusted for healthy catering.

This recipe relies on the external fat on the topside to keep it moist during roasting. Putting the meat on a trivet keeps it clear of the fat which runs out of the meat during cooking.

Roast beef with mustard and black peppercorn crust

by Meat and Livestock Commission

SERVES 4 to 6

900 g–1.35 kg	beef topside	2–3 lb
15 ml	black peppercorns, crushed	1 tbsp
45 ml	English mustard	3 tbsp
30 ml	fresh parsley, chopped	2 tbsp
5 ml	oil	1 tsp
25 g	breadcrumbs	1 oz

1   Press the crushed black peppercorns all over the surface of the joint, and place on a trivet in a roasting tin. Roast at 180°C for the calculated time. ← See table below for roasting times.

2   Remove joint from the oven 15 minutes before the end of cooking. Spread the mustard over the surface. Mix the breadcrumbs with the oil and parsley, and press on to the mustard.

3   Return to the oven for the final 15 minutes until the breadcrumbs are golden.

4   Allow the joint to stand for 10 minutes before carving.

Roasting – cooking times

	per 450 g (1 lb)	Plus
Beef: rare	20 mins	+ 20 mins
Beef: medium	25 mins	+ 25 mins
Beef: well-done	30 mins	+ 30 mins
Pork: well-done	35 mins	+ 35 mins
Lamb: medium	25 mins	+ 25 mins
Lamb: well-done	30 mins	+ 30 mins

Joints weighing less than 1.25 kg (2½ lb) may need 5 minutes per 450 g (1 lb) extra cooking time.

with thanks to Meat and Livestock Commission

Roast rack of lamb with herb crust

Preparation:

1   Roast in a suitable pan until cooked to the guests' requirements.

2   Brush the aubergine with olive oil and char grill both sides.

3   Arrange the herb crust on top of the rack, place in oven to brown the crust.

4   Upon request, arrange the rack and rosti potato on to a hot service plate, garnish with the hot pepper jelly and herbs.

Char grilled double breast of chicken

Preparation:

1   Brush the chicken with olive oil, season with star anise, char grill on both sides, place on to a suitable tray and finish cooking in the oven until the juices run clear.

2   Upon request, arrange the chicken and fries as shown.

Grilled rump steak

Garnish with herbs, and serve with baked tomato, fries and grilled field mushrooms.

Braised gammon in mushroom sauce

by Pork and Bacon Promotion Council and others

SERVES 10

1.25 kg	gammon joint (boneless)	2½ lb
600 ml	brown stock (hot)	1 pt
50 g	margarine	2 oz
25 g	tomato paste	1 oz
100 g	button mushrooms, sliced	4 oz
25 g	flour	1 oz
50 g	onion, finely chopped	2 oz

1 In the braising pan which you will be using to cook the meat, shallow fry the onion and mushrooms in the margarine.

2 Stir the flour in thoroughly. Cook for a few minutes, stirring all the time.

> This is similar to the method for making a roux-based sauce (see Section 10).

3 Add the tomato paste and mix well.

4 Gradually add the hot stock, stirring thoroughly with each addition until you get a smooth paste.

5 When all the stock has been added (by this time the sauce will be fairly thin), bring to the boil and season.

6 Place the gammon in the sauce, baste well with the sauce, cover the pan and place in the oven at 180°C for 70 minutes. Baste from time to time with the sauce.

7 When cooked, allow the gammon to rest for 10 minutes before carving.

> This recipe involves frying the meat. To finish, the dish is baked in the oven.

Bacon and leek gratin

by Potato Marketing Board

From *Catering for the Elderly*, a booklet of recipes for use in residential homes.

SERVES 10

450 g	bacon, derinded and chopped	1 lb
450 g	leeks, trimmed and sliced	1 lb
1 × 397 g	can chopped tomatoes	1 × 14 oz
15 ml	cornflour	1 tbsp
150 ml	water or stock	5 fl oz
900 g	potatoes, peeled and sliced	2 lb
50 g	grated cheese	2 oz
	seasoning to taste	

1 Fry the bacon and leeks together for 10 minutes. Add the tomatoes and continue to cook for 5 minutes. Season. Dissolve cornflour with the water or stock and add to the pan.

> Another way of thickening the cooking liquid.

2 Meanwhile, boil the sliced potatoes for a few minutes. Drain.

3 Lay half the potatoes on the base of a lightly oiled 25 cm (10 inch) ovenproof dish. Place the bacon mixture on top and finish off with another layer of potatoes. Sprinkle the cheese on top.

4 Put in the oven to bake at 200°C for 30 minutes or until the potatoes are cooked and the cheese is browned. Serve.

> For a milder chilli, omit fresh chilli, or reduce amount of chilli powder

Chilli-con-carne

by Meat and Livestock Commission

. Serve with brown rice. Can also be used as a filling for jacket potatoes.

SERVES 4

450 g	braising steak, cubed	1 lb
30 ml	vegetable oil	2 tbsp
1	large onion, finely chopped	1
1	clove garlic, crushed and peeled	1
30 ml	malt vinegar	2 tbsp
	seasoning to taste	
5 ml	dried oregano	1 tsp
5 ml	chilli powder	1 tsp
1	fresh green chilli, deseeded and finely chopped	1
30 ml	tomato purée	2 tbsp
150 ml	beef stock	5 fl oz
1 × 397 g	can chopped tomatoes	1 × 14 oz
1 × 397 g	can red kidney beans, drained and rinsed	1 × 14 oz

1 Heat oil in large pan and fry onion and garlic until softened. Add beef and cook until well browned.

2 Add the remaining ingredients with the exception of the kidney beans. Bring to the boil, cover and simmer for about 90 minutes or until meat is tender and sauce has become rich and thick.

3 Add kidney beans and continue cooking for 15 minutes. Serve.

> Avoid all contact with the seeds of fresh chilli. Should you touch them and then your eyes, you will experience a painful burning.

Dish production guide

Hot smoked chicken, ham and pineapple salad

Preparation and cooking:

- estimate daily sales in advance
- wash and prepare all salad items
- cut chicken into strips
- dust chicken with seasoned flour, and shallow fry for about 4 minutes, stirring all the time
- add soy sauce towards the end of cooking.

Presentation:

- place lettuce on to plate
- arrange cucumber twist, tomato wedges, batons of red pepper and sliced celery on the lettuce
- place hot chicken (see photograph by question 13 on page 108)
- add rolled ham, orange slices, diced pineapple, and spring onion
- serve immediately, accompanied by new potatoes.

1 Give two general quality points you should check when receiving meat, poultry or offal.

2 What are the rules for defrosting food?

3 What do you remember when seasoning with salt, for health reasons?

4 To reduce the risk of an accident, what precautions should you take before using a chopping board?

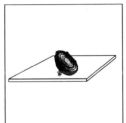

5 What safe practices do you follow when using a knife?

6 When should you use a trolley to carry food and equipment? Why is it safer?

7 Before you let this person handle food, what would you have to say about the hair, uniform and jewellery?

8 What could get into food in a kitchen, which would make the food unsafe to eat?

9 What can happen if food is kept at the wrong temperature for too long?

10 What is the safe temperature for storing meat, poultry and offal before cooking?

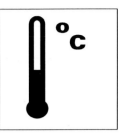

11 For each of the eight basic preparation methods, give some examples of meat, poultry and offal dishes which use them.

1 There are two types of offal in this photo, and one type of meat. Identify them.

2 Look at the photo above again. At least four methods of preparation have been used. What are they?

5 Imagine the chef in this photo is approached by someone who started working in the bar that day, and doesn't know much about food hygiene.

'You've got a sharp knife there chef, and a nice board. I need this lemon sliced urgently for a gin and tonic. Would you do it for me, please?' Assuming he wants to help, what should the chef do?

9 This food has been shallow fried. What has gone wrong to lead to the result shown here?

10 And why has this happened?

3 The cooking untensils sitting on top of, and in the oven of this cooking range, are made of two types of metal (shown as A and B in the key below):
a) identify the two metals
b) for each of the types of metal, state one advantage and one disad-vantage.

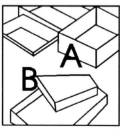

6 What sort of grill is this piece of lamb's liver being cooked on:
(a) infra-red,
(b) overhead or salamander,
(c) simulated charcoal? Circle the relevant picture on the right.

11 And this?

12 Comment on the presentation of this dish, *Steak and smoked chicken.*

7 Name the other two grills illustrated.

13 In what order would you assemble this dish, *Hot smoked chicken, ham and pineapple salad*?

4 Which pan would you use for cooking the following: (a) 6 roast chickens; (b) steak pie; (c) roast topside of beef; (d) 30 portions of lamb hotpot

8 In the photo by question 6, the liver is being turned using a pair of tongs. Why should tongs be used and not a fork?

14 This dish is for children: *Chicken teddies and chicken smiles.* How would you describe its quality points?

Photographs by questions 12 to 14 are from the Toby Restaurants training manual.

For help to answer questions relating to:

Health and safety

? **safe working practices**

The hazards include use of knives, handling large/heavy/awkward objects (e.g. joints of meat), hot cooking equipment (burns).

? **fat/oil approaching flash point**

This happens in frying when the fat or oil gets too hot. Quite suddenly it bursts into flame. Fortunately, you get a few moments' warning – dark smoke coming off the surface of the oil and an unpleasant smell. The temperature at which this happens depends on what oil or fat you are using, and the condition it is in – oil which is old, or has not been well looked after, has a lower flash point.

? **what to do if fat/oil reaches flash point**

You are dealing with a fire. Prompt action is essential: turn off the fryer at the main switch/gas supply, use the fire blanket to smother the fire, and get help. See pages 14 and 131.

Food hygiene

? **importance of good hygiene**

Meat is a high risk food because it supports the growth of harmful bacteria. Sometimes, the meat is already carrying bacteria when it comes into your kitchen (see page 51). Keeping preparation areas and equipment clean reduces the risk of these bacteria spreading from one food to another. And because the bacteria are impossible to see (being so small in size), the cleaning must be thorough.

? **main contamination threats**

You have just been considering one threat: harmful bacteria. Some of the other things which can make food unsafe to eat are about you in the kitchen. Many are safe in their proper place, e.g. cleaning materials. The danger is when they contact or get into the food unnoticed.

Other dangers arise from poor standards of personal hygiene (e.g. hair falling in food), or inadequate cleaning of equipment and work surfaces (e.g. burnt remnants of food falling from the oven shelf into a tray of roast potatoes).

? **importance of time and temperature**

One of the reasons for cooking meat is to make it safe to eat. The problems occur when the food is in the warm kitchen – during preparation, waiting to be cooked, or after cooking. At these temperatures bacteria multiply – in minutes they start doubling in number. So in 10 minutes, 1000 bacteria become 2000. Left another 10 minutes, there will be 4000!

A particular danger comes from those bacteria which can survive cooking. Given the chance (e.g. if the food is kept warm for a long time after cooking) they revive.

? **products not for immediate use**

Bacteria do not increase in numbers at temperatures below 5°C and above 63°C. This is why prepared meat must be kept refrigerated until required. And if there is a delay in serving meat after it has finished cooking, it must be kept piping hot, or cooled quickly and then chilled.

Product knowledge

? **quality points of fresh meat**

The meat should be chilled, and not beyond the date stamp on the packaging. The other points depend on having the experience to recognise what is right or not right. Make a point of noticing the appearance and smell of meat you handle at work (which you know from your manager is the right quality), and in butcher shops and the meat counters of supermarkets.

? **quality points of cooked meat**

The dish should be *freshly cooked*. Whether this means minutes or hours depends on the dish, and you should follow workplace guidelines on how long food can be kept hot.

The *quantity* or portion size should be right. There will be clear standards to follow in your workplace. If you give too much, you put profits at risk. If you give too little, you are cheating the customers. When menus state portion size, this will be an offence under trade descriptions law.

The other quality points are harder to quantify, but experience and guidance from your manager will help you know what *texture, aroma, flavour* and *appearance* to look for.

? **preparation methods**

These are: defrosting, washing, skinning, dicing, trimming, slicing, seasoning, coating. To relate them to different types of meat, etc., you might find it helpful to start with those methods you use regularly at work, and the various meat dishes you prepare.

⸹ Sutcliffe

Chicken and black bean sauce with crispy vegetables

10 portions		25 portions
1 1/4pt/750ml	Uncle Ben's Black Bean sauce	3 pints/1.75litres
2 1/2lb/1.125kg	Chicken breast, cut in 2" strips	6 1/4lb/2.8kg
5 tbs/75ml	Light soy sauce	6fl.oz/175ml
1 tbs/15ml	Vegetable oil	2 tbs/30ml
10 oz/250g	Onions, cut in strips	1 1/2lb/675g
10 oz/250g	Celery, sliced diagonally	1 1/2lb/675g
10 oz/250g	Carrots , cut in strips	1 1/2lb/675g
12 oz/350g	Green peppers, cut in strips	2 lb/900g
1/2 bunch	Spring onion, finely sliced	1 bunch
1 lb/450g	Uncle Ben's long grain rice	2 1/2lb/1.125kg

1. Place the chicken in a large bowl, add the soy sauce and mix well. Cover and refrigerate for 4-6 hours.
2. Transfer the chicken strips onto a shallow baking sheet and steam for 10 - 12 minutes.
3. Meanwhile, heat the oil in a wok or large pan, stir fry the onion, celery and carrot. Remove from the pan.
4. Blanch the pepper strips in boiling salted water, keep crisp. Drain and refresh.
5. Heat Uncle Ben's Black Bean sauce in a large pan, stir in the vegetables. Drain excess liquid from the chicken strips and add to the sauce. Simmer for 5 - 10 minutes.
6. Turn into serving dishes and sprinkle with spring onion. Serve with Uncle Ben's Long grain rice.

CHINESE

Calories	Under 300K Cal ☐	Under 400K Cal ✓	Under 500K Cal ☐
Fat	Low ✓	Medium ☐	
Fibre	Medium ✓	High ☐	

⸹ Sutcliffe
Your Quality Partner

Nutrition policy

We are committed to helping our customers move towards a healthier diet, should they wish to do so. To this end, we have a responsibility to:

- provide sufficient variety and choice within our menus so that customers can select healthier food combinations or meals

- adapt our methods of preparation and service, to avoid excessive use of fat (particularly saturates), salt and sugar, while increasing the use of starchy, fibre-rich foods, fruits and vegetables

- play an active role in promoting good nutrition by the provision of sound nutrition information.

This is one of the dishes which feature on the menu as the healthy eating Choice of the day *at restaurants run by the contract caterers Sutcliffe Catering.*

? cooking methods

Nine cooking methods have been covered in this section: the *dry processes* of roasting, grilling, frying and baking; and the *wet processes* of boiling, stewing, braising, steaming and combination cooking.

Match the methods used in your workplace to the different types of meat, poultry and offal you cook. You will find there is a strong link between, on the one hand, the speed of cooking and the temperatures used, and on the other hand, how tender/tough the meat is and therefore its price.

Cuts of meat which come from parts of the animal that do a lot of work – generally in the forequarter – need slow, moist cooking, such as stewing or braising. They are the less expensive cuts. Cuts which come from muscle areas not so heavily used by the animal – generally in the hindquarter – can be cooked by the faster, dry methods, such as grilling, roasting or frying. They are the most expensive cuts.

Developments in the agriculture industry, in butchery techniques and in cooking have increased the range of cuts which can be cooked by the quicker methods.

? identifying when meat is cooked

Answer this question for some of the dishes you regularly prepare and cook. If you have photographs or workplace guidelines (see examples reproduced here) these will set out what the finished dish should look like. The temperature at the centre of the food is another key factor.

Healthy catering practices

? replacing high fat ingredients

The traditional coating of flour, eggwash and breadcrumbs for many shallow fried dishes (e.g. escalopes of pork, chicken or turkey) adds a certain amount of fat (in the eggwash). The coating also absorbs more fat during cooking. If the recipe allows variations, you could use flour on its own as the coating, or omit the coating altogether.

? increasing fibre content

Too little fibre in the diet can cause constipation. It is also associated with cancer of the colon and with other medical problems. The fibre content of meat, poultry and offal dishes can be increased by using wholemeal flour and wholemeal breadcrumbs as the coating ingredients, and by using as ingredients, accompaniments, or the garnish: rice, pulses, pasta, potatoes and other vegetables.

? reducing salt

A high salt intake can contribute to high blood pressure and most people, according to government health advisers, eat too much salt.

Unsalted food may appear rather tasteless to people used to having salt on their food. On the other hand, the health of customers has to be considered – and they can, of course, add their own salt.

There are three steps you can take: add less salt when cooking, use herbs and other flavourings (e.g. lemon juice) in place of salt, taste the dish before adding salt.

? fats/oils for healthy eating

A high proportion of polyunsaturated fats and a low proportion of saturated fats are best from a health point of view. Soya and sunflower oils come into this category. Other advantages are their light, fairly neutral flavour, high smoke point (which means they are suitable for frying) and medium price.

Grapeseed and corn oils are high in polyunsaturated fats and low in saturated fats. Grapeseed oil is aromatic, but expensive. Corn oil is economical, but has quite a strong frying smell.

Palm oil is economical and has a high smoke point, but a high proportion of saturated fats.

Use soya or sunflower oil for roasting in place of dripping and lard (both high in saturated fats and low in polyunsaturated).

For blended oils, check the information on the label carefully.

? cooking methods, etc. to reduce fat

Where you have a choice you can grill or bake a dish instead of frying, e.g. pieces of chicken and turkey coated in breadcrumbs. Grilling requires less fat or oil than shallow frying. Furthermore, any fat or oil which comes out of the food during cooking runs through the grill bars instead of being trapped in the pan. But grilling food on a tray means it is sitting in the fat.

Coatings on fried food give a crunchy texture, but absorb the oil. If the oil is not hot enough when you put the food in the pan, or you have too much oil in the pan, even more will be absorbed.

Non-stick frying pans require little or no oil, provided you control the heat carefully.

Boiling, steaming and baking involve no fat at all. Stewing does if the food has to be shallow fried first. Any fat which rises to the surface during boiling and stewing must be skimmed off carefully and often. If the boiling action is too vigorous, this becomes more difficult as the fat breaks up into small droplets.

Use this to check your progress against the performance criteria.

Element 1

Prepare meat, poultry and offal for cooking

Get your preparation areas and equipment ready for use ☐ PC

Select meat, poultry and offal of the type, quality and quantity required ☐ PC

△ Meat: beef, lamb, pork, bacon; poultry: chicken, turkey; offal: kidney, liver

Identify problems with the quality of meat/other ingredients & report them ☐ PC

△ Other ingredients: flour, melted butter, breadcrumbs, milk, egg wash

Use basic preparation methods and combine with other ingredients ☐ PC

△ Preparation methods: defrosting, washing, skinning, dicing, trimming, slicing, seasoning, coating
Other ingredients: flour, egg wash, breadcrumbs

Correctly store meat, poultry and offal not for immediate use ☐ PC

Clean preparation areas and equipment after use ☐ PC

Prioritise and carry out your work in an organised, efficient and safe manner ☐ PC

Element 2

Cook basic meat, poultry and offal dishes

Get your cooking areas and equipment ready for use ☐ PC

Cook meat, poultry and offal dishes ☐ PC

△ Dry cooking methods: roasting, grilling, frying, baking
Wet cooking methods: boiling, stewing, braising, steaming, combination cooking

Finish dish using appropriate method ☐ PC

△ Methods: garnishing, glazing, coating

Correctly store meat dishes not for immediate service ☐ PC

Clean cooking areas and equipment after use ☐ PC

Identify problems with the quality of the dish and report these promptly ☐ PC

Prioritise and carry out your work in an organised, efficient and safe manner ☐ PC

Preparing fish for cooking

Customers are now more adventurous, willing to try new varieties of fish, and different ways of preparing and cooking them. One reason is that some of the great favourites, e.g. cod and herring, are declining in numbers and this has put the price up. On the other hand, commercial fish farming has meant that trout and salmon are no longer luxury items.

Types of fish

There are various ways of classifying fish:

- their condition when purchased: frozen, chilled, canned, smoked, salted, 'wet': meaning fresh as opposed to salted

- where they come from: sea, or freshwater, farmed or wild (e.g. salmon), exotic (imported from all corners of the world: examples include snapper, shark, parrotfish and tuna). Freshwater fish are sometimes divided into river and lake fish.

But perhaps the most useful way of classifying fish for caterers is:

- by their shape, whether they are *flat* or *round*

- by the general characteristics of their flesh, whether they are *white* or *oil-rich*.

Flat fish, such as sole and plaice, because of their shape, are filleted in a different way from round fish, such as cod, hake, whiting, salmon and herring.

The flesh of the last two examples, salmon and herring, has a different and easily detectable characteristic: it is oily. Other oily fish are mackerel, tuna, anchovy and sardine, quite different in flavour and taste from white fish such as turbot and halibut.

Quality points to look for with fresh, whole fish

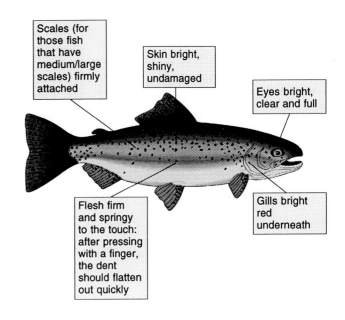

Scales (for those fish that have medium/large scales) firmly attached

Skin bright, shiny, undamaged

Eyes bright, clear and full

Gills bright red underneath

Flesh firm and springy to the touch: after pressing with a finger, the dent should flatten out quickly

Quality points

Points to look for are:

- *temperature* – fresh fish should be very well chilled to protect its eating quality, around 0°C is best, but not below –1°C, otherwise the fish will begin to freeze (under these conditions, freezing is slow and damages the structure of the fish)

- *appearance* – with so many varieties of fish, there is no set of rules which hold true for all types. The illustration gives the main points for whole fish. Pre-prepared fillets should be well trimmed, with no area of discolouration (e.g. blood clots or bruising)

- *aroma* – a mild, sea-fresh smell. Fresh skate sometimes smells slightly of ammonia until cooked. However, if this aroma remains after cooking, the fish is of poor quality.

Basic preparation methods

With practice, a very sharp knife of the right sort (see page 53) and determination to learn the right way, you will become fast, neat and waste little or nothing.

Washing

Before starting any preparation, wash the whole fresh fish thoroughly under cold, running water. This removes any slime. Use a food preparation sink. Be sure it is clean before you start, and after you finish. Fish easily picks up smells from other food. It can just as easily give its smell to other food.

You should wash fish after gutting (removing the intestines), descaling, trimming and skinning. Once you have filleted the fish, wash the fillets.

Washing helps remove any remaining scales, or loose bits of flesh. Handle the fish carefully so as not to damage the delicate flesh.

Descaling (or scaling)

This can make a mess, with scales shooting everywhere, so do it carefully and in a part of the kitchen where it will be easy to clear up thoroughly afterwards:

- use a firm-bladed knife, ideally a cook's knife

- if you have not had much experience, it is advisable to use the back of the knife blade. This will reduce the risk of accidentally damaging the skin of the fish

- hold the knife at a slight angle and scrape the scales from tail to head, so that the knife is lifting the scales up and away from the body

- while doing this, hold the fish firmly by the tail.

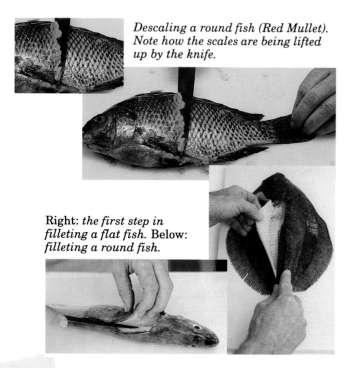

Descaling a round fish (Red Mullet). Note how the scales are being lifted up by the knife.

Right: *the first step in filleting a flat fish.* Below: *filleting a round fish.*

Gutting

Take care not to puncture the internal organs or damage the flesh. Hold the fish so that you are cutting away from yourself. Then, if the knife does slip, you are less likely to injure yourself.

For a *round* fish:

- make a slit along the belly from below the head, to extend two-thirds of the length of the fish

- using your fingers or the handle of a spoon, pull out and discard the internal organs

- scrape or wash away any dark membrane (looks like black skin) from inside the cavity

- scrape away any congealed blood lying along the back bone.

After gutting, thoroughly wash inside and outside of the fish under cold running water. There should be no trace of blood left.

Flat fish are gutted at sea, immediately after they have been caught.

Filleting

A filleting knife, with its flexible blade, is ideal for this task.

Trim off any large, spiky fins first (e.g. on monkfish).

Flat fish are prepared in two ways, depending on their size. Larger fish make four fillets, two from each side. This is called *quarter-cutting*. This is what you do:

- place the fish on the chopping board, dark side up, with the tail end nearer you

- cut around the head, then down the centre line of the fish, through to the backbone

- work the blade of the knife into the cut, and gently lift the flesh up

- keep the knife blade almost horizontal, as close to the bones as possible, and use a light stroking movement, to gradually free the fillet from the backbone

- turn the fish around, so that the head is facing you, and remove the second fillet

- turn the fish over to get two more fillets.

*Skinning a fillet
of plaice.*

Small flat fish – up to 450 g or so – are usually cut into two fillets only, one from each side. This is known as *cross-cutting*:

- lay the fish on the board, head facing you, cut around the head

- insert a knife into the flesh at one corner near the head, with the blade facing away from you

- with a sawing movement, work the knife blade across and down the backbone, to free the fillet

- turn the fish over and remove the other fillet in the same way.

There are also two ways for *round* fish. A round fish has only two fillets, one on each side. To remove them:

- lay the fish on one side on a chopping board, cut around the head

- working towards the tail, cut down the backbone using the knife blade to feel along the rib bones

- lift the fillet away as you cut, in order not to get a ragged filled

- turn the fish over, and remove the second fillet in the same way.

Some chefs find it easier to remove the head first, and to trim the fins.

The second method for round fish produces butterfly fillets. It should only be attempted with very fresh mackerel, herring, sardines and sprats:

- gut and trim the fish

- cut along the full length on the underside, to split the fish

- open the body out, and place on a chopping board with the skin uppermost

- using your thumbs or the heel of your hand, press firmly along the back of the fish to help release the backbone from the flesh

- turn the fish over and ease the backbone away from the flesh, starting at the head and working towards the tail.

Skinning

For skinning fillets a medium-sized cook's knife is probably the best choice, since it is firm. Some chefs prefer to use a filleting knife, with its more flexible blade.

To skin a *fillet* (round, flat or smoked):

- place the fillet on the chopping board, skin down

- cut through the flesh to the skin at the tail end

- with one hand, hold the skin firmly by the tail end

- with the other hand, hold the blade at a slight angle, and using a sawing movement, push the knife down and forwards at the same time

- keep the blade as close to the skin as possible, without cutting through it.

If you do cut through the skin, try to correct the situation quickly, because it can be quite difficult to cut away any bits of skin that are left on the fillet.

For whole *flat* fish, work from head to tail:

- with the point of a knife, loosen the skin from around the head

- work your thumb carefully between the skin and the flesh

- when enough skin has been worked loose to get a good grip, press the palm of one hand firmly on the head/skinned area of the fish, to hold the fish firmly

- tightly grip the flap of skin using the fingers of your other hand, and pull to tear the skin away.

Dover sole is skinned from tail to head.

Trimming

Fillets may need trimming. Cut away jagged or loose pieces of flesh, and any pieces of bone or skin.

For fish which is to be served whole, it is usual to trim the fins and, in some cases, the head.

To trim the fins, use a pair of kitchen scissors, cutting against the natural lie of the fins. Alternatively, use a cook's knive: with the fish firmly on the board, fan out the fins with the back of the knife point, then use the (sharp) cutting edge to remove them.

When the head is to be left on, open the gill slit, use scissors or a knife to cut the gill free at each end, and remove. Then use the point of a sharp knife or peeler to hook each eye out.

To remove the head entirely, for:

- a round fish, cut it off just below the gills

- a flat fish, cut from both sides of the head towards the body, forming a V-shaped cut.

Portioning

Management usually decides on portion sizes, to reflect the style of service, prices charged, and what customers want. You have an important role to play in keeping to these guidelines: too small and customers will be cheated, too generous and the business costs will rise.

The guidelines are often based on weight, e.g. 175 g per portion for fish off the bone, 225 g for fish on the bone. If fish is purchased at a standard size, then it is more usual – because it is easier for everyone – to say that a portion is two fillets or one fish.

Basic coating

Many fish dishes – especially those that are fried or grilled – require a coating. Besides adding flavour, the coating helps:

- the surface to brown and crisp
- the delicate flesh of the fish to retain its moist texture and flavour, without absorbing too much oil or fat during frying.

There are three basic groups of coating: flour, breadcrumbs and batter. Battered coatings are dealt with in Section 23.

For a *flour coating*:

- traditionally, white flour is used, seasoned with salt and pepper to add flavour
- for grilling and shallow frying, the fish is lightly coated in the flour immediately before cooking. The flour will stick quite easily to the moist (but not wet) surface of the fish
- for deep frying, the fish is dipped in milk and then coated with flour, immediately before cooking. The combination of milk and flour gives a thicker coating. A disadvantage is that flour particles fall into the oil during cooking, causing it to spoil.

For a *breadcrumb coating*, the fish needs preparation in some way so that the crumbs will stick:

- brushed with oil or melted butter, then breadcrumbed – for grilling or shallow frying
- lightly coated with flour (seasoned if required), dipped in egg wash (raw egg, beaten with a little water or milk), and then in breadcrumbs – for deep frying or shallow frying
- breadcrumb coatings can be prepared in advance, when the fish should be placed on layers of greaseproof paper, not more than two or three layers per tray – see page 95 for advice on applying the coating.

For a healthier dish, use:

- freshly ground black pepper (but not on steamed white fish, because it spoils the appearance) and/or herbs and spices (e.g. paprika, parsley) of your choice, but not salt
- wholemeal flour/brown breadcrumbs (to increase the fibre)
- in place of flour/breadcrumb coatings, use oatmeal, matzo meal, barley or crushed breakfast cereals such as bran flakes (all fibre-rich)
- oil high in polyunsaturates.

Fish cuts

Fish sometimes cooked and served whole include herring, mackerel, whiting, trout and sole. The single portion size of fish will be around 200 g, perhaps as much as 300 g for a whole sole served as a main course dish. Whitebait, very tiny fish, are also cooked and served whole, many to the portion.

Whole flat fish can be prepared as *fillets* (as described above).

To produce small pieces of fish, fillets of flat fish can be cut into *goujons*. These are thin strips, cut at a slant across the fillet. Each strip is 60 to 80 mm long, and about 15 mm wide.

Whole flat fish of the thicker type (e.g. turbot and halibut) can be cut through the bone to make a *tronçon* or steak.

Whole round fish can be cut into a *darne* or steak.

For a special presentation, a fillet can be folded in two as *delice*, or rolled up into a cylindrical shape as *paupiette*.

Storing fish not for immediate use

Fish should be stored separately from other foods to prevent transfer of smells and flavour, ideally in a fish refrigerator. This keeps the fish at around 0°C (a few degrees colder than other foods are kept). It has drawers in which the fish are placed, surrounded by ice. Drain holes at the bottom of each drawer allow water from melting ice to run off.

Keep prepared fish separate from unprepared fish (which will not have been washed). To reduce the risk of confusion (thinking that a fillet of turbot is cod or halibut), and the transfer of smells and flavour from the stronger types, it is best to keep different varieties of fish apart.

Ready-to-eat cooked fish, such as smoked mackerel, should be stored on the shelves above raw fish and other raw foodstuffs to avoid cross contamination.

Cooking and finishing basic fish dishes

People are becoming more adventurous in the varieties of fish they are willing to try, and in the ways in which they are cooked. Travel abroad and the popularity of ethnic restaurants are big factors in this trend.

Dry cooking methods

Fish has tender flesh, which does not take long to cook. This means that small whole fish and the various cuts of fish can be fried, grilled or baked. The combination of high temperatures, dry heat and short cooking times emphasises the natural flavour and moistness of the fish.

Careful timing and control of temperatures are essential, with no delay between the finish of cooking and service, otherwise the dish will be spoilt. If the temperature is too high, or cooking too long, the fish can get dried out, burnt, and break apart. If the temperature is too low, the fish can become soggy and pale in appearance. To avoid these problems:

- check the oil or the grill is hot before starting to cook the fish

- cook the presentation side (i.e. the better-looking side) of the fish first – for a fillet, this is the side which was nearer the bone; for a whole flat fish, it is the unskinned side (when the white skin has been left on)

- keep an eye on the fish throughout cooking – because the dry methods are so fast, even a few minutes' lack of attention can spoil the food

- turn the fish halfway through cooking, so that both sides brown: this is only necessary in deep frying if the fish floats to the surface

- reduce the temperature during cooking for larger cuts and whole fish (so that the fish is cooked through to the centre, but not overcooked on the outside)

- do not put too much fish at one time in the pan, grill or fryer. Because the pan/fryer is so crowded, it will be very difficult to handle the fish without damaging it. The temperature of the frying oil will drop, so the fish cooks more slowly and absorbs oil.

Constant attention to the fish during cooking is also necessary for safety. The high temperatures mean there is a risk of fire. Oil or fat will start to smoke when it is too hot and, if left on, the heat will cause the oil to burst into flames. See Section 2.

Fire safety in frying

1 Do not overfill the fryer with fat or oil. The pan should be no more than two-thirds full when the fat is hot – remember fat and oil expand when hot.

2 Never use the fryer beyond the operating temperatures. Check thermostats regularly.

3 Never plunge wet foods into hot fat – excess water can cause a fat 'explosion'. Always drain or dry foods first.

4 Drain and filter oil daily.

5 Change oil when it begins to discolour and 'break down' – the taste of the food, smell of the fat and effects on food colour are good guides to this. Remember, fat which is in this condition will have a lower 'flash point' temperature than clean fat – and presents a real fire hazard (as well as spoiling food).

6 Do not rest trays or pans on the edge of the fryer. If it is 'knocked into the pan', fires or serious splash burns could occur.

Frying

There are three ways of frying fish:

- *shallow frying* – the fish is cooked in a pan on top of the stove, with a little oil or fat

- *stir frying* – the fish, cut into small pieces, is cooked very quickly in a wok or frying pan, alongside the other ingredients for the dish

- *deep frying* – the fish is entirely submerged in oil or fat in a deep fryer (more details of this method are given in Section 21).

The oil or fat helps carry heat to the fish. It needs to withstand the high temperatures of frying – butter, for example, will smoke and burn before getting hot enough to cook the fish. Flavour is another consideration: it should complement and never dominate the fish. For health reasons, products high in polyunsaturates and low in saturates are best.

If some of the coating or small pieces of fish fall off during cooking, scoop them out of the pan before they burn and spoil the flavour of the oil. When you are shallow frying large batches, change the oil or fat from time to time, and wipe the pan clean with absorbent kitchen paper.

Most varieties of fish can be fried, although oil-rich fish (e.g. mackerel, herring, sprat, tuna, anchovy and salmon) is not usually deep fried. A coating (of breadcrumbs, for example) helps the dish colour attractively, keeps the natural moistness of the flesh, and prevents too much oil being absorbed.

Grilling

Whole fish is scored before grilling. Make two or three short parallel cuts through the skin on each side of the thickest part of the fish. This helps the heat get to the flesh, and stops the skin splitting open of its own accord, which looks untidy. (Crimping is another name for scoring.)

During grilling, brush or spoon a little oil or fat over the fish. This prevents the flesh from drying out. Fish such as herring and mackerel, which are protected by natural oils, may not require basting.

Where possible, use a special wire fish holder or tray to make handling the delicate fish easier. Grease the holder (or the grill bars if you are not using a holder or tray), to stop the fish from sticking.

Baking

The fish needs protection from the direct heat of the oven. This is why it is enclosed in a coating of some sort (e.g. breadcrumbs), or placed in a covered ovenproof dish or parcel of foil, paper, vine leaves, etc. Another way is to brush the fish with oil or butter before cooking (some chefs call this roasting), or with a marinade, wine or other flavouring liquid before and during baking.

Follow recipe cooking times and temperatures carefully, so that you can be sure the fish is cooked. If there is any doubt, use a temperature probe to check. The centre of the fish should be 70°C to 75°C.

Grilling mackerel, using a tray (on left), and wire fish holder (on right).

Deep poaching salmon. Below: the ingredients for the cooking liquid (court-bouillon).

Wet cooking methods

The moistness of fish makes it a good partner with the gentler cooking that occurs in poaching, steaming and boiling. Spices, herbs, lemon juice, wine, vinegar, chopped onions or shallots, and sliced mushrooms are some of the ingredients that can be used to add flavour to the cooking liquid, and to the fish. The liquid can become the basis for a delicious sauce.

Poaching

This is a popular way of cooking most varieties of fish, and in particular those with a more delicate flavour or texture. Larger cuts and whole fish are completely covered by the cooking liquid – this is called *deep poaching*. Smaller cuts and fillets are usually partially covered – called *shallow poaching*.

For deep poaching, there are special pans (called kettles) which have a close fitting lid, a perforated tray for lifting the fish in and out, and come in various shapes and sizes to suit the fish. Cooking is done on top of the stove.

A low-sided saucepan, which has a tight-fitting lid and ovenproof handles, can be used for shallow poaching. Cooking is started on the top of the stove, although some chefs prefer to put the fish straight in the oven.

Once the fish has been added, the liquid should be kept just below boiling point. For deep poaching whole fish, and for shallow poaching, the liquid is usually cold to start with. For deep poaching cuts of fish, the liquid is normally hot.

If the fish is not covered with the liquid, as in shallow poaching, place a piece of greased, greaseproof paper over it (cut to fit the shape of the pan). It is best to use a lid as well, to trap the moist air around the fish.

In deep poaching, the fish is often allowed to cool in the cooking liquid. This helps the flavours to develop more fully, and to keep the fish moist. Cooling must happen quickly to avoid the risk of food contamination. Place the kettle in a cool room, or in a sink with cold water. Replace the water regularly until the cooking liquid has cooled. Transfer the fish to a clean container, with some of the poaching liquid, cover and put in the refrigerator.

Steaming

Steaming is suitable for fillets of white fish, and for various cuts (but not the small ones). Small whole fish can also be steamed. Oily fish is not usually steamed.

Before cooking, lightly moisten the fish with a little fish stock, lemon juice, milk or water (or follow specific recipe instructions). Season to taste (but avoid black pepper which will look unappetising against the white background of the cooked fish).

Boiling

Some recipes require fish to be boiled, for example if you are making a fish stew (e.g. bouillabaisse) or a fish soup. The fish does not need long cooking, around 10 minutes being typical.

Combination cooking

If your workplace has a combi-oven, this means the normal oven operation can be switched to introduce steam into the compartment. This means you can use higher temperatures than a steamer (so cooking time is reduced), while there is less risk of the fish drying out (which might happen in baking).

Finishing and presenting

There are a number of ways of testing whether fish is cooked enough. Choose the method that is least likely to damage the appearance of the finished dish:

- press gently with the back of a teaspoon – it should give under the pressure and not spring back

- insert a cocktail stick into the thickest part of the flesh – there should be little resistance

- cooked fish flesh loses its translucent (see-through) appearance and becomes opaque. This is particularly noticeable on white fillets.

If the fish breaks up, it is overcooked.

When fish is cooked correctly, it can be easily taken off the bone.

Portioning

For fillets and goujons, you will be told the number per portion. Darnes will normally be in single-portion size (having been cut to the correct size before cooking). With whole fish, it will either be one fish per portion (e.g. trout, herring), or for large fish (e.g. salmon), so many portions per fish. With whitebait, which are tiny, portioning is usually by weight. Sardines can be small, when you might have to serve three or four per portion.

Saucing

Some sauces are made with the cooking liquid (after poaching). This is done quickly, while the cooked fish is kept warm in the hot cupboard. The fish is then coated with the sauce, sufficient to cover it all over, but not so much as to overwhelm it. Sometimes the assembled dish is placed for a few moments under the hot grill, so the surface of the sauce browns attractively.

Take care to drain the fish well, otherwise the added sauce will turn rather watery, or become streaky.

Dressing

This has two meanings: garnishing (see overleaf) and accompanying by sauce, e.g. some grilled and deep fried fish dishes are traditionally accompanied by tartare sauce. The sauce is offered separately, or put to one side of the fish on the plate. Do not put the sauce over the fish or it will spoil the crisp texture. Besides, not all customers want the sauce.

Gratinating with cheese

Some fish dishes have grated cheese added at the last moment. The serving dish is placed under a hot grill, until the cheese melts, bubbles with the heat and turns an attractive brown colour. Some fish sauces are browned in this way. And fish can be gratinated in the oven, coated with breadcrumbs and melted butter.

117

Garnishing

Simple garnishes which work well with fish dishes include:

- parsley (fresh or deep fried)
- slices or segments or halves of lemon
- fresh herbs such as dill and fennel

and with deep fried dishes:

- salad arrangement, e.g. lettuce, slices or shapes of cucumber, quarters or slices of tomato
- pickled vegetables, e.g. cucumber, gherkins.

If you have to make up your own garnish, choose items that will provide a good balance and contrast of colour, flavour and texture.

Quality points of finished dish

The finished dish should look right, and have good flavour, texture and aroma. If you do not have a photograph to compare the appearance with, your manager and more experienced colleagues will give you guidance. Once you are familiar with the dish, you will have a clear idea of what to expect.

Many problems with quality happen because there is too much delay between the finish of cooking and service. If this happens, deep fried fish should not be covered (but even then, it will loose its crisp texture quite quickly).

Fillets of sole meunière

SERVES 1

2 × 75 g	fillets of sole	2 × 3 oz
12 g	butter	½ oz
5 ml	oil	1 tsp
	flour, seasoned if required	

For finishing

25 g	butter	1 oz
3	slices peeled lemon	3
	squeeze of lemon juice	
	fresh parsley, chopped	

1 In a suitable frying pan, heat the oil, then add the butter.

2 Lightly coat both sides of the fillets in the seasoned flour, shake off any surplus and place the fish into the pan, presentation side downwards.

> This is the side which will look best after cooking, the side which was nearest the bone of the fish. →

3 Half way through cooking, turn the fish over. A small fillet will take 3 to 5 minutes to cook a golden brown.

4 Place the fish in a warm serving dish, presentation side upwards. Sprinkle with chopped parsley.

> Some chefs put the chopped parsley in with the hot butter (step 5). →

5 Place the butter into a clean, hot frying pan, shake the pan until the butter has turned an even golden brown colour. Add the squeeze of lemon juice. This will cause the butter to froth. Pour over the fish, decorate with the lemon slices and serve at once.

> Butter done this way is called *beurre noisette*. →

Fruity plaice turbans

The Rice Bureau

SERVES 6

6	fillets of plaice	6
25 g	butter, melted	1 oz
Stuffing		
100 g	cooked risotto rice	4 oz
25 g	sultanas	1 oz
40 g	raisins	1½ oz
2	sticks celery, finely chopped	2
40 g	butter, melted	1½ oz
75 g	peeled prawns	3 oz

> Skinned and trimmed. →

> The stuffing ingredients are all mixed together. →

1 Fold the fillets in half lengthways, skin side innermost. Brush with the butter and curl loosely.

3 Put in an ovenproof dish. Spoon stuffing into the centre of the fish, and around it.

4 Cover with foil and bake at 190°C for about 15 minutes.

> ← Garnish with prawns, lemon slices and sprigs of dill.

This method is suitable for *small whole fish*, e.g. herrings, trout, sardines, *whole flat fish*, e.g. lemon or Dover sole, *fillets* e.g. plaice, and *steaks*, e.g. halibut.

By using wholemeal macaroni, the fibre content of this dish would be increased (see Section 15).

Tartare sauce is the traditional accompaniment to this dish.

Deep fried goujons of plaice

SERVES 2

4 × 75 g	plaice fillets cut into goujons	4 × 3 oz
2	lemon wedges	2
2	sprigs parsley	2
50 g	flour, seasoned if required	2 oz
1	egg beaten with little milk	1
50 g	breadcrumbs	2 oz

1 Coat the goujons with the flour, beaten egg and breadcrumbs. Shake off any excess.

> Coat the goujons one at a time!

2 Roll each goujon lightly between the palms of your hands to neaten the shape.

3 Deep fry at 185°C until crisp and golden brown (about 2 minutes).

4 Drain well, then place on a warm serving dish lined with a dish paper. Decorate with the lemon wedges and plain parsley (or deep fried).

> Do not cover. Serve at once.

If you are using frozen cod steaks, do not defrost, and increase cooking time to 15 minutes.
For a larger portion, use 225 g (8 oz) steaks

Grilled salmon steaks

SERVES 4

4 × 225 g	salmon steaks	4 × 8 oz
Coating		
50 g	flour, seasoned if required	2 oz
50 g	oil or melted butter	2 oz
	seasoning to taste	
Garnish		
4	lemon wedges or halves	4
8	slices parsley butter (page 105)	8
	sprigs of parsley	

1 Coat the fish with the seasoned flour. Shake off any surplus, then brush lightly with oil or melted butter.

> Brand the salmon before grilling, for an attractive presentation.

2 Grill until the fish develops a good colour. Turn over when half-cooked (after about 6 minutes) and continue grilling until the fish is cooked (about another 6 minutes). Brush with more oil or melted butter if the fish starts to dry out.

3 Arrange the steaks on a warm serving dish. Decorate with the parsley and lemon. Serve accompanied by slices of parsley butter (placed in a sauceboat or dish with iced water).

This uses a variation on mayonnaise (page 125)

Fish and pasta creole

by Sea Fish Industry Authority

SERVES 20

100 g	butter	4 oz
1–2	cloves garlic, crushed and peeled	1–2
10 sticks	(1 head) celery, washed and diced	10 sticks
1½ litre	fish stock	2½ pt
900 g	sweetcorn (frozen or tinned)	2 lb
3–3½ kg	coley or monkfish fillets, cubed	7½ lb
1	bay leaf	1
450 g	macaroni	1 lb
4 × A2½ cans	whole tomatoes	4 × A2½ cans
	seasoning to taste	
	fresh parsley, chopped (garnish)	

1 Melt the butter in a large saucepan and lightly fry the garlic and celery.

2 Add the stock, sweetcorn, fish, bay leaf and macaroni. Season and gently simmer for 10 to 12 minutes until the fish and macaroni are tender.

3 Add tomatoes (drained). Reheat briefly, adjust seasoning. Remove bayleaf.

4 Serve hot, decorated with chopped parsley.

> For easier eating and better presentation, remove the bone (pierce with the point of a sharp knife) and the skin (pull away carefully with a knife, or roll round the prong of a fork).

Poached salmon steaks with sherry mayonnaise

by Dufrais

SERVES 4

15 ml	sherry vinegar	1 tbsp
2.5 ml	French mustard	½ tsp
15 ml	pasteurised egg yolk (1 yolk)	1 tbsp
	pinch of sugar, salt and freshly milled black pepper	
150 ml	oil	¼ pt
4 × 150 g	salmon steaks	4 × 6 oz
150 ml	fish stock	¼ pt
15 ml	sherry vinegar	1 tbsp

1 Place the egg yolk, sugar, salt, pepper and mustard in a small bowl. Beat in the vinegar. Beat in the oil a drop at a time until thick and creamy.

2 Poach the salmon in the fish stock and vinegar for about 15 minutes. Drain and serve with the sauce.

Cheesy baked cod steaks

by Sea Fish Industry Authority

SERVES 4

4 × 175 g	cod steaks	4 × 6 oz
	knob of butter or margarine	
15 ml	Worcestershire sauce	1 tbsp
1	small packet plain potato crisps	1
50 g	grated cheese (e.g. Cheddar)	2 oz

1 Arrange fish in an ovenproof dish. Dot with butter or margarine. Sprinkle with Worcestershire sauce.

2 Bake for 10 minutes at 200°C.

3 Crush crisps and mix with cheese. Sprinkle over fish and bake for a further 10 minutes or so: the crisps will brown quickly.

1 What chopping board should you use for preparing fish? What must you check about the board before using it?

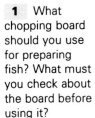

7 Describe some of the things you might notice about 'fresh' fillets of fish which would make you doubt their freshness.

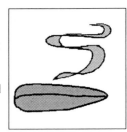

13 Identify the preparation methods used for the fish in the photograph below. (Some involve more than one.)

2 What sink do you use to wash fish, and what should you check before starting?

8 What do you do if you find some fillets of fish, which you need to prepare immediately, are frozen because the fridge has been turned too cold?

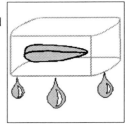

3 What are your workplace rules for storing fish before preparation?

9 What is special about the knife used for filleting flat fish?

14 Name two dishes which use a) whole fish, b) fillets of fish.

MENU

Grilled Lemon Sole

Poached Halibut fillet

4 What are your workplace rules for storing fish after preparation and before cooking?

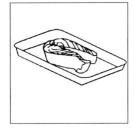

10 Is this fish flat or round? When it is filleted in the way shown, how many fillets will you get?

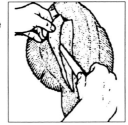

15 Name two fish dishes which use a) goujons, b) darnes or steaks.

MENU

Deep fried goujons of plaice

Baked salmon steak

5 Is fish high or low risk food in terms of food safety? Give the reason for your answer.

11 Name the cut being prepared in this illustration. How many pieces would you serve per portion for a) starter, b) main course?

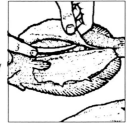

6 Describe the general points which indicate that whole fresh fish is of the right quality.

12 Name the cut in this illustration. Approximately what weight of fish would you prepare for a) starter, b) main course?

1 For two tasks involved in cooking fish, describe the safety procedures you must follow.

2 Identify some ways by which bacteria might contaminate fish during its preparation and cooking. What can you do to reduce the risk?

7 Name the cooking utensil, shown here, b) state the cooking method is it used for, c) name two types of fish that might be cooked by this method, d) give the purpose of adding the various ingredients shown to the cooking liquid.

12 Comment on the presentation of the two fish dishes shown here. Say what you like, and what you would do differently, and why.

3 What is the maximum time for keeping hot 3 of the fish dishes you cook? What happens to the dish then?

8 If a customer asks for a low-fat fish dish, what cooking method would you suggest?

13 When the sauce is too thin for a fish dish you serve at work, what can be done to correct it?

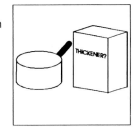

4 Why is this oil a fire hazard? How do you stop oil spoiling in this way?

9 Describe some ways of telling that fish is cooked.

14 What can you do to make sure that fish which has been fried does not look greasy on the customer's plate?

5 This oil is clean. The chef is lowering the food in carefully so as not to splash himself with hot oil. But what else should he be careful not to do?

10 What happens to fish if it is overcooked? How can you prevent this happening?

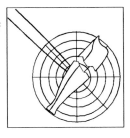

15 If a customer at your workplace complains about a fish dish, what is the procedure you should follow?

6 Not much care being taken here! What are the rules when shallow frying to avoid this happening?

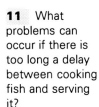

Cartoon with thanks to De Vere Hotels.

11 What problems can occur if there is too long a delay between cooking fish and serving it?

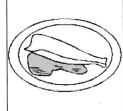

16 If the complaint is because the fish was not hot, what might have caused the problem? How can you check that fish is at the right temperature when served?

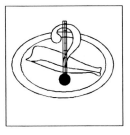

Photographs of finished dishes on this page and page 117, with thanks to Forte Crest, Metropole Hotels and Toby Restaurants.

? Knowledge check
Prepare and cook basic fish dishes

Skills check
Prepare and cook basic fish dishes
Unit 2ND2

NVQ SVQ

level 2

For help to answer questions
relating to:

Health and safety

? safe working practices

Hazards include the use of knives,
pieces of equipment, trays of fish,
etc. which are heavy or difficult to
handle, and burning yourself from
hot surfaces and liquids.

Fish which is wet can be slippery.
Some varieties (e.g. trout) are
particularly slippery, because the
skin is covered in slime.

The fins of some fish are quite sharp.
Take care not to pierce yourself.

The kettles used for poaching whole
fish are heavy when filled. The
bigger ones can be awkward as the
liquid sloshes up and down if you are
not careful. Fill the kettle by pouring
from a smaller container. Ask
someone to take the other end, when
you have to move a full kettle.

Frying with oil is one of the most
dangerous kitchen tasks, because of
the risk of the oil bursting into
flames (see pages 14 and 31 for
advice).

Food hygiene

? importance of good hygiene

Like meat, fish is a high risk food.
Its high moisture content suits
certain types of bacteria including
Staphylococcus aureus which is often
carried by people (see page 38).

Some raw fish will already be
carrying harmful bacteria. This can
happen at any stage when it has
been handled, or because of pollution
in the sea.

? importance of time and temperature

Bacteria increase rapidly in numbers
at the right temperature. The
dangers are increased when the fish
is kept hot for a long time, and if the
fish is to be served cold.

? main contamination threats

Other food (e.g. fresh vegetables/
fruit), food handlers, dirty
equipment/work area, harmful
cleaning substances, foreign bodies
(e.g. piece of broken glass).

? products not for immediate use

Store above 63°C or below 5°C.

Product knowledge

? quality points for fresh fish

The fish should be very well chilled.
The appearance and the smell should
be right for the type of fish, e.g.:
whole salmon: *skin* bright, shiny and
undamaged, *scales* firmly attached,
eyes bright, clear and full, *gills*
bright red, *flesh* firm and springy to
the touch, *smell* fresh.

? quality points for cooked dishes

Describe how the dish should look
(appearance, consistency), smell
(aroma), and taste *(texture, flavour)*.

? preparation methods

These are washing, trimming,
gutting, descaling, filleting, skinning,
portioning, coating.

? cuts of fish

These are fillet, goujon, whole,
tronçon and darne.

? cooking methods

These are: baking, grilling, frying,
poaching, steaming, combination
cooking, boiling. Some are not
suitable for certain fish, e.g. oil-rich
fish is not normally deep fried or
steamed.

? identifying when dishes are cooked

Some methods were given in the
text: using a cocktail stick, pressing
with a spoon, looking at the
appearance, and removing the bone.

Healthy catering practices

? replacing high fat ingredients

A plain flour coating adds no fat to
the fish, but a breadcrumb coating
will if the egg wash method is used
(there is fat in the egg yolk), rather
more if butter is used. Remind
yourself of the tips on page 130 for
replacing cream, butter, etc.

? fats/oils for healthy eating

See page 110.

? cooking methods, etc. to reduce fat

You can begin by eliminating frying.
Since this involves cooking in oil, the
fish will have more oil by the time it
is served. There are ways in which
the potential harm to health can be
reduced (e.g. by cooking at the right
temperatures, and using good quality
oil which is high in polyunsaturates,
see page 110).

Grilling involves some oil, to keep
the fish moist. In place of this, you
could consider using a marinade
which has only a little oil or lemon
juice.

Baking, steaming and poaching do
not require oil (but watch for recipes
which use butter or margarine for
flavour or to provide moistness).
However, the sauce which
accompanies a poached fish dish can
be quite rich, especially if butter and
cream have been added. Low-fat
yogurt, quark and fromage frais are
healthier alternatives.

? increasing fibre content of dishes

Coatings made with wholemeal flour
will have higher fibre content.

? reducing salt

See page 110.

Use this to check your progress against
the performance criteria.

Element 1

Prepare fish for cooking

Get your preparation areas and
equipment ready for use ☐ PC

Select fish of the type, quality and
quantity required ☐ PC

△ Fish: flat white fish, round white fish, oily fish

Identify problems with the quality of
fish/other ingredients and report them ☐ PC

△ Other ingredients: flour, melted butter,
breadcrumbs, milk, egg wash

Use basic preparation methods
appropriate to the fish cut ☐ PC

△ Preparation methods: washing, trimming, gutting,
descaling, filleting, skinning, portioning, coating
Fish cut: fillet, goujon, whole, tronçon/darne

Combine fish with other ingredients
to meet dish requirements ☐ PC

Correctly store fish not for
immediate use ☐ PC

Clean preparation areas and
equipment after use ☐ PC

Prioritise and carry out your work in an
organised, efficient and safe manner ☐ PC

Element 2

Cook and finish basic fish dishes

Get your cooking areas and
equipment ready for use ☐ PC

Cook fish using appropriate method
for type of fish and fish cut ☐ PC

△ Methods: baking, grilling, frying, poaching,
steaming, combination cooking, boiling

Finish dish using appropriate
method ☐ PC

△ Methods: dressing, garnishing, saucing,
gratinating with cheese, portioning

Correctly store fish dishes not for
immediate service ☐ PC

Clean cooking areas and equipment
after use ☐ PC

Identify problems with the quality of
the dish and report these promptly ☐ PC

Prioritise and carry out your work in an
organised, efficient and safe manner ☐ PC

Preparing and cooking basic
sauces and soups

Preparing and cooking sauces

There are many hundreds of sauces, especially when you take into account the creations of individual chefs. A good sauce adds interest to the food – meat, poultry, fish, vegetables, pasta, etc. It can give variety of texture, of flavour, or colour, and give the dish a delicious aroma.

Some sauces are designed to complement the food's flavours (e.g. gravy with roast meat), others to provide contrast (e.g. cranberry with turkey). Some sauces are rich, using butter, cream, egg yolks, etc. Others have no fat at all, and help balance the rich food (e.g. apple sauce with pork).

The consistency of a sauce – whether it is thin or thick – is another factor. Gravy, made in the traditional way with the juices from the roasting meat and stock, is thin and clear, like stock, but most other sauces are thick naturally (e.g. apple sauce), or because a thickening agent (e.g. flour and cornflour) has been added.

Vinaigrette may be quite thin, depending on the oil which has been used. Mayonnaise uses the binding ability of egg yolk as a thickener, while fresh egg custard (which has to be cooked) uses the setting ability of egg yolk.

As these examples indicate, most sauces are variations on a few, basic methods. This section deals with two ways of thickening hot sauces, and four cold sauces.

Hot sauces

A *roux* sauce is thickened at the start of cooking, by heating fat or oil and flour together. Other ingredients may also be present, e.g. chopped vegetables. The recipe liquid is then added, a little at a time and stirring well.

The flour thickens the liquid. The fat or oil coats the tiny granules of flour, and helps keep them apart. Otherwise you would get a very lumpy mixture. Vigorous stirring is the other way of keeping the flour granules from sticking to each other.

Béchamel/Mornay sauce

Makes 1 litre (2 pts)

100 g	margarine or butter	4 oz
100 g	flour	4 oz
1 litre	milk	2 pts
1	onion, with bay leaf attached to it by a clove (*onion clouté*)	1
	seasoning to taste	

For mornay sauce

100 g	grated cheese (Cheddar, or half Gruyère, half Parmesan)	4 oz

1 In a saucepan, gently warm the milk with the onion clouté for 5 to 8 minutes. This is known as *infusing*.

2 Melt the fat in a second saucepan, add the flour and mix. Cook over a low heat for 4 to 5 minutes, making sure that the mixture does not start browning.

3 Remove the onion from the milk and set aside. Slowly blend the hot milk into the roux, stirring till smooth with each addition of milk.

4 Return the onion clouté to the sauce and bring to the boil. Reduce the heat and simmer gently for 20 minutes. Skim off any fat or impurities that rise to the surface.

5 Discard the onion. Pour the sauce through a conical strainer.

6 Check seasoning and consistency – the sauce should be creamy and smooth enough to pour.

7 You have now made *béchamel sauce*. To turn it into *mornay sauce*, add the grated cheese, and stir until thoroughly blended.

> A roux is a blend of flour and fat (usually in equal quantities) cooked for a few minutes to make a white roux (as in this recipe), or for longer to make a blond roux (sandy colour) or brown roux (light-brown colour).

> When you add the first liquid, there may be a quite vigorous reaction in the pan. If this happens, let the roux cool before adding any more. Blond and brown roux get much hotter than white roux, so always allow to cool slightly before adding liquid.

> Don't add more liquid until the roux mixture is smooth. Vigorous mixing should do the trick!

A *starch-thickened* sauce is made differently. The thickening agent is added to the simmering liquid. The liquid is brought back to the boil, and simmered until the starch flavour has gone (between 5 and 15 minutes).

Recipes say which method to follow. By comparison, you will probably find starch-thickened sauces easier and quicker than making a roux.

Cornflour (made from maize) and arrowroot (made from the root of a West Indian plant) blend easily with liquid (thanks to the very fine particles) and thicken quickly (because of the high starch content). Nevertheless, it is best to blend the flour with a little cold water or some of the recipe liquid. Once you have a smooth paste (this won't take more than a few minutes of stirring), add it to the liquid, stirring all the while.

Fécule (or potato flour), rice flour, besan flour (made from chick-peas) and plain flour can also be used. These should also be mixed to a paste first, with some of the recipe liquid. Flour can be mixed with butter to form *beurre manié*.

Some cold sauces

People have different views on the way to make a *vinaigrette*: what ratio of oil to vinegar to use, what oil (olive oil is a favourite, for its fine flavour, but it is expensive), which vinegar (or whether lemon juice is preferable) and the type of mustard.

The traditional recipe is given opposite. Popular variations are: adding garlic, using cider or wine vinegar, or a vinegar flavoured with herbs, or adding fresh herbs.

Mint sauce, usually offered with roast and grilled lamb, combines the strong, characteristic flavour of freshly chopped mint with vinegar. A little sugar is added to counteract the sharpness of the vinegar. Wash the mint well under cold running water, and pick the leaves away from the stalks (which you do not use). Some chefs chop the leaves with sugar, otherwise the sugar can be added later. To give the flavours time to develop, prepare the sauce about half an hour before use, longer than this, the mint looks tired.

Another variation is to soak the chopped mint for half an hour in a little hot water and the sugar. Vinegar (or white wine) is added before service.

You will find fewer variations between recipes for fresh *horseradish sauce*, a traditional accompaniment for roast beef and smoked trout. The main ingredient is the root of the horseradish plant, thick, white, with a pungent smell. It is peeled, then finely grated. A little vinegar is added, possibly some mustard and sugar, then the mixture blended with lightly whipped cream. Chill before serving, to give the flavours a chance to develop.

Getting a good balance of flavours is the main skill in making vinaigrette, mint and horseradish sauces. With *mayonnaise*, a greater challenge (at least until you are well practised at making it) is getting a thick, smooth sauce, that does not separate. Some tips:

- collect all your ingredients, so that once started you can proceed without interruption

- use oil which is at room temperature, and take the egg yolks out of the refrigerator half an hour or so in advance

- dribble the oil in very slowly at first (see photograph); you can pour faster for the second half of the oil, provided you see the mixture is holding together

- if the mixture does separate, begin again with fresh yolks and a little cold water, dribbling and whisking the unsuccessful mixture into it

- alternatively (if you are more confident) begin again with a warm water, whisking the mixture into this.

In view of the risks of *salmonella* being present in the eggs, you should only use pasteurised egg yolks to make fresh mayonnaise. Because mayonnaise is not cooked, any bacteria introduced by using fresh egg yolks (the traditional method) would multiply and could cause food poisoning.

Vinaigrette

MAKES 100 ml (4 fl oz)

75 ml	salad oil	3 fl oz
25 ml	vinegar	1 fl oz
½ tsp	French mustard	½ tsp
	seasoning to taste	

1 Place all the ingredients into a mixing bowl and whisk together thoroughly until combined.

2 Before use, whisk again.

> Oil and vinegar do not mix naturally. Hence need to whisk.

> The droplets of oil stay suspended in the vinegar for only a short time. The longer the mixture is shaken or stirred, the smaller the droplets become, and the longer the emulsion will last.

Mayonnaise

MAKES 1 litre (2 pts)

125 ml	pasteurised egg yolks (equivalent to 5 yolks)	¼ pt
½ tsp	mustard	½ tsp
75–125 ml	white vinegar	3–4 fl oz
1 litre	olive (or salad) oil	2 pt
	squeeze of lemon juice	
	seasoning to taste	

1 Place the egg yolks into a large mixing bowl.

2 Add the seasoning, and the mustard diluted in half the quantity of vinegar.

3 Whisk until thoroughly combined.

4 Add the oil (which should be at room temperature) in a thin stream, while whisking continuously. When the sauce becomes very thick, thin it as required using the remaining vinegar. The mayonnaise should be thick enough to hold its shape when placed on a serving spoon.

5 Finish with the lemon juice and check the seasoning.

> Some chefs use all the vinegar at the beginning. If the mayonnaise ends up too thick, you can add a little hot water.

> The photograph on the opposite page shows the oil being added.

> Unlike vinaigrette, mayonnaise will stay mixed. This is because lecithin (in the egg yolk) forms a thin, slightly sticky layer around each droplet of oil.

> Beating the mayonnaise thoroughly gets very tiny droplets of oil, forming a relatively stable network thanks to the lecithin.

Preparation methods for basic sauces

Chopping – cutting into pieces. Onions, carrots, herbs, bacon, eggs and apples are examples of ingredients which are chopped before going into sauces. If the purpose is mainly to give flavour, and the sauce is later strained or blended in a food mixer, then the recipe will say 'roughly chop'. If the chopped ingredients will be part of the final sauce, then they should be cut quite small and evenly, or to a specific shape if the recipe says this.

Grating – this requires the use of a grater, so that you get fine shreds of the food. The hard varieties of cheese (e.g. Cheddar and Parmesan) are usually grated for use in a sauce. This is more practical than trying to chop the cheese with a knife.

Mixing – combining ingredients together. When recipes say 'mix' they usually mean stir with a spoon, until all the ingredients are evenly distributed in the sauce. There is no need to get air into the mixture (which is the purpose of whisking, see below). Nor is care required to avoid beating air out of the mixture (if this is a concern, then the term 'folded' is used, see page 178).

Whisking – this is normally done with a whisk. The shape of the whisk, when used vigorously, is very effective at beating the liquid. The egg yolks in mayonnaise are whisked to make the oil break up into tiny droplets. Double cream is whisked to incorporate enough air bubbles for the cream to thicken. With egg whites, the whisking is most vigorous, so that millions of tiny air bubbles are trapped in the mixture, giving it lightness and much greater volume.

Blending has two meanings: a) thoroughly mixing two or more ingredients, b) using a liquidiser or food processor. The mechanical method results in a thorough mixing and, when there are chopped vegetables, etc. in the mixture, these are puréed at the same time. Some chefs prefer to make mayonnaise in this way. The rapidly rotating blades of the processor break the oil up into minute droplets.

Straining – pouring the sauce through a strainer (usually a conical shaped one). The fine mesh of the strainer traps the solids, allowing the liquid to pass through. Sometimes thicker sauces are agitated with a ladle to help them filter through.

Chef's Tip

Using a metal spoon for stirring in a metal pan can discolour the sauce or soup (especially if an aluminium pan is used). A plastic spoon or wooden spatula is best.

Many chefs use a spatula when making a roux. The straight edge makes it easier to keep food from sticking to the bottom of the pan and burning.

Here are some ways to prevent a skin forming on a sauce when it is cooling:

- place small pieces of butter on the surface, or brush over with melted butter
- rest a circle of greaseproof paper over the surface
- float over the surface a thin film of milk, stock or water (as appropriate to the flavour of the sauce).

Cooking methods

Roux and starch-thickened hot sauces have to be *boiled* or *simmered* for a time. This is to get the starch to do its job as a thickener.

There is a common view on what boiling means: bubbling at the surface, and the liquid is at 100°C (although the exact temperature depends on how far your kitchen is above or below sea level).

Simmering is a gentler cooking. Some say that the temperature should be a few degrees below boiling. What everyone agrees is that the bubbling at the surface of the liquid should be kept very gentle.

With most sauces, 20 to 60 minutes is long enough for the boiling/simmering stage, but if various ingredients need more time to become tender, or if the volume of the liquid has to be reduced (to give a stronger-flavoured sauce) this could be a few hours.

When sauces are simmering, you may see a scum forming on the surface – this is impurities and fat. Scoop them away using a ladle or large spoon. The aim is to collect the scum, not the sauce.

Stir sauces from time to time while they are cooking. This keeps all the sauce at the same temperature, encourages the flavours to blend, and reduces the risk of burning at the bottom of the pan. If the sauce is thickening too much, add more recipe liquid.

Judging quality

The *quality* of the final sauce can be compared with what you know it should be. It is more than personal preference, e.g. you may dislike the taste of horseradish sauce. Quality is what people see, taste and smell, experiences that are not easy to put in words. There are several aspects, many of which overlap:

- texture – smooth, cream, oily, thin, chunky, etc.
- flavour – sharp, sweet, of particular ingredients (e.g. mint, fish stock, herbs)
- aroma – some sauce ingredients have a distinct and quite strong aroma, e.g. garlic, mint, vinegar, wine
- appearance – colour mainly, but also texture and consistency
- consistency – thickness or thinness.

Finishing methods

Straining the sauce before it is served is recommended when a skin has formed while the sauce was kept hot. This may happen with roux-based and starch-thickened sauces. Another reason for straining is to remove any lumps left from the thickening stage.

Do not strain sauces which are meant to have chopped or sliced vegetables, herbs, etc. in them. Horseradish and mint sauces are not strained for this reason. Vinaigrette and mayonnaise are not strained because there should be no need (and the straining process would encourage the oil to separate).

If the sauce incorporates cooking juices (from the pan used for roasting, frying or poaching), then the recipe will usually tell you to strain it. Otherwise the appearance of the sauce will be spoiled by burnt pieces of food, etc.

After straining hot sauces, reheat before serving.

All sauces should be checked for *seasoning* at some stage. This means tasting the sauce (use a clean spoon each time you taste). If the sauce has been simmering, or even if it has been kept hot for some time, you should check the seasoning again, just before service.

Seasoning is a matter of personal preference. You need to strike a balance, so the sauce tastes right to most customers. Those who want extra salt or pepper can always add their own. It is very difficult (for you and for customers) to do anything about food that is overseasoned. Experience and the advice of colleagues will tell you what to look for.

The other final step sometimes necessary is to *adjust the consistency* (thickness/thinness) of the sauce. If roux-based or starch-thickened sauces are:

- too thick, add a little more of the recipe liquid (e.g. stock, wine), or cream (if the sauce is a rich one)
- too thin, boil the sauce vigorously to reduce the liquid content, or add a little more thickener. With a roux-based sauce, you will need to use arrowroot, cornflour, or one of the other starch thickeners.

Get the consistency of mayonnaise right at the time you make it (see recipe). With vinaigrette, the flavour and thorough blending of the oil and vinegar are the important points. Some oils give a thicker vinaigrette. For the other two cold sauces, you can add a little extra vinegar to compensate for too much chopped mint, and some more cream to the horseradish.

Preparing and cooking soups

Soups can be placed in categories, e.g. cream, broth and purée. The classification helps explain how they are cooked, and often forms part of the name, e.g. cream of mushroom soup.

Some names give nothing away about the method or the ingredients. Vichysoisse is an example. Made with potatoes and leeks which are puréed to give thickness, cream is often added as a finishing touch.

Preparation methods

Those explained earlier in this section (box on page 125) are: *chopping, mixing, blending* and *straining*.

When a recipe tells you to use chopped onion, it means an onion cut into small pieces. Finely chopped would be smaller than a pea, roughly chopped into pieces about 10 mm square.

Slicing produces differently shaped pieces. When a carrot is sliced, it is cut across the length of the carrot into coin-shapes. An onion sliced whole produces rings, or if cut in half and then sliced, half-rings.

While soups are being cooked, impurities and fat may rise to the surface and form a scum. This must be *skimmed* off before the impurities are boiled back into the liquid. Move the lip of a ladle around the surface of the soup, just under the scum, so that you scoop as much up as possible of the impurities, and the minimum amount of the soup.

When soups are *puréed*, this is done in a food processor, blender or liquidiser. Before such machines were widely available, chefs had to use a soup machine for large quantities, or a sieve for smaller amounts, pushing the vegetables, etc. through with a wooden mushroom.

More on creams, broths and purées

Cream – a thick soup to which cream is traditionally added. Most cream soups start with a roux, but purées can also be turned into a cream soup. Low fat yogurt is sometimes used to give a similar creamy texture, and a slightly sharp flavour.

Broth – plain-boiled soups served as they are cooked, with chopped vegetables and often barley, rice or pulses.

Purée – a thick soup with vegetables and/or pulses, puréed or blended in a food processor or liquidiser, e.g. lentil soup and potato soup.

Finishing methods

Adding cream is done to give the soup a rich flavour, and a creamy-colour. Cream soups have that name because cream is added as part of the recipe (it would be wrong to serve a cream soup without cream).

The cream is always added last, and then the soup carefully reheated without boiling. This is because cream is likely to separate when boiled, leaving fat globules floating around the top of the soup. This looks unpleasant, and the taste will become a fatty one.

Adding butter to a soup gives it a glossy appearance and rich taste. Use small pieces and stir in sufficiently for the butter just to melt. Serve the soup immediately.

Adjusting consistency and the *seasoning* of soup are approached in the same way as sauces (see earlier in this section). With a cream soup, remember that adding the cream will thin it slightly. Remember too, that you can't boil the soup after adding cream. If the soup is too thin, you will need to add cornflour (or similar thickening agent) and bring back to the boil at least five minutes before service, and before adding the cream.

Broths do not need thickening, although you may want to add a little extra stock if there is not enough liquid for the pieces of vegetable, rice, meat, etc. The ratio should be two-thirds liquid, one-third solids.

Purées should not be thickened either. The thickness comes from the breaking down of the ingredients (e.g. potato). You may need to thin the soup slightly, with some stock.

The flavours of any soup develop throughout the cooking. If you are using stock cubes or bouillon, these are often quite salty. While the soup is boiling or simmering, it reduces a little in quantity. For all these reasons, it is best to add the seasoning towards the end of cooking.

Garnishing is adding chopped parsley, leaves of watercress, croûtons (cubes of bread, fried in butter), decorative pieces of the main ingredient (e.g. cubes of cooked chicken breast in a chicken soup), dusting of cayenne pepper, a swirl of thick cream, yogurt, etc.

Garnishing is done to improve the appearance of the soup. What you are using should be appropriate for the soup. It can tell people something about the soup (e.g. pieces of sweetcorn in a sweetcorn soup).

The *quality points* to look for in the finished soup are similar to those for sauces: texture, flavour, aroma, appearance and consistency. If the vegetables in a broth are very soft, then the soup has been cooked too long.

1 How should you lift the lid off a saucepan of boiling liquid?

7 Why should a sauce or soup be covered while cooling?

13 What should you remember when tasting a sauce or soup, from a hygiene point of view?

2 What should you do if a saucepan is too large or heavy for you to lift safely?

8 What is a safe temperature for keeping a sauce or soup hot?

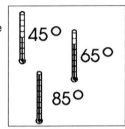

14 Say what you should pay special attention to when cleaning a sieve or food processor/liquidiser.

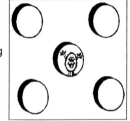

3 What sort of utensil should you use for stirring in an aluminium saucepan?

9 If after reheating a sauce or soup for the second time, there is still some left, what should be done with it? Why?

15 Give some ways in which you can garnish a soup (some ideas in the photo below). What is important to consider when choosing a garnish?

4 Say how you cool a hot sauce or soup. Why is this best from a food safety point of view?

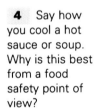

10 What can happen if you boil a soup or sauce which has already had cream added?

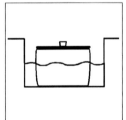

5 Why is it wrong to put a hot sauce or soup into the refrigerator or cold room?

11 For each of the preparation methods shown, name a sauce which uses that method.

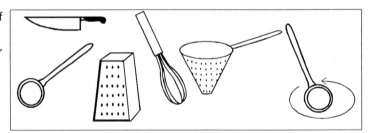

6 What is the average time for 2 bacteria to become 4, and 4 to become 8, if the conditions are right?

12 For each of the preparation methods shown, name a soup which uses that method.

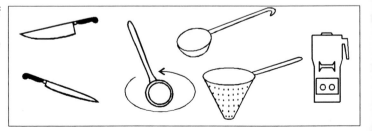

Study the recipes on this page and comment on:

a) their name in relation to how they are made and their ingredients

b) how you would suggest they were described on the menu/to customers (to make them sound appealing)

c) what you would stress from the healthy eating point of view

d) what ingredients you would change or omit so the soup was suitable for vegetarians

e) what preparation and cooking methods each use

f) how each soup is thickened (if at all)

g) what quality points you would look for in the finished dish.

Tomato and haricot bean soup

by The Fresh Fruit and Vegetable Information Bureau

SERVES 4

00 g	haricot beans, soaked for 12 hours	4 oz
00 g	streaky bacon, chopped	4 oz
	medium onion, finely chopped	1
	sticks celery, chopped	2
50 g	tomatoes, skinned, deseeded and chopped	1 lb
	clove garlic, peeled/crushed	1
litre	beef stock	2 pt
0 ml	tomato purée	2 tbsp
	seasoning to taste	
0 ml	fresh parsley, chopped	2 tbsp

Fry the bacon gently, add the onion and celery, and cook in the bacon fat for 2 to 3 minutes.

Add the remaining ingredients apart from the parsley, and simmer gently until the beans are tender, for about 60 minutes.

Blend or liquidise until smooth. Return to the pan, add parsley and heat through to serve.

Cream of mushroom soup

by The British Egg Information Service

SERVES 4

150 g	button mushrooms	5 oz
50 g	polyunsaturated margarine	2 oz
15 ml	brown or white plain flour	1 tbsp
300 ml	chicken stock (hot)	½ pt
575 ml	skimmed milk (hot)	1 pt
	seasoning to taste	

To finish

30 ml	low fat yogurt	2 tbsp
2	egg yolks	2
	parsley, freshly chopped	

1 Coarsely chop the mushrooms into even-sized pieces for a chunky soup, or slice finely.

2 In a heavy-based saucepan, melt the margarine and add the mushrooms. Stir for 1 to 2 minutes over a gentle heat without browning.

3 Take off the heat and stir in the flour. Return to the heat and cook for about 1 minute. Slowly pour in the hot chicken stock, then the hot milk, stirring well with each addition.

4 Bring to the boil, then simmer for about 10 minutes, covered.

5 Blend together the yogurt and egg yolks until evenly mixed.

6 Take the soup off the heat and stir in the yogurt mixture. Season to taste. Serve at once, with a sprinkling of chopped parsley.

Scotch broth

SERVES 4 to 5

1 litre	white stock	2 pt
25 g	pearl barley, washed	1 oz
50 g each	onion, carrot and turnip, finely chopped	2 oz each
25 g each	celery and leek, finely chopped	1 oz each
	chopped parsley (optional garnish)	
	salt and white pepper to taste	

1 Bring the stock to the boil. Add the barley, and simmer for about 1 hour. Top up with stock as required.

2 Add the onion, carrot, turnip and celery. Simmer for 10 to 15 minutes.

3 Add the leeks, then simmer until all the vegetables are cooked, about another 10 to 15 minutes.

4 Skim off any fat, and check seasoning.

NVQ SVQ

Skills check
Prepare and cook basic sauces and soups
Unit 2ND2

level 2

Use this to check your progress against the performance criteria.

Element 1

Prepare and cook basic hot and cold sauces

Get your preparation/cooking areas and equipment ready for use — PC1 ☐

Select ingredients of the type, quality and quantity required — PC2 ☐

Identify and report problems with the freshness or quantity of ingredients — PC3 ☐

Prepare/boil/simmer sauces using appropriate methods — PC4 ☐

△ Preparation methods: chopping, blending, whisking, mixing, straining, grating
Hot sauces: roux, starch-thickened
Cold sauces: vinaigrette, mayonnaise, mint, horseradish

Finish sauces to get right consistency, texture, aroma, flavour, appearance — PC5 ☐

△ Finishing methods: adjusting consistency, seasoning, straining

Correctly store sauces not for immediate use — PC6 ☐

Clean preparation areas and equipment after use — PC7 ☐

Prioritise and carry out your work in an organised, efficient and safe manner — PC8 ☐

Element 2

Prepare and cook basic soups

Get your preparation/cooking areas and equipment ready for use — PC1 ☐

Select ingredients of the type, quality and quantity required — PC2 ☐

Identify and report problems with the freshness or quantity of ingredients — PC3 ☐

Prepare and cook cream/broth/purée soups using appropriate methods — PC4 ☐

△ Preparation methods: chopping, slicing, blending, mixing, straining, serving

Finish soups to get right consistency, texture, aroma, flavour, appearance — PC5 ☐

△ Finishing methods: adjusting consistency, seasoning, adding cream/butter, garnishing

Correctly store soups not for immediate use — PC6 ☐

Clean preparation areas and equipment after use — PC7 ☐

Prioritise and carry out your work in an organised, efficient and safe manner — PC8 ☐

For help to answer questions
relating to:

Health and safety

safe working practices

You must take special care handling
heavy and large saucepans (see
page 60). It is easier to fill big
saucepans at the stove, by carrying
jugs of water from the sink.

Use a dry oven cloth when moving
hot pans, to avoid burns. Lift the lid
off away from you, so it acts as a
shield, protecting your face from the
escaping steam.

When you are making a roux, adding
the first liquid can cause a violent
spitting. This happens when the
flour/fat mixture is very hot (which
it will be with a brown or blond
roux), and it comes into contact with
a hot liquid. Allow the roux to cool a
little.

Take care to avoid splashes of hot
liquid, when you are sieving,
puréeing or blending a hot soup or
sauce. Do not overfill the sieve or the
liquidiser. Check that the lid is
properly on liquidisers or processors
before turning the machine on.

Food hygiene

importance of good hygiene

Most sauces and soups are high risk
foods (the vinegar in mint sauce
means that it is not). Mayonnaise
should be made with pasteurised
eggs. Because the sauce is not
cooked, any salmonella present in
the raw eggs will multiply very
rapidly while the mayonnaise is at
room temperature (e.g. on a buffet
table, or in a sandwich which is not
chilled).

importance of time and temperature

Bacteria spread through unhygienic
handling, dirty equipment, etc., will
multiply rapidly during any period
the sauce or soup is in the
temperature range 5°C to 63°C.

main contamination threats

'Waiter, there's a fly in my soup' is
not an original joke, but it will start
you thinking about the things that
can fall in sauces and soups.

products not for immediate use

When cooling is necessary, this
should be as rapid as possible –
ideally in a blast chiller. Otherwise
place the saucepan in a sink,
surrounded by cold water. A cool
room is the other alternative. As
soon as the sauce or soup has cooled,
place it in the refrigerator.

Hot sauces and soups being kept for
service should be hotter than 63°C.
Cold sauces must be below 5°C.

When reheating a sauce or soup,
bring it to the boil for a few minutes.
(Do not attempt to reheat something
that has had cream added to it, as
the cream will curdle.) Sauces and
soups should never be reheated more
than once. Some bacteria can survive
boiling, and reactivate themselves as
soon as the liquid has cooled.

If you are using a fresh stock to
make the sauce or soup, it must be
made on the day required.

Product knowledge

preparation methods

These are: chopping, blending,
mixing and straining for sauces and
soups, plus whisking and grating for
sauces, and slicing and serving for
soups.

quality points

In your answer, try to cover what the
sauce or soup should look like
(overall colour, and contrast, if any,
provided by ingredients, no fat, skin
or impurities on the surface, etc.),
the texture of any vegetables which
are part of the finished dish, the
aroma or smell and flavour (mention
what should be the dominant
ingredient, make comparisons with
the flavour of fruits, etc.), and the
thickness or thinness (consistency).

when sauces/soups are cooked

If you prepare the ingredients as
stated in the recipe, and keep the
sauce or soup simmering for the time
stated, you should not have a
problem. It is much less complicated
than roasting meat, for example,
where the time taken for the
temperature at the centre to reach a
safe level depends on many factors.

The flavour is a good guide. If this
has not developed fully, or there is a
starchy-taste, you have probably not
cooked the dish for long enough (but
the problem could be to do with the
quality or quantity of ingredients).

The texture of any solids in the sauce
or soup is another guide. Vegetables,
meat, rice, pulses, etc. should be
tender. If the soup is being puréed, a
soft texture is essential.

Healthy catering practices

replacing high fat ingredients

If the decision is yours, use:

- low fat yogurt, fromage frais or
  quark in place of cream or butter
- half cream (which has about
  12% fat) in place of single cream
  (18% fat)
- low fat cheese
- arrowroot, cornflour or similar
  starch to thicken sauces, rather
  than using a roux base (which
  requires oil or fat).

fats/oils for healthy eating

Use oils or fats high in
polyunsaturates and low in saturates
(which means avoiding butter).

increasing fibre content of soups

Use a paste of half besan flour, half
white flour and some of the recipe
liquid, instead of a roux base, to
increase the fibre content and reduce
the fat. Offer more soups which
include pulses and vegetables that
are high in fibre.

reducing salt

Add less or no salt. Many stock cubes
and bouillon preparations make the
addition of further salt unnecessary.
Herbs, spices and freshly ground
pepper can often provide sufficient
flavour, without requiring salt at all.

Unit 2ND18, Element 1

Preparing vegetables for hot dishes and salads

For maximum flavour and nutritional value, vegetables should be washed, prepared and cooked as near to service time as possible. Do not leave vegetables to soak in water, as this causes loss of Vitamin C and other water-soluble vitamins. Peeled potatoes must be kept in water, or they will discolour.

Careful storage of vegetables will keep them in better quality, and for longer (see pages 2 and 62). Discard any vegetables on which you find signs of mould or rot. These problems spread quickly.

Categories of vegetable, their quality points and preparation

There are a great many types of vegetable, but they can be put into categories according to the part of the plant they come from, or the type of plant. You may come across other classifications, e.g. broccoli and cauliflower are members of the brassica or cabbage family.

General quality points for vegetables

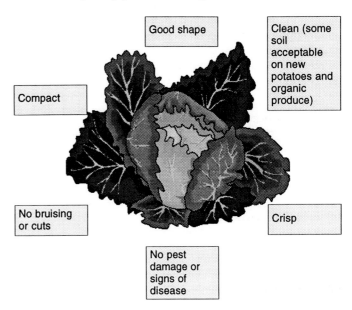

Good shape

Compact

Clean (some soil acceptable on new potatoes and organic produce)

No bruising or cuts

Crisp

No pest damage or signs of disease

Roots

The root anchors the plant to the ground, and absorbs and transports moisture and nutrients from the soil up to the rest of the plant. Carrots, parsnips and turnips are root vegetables.

Carrots should feel hard, and snap easily. Store in a cool, dark place, or refrigerator. New carrots may not require peeling. Wash well, scrape off any blemishes, trim off the top (stalk end) and the wispy tail. Peel older carrots thinly, top and tail.

Parsnips should be white and look fresh, with few whiskers and knobbles. They should snap easily. Brown patches indicate they are rotten inside. Top and tail, and peel thinly. Cut out the core of large parsnips, as it tends to be woody.

Turnips (in Scotland called swedes) should feel firm, with smooth skin that is white, pale green or violet. Scrub or thinly peel the younger ones. You need to peel the older ones more thickly.

Tubers

A tuber is an underground stem, which carries nutrients from the roots to the rest of the plant. It can also store nutrients.

Potatoes are tubers. They should be a good shape. Avoid greening or scuffed skins, deep eyes and new shoots. Keep in a cool, dry, dark atmosphere, away from strong-smelling foods. If the skin has turned green, potatoes should be thrown away, or at the very least heavily peeled.

New potatoes are often preferred with their skin on (washed well and, if necessary, scrubbed). Otherwise scrape the skin off with a knife. It comes away quite easily.

Peel old potatoes thinly, and cut out any eyes.

There are many different ways of preparing potatoes, from the well known chip, to elaborate chains, star shapes, etc. One of the more recent developments is the *wedge*. Cut the unpeeled potato into half lengthways. Then cut each half lengthways again, and so on until you get eight equally sized wedges (like segments of an orange).

Bulbs

Bulbs are leaf bases swollen with water and carbohydrate stored for the next year's growth. Left unpicked, their many layers would eventually form leaves. Onions, leeks and garlic are bulbs.

Onions should be firm, with no green shoots or brown marks. Keep in a cool, dry, dark place. To chop finely:

- cut the washed, peeled onion in half from top to bottom and place each half flat side down on the chopping board

- trim the root end carefully (if you trim off too much the onion will fall apart)

- slice the onion towards the root end (without cutting through the base so that the onion is still just held together). The size of these slices decides how big the dice will be

- cut a series of vertical slices towards the root (again not cutting through the base)

- now cut across the onion at right angles to form dice. If some of the dice are too big (this tends to happen with the slices that come from the curved outer edges), chop them smaller on the board.

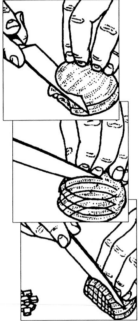

Left: *slicing onion.*

Below: *chopping parsley.*

Leeks should have firm, white bulbs, and bright green unwilted leaves which have been trimmed. Avoid any which have had the base of the root removed, as these deteriorate quickly. Keep cool or store in refrigerator.

Soil can penetrate the layers of the leek. To clean:

- cut away the dark green top, and pull off any old outer leaves

- trim off the roots, but do not cut into the base of the leaves (or the leek may fall apart during cooking)

- with a pointed knife, pierce the leek where the white base and green top meet, and draw the knife through to the top, splitting the leaves open

- fan out the leaves and wash under cold running water until all grit has gone.

Cloves of **garlic** should be plump and firm. Avoid those with green shoots. Store in airy, dry place.

To prepare garlic, pull off required cloves, smash with the flat side of a heavy knife, discard the skin and chop as finely as you require (some chefs add a little salt). Alternatively, peel and put through a garlic squeezer.

Basic preparation methods

Peeling – removing the outer skin of vegetables, because it is inedible (e.g. onions, parsnips), or for preference (e.g. cucumbers are sometimes peeled). Old potatoes are usually peeled, but not if they are to be baked.

Skinning – has the same meaning as peeling, but people usually refer to 'skinning tomatoes', rather than 'peeling tomatoes', perhaps because the skin of a tomato is so thin, and distinct from the flesh.

Shelling – removing the hard, outer covering, or the shell. Removing peas and broad beans from their pod is called 'shelling'.

Chopping – cutting into pieces, e.g. chopping onion, but sometimes means a more vigorous chopping action with the knife, e.g. chopping parsley or garlic.

Shredding – cutting into long, narrow strips or strands. Examples are lettuce for a salad (instead of whole or part of the leaves), and cabbage for a coleslaw salad.

Cutting – a less precise term than chopping or slicing, e.g. 'cut up the vegetables for the salad' (meaning slice the cucumber, chop the spring onion, cut the tomatoes into quarters, etc.).

Slicing – cutting through the vegetable to form slices, often circular in shape (e.g. of tomato, onion, carrot, beetroot).

Trimming – cutting off untidy pieces, parts which are not eaten, e.g. root of a spring onion.

Grating – rubbing against the serrated edge of a grater to produce fine shreds, e.g. of carrot for coleslaw salad.

Topping and tailing – cutting both ends off a whole carrot or French bean, for example.

Aqueous

Aqueous means containing water. Examples are courgettes, marrows and cucumbers, which have a high water content. *Squash* is another name for this group.

Courgettès and **marrows** should be firm, with smooth skins. Avoid any marrows longer than 20 cm as these tend to have a watery, rather bitter flesh.

Keep courgettes and marrows refrigerated, and use as soon as possible. Wash, then trim both ends. There is no need to peel courgettes and marrows – sprinkle the outer flesh lightly with salt half an hour or so before cooking. The salt absorbs the excess moisture.

Cucumbers should have a good colour, and not be bruised, wrinkled or broken. The stalk end should be firm. Store in a cool place or in the refrigerator. Leave any shrink wrapping on until ready to use.

For a salad, slice the cucumbers thinly. If preferred, cucumbers can be peeled. Alternatively, cut shallow, V-shaped grooves out of the skin down the length of the cucumber, so that when round slices are cut, they have a decorative edge.

To draw out some of the excess water from the cucumber before serving, sprinkle the slices with salt and set aside for 30 minutes. Then wash the slices quickly under cold running water and drain well.

Leaves

In a process called photosynthesis, leaves use sunlight to produce food (in the form of sugar) plus oxygen. Cabbage, Brussels sprouts, spinach, watercress and lettuce are leaves.

Cabbage should feel firm, with crisp, bright looking leaves. To store, remove excess leaves, and keep in a cool, dry, airy place, or in the refrigerator. Looser varieties (e.g. greens, spring and savoy) will keep 2 to 3 days, hard white and red cabbages 5 to 6 days.

Remove coarse, outer leaves and trim the stalk. Other preparation steps depend on how the cabbage will be served, e.g. cooked whole then roughly chopped before service, sliced thinly and stir fried (for white cabbage).

Brussels sprouts should be a good even colour, with tightly packed leaves and white stalked base. Cut away any loose outer leaves. It should not be necessary to cut a cross in the base.

The stalks of **spinach** should be tender. Avoid flowering shoots and yellow leaves. Cut or tear off the large stalks. Place the leaves in a large colander and plunge in and out of cold water until all the grit has been removed. Pat dry and use.

For a salad, tear the spinach into bite-size pieces.

Watercress should be dark green. Remove discoloured or wilted leaves, rinse well in cold water and cut off the ends of the stems.

Lettuces should be firm, not drooping or wilting. Varieties include cos, round, iceberg, Webbs wonder, little gem, oakleaf and lollo rosso. Store in the refrigerator, in the plastic bag.

To separate the leaves, take firm hold of the core, twist and pull out. Tear rather than cut lettuce leaves, as they bruise and discolour easily. If a knife has to be used, for example, to shred the lettuce, use one with a stainless steel blade to reduce the risk of browning.

Wash the leaves carefully, then drain thoroughly. With iceberg varieties it is a good idea to run water into the hole left by the core. The lettuce can then be turned upside down to drain.

Flower heads

Left to grow, these would eventually produce seeds. Cauliflower and broccoli are examples.

Cauliflower should have a clean, white head, and crisp green outer leaves. Immerse in cold salty water for 30 minutes or so to clean. If cooking whole, cut out the centre of the core from the stalk using a sharp knife or apple corer. This speeds up cooking.

Broccoli should be bright green and feel firm. Shoots should snap easily. Avoid woody stalks on large heads. Discard any tough leaves attached to the stalk, and trim very long stalks. Swirl in a sink of cold water to dislodge any dirt in the head.

Stems

When sold, celery and fennel usually have the roots trimmed, but some of the leaves left on. Asparagus is a stem with the bud.

Celery should have regular shaped stalks, greenish-white or green depending on variety. Keep in its plastic sleeve, and store in the refrigerator. Remove any damaged stalks and excess leaves. Break off stalks individually, scrub if necessary to remove dirt, and slice or cut into pieces. For cooking whole, trim the root end and remove any blemishes with a peeler or small knife.

Fennel should be well-rounded, and pale green or white in colour. Trim leafy stems close to the root. Feathery leaves can be added to the cooking liquid for extra flavour or finely chopped for a garnish.

Asparagus spears should be of even length and thickness. The straighter the shoot and the more compact the tip, the better the quality. Store in a cool, humid place. Trim off any woody ends. Less tender asparagus may have to be lightly peeled.

Fungi

These are almost the only vegetable foodstuff that does not derive from a green plant.

Mushrooms are fungi. There are many varieties. Of the three more common groups, button (buds that have not opened) and cups (larger, showing gills) should have clean firm, white caps and fleshy stems. Flats should be opened, and a darker colour. Mushrooms dry out quickly. Store unwashed in a closed container in the bottom of the refrigerator.

There is no need to peel cultivated mushrooms, and a light washing is usually adequate. Do not soak in water, as this dilutes their taste and causes vitamin loss.

To slice, cut through the cap and stem to form slices in an umbrella shape. If the mushrooms need to be a sturdier shape, cut each in half and then in quarters.

Vegetable fruits

When animals eat fruit, seeds pass straight through the digestive system, and get scattered far and wide. Peppers and tomatoes are examples.

Peppers (also called sweet peppers or capsicums) should have a firm texture and bright appearance. Their various colours include green, red, white, yellow and deep purple. Before use, remove the seeds and pale-coloured pith-like matter from inside the pepper.

To peel, place quarters or slices of pepper, skinside uppermost under a hot grill. Remove when the skin has blackened. It will pull off easily. Or else, plunge into boiling water for a minute or so, until the skin peels off.

Tomatoes should be firm, with the skin unflawed and bright in colour. Keep in the refrigerator. Soft tomatoes can be used for sauces, soup, etc., but use at once, chilling will only make them softer. Green and hard tomatoes will ripen in 2 to 3 days in a sunny room.

Remove the stalks and prepare as required. To skin:

- place the tomatoes in boiling water for 10 to 20 seconds (this loosens the skin)
- cool immediately under cold running water
- pull away the skin with a sharp knife. If you have kept the tomatoes in the boiling water for the right length of time, this should be fairly easy.

To prepare tomato concassé (chopped tomato flesh), cut the tomatoes in half. With a teaspoon, scoop out the seeds (these can be used in stock or soup). Cut the flesh into neat cubes.

For whole, grilled tomatoes, cut out the eye (where the stalk was attached), and make an X-shaped cut in the top of the tomato just deep enough to penetrate the skin. Alternatively, cut larger tomatoes in half.

Legumes or seeds

With French beans and runner beans, the seeds are eaten complete with their seed case. With broad beans and garden peas, only the seeds are eaten.

Beans should have firm, crisp pods, look fresh and be bright green. Avoid any which are wrinkled or discoloured.

Trim both ends of French beans and runner beans – 'top and tail'. Sometimes runner beans are cut into long, thin strips. Shell broad beans.

Peas (or garden peas) in their pod should be bright coloured, with the pod firm and plump. Shell before use.

Mangetout (or sugar peas) should be bright green, fresh and juicy. The row of little peas down one side should be just visible. Top and tail before use.

Finishing salads

Salads are at their best prepared to order, from good quality ingredients. Too much moisture will produce a soggy result, so drain ingredients well after washing. Pat dry with kitchen paper if necessary.

When salad ingredients have been washed and prepared in advance, store in the refrigerator, in a covered container. Do not pack too tightly.

Seasoning should be done with care to bring out the flavour of the ingredients. No seasoning may be necessary if the salad is to be dressed.

The different colours and shapes of salad ingredients often make *garnishing* unnecessary. For those that have a rather bland appearance, garnishes which can add interest include sprigs of fresh herbs, slices of cucumber, tomato, stuffed olive, hard-boiled egg, croûtons, rings of pepper or onion, etc.

Dressing a salad means adding a flavouring liquid or sauce. Vinaigrette (an emulsion of oil, vinegar, mustard and seasoning, see page 125) is an example.

Thin dressings (e.g. vinaigrette) are best for soft, delicate salads. The thicker dressings (e.g. mayonnaise) are good with firm ingredients, e.g. potato.

Dressings which contain acids (e.g. vinegar or lemon juice) should not be put on green salads until half an hour or so before they are due to be eaten, otherwise the salad will go limp and lose colour and flavour. Some people consider half an hour too long.

Tossing the salad means gentle mixing, so as to coat all the ingredients with the dressing, but not squash, bruise or damage the softer ones. Using two large spoons, lift the salad up into the air, and let it gently tumble back into the bowl. Repeat two or three times.

Cooking vegetables

Shorter cooking times and minimum delay between preparation, cooking and service help keep the flavour, texture and nutritional value of vegetables.

Boiling

The boiling water is in direct contact with all or most of the food, so heat transfer is quick and efficient. To keep as much of the nutritional value as possible:

- use the minimum amount of water
- bring the water to the boil before adding vegetables – this applies to green vegetables, and also those which grow below the ground (e.g. new and old potatoes and carrots)
- keep the lid on the pot during cooking, but lift from time to time to allow any volatile acids (created during the cooking of cauliflower, broccoli, Brussels sprouts, etc.) to escape
- keep liquid movement to a gentle simmering action, to avoid damaging the vegetables.

Blanching

Blanching has two meanings. For chips or French fries it refers to a preliminary deep frying, sufficient to cook the potatoes but not brown it. They can then be kept chilled until required (preferably not more than 4 to 6 hours). Final cooking (at a higher temperature) takes a few minutes to produce an attractive brown, crisp chip.

The second meaning refers to boiling vegetables for a short time until they are partly cooked. Cooking is completed as a second stage, with further boiling, or sometimes by a different method (e.g. baking, roasting or frying). The main purpose is to reduce the time of the final cooking. This can be done minutes before the vegetables are served. There are other purposes, e.g. to skin tomatoes, or to remove the somewhat bitter flavour of celery and cabbage before they are braised.

Place the vegetables for a short time in sufficient boiling water to cover them. How long depends on the purpose of blanching and the degree to which the vegetable should be cooked.

To *refresh* the vegetables – that is, to stop them cooking – plunge the basket of vegetables into cold water, or run cold water into the saucepan through a sieve. The sieve breaks the force of the water. It also prevents the vegetables from washing over the edge of the pan, a problem with peas and other small items.

Reheating

To reheat blanched vegetables for service, plunge them into boiling water for a few minutes. Alternatively, use a microwave oven.

Steaming

In some respects, steaming is the ideal way of cooking vegetables. The food remains still and does not roll around as it does in a boiling liquid, so it is less likely to break up. Two or more vegetables can be cooked at the same time, without transfer of flavours.

Fewer of the water-soluble Vitamins B and C are lost. Loss of vitamins through contact with air is also reduced, especially in pressureless convection and high-pressure steamers. In these sorts of steamer, cooking is very fast. This means that cooking can be left until just before the vegetables are served, even from a frozen state. Cooking times can be worked out in advance and the steamer set to turn itself off automatically.

Roasting

Potatoes and parsnips are traditional accompaniments to the British roast meal. Sweet potatoes are sometimes roasted, as are onions and Jerusalem artichokes.

Leave small potatoes and parsnips whole, but cut larger ones to a similar size. There are different preferences for roasting. Some chefs:

- use a little oil and baste the vegetables regularly
- parboil the vegetables first (i.e. boil them until partly cooked)
- shallow fry them first, in the fat in the roasting tray for 3 to 4 minutes
- season with salt and pepper, others with salt only.

For a healthier result, do not parboil or shallow fry, but brush lightly with polyunsaturated oil and place on a flat baking sheet. Do not turn or baste while roasting.

Baking

This is mostly used for potatoes and sometimes tomatoes. The skin provides a natural protection from the dry heat. Some vegetables, e.g. courgettes and marrows, are stuffed and baked.

Wipe the washed potatoes dry, then pierce once or twice with the prongs of a fork (to avoid bursting potatoes). If you are using a baking tray, sprinkle a thin layer of cooking salt on it (to prevent the potatoes scorching where they touch the tray). If a soft skin is required, rub the potato with oil before cooking.

Grilling

Tomatoes and mushrooms are popular grilled vegetables, and peppers, courgettes and aubergines are good. Brush lightly with oil or butter before cooking. Other vegetables are likely to dry up in the intense heat.

Shallow frying

Most vegetables can be shallow fried. Mushrooms, onions, tomatoes, aubergines, courgettes and peppers are commonly cooked by this method. Potatoes are usually boiled or steamed before slicing and *sautéing* (as they are called when shallow fried).

Other vegetables, such as French beans, are sometimes shallow fried as a means of finishing just before service, having first been boiled or steamed.

Sweating vegetables means very gentle shallow frying, without browning. Keep the pan covered (to trap the steam around the vegetables, discouraging browning), and stir from time to time (to prevent any sticking to the pan bottom and burning).

Deep frying

Potatoes (as chips, see Section 23, French fries, or speciality cuts), onions (as rings), aubergines and courgettes (as round slices or pieces), and mushrooms are deep fried.

With the exception of potato chips, vegetables which are deep fried are usually coated first in flour, breadcrumbs or a batter.

Combination cooking

Microwave ovens which combine microwave energy with conventional heat, bake potatoes in less time than a normal oven. The second heat source gives the potato skin a crispness that it would otherwise lack.

Potato wedges baked in the oven require steam (since the potato is not protected by its skin, as in baking). If you do not have a combi-oven that does this, use a closed cooking container, with a small amount of water surrounding the potatoes.

Chef's Tip

Healthier options: alternatives to salt

With potatoes – mint, parsley, onion

With green beans – lemon juice, dill

With peas – mint, parsley

With cabbage – thyme, nutmeg, apple, sultanas

With carrots – parsley, cloves, tarragon, lemon juice

With tomatoes – basil, oregano, marjoram, vinaigrette

With thanks to Safeway Nutrition Advice Service

Finishing vegetables

Vegetables are cooked to the point at which they become tender. Some people prefer green vegetables to be slightly firm or *al dente*. Few people like soggy, overcooked, colourless vegetables which have lost most of their nutritional value. The difficulty is that one or two minutes can make the difference between cooking and overcooking.

Careful timing is a must. You do need to check towards the end of cooking, prodding the vegetable with a cocktail stick or the point of a thin knife.

Flower vegetables, e.g. cauliflower and broccoli, are quite difficult because the flower is more delicate than the stalk. If you find the flower is overcooked before the stalk has got tender (which may happen with particular batches of vegetables, or at certain times of the year), trim more of the stalk off before cooking, or divide the vegetable into florets and discard the stalk.

To test a baked potato is cooked, place one of the potatoes in a clean towel and squeeze lightly. You should feel the inside giving way.

When vegetables have been blanched, they will require *reheating* before service (described on page 135).

Seasoning is done during cooking (e.g. salt in the boiling water) or after cooking (when salt can help keep fried potatoes crisp). Preferences vary, so remember that customers can always add their own salt and pepper.

Careful *draining* after cooking will avoid the vegetable swimming in water or fat on the service dish. Some chefs use a wire basket to lift blanched vegetables into and out of the reheating water (similar to the basket used in deep frying). A perforated spoon or spider is helpful for taking vegetables out of water or fat. Alternatively, place the cooked vegetables into a colander. Sautéed potatoes can be put on a tray lined with kitchen paper.

Brush off any salt from the surfaces of baked potatoes before service. Cut a deep cross in the tops and place them on a warm serving dish. Garnish as required.

1 Comment on the hand position shown here. Why is it safe?

2 Describe what you should look for when checking the quality of vegetables.

3 What problems could result from not washing vegetables properly?

4 When should the dressing be put on a salad?

5 Describe how you mix the dressing into a salad.

6 When you prepare salads in advance, how are they stored?

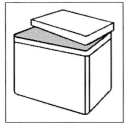

7 What is important about the knife and chopping board you use for preparing vegetables for a salad?

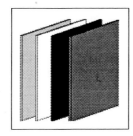

8 What might have caused the problems shown here?

9 Say how you can reduce vitamin loss when preparing vegetables.

10 Name the ten categories of vegetable. (There are 6 in this photo on the right, the others are represented in other photos on this page.)

11 For each category, give one or two examples of its vegetables, and state a method of preparation used.

12 Describe how you wash:
a) cauliflower,
b) leeks,
c) broccoli, and why special care is needed.

14 For what dishes can the skin be left on potatoes? Why is this good healthy catering practice?

15 What do you like about the presentation of this winter salad, and why? What would you change, and why?

Winter salad, with thanks to Forte Crest

For help to answer questions relating to:

Health and safety

safe working practices

The main hazards are from using knives, graters (it's easy to catch your knuckles against the sharp edge), and hot equipment.

heavy/bulky items

Large quantities of vegetables are heavy, and quite often awkward to lift. Plan how you are going to approach the task, check your route is clear, and use the manual handling skills you have been shown (see also pages 34, 40 and 60).

Food hygiene

importance of good hygiene

One of the ways food poisoning bacteria come into kitchens is on raw vegetables. This is because *Clostridium perfringens* and *Bacillus cereus*, two of the most harmful types, are found in the soil. Other bacteria may be spread by the people picking and handling the food. Water-borne and soil-borne viruses (e.g. of the type which cause tetanus) can also be carried on vegetables.

Vegetables may be contaminated with insecticides and other chemicals (used during their growing, harvesting and storage), with grit and soil and with insects (e.g. caterpillars and ants). Some mushrooms are poisonous (this is only a concern if you are preparing mushrooms picked from the wild by someone lacking knowledge on which varietes are safe to eat).

Once in the kitchen, vegetables can pick up bacteria from other foods and from food handlers (through cross contamination, poor hygiene practices, equipment which has not been properly cleaned, etc.).

Care is needed at all stages to avoid these problems affecting other food (e.g. from equipment or handling). An equal concern is preventing harmful bacteria from spreading to cooked vegetables from raw meat or similar high-risk foods.

main contamination threats

Soil from unwashed vegetables, insects brought in on vegetables, cleaning agents incorrectly stored, etc.

washing vegetables

Thorough washing of all raw vegetables is protection against many of the risks described above. If you are using a sink which is also used for washing kitchen equipment, clean and sanitise the sink before starting.

removing from packaging

For many vegetables, good air circulation keeps their quality. In particular, it reduces the risk of mould and rotting. But some types dry out (e.g. mushrooms) and, for longer keeping, should be covered or placed in a sealed bag in the refrigerator.

importance of time and temperature

Bacteria multiply very rapidly at temperatures between 5°C and 63°C.

products not for immediate use

Ideally (to protect nutritional content and eating quality), there should be little delay between preparation and use of vegetables. When advance preparation is necessary, keep the vegetables cool or chilled (depending on variety, see text), and well apart from unprepared vegetables and other possible sources of contamination.

Vegetables which are to be reheated before service must be kept apart from, and well protected from, all sources of contamination, and well chilled. It is unlikely that the short reheating time will kill harmful bacteria which have somehow got on to the vegetables before then.

Product knowledge

categories of vegetables

Ten categories were given in the text. To help you remember them, list all the vegetables you know, then for each one think what part of the plant it comes from. Finally think of the categories that are to do with water content and type of plant.

preparation methods

Use the list you have just prepared, and this time attach one or two preparation methods to each vegetable. The methods are: peeling/skinning/shelling, choping/shredding/cutting, slicing, trimming, grating.

quality points of cooked vegetables

Give your answer in terms of *texture* (e.g. not too soft, nor too hard), *flavour* (e.g. no taste of cooking oil on chips, fresh taste for green vegetables), *aroma* (e.g. no strong smell, as you get with overcooked cabbage), and *appearance* (e.g. cauliflower white, broccoli bright green).

cooking methods

Begin with the vegetables and the methods you use to cook them. It will help to consider why that method is preferred (e.g. steaming is fast and practical), and why others are not suitable (e.g. Brussels sprouts are not suited to roasting, grilling or deep frying).

testing when vegetables are cooked

The texture and colour are good guides, e.g. roast potatoes should be crisp on the outside, tender on the inside and attractively browned.

Until you know what to look for, you might find it helpful to eat a small sample of the cooked vegetable. This is also a good way of experiencing the flavours of different vegetables and the ways they are cooked.

boiling gently

The movement of water which is boiling vigorously will damage the appearance of vegetables, e.g. potatoes will break up into a pulp if you are not careful.

sweating vegetables

Sweating is a very slow, gentle shallow frying, with the lid on the pan to trap the steam. When courgettes, cucumbers, aubergines and peppers are cooked in this way, it means you can cook quite chunky pieces, or small whole vegetables. The slow cooking allows the whole vegetable to develop a good flavour and become tender, without risk of burning.

Health catering practices

increasing fibre content

Vegetables are one of the main sources of fibre in people's diets. Unpeeled potatoes have twice the fibre content of peeled ones. This is one reason why many people like their new potatoes scrubbed, not peeled, and why potatoes baked in their jackets and potato wedge dishes (which include the skin) are popular.

Leaving the skin on courgettes, cucumbers and peppers also increases the amount of fibre.

cooking methods, etc. to reduce fat

You can start by ruling out the cooking methods that use fat, i.e. frying and roasting. In grilling, a little fat may have to be used, to stop burning.

Fried and roasted vegetables can be made healthier by using oil which is high in polyunsaturates and low in saturates. See page 135 (on roasting potatoes) for other steps.

reducing salt

Try adding less salt to the cooking water for plainly-cooked vegetables. Re-read the Chef's tips on page 136 for some alternatives to salt.

Nutty vegetable stir fry

by Sarsons

SERVES 4 to 6

ml	untoasted sesame oil	2 tbsp
50 g	red cabbage, shredded	12 oz
75 g	fresh spinach, shredded	6 oz
25 g	fresh beansprouts	8 oz
g	pine nuts	2 oz
ml	soy sauce	3 tbsp

1 Heat oil in a wok, then stir fry cabbage for 2 minutes. Add spinach and beansprouts, cook for a further 2 minutes. Add pine nuts and soy sauce, cook for a final 2 minutes.

Cooking times are very short with stir fried dishes

Potato, cheese and onion pie

by The Fresh Fruit and Vegetable Information Bureau

SERVES 4

	medium onion, thinly sliced	1
5 ml	vegetable oil	1 tbsp
	large potatoes	3
	leeks	2
00 g	curd cheese	4 oz
0 ml	chives, freshly chopped	2 tbsp
	tomatoes, skinned, deseeded and chopped	6
	clove garlic, crushed and peeled	1
	seasoning to taste	
0 ml	chicken stock	4 tbsp
0 ml	Parmesan cheese, grated	2 tbsp

1 Boil the potatoes in their skins for 10 minutes. Peel and thinly slice.

You can peel the potatoes much more thinly this way.

2 Slice the leeks into rings, then boil for 3 minutes.

3 Fry the onion gently in the oil.

4 Layer the onion, potato and leeks in an ovenproof dish with small knobs of cheese between each layer.

5 Mix the chives, tomatoes, garlic, seasoning and chicken stock together. Spoon over the potato mixture. Sprinkle with Parmesan cheese.

6 Bake at 190°C for 25 minutes. Serve hot.

This is an example of a dish which does not strictly follow any of the traditional cooking methods.

You could adapt the dish by cooking the vegetables in a casserole dish in the oven.

Vegetable medley

by The Dutch Dairy Bureau

SERVES 4

50 g	unsalted butter	2 oz
1 kg	potatoes, finely sliced	2 lb
225 g	onions, finely sliced	8 oz
275 g	Gouda cheese, coarsely grated	10 oz
1 each	red and green pepper, deseeded and chopped	1 each
	black pepper	

1 Melt butter in a frying pan. Place the potatoes, onions, cheese and peppers in alternate layers, seasoning well between each layer. Finish with a layer of cheese.

2 Cover with a piece of foil, cook over a gentle heat for 35 to 40 minutes.

---

1 Describe what you can do to reduce vitamin loss when cooking green vegetables.

2 Describe what sort of boiling action (gentle/vigorous) is better for cooking vegetables. Why?

3 When opening an oven or taking the lid off a pan, what should you remember?

4 Name two vegetable dishes which can be cooked in a combi-oven (shown at left in the photo below).

5 Name two vegetables which are often cooked in a high-pressure steamer (shown on the right in the photo below). What are some of the advantages of using high-pressure steamers?

6 For each of the vegetables shown here, give one method of cooking, and say how the vegetable would be prepared. Try to include a variety of cooking methods in your answer.

7 The platter of char grilled vegetables (below) includes peppers (red, yellow and green), baby corn, courgette and aubergine. Identify them on the dish, and state how each would be prepared.

8 What do you like and dislike about the presentation of the char grilled vegetables in the photo below, and why?

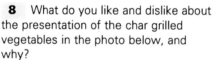

Char grilled vegetables with thanks to Forte Crest

9 For a healthy diet, what are some advantages of vegetables. What methods of cooking maximise these advantages?

10 Have another look at the photograph below. For each of the vegetables shown, say roughly how long it would take to boil, and how can you tell when the vegetable is cooked.

11 How would you cook this vegetable? Describe the colour and texture it should be when cooked.

12 Describe how you would blanch a) tomatoes, b) Brussels sprouts, c) chips. What is the purpose of blanching in each case?

Preparing and cooking basic
vegetable protein dishes

Preparing vegetable protein dishes

More people are becoming vegetarian. Some of these still like the taste and texture of meat. Others want nothing to do with meat but want a protein-rich, convenient food to add interest to vegetables and pulses. Yet others want to limit their meat intake, by avoiding those cuts and dishes which have a high saturated fat content.

To meet this market, there is a choice of high quality, vegetable protein products. These are the result of years of research and development, and millions of pounds of investment. They are manufactured. They use natural ingredients, but they are not grown, as are the animals which give beef and other meats, or the crops which produce vegetables for the table.

There are different types of vegetarianism (see box on page 144). Some people will not eat eggs, for example, others exclude all foods of animal origin. What everyone needs in their diet is protein. Protein cannot be stored by the body. This means that each main meal should include sufficient protein. And a good way of doing this, is to serve a dish based on vegetable protein.

Some people – vegetarians and non-vegetarians – have special dietary requirements for health reasons. For example, some people get seriously ill if a dish they eat contains nuts. Others are unable to digest dairy products.

This means you have to look carefully at all the ingredients of a dish, before recommending it to customers with special dietary needs. If you are not sure, give the customer all the facts (e.g. from labels on packets and lists of recipe ingredients), so that he or she can make the decision.

When preparing vegetarian dishes alongside those containing meat or fish, or vegetarian dishes which contain dairy products, for example, you must use separate sets of equipment (chopping boards, knives, mixing bowls, etc.). The dish will in effect be contaminated if pieces or even traces of non-vegetarian food have got into it.

Quorn pieces (on board, main photo)*, and minced* (smaller photo)*, one of the leading brands of vegetable protein.*

Quality points and preparation methods

The soya bean, which is very rich in protein, forms the basis of many vegetable protein foods. But the names of these foods come from a variety of sources. Tofu is the Japanese word for unfermented soya-bean curd. Textured vegetable protein, which has the ring of a food scientist about it, describes the outcome of a manufacturing process. Quorn is the name given to the product mycoprotein, by its makers. It is a registered trade name, so no other manufacturer can use it.

Tempeh

Tempeh is made from soya beans that have been injected with a special fungus and left to ferment. The distinctive black specks are similar in nature to the blue veins in some cheese, and do no harm.

Tempeh is chewy and has its own flavour. It is high in protein, and free from gluten (which some people are allergic to) and salt.

Textured vegetable protein (TVP)

TVP is basically a dried foam made from soya flour. The flour which is left behind after the oil has been extracted is mixed with water to form a dough. This is heated under pressure, and then forced through a small nozzle. The fall in pressure causes the TVP to expand as it leaves the nozzle. The resulting texture is rather like sponge. It is then cut into chunks or flakes, ground up to form mince or powder, sometimes flavoured to resemble meat, and sold in this dried form.

Food manufacturers are the main users of TVP. They use it in place of some or all the meat in pies, casseroles, sausages and burgers. It is inexpensive, yet high in protein and dietary fibre, and very low in fat.

The product VegeMince (from Haldane Foods) contains some TVP but is mostly based on wheat gluten. It is a vegetarian alternative to beef mince (the egg content is from free range eggs). VegeMince is sold pre-cooked and frozen. It can be used straight from the freezer in dishes that would otherwise use minced beef. If you are following a meat recipe, add extra liquid as some will be absorbed by the VegeMince.

Preparation methods for vegetable protein

Soaking – this means leaving the food in a liquid for some time. Vegetable protein is sometimes soaked or *marinated* to absorb flavour. Dried fruit (used in some vegetable protein dishes) is sometimes soaked in water, so that it becomes plump and moist again (e.g. prunes), or in wine, sherry or port so that it also acquires the flavour of the liquor.

Mixing – combining the ingredients. The recipe may say that the mixing should be 'thorough' (to ensure everything is blended), or 'gentle' (to avoid damaging the shape of ingredients).

Slicing – usually means cutting thin pieces (compare with chopping, below).

Chopping – cutting into cubes. The recipe may say 'finely chop' (meaning very small pieces), or 'roughly chop' (meaning that pieces do not have to be evenly shaped, or of the same shape and size).

Tofu

Tofu is soybean curd. Not many years ago, the only types available were the Morinaga, imported from Japan, and home-made tofu bought at Chinese stores. The choice from wholefood suppliers has expanded considerably, ranging from very soft to quite firm, and including smoked.

The protein value of tofu is as high as chicken. High in essential amino acids, which most grains lack, tofu also boosts the protein value of foods that it is served with. For example, stir fried tofu and vegetables, with rice, millet buckwheat or couscous, is a sound meal, being richer than it would seem. A tofu filling for a wholemeal sandwich is another good combination.

Tofu has a fairly bland taste:

- the very soft types can be used at once for puddings, when you need a smooth, thick sauce, or drained and left for a day before cutting
- mashed up it can be used in cheesecake, ice cream or blended with soft fruits
- thinly sliced smoked tofu makes a tasty first course served with sliced avocado and a fruit like mango or pawpaw, and dressed with a lime vinaigrette

To help tofu absorb the flavour of a marinade, lightly score the cubes of tofu. Cubes of tofu can also be rubbed with herbs and spices.

Quorn

Quorn is vegetable in origin, a distant relative of the mushroom. Although it occurs naturally in the soil, very precise conditions have to be created for its production in commercial quantities.

Quorn is high in protein and fibre, and low in fat. It has a mild savoury taste and firm but tender texture. It can be used in place of meat or fish in most recipes for grills, casseroles, stews, quiches and similar dishes, including those which are microwaved and stir fried.

Quorn is not suitable for vegans as it contains egg white. Some vegetarians do not use it because the eggs are not free range.

Quorn readily picks up the flavours of other ingredients with which it is cooked. When using strong flavours (e.g. garlic, wine, lemon and herbs), halve recipe quantities. Limit marinating time to 30 minutes.

Store Quorn in the refrigerator, and use before the date on the packet. Quorn freezes very successfully, and will keep in the freezer for up to 3 months. Use frozen, or place in the refrigerator overnight to thaw. Use within 24 hours of thawing.

As a guide, 225 to 350 g of Quorn will serve 4 people, depending on the recipe.

Wheatpro

Wheatpro, from Lucas Ingredients, has similar characteristics to top quality TVP products. The raw material in this case is gluten, obtained by washing away other water-soluble proteins and starches from wheat flour.

Catering suppliers may sell pre-prepared products made from Wheatpro, for example burgers. Convenience vegetarian and vegetable dishes may also include Wheatpro.

Wheatpro mixes for burgers, pastry rolls and pies should be stored in dry, well ventilated conditions, away from sunlight and strong odours. Do not store for more than 6 months.

Once reconstituted, Wheatpro should be handled and stored as fresh meat.

Other ingredients

Vegetable protein products are not intended to be eaten or cooked on their own. They are made to blend with and take on the flavours of a wide range of accompanying ingredients. There is much scope for adventurous combinations. If you are adapting recipes, be careful not to introduce ingredients which clash with others, or which do not lend themselves to the preparation or cooking process you are following.

Fresh vegetables and fruit – all types (see Section 11) are suitable. Jains (a Hindu sect) do not eat onions, garlic and root vegetables.

Leaves (e.g. spinach, watercress, lettuce and cabbage), stems (e.g. celery and fennel), flowers (e.g. broccoli), fruits and aqueous vegetables (e.g. marrows, tomatoes and courgettes) contain little or no protein. Tubers (e.g. potatoes) and roots (e.g. carrots and turnips) contain some protein.

Preserved vegetables and fruit – also called *pickled vegetables* and *dried fruits*. The preserving, pickling or drying process extends the life of the food, and often means it can be stored safely at room temperature.

Onions, gherkins and beetroot are examples of pickled vegetables. Chillies are available dried, and there are dried potato and onion products.

Apricots (which are very high in dietary fibre), prunes, bananas, dates, figs, raisins and sultanas are popular in their dried form. Glacé cherries and mincemeat may not be suitable as the colouring is derived from the cochineal beetle.

Cereals – not the breakfast-table sort, but *grains* such as barley flakes, buckwheat (roasted or unroasted, also as flour and noodles), cornmeal and cornflour (gluten-free), millet (flakes or flour, also gluten-free), oats (whole, flakes and rolled oats) and couscous (a North African product, made from wheat). All are a valuable source of protein.

Seeds – of plants, used for flavour, texture and sometimes as a source of protein, e.g. fennel, poppy, sesame, cumin, cardamom, sunflower and pumpkin.

Nuts – these add texture, colour, flavour and protein. The choice includes almonds, cashews, walnuts, peanuts, pistachios and Brazils. Because a few people have an acute allergic reaction to nuts (mainly peanuts), menu and dish descriptions should make it clear that nuts are one of the ingredients.

Always read a recipe through before starting on step 1 of the instructions. Collect and prepare all the ingredients you need. Weigh/measure quantities. Assemble the stirring spoons, pans, knives, chopping boards, etc. you need.

Quorn and rice risotto
by Crosse & Blackwell

SERVES 4

Metric	Ingredient	Imperial
225 g	long grain brown rice, cooked	8 oz
30 ml	oil	2 tbsp
1	large onion, chopped	1
2	cloves garlic, crushed and peeled	2
225 g	aubergine, sliced	8 oz
1	red pepper, deseeded and sliced	1
350 g	courgette, sliced	12 oz
10 ml each	fresh sage and thyme, chopped	2 tsp each
15 ml	lemon juice	1 tbsp
30 ml	stock	2 tbsp
3	tomatoes (skinned, deseeded, chopped)	3
30 ml	tomato purée	2 tbsp
1 x 250 g	packet Quorn	1 x 9 oz
	seasoning to taste	

For a vegetarian dish, what sort of stock should this be?

Failing to prepare would get you in immediate difficulty with this recipe. Having cooked the onion and garlic, you realise you have to prepare the aubergine, pepper, courgettes, herbs and lemon juice!

1 Heat oil and cook onion and garlic until soft. Stir in aubergine, red pepper, courgettes, herbs, lemon juice and stock. Cover and cook gently for about 15 minutes. Stir occasionally.

2 Stir in tomatoes, tomato purée and Quorn, cover and cook for 10 minutes. Stir in rice, seasoning and heat through.

Oops! The rice should have been cooked first!

Ingredients to avoid

When preparing dishes for vegetarians, you must check before using any products connected with animals, or for those with special dietary needs.

No vegetarian dish should contain any of the following:

- fresh stocks made with meat or fish, stock cubes or bouillons containing meat or fish – use vegetarian stock cubes
- suet and lard (because they are animal fats) – use vegetable oils and fats
- margarine (because it may contain fish oil or other animal products) – use a vegetarian margarine
- pre-prepared pastry (because it may have been made from unsuitable margarine) – use vegetarian product or make your own with suitable products
- sauces made with animal products (e.g. anchovy sauce)
- gelatin and aspic – use agar agar (made from seaweed) or vegetarian jelly
- cheese made with rennet or pepsin – use vegetarian cheese
- yogurts, fromage frais, etc. which have been made with animal rennet – use vegetarian products (e.g. soya yogurt).

Ingredients to consider before use

Eggs (free-range, not battery-farm hens since they may have been fed with fish meal) and *dairy products* are acceptable to some vegetarians (see box). For this group, a product similar in its uses to vegetable protein, called *Paneer*, is available. From the cheesemakers, Clawson, it is made from fresh whole milk (so it is protein rich, but does contain fat) and acetic acid.

Paneer has a firm consistency. It can be grated, chopped, cubed, crumbled or puréed. With a mild flavour, it can be used as the main or one of a number of ingredients in both savoury and sweet dishes: casseroles, pastas, cheesecakes, as a topping on pizzas, in salads, etc.

For vegetarians who do not eat eggs, you should not use products that contain egg by-products (e.g. Quorn).

Some vegetarians avoid all *alcoholic drinks* as part of their lifestyle. Others avoid them because the refining process often involves animal products. For this group, use vegetarian wines.

Additives from non-vegetarian sources (many of the E-numbered products you see listed in small print) are not suitable.

Crisps, bought-in cakes and biscuits may contain hidden animal products (e.g. in the margarine or an additive).

To avoid doubt, use products which are labelled suitable for vegetarians. This will be stated by the maker, or indicated by the use of the easily recognisable V-logo of the Vegetarian Society (for which a fee is paid to the Society).

Uncooked vegetable protein dishes

As indicated above, many vegetable protein products do not need to be cooked. They can be chopped and sliced to go into salads, or puréed for a salad dressing.

More on vegetarianism

The most common reason vegetarians do not eat meat, poultry or fish is their dislike of killing animals for food. Religion and health are the other main reasons.

Some vegetarians will not eat any foods of animal origin, e.g. eggs, milk, cheese, honey even though they do not involve the death of animals. Some will not wear clothes, shoes or accessories which are made from leather. Some will not eat particular vegetables (e.g. onions and garlic).

Vegetarians tend to feel that it is wasteful and/or unhealthy to eat foods which are over-refined, e.g. white flour and white rice, or have the major part of the protein, mineral and fibre content removed.

Some people are *wholefooders*, but not actually vegetarian. They prefer foods which are as unrefined or unprocessed as possible.

Types of vegetarian

The various degrees of vegetarianism have names:

Semi-vegetarian or *demi-vegetarian* – those who eat a mainly vegetarian diet, but occasionally eat meat or fish.

Ovo-lacto-vegetarian – diet includes milk, dairy products and eggs (preferably free-range). The majority of vegetarians in the UK are of this type. Besides meat, fish and poultry, they will not eat products made from dead animals, e.g. suet, lard, gelatin, aspic (made from animal bones) and animal rennet (used to produce many types of margarine and fromage frais).

Lacto-vegetarian – eggs are also excluded from the diet.

Ovo-vegetarian – includes eggs, but not milk or milk products (e.g. yogurt and cheese).

Vegan – eat vegetables, fruit and other products of plants (e.g. milk, cheese and yogurt made from soya). All foods of animal origin are excluded (meat, fish, dairy products, eggs, honey, etc.).

Fruitarian or *fructarian* – diet consists of only raw fruit, nuts and berries. They usually exclude all grains and processed foods. Honey may not be acceptable.

With thanks to Mary Scott Morgan, Caterveg, The Association for Vegetarian Catering, East Langton, Leicestershire.

Cooking vegetable protein dishes

When cooking dishes that are described as suitable for vegetarians, be careful not to taint the food with non-acceptable products. This can happen by cooking vegetarian and non-vegetarian dishes at the same time, or using the same utensils to handle both foods. To avoid problems of this sort:

- keep the oil for deep frying vegetarian dishes only for that use. These must be vegetable oils; dripping and lard are unacceptable, being animal-derived products. If you use groundnut oil, or blended products which might contain nut oils, customers should know this, in case they have an allergy

- never use the oil left over from shallow frying meat or fish dishes for frying a vegetarian dish

- grill vegetarian dishes separately from non-vegetarian dishes, making sure first that there are no remnants of meat or fish on the grill

- when you are shallow frying, keep pans cooking meat or fish to the other side of the stove, in case fats spit on to vegetarian dishes

- use a different set of tongs, spoons, knives, chopping boards, etc. for vegetarian foods

- keep vegetarian and non-vegetarian foods well apart in the hot cupboard, refrigerator, freezer, etc.

Cooking methods for vegetable protein dishes

Vegetable protein does not require cooking to make it tender (as do meat and vegetables). It is almost always used as part of a more complex dish. The aim is to allow the different ingredients and flavours to blend together, and for the dish to be heated through to the right temperature.

The cooking method therefore depends on the type of dish that you are preparing, e.g. a casserole or a roast. Cooking times will reflect how long the accompanying ingredients take to become tender, and/or the sauces to develop their full flavour.

Examples of the sort of dishes you will come across and the cooking methods involved are:

- nut roasts – *baking* if only the dry heat of the oven is used, *roasting* if the dish is basted in fat during cooking, and *braising* if the food is partly covered in a flavouring liquid or sauce during cooking

- kebabs – *grilling*

- burgers – these can be *grilled, shallow fried, deep fried* or *baked*, depending on the recipe

- stir fried vegetables, etc. – *stir frying*, as the name implies

Creamy Quorn casserole
by Marlow Foods

SERVES 4

30 ml	vegetable oil	2 tbsp
250 g	Quorn	9 oz
1	small onion, chopped	1
100 g	mushrooms, sliced	4 oz
1 × 200 g	can sweetcorn	1 × 7 oz
275 ml	vegetable stock	½ pt
30 ml	dry white wine	2 tbsp
30 ml	wholegrain mustard	2 tbsp
2.5 ml	ground cumin	½ tsp
50 g	full fat soft cheese	2 oz
15 ml	cornflour	1 tbsp
	seasoning to taste	
30 ml	half fat cream	2 tbsp

1 Heat the oil in a large saucepan. Fry the Quorn and onion, cooking until the onion softens.

> The Quorn does not need cooking in the usual meaning of the word. Adding it at this stage helps the Quorn absorb the flavour of the onion.

2 Add the mushrooms and fry for another 3 minutes. Add the sweetcorn, stock, wine, mustard, cumin and cheese. Bring to the boil, stirring continuously.

> Check with Section 10 (page 124) for the reason why the cornflour is mixed with a little water first.

3 Blend the cornflour with a little water. Add to the Quorn mixture, stirring until the sauce thickens. Season.

4 Remove from the heat and stir in the cream. Serve with wholegrain rice.

> Check with Section 10 (page 127) for the reason the cream is added at this stage. Should you check the consistency of the casserole before adding the cream?

> What group of vegetarians would this recipe NOT be suitable for?

- casseroles – *stewing* (but all the cooking may be done in the oven). Casseroles may also involve *frying* (e.g. as a first step to colour or cook some of the ingredients) and *boiling* (e.g. to thicken the sauce once cornflour has been added)

- risotto – *boiling* or *simmering* of ingredients to combine flavours and cook vegetables and rice until tender.

For help to answer questions
relating to:

Health and safety

❓ safe working practices

The main hazards are from using
knives, hot equipment, handling
heavy items.

Food hygiene

❓ importance of good hygiene

Vegetable protein must be stored and
handled as any other fresh food, to
protect it from sources of harmful
bacteria.

❓ importance of time and temperature

Bacteria increase rapidly in numbers
at the right temperature.

❓ main contamination threats

Other food (e.g. fresh vegetables/
fruit), food handlers, dirty
equipment/work area, harmful
cleaning substances and foreign
bodies (e.g. piece of broken glass).

❓ products not for immediate use

Store above 63°C or below 5°C.

Product knowledge

❓ types of protein and their uses

Re-read pages 141–143. To add
texture and interest to dishes, as
source of protein, as meat substitute.

❓ other alternatives for vegetarians

There is a vast range of delicious
dishes that can be created with fresh
vegetables, fruit, pasta, rice, etc. But
first, re-read the text and box on
page 144 to know what NOT to
include.

❓ quality points for different products

Remind yourself of the general
quality checks (page 141). Look at
the packaging, the date mark, the
temperature, and the appearance.

❓ quality points for cooked dishes

Describe how the dish should look
(*appearance, consistency*), smell
(*aroma*) and taste (*texture, flavour*).

❓ preparation methods

These are: soaking, mixing, slicing
and chopping. It may help to base
your answer on dishes that you are
familiar with.

❓ cooking methods

This depends on the sort of dish you
are preparing. Try to think of an
example for each cooking method.

❓ identifying when dishes are cooked

The main reason for cooking
vegetable protein is to produce a
well-flavoured dish at the right
temperature. But other ingredients
will have to be tender (e.g.
vegetables).

Healthy catering practices

❓ replacing high fat ingredients

Remind yourself of some of the tips
on page 130 for replacing cream,
butter, etc.

❓ fats/oils for healthy eating

See page 110.

❓ cooking methods, etc. to reduce fat

See page 138.

❓ increasing fibre content of dishes

Most vegetarians prefer foods which
are as unrefined or unprocessed as
possible, and recipes reflect this,
making use of brown rice, wholemeal
flour, etc.

❓ reducing salt

See page 110.

Self-check questions

1 When using a knife to prepare
vegetables, give three safe practices
you should follow.

2 How can you protect yourself from
burns when cooking?

3 For one vegetable protein product,
describe how it should be stored and
handled to prevent contamination from
harmful bacteria.

4 What dishes on your workplace menu
would be suitable for a customer who
is a) a vegan, b) a lacto-vegetarian?

5 State four food items you should
never use when making a dish for
vegetarians. For each, give an
alternative product.

6 If you are cooking dishes for
vegetarians alongside meat and fish
dishes, what precautions should you
take and why?

7 Why is it important that a main course
vegetarian dish should be protein-rich?

8 Give three dishes that are suitable as
main courses for a vegetarian.

Skills check

NVQ SVQ — Prepare and cook basic vegetable
protein dishes
Unit 2ND19 — level 2

Use this to check your progress against
the performance criteria.

Element 1

Prepare basic vegetable protein dishes

Get your preparation areas and
equipment ready for use — ☐ PC1

Select ingredients of the type,
quality and quantity required — ☐ PC2

▲ Vegetable protein: reconstituted textured
vegetable protein (TVP), tempeh, tofu, Quorn
Other ingredients: fresh vegetables/fruit,
preserved vegetables/fruit, cereals, nuts, seeds

Identify and report problems with the
quality or quantity of ingredients — ☐ PC3

Correctly combine vegetable protein
with other ingredients — ☐ PC4

Prepare vegetable dishes using
appropriate methods — ☐ PC5

▲ Preparation methods: soaking, mixing, slicing,
chopping

Clean preparation areas and
equipment after use — ☐ PC6

Prioritise and carry out your work in an
organised, efficient and safe manner — ☐ PC7

Element 2

Cook basic vegetable protein dishes

Get your cooking areas and
equipment ready for use — ☐ PC1

Identify and report problems with the
quality or quantity of dishes — ☐ PC2

Cook vegetable protein dishes — ☐ PC3

▲ Cooking methods: grilling, shallow frying, stir
frying, boiling, braising, stewing, deep frying,
roasting, baking

Finish vegetable protein dishes — ☐ PC4

Correctly store vegetable protein
dishes not for immediate use — ☐ PC5

Clean cooking areas and
equipment after use — ☐ PC6

Prioritise and carry out your work in an
organised, efficient and safe manner — ☐ PC7

Preparing and cooking basic **pulse** dishes

Preparing pulse dishes

Pulse is a collective name for the edible seeds of plants grown in various countries of the world. As people in Britain have become more knowledgeable about the cuisines of China, Argentina, Thailand, the USA and other distant places, so the range of pulses in our shops has increased.

Pulses are low in fat, and a very good source of fibre, Vitamin B and minerals. They also have a high protein content. This means that they can be the centre-point of a meatless meal.

As pulses are low in some essential amino acids, they need to be eaten with a cereal such as rice or wholemeal bread, or nuts or seeds to make a balanced, healthy diet. Meals for vegetarians should take this into account.

Pulses can be eaten on their own as a vegetable course, or in stews, soups, casseroles, burgers, kebabs, salads and pancakes.

Types of pulse

Most pulses come dried, which means they are easy to store and have quite a long shelf-life. Canned pulses have similar advantages, and being cooked, are convenient to use.

The many different varieties can be put into three groups. The first is those which have the word 'pea' in their name, e.g.:

- *Chickpeas* – sometimes spelt as two words, from various countries, including the USA and India. Small, round, distinct knobbly shape, and golden brown colour. Nutty taste. Firm texture, even when cooked. Main ingredient in humus (a paste, flavoured with garlic, paprika and lemon). Used in many dishes from the Middle East and India

- *Marrowfat peas* – any of several varieties of pea plant that have large seeds

- *Green split peas* and *yellow split peas* – break up when cooked, so good for thick soups and (green split peas) for pease pudding.

In the second group – and there are rather more of these – are those with the word 'bean' in their name, e.g.:

- *Aduki beans* – from China. Also spelt *Adzuki*. Small, reddish, round bean with a strong, sweet, slightly nutty flavour. Used in some recipes for cakes and desserts

- *Black-eye beans* – from the USA. Small, creamy white bean with black splash at the 'eye' of the bean. Popular in salads and in creamy sauces. More easily digested than most other pulses

- *Black bean* – from USA. Small, stays black while giving inky colour to the cooking liquid. Good for rich and spicy stews

- *Butter beans* – from USA. Also called *Lima beans* (from Peru). Large, cream-coloured, creamy texture and nutty flavour. Breaks down easily when cooked, so good for sauces, soups and dips

- *Cannelini beans* – from Italy. Small white beans, can be used in the same way as haricot beans

- *Flageolet beans* – mainly from Argentina. These are the seeds of a variety of dwarf green bean, picked when young. Pale green and tender

- *Haricot beans* – also known as *navy beans*, from North America. Small, white, used in hot and cold dishes. This is the bean you get in a can of baked beans

- *Mung beans* – from Thailand. Often used as sprouting bean. Moss green colour, with sweetish flavour. Hold their shape well

- *Pinto beans* – from the USA. Medium sized, speckled pink/brown colour with creamy texture

- *Red kidney beans* – from the USA. Colourful, large red haricot bean, with mealy texture. Good in spicy dishes and salads.

The third group, *lentils*, are the seeds of one particular plant (it grows mainly in the Mediterranean and West Asia). They come in a range of colours, whole and split. Split lentils are inclined to break up if overcooked. *Brown lentils*, from Canada, retain their shape well during cooking.

Quality and storage points

Check the date stamp. Although dried pulses keep well, it is best to eat them as fresh as possible. Old pulses take longer to cook and are more difficult to digest.

The packaging should be in good condition – no signs of insect damage, cans not blown and the seals sound. Once a packet of dried pulses is open, transfer unused contents to an airtight container. Keep dried pulses in a cool place, out of direct sunlight, and away from any moisture or dampness.

There is sometimes grit among dried beans. This should be picked out, or rinsed away.

With a range of colours and shapes, pulses can add visual interest to dishes, as well as contrast of texture and nutritional value. (The self-check questions on page 152, will help you identify the names of the pulses in the photograph.)

Other ingredients

With the extensive range of pulses available, there are types that go well with most of the ingredients usually found in catering kitchens. Many successful combinations are based on the inexpensive cuts of meat, e.g. chilli con carne (usually with minced beef, or in the Mexican way with minced pork), and various bean stews and cassoulets (with pork belly, ham bones, etc.). Pulses also go well with fish, to make tasty soups, a variation on kedgeree and various baked dishes.

Since they are rich in protein and produce a flavourful dish when combined with vegetables and fruit (fresh and preserved), cereals, nuts and seeds, pulses make a key contribution to many vegetarian dishes. (See page 143 for notes on these other ingredients.)

When cooking for vegetarians, be careful not to use any animal products (see page 144).

Preparing pulses

Pulses do not require peeling, trimming or other preparation tasks that, for example, vegetables need. But with dried pulses, advance planning is essential because of the need to soak most pulses before cooking.

Draining

Canned beans require draining – about one-third of the weight shown on the can is water.

Open the tin and pour the contents into a colander (resting on the sink draining board or over a bowl to catch the juices). Leave for a few minutes until the juices have run off.

Soaking

Dried pulses cook faster and more easily when they have been soaked. But red lentils and split peas do not need soaking.

Check a day in advance what the instructions are for soaking, since soaking for up to 12 hours is often recommended, and 3 to 4 hours is quite normal:

- put the pulses in a large bowl, and cover in plenty of cold water – at least twice the amount of water to pulses
- leave for the recommended time in a cool place or the refrigerator – cover the bowl with a clean cloth
- drain the pulses in a colander, then rinse well under cold running water.

If the pulses have started to smell rotten and ferment – which might happen if they have been soaked for too long, or in a warm place – then they should not be used.

Blanching

Beansprouts (small shoots grown from Mung beans, but not strictly speaking, pulses) are sometimes blanched before use in a salad or a stir-fried dish:

- place the sprouts in a sieve or colander sitting in a large stainless steel bowl
- pour boiling water over, sufficient to cover the sprouts
- immediately lift the sprouts out, and keeping them in the sieve or colander, plunge into a sink full of fresh, cold water.

The term blanching is sometimes used to describe the pre-boiling of dried pulses.

Pre-boiling of dried pulses

Dried pulses may contain poisonous substances – red kidney beans are very likely to, and other pulses should be treated as if they do. The only exceptions are lentils and split peas.

When the toxins (as these substances are called) survive cooking, they can cause inflammation of the stomach and intestines. In a few serious cases, this has led to the death of the person affected.

Fortunately, a short period of vigorous boiling drives off the toxins. Often this step forms part of the first stage of the recipe you are following. But you may need to do this separately:

- after soaking, put the pulses in a large saucepan
- cover with cold water (twice the amount of water to pulses)
- bring to the boil – do not cover the pan – and boil vigorously for 10 minutes
- drain off the pulses.

Continue, as required by the recipe.

Refreshing

The recipe may tell you to refresh the pulses after blanching or pre-boiling. This means cooling them quickly to stop the cooking. To do this, leave the pulses in the pan, and place under the cold water tap, with a sieve to break the force of the water. Let the water run until all the pulses are cold.

Other preparation methods

When you are using canned pulses, or dried pulses which have been previously cooked, for a salad or other cold dish, this is likely to involve:

- *mixing* – to combine the various ingredients. Do this carefully, so that you do not crush any of the softer items. The aim is to distribute the different ingredients evenly, and to coat them in any dressing or sauce which is being used
- *slicing* – vegetables (e.g. onions and tomatoes) and fruit (e.g. apples) may have to be sliced
- *chopping* – this might also apply to vegetables and fruit, when small cubes are required, and to nuts if they are to be cut into smaller pieces.

For some soups, sauces, burger and patty recipes, the pulses are puréed or blended in a food processor so they produce a creamy consistency.

Cooking pulse dishes

Dried pulses have to be soaked, boiled vigorously to drive off the poisons, and then cooked until they are tender. All or some of this last stage is often combined with the cooking of the other ingredients – by boiling, stewing, braising or baking – so that all the flavours develop and blend together. Alternatively, the pulses are boiled or steamed on their own until tender, then mixed with various ingredients, and grilled or fried.

Canned pulses have already been cooked until they are tender. After draining, further cooking should only be sufficient to heat them up, and to combine their flavour with other ingredients in the dish.

Cooking times for pulses, even for the same variety, vary considerably. At regular intervals during the second half of the recommended recipe cooking time, remove a few pulses and test. If they crush easily, they are cooked.

With soups and some sauces, it is intentional that the pulses should break up, so that they thicken the liquid.

Boiling (dried) pulses

When boiling pulses, keep quite a high heat under the pan until the pulses have boiled rapidly for about 10 minutes (to get rid of the poisonous substances). After this time, turn the heat down so the pulses simmer gently. Skim off any scum which forms on the surface.

In some recipes, the initial boiling is a separate step, using plenty of water. Afterwards, the cooking water is thrown away, the pulses drained, and cooking continues more gently. Less cooking liquid is used, and it may include ingredients to add flavour, e.g. chopped vegetables, wine, beer or cider.

Some recipe quantities are worked out so that the pulses have absorbed all the liquid by the end of cooking.

If using salt, do not add to the cooking water until the end of the cooking time. Otherwise the salt will make the pulses tough. Acids (e.g. lemon juice and vinegar) also toughen pulses.

Do not add bicarbonate of soda to the boiling water. Although it is said to soften the pulses during cooking, it destroys the B vitamins.

If you are cooking a vegetarian dish, use different utensils and equipment, and different cooking oil, so that there is no risk of tainting the dish with meat, fish or any product derived from animals.

Types of dish and their cooking methods

Pulse dishes fall into four main groups, each of which uses one or more cooking methods.

Loaves/bakes

The pulses (unless canned) are *boiled* or *steamed* first. Other ingredients may also be pre-cooked, e.g. shallow frying the chopped vegetables. Everything is mixed together, with spices, nuts, herbs, etc. according to the recipe. Often raw egg is added, to help the mixture set during *baking*. Use a deep-sided baking container, to produce the shape of a loaf of bread.

Unless the container is non-stick, you should line and/ or lightly oil it first, so that the cooked mixture will turn out easily. It may be necessary to cover the mixture for the first part of baking, so the top does not burn. Some recipes require a moist oven for some or all of the cooking time (i.e. the cooking container is placed in another, larger one containing water).

Casseroles/curries

These may involve *shallow frying* some of the ingredients, as a preliminary stage to *stewing* or *braising*. When the different ingredients are added will depend on their cooking time. Usually it is easier to do most of the cooking in the oven. Even-all-round heat reduces the risk of burning (compared with cooking on top of the stove).

Rissoles/burgers

Take care to get the right consistency in the mix for rissoles and burgers, otherwise they will fall apart during cooking and handling. A problem can occur if you do not follow recipe instructions carefully and, for example, the pulses are boiled for too long or in too much liquid, or not adequately drained.

Most burgers and rissoles can be *grilled* (when they may need to be brushed with a little oil to prevent drying out), or *shallow fried* (for health reasons, use the minimum amount of oil, and one that is high in polyunsaturates).

Some types can be *baked*, when you will probably not have to use any oil. Some can be *deep fried*, which produces a crispy outer surface but results in some oil being absorbed by the food (a disadvantage for health reasons).

Stir fried dishes

Some stir fried dishes use pulses. Much of the point of *stir frying* is to produce a tasty dish of quickly and lightly cooked foods which retain a certain crispness and individuality. Pulses can add colour to such dishes, and also protein (which a vegetarian main course dish should have).

Only pulses which retain their shape are suitable for stir fried dishes. Avoid overcooking the dried variety in the preliminary stage. When adding them to the wok or frying pan, keep stirring so that you do not get pulses sticking together to form a clump.

Curried peas

by Chris Hardisty for The Vegetarian Society

SERVES 2

100 g	split peas, soaked for 2 hours	4 oz
1	small onion, finely sliced	1
1	small carrot, diced	1
15 ml	vegetable oil	1 tbsp
10 ml	flour	1 dstsp
10 ml	curry powder	1 dstsp
1	small apple, diced	1
	small handful sultanas	
75 ml	milk or soya milk	3 fl oz
	pinch salt	

1 Drain the peas, cover with fresh water and bring to the boil. Simmer for 30 minutes until soft.

2 Meanwhile, gently fry the onion and carrot in the oil until softened.

3 Drain the peas, reserving the cooking liquid. Add the peas to the onion and carrot, together with the flour, curry powder, apple and sultanas, and cook for a minute or two. ← *This is preparing a roux, as in making a sauce, see Section 10 (page 123).*

4 Slowly add the milk, then 275 ml (10 fl oz) of the reserved cooking liquid and stir until thickened. Season and simmer for 20 minutes. Stir occasionally.

5 Garnish and serve.

Black bean salsa

by the US Quality Bean Information Bureau

SERVES 20 as first course

1 kg	black beans	2 lb
4	cloves garlic	4
1.5 kg	tomatoes, skinned, seeded and diced	3 lb
1 tsp	chilli paste	1 tsp
6 tbsp	fresh coriander leaves, chopped	6 tbsp
12	spring onions, chopped	12
4 tbsp	olive oil	4 tbsp
4	lemons or limes, juice of	4
	salt to taste	

1 Soak beans overnight.

2 Drain and put into a deep saucepan. Cover with fresh water. Bring to the boil, and boil vigorously for 10 minutes. ← *This is an essential safety step.*

3 Reduce to a simmer, add garlic and cook for 45 minutes or until the beans are tender.

4 Drain and remove garlic. While still warm, stir in other ingredients and serve immediately. ← *Or, chill quickly and serve cold (as a first course or salad accompaniment).*

This recipe, for a casserole-type dish, involves frying, boiling and baking.

Lentil savoury

by The Vegetarian Society

SERVES 4

175 g	red lentils	6 oz
2.5 ml each	basil and mixed herbs	½ tsp
50 g	margarine	2 oz
2	onions, chopped	2
30 ml	tomato purée	2 tbsp
	seasoning to taste	
1 × 340 g	can tomatoes	1 × 14 oz
5 ml	brown sugar	1 tsp
175 g	vegetarian Cheddar cheese, sliced	6 oz
150 ml	soured cream	5 fl oz
	seasoning to taste	

1 Place lentils in a pan with enough water to cover them. Add herbs and simmer until tender, for about 50 minutes. Drain.

2 In a saucepan, fry the onion in the margarine until soft. Add the lentils, tomato purée, tomatoes and sugar. Season. Simmer for 15 minutes.

3 Pour into a greased ovenproof dish. Cover with cheese and cream. Bake for 5 to 10 minutes at 180°C until the cheese has melted. Serve at once.

For help to answer questions relating to:

Health and safety

❓ safe working practices

The main hazards are from use of knives, hot equipment and lifting.

Food hygiene

❓ importance of good hygiene

Pulses must be stored and handled as any other fresh food, to protect them from sources of harmful bacteria.

❓ importance of time and temperature

Bacteria increase rapidly in numbers at the right temperature.

❓ main contamination threats

Other food (e.g. fresh vegetables/fruit), food handlers, dirty equipment/work area, harmful cleaning substances and foreign bodies (e.g. pieces of grit).

❓ products not for immediate use

Store above 63°C or below 5°C.

Product knowledge

❓ quality points for pulses

Remind yourself of the general quality checks (page 148). Look at the packaging, the date mark, the condition of the can, the appearance of the pulses themselves.

❓ quality points for cooked dishes

Describe how the dish should look (appearance, consistency), smell (aroma) and taste (texture, flavour). .

❓ preparation methods

These are: soaking, draining, mixing, blanching, slicing and chopping. It may help to base your answer on dishes that you are familiar with. Remember that pulses need to be boiled vigorously to drive off poisons.

❓ cooking methods

This depends on the sort of dish you are preparing. Many involve two or three methods. Try to think of an example for each cooking method.

❓ identifying when dishes are cooked

Dried pulses are cooked to make them moist and tender. Some break up when cooked, and are therefore favourites for soups, burgers and patties which involve mashing or puréeing the cooked pulses. For other dishes, you need to be careful not to overcook the pulses, so they retain their shape and do not taste mushy. Canned pulses are already cooked, but need time to absorb the flavours of the other ingredients, and to get hot (for a hot dish).

Healthy catering practices

❓ replacing high fat ingredients

Remind yourself of some of the tips on page 130 for replacing cream, butter, etc.

❓ fats/oils for healthy eating

See page 110.

❓ cooking methods, etc. to reduce fat

See page 138.

❓ increasing fibre content of dishes

Any dish based on pulses will be a good source of fibre. Some vegetables will further increase the fibre content (see page 138).

❓ reducing salt

See pages 110 and 138.

Self-check questions

1 When using a knife to prepare the ingredients for a pulse dish, give three safe practices you should follow.

2 Why should pulses be covered while they are soaking? Where should they be kept during this time?

With the help of the photograph on page 148, and the description of various pulses:

3 name two pulses of the same group, the only difference being their colour

4 state what bean is mainly cream coloured, but has a black splash

5 state what bean has a knobbly shape

6 name the largest bean

7 state what bean is sometimes sprouted.

Use the key below to check your answers.

8 What bean must definitely be boiled vigorously at the start of cooking?

9 Why should all pulses (with the exception of lentils and split peas) be boiled vigorously for 10 minutes?

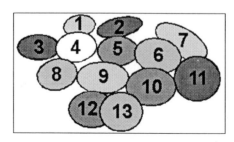

1) Mung beans, 2) aduki beans, 3) haricot beans, 4) butter beans, 5) pinto beans, 6) red kidney beans, 7) yellow split peas, 8) green lentils, 9) red split lentils, 10) marrowfat peas, 11) green split peas, 12) chickpeas, 13) blackeye beans.

NVQ SVQ
Skills check
Prepare and cook basic pulse dishes
Unit 2ND5

level 2

Use this to check your progress against the performance criteria.

Element 1
Prepare basic pulse dishes

Get your preparation areas and equipment ready for use ☐ PC1

Select ingredients of the type, quality and quantity required ☐ PC2

⚠ Pulses: beans, peas, lentils
Other ingredients: fresh vegetables/fruit, preserved vegetables/fruit, cereals, nuts, seeds

Identify and report problems with the quality of ingredients ☐ PC3

Prepare and combine pulses with other ingredients ☐ PC4

⚠ Preparation methods: soaking, draining, mixing, blanching, slicing, chopping

Correctly store pulses not for immediate use ☐ PC5

Clean preparation areas and equipment after use ☐ PC6

Prioritise and carry out your work in an organised, efficient and safe manner ☐ PC7

Element 2
Cook basic pulse dishes

Get your cooking areas and equipment ready for use ☐ PC1

Cook pulse dishes ☐ PC2

⚠ Pulse dishes: loaf/bake, casserole/curry, rissoles/burgers
Cooking methods: baking, grilling, shallow frying, stir frying, braising, stewing, steaming, deep frying

Finish pulse dishes ☐ PC3

Correctly store pulse dishes not for immediate use ☐ PC4

Clean cooking areas and equipment after use ☐ PC5

Identify and report problems with the quality of pulse dishes ☐ PC6

Prioritise and carry out your work in an organised, efficient and safe manner ☐ PC7

Preparing and cooking basic
rice dishes

Preparing rice dishes

With the increased interest in the foods of different parts of the world – in particular, the Indian continent, Far East and Middle East – rice appears much more often on menus. The many varieties offer a wide range of textures, flavours and colours.

As a result, there are few rules which apply to all types of rice. Distinctions once made – such as short grain rices are for puddings, long grain rices for savoury dishes – no longer hold true.

Rice is convenient for caterers. It requires little preparation. It is easy to store – dried rice can be kept in a cool, dry place for weeks or months (but do not use beyond the best-before date). It can be cooked in a number of interesting ways, fairly quickly and easily.

Rice is gluten free (even the variety called glutinous rice). It can be offered to customers who are not able to eat foods which contain wheat flour (pastas are not suitable for a gluten-free diet.)

Some types of rice (clockwise from centre top): Long grain, wild rice mixed with brown, long grain Patna, short grain dessert, long grain brown, Basmati.

Types of rice and their quality points

The different varieties of rice can be put into four broad groups. Some types could go in two or more of these groups, but the classification provides a starting point.

Brown rice

The colour is the distinguishing feature. Another name is wholegrain rice. Both give clues about the character of the rice – it is rice which has undergone minimal milling. This removes the husk, but retains the bran layer and thus more of the vitamins, minerals and fibre.

Brown rice has a long grain, and a distinctly nutty flavour. It is also available in easy-cook form.

Long grain rice

Long grain rice is milled to remove the husk and bran layer. The grain is white, slim and four to five times as long as it is wide. On cooking, the grains separate to give an attractive fluffy effect.

Long grain rice has a subtle flavour which complements both rich and delicate sauces.

Easy-cook long grain white rice has a full flavour and golden colour which turns to white on cooking. Unlike regular rice which is milled direct from the field, it is steamed under pressure before milling. This hardens the grain, reducing the possibility of over cooking. More of the nutritional value is retained.

The main speciality rices, particularly suited to ethnic dishes, are:

- *Basmati rice* – very long grained. Grown in the foothills of the Himalayas it has a fragrant flavour and aroma and is the rice used in Indian dishes such as biryani and pilau rice. Easy-cook and brown basmati are also available

- *Jasmine rice* (also called *Thai fragrant rice*) – another aromatic rice, although its flavour is slightly less pronounced than that of basmati. Originating in Thailand, it differs from other long grain rices in that it has a soft and slightly sticky texture when cooked. This rice is good with both Chinese and south east Asian food

- *Risotto rice* (also called *Arborio rice*) – a medium grain rice. It originates in Italy, and has given its name to the dish risotto, in which it is used. Risotto rice absorbs up to five times its weight of liquid. During cooking, starch is released to give the creamy texture characteristic of the classic risotto.

Short grain rice

More accurately called *pudding rice*, the grains are short, tubby and chalky in appearance and cling together on cooking.

Pudding rice typically comes from Italy and is the one to use for puddings and sweets.

Glutinous rice (also called *sweet* or *sticky rice*) has a round, pearl-like grain which turns sticky when cooked. It tastes slightly sweet, and is used in some Japanese savoury dishes.

Wild rice

Wild rice is not true rice at all, but an aquatic grass. The grains are long and slim, and range in colour from dark brown to black. It is grown in the USA and Canada where it was the traditional food of the American Indians. It is often mixed with other types of rice such as white or brown long grain and basmati, providing an attractive contrast of colour and flavour.

Wild rice is expensive.

Preparation methods for rice

Washing – most rices are intended to be used straight from the packet. Washing these types of rice may lead to a rather sticky, finished dish. But you should always check – and follow – the directions for use on the packet (or workplace recipes). If you are told to wash the rice, place it in a large bowl and fill with cold water. Stir the rice. Once it has settled, pour off the cloudy water. Sometimes this process must be repeated until the water is clear. For some recipes, basmati rice is soaked first, in plenty of cold water.

Draining – after washing or soaking, drain the rice carefully so you don't lose any in the sink. A fine sieve is best.

Mixing – stirring rice and the other recipe ingredients to blend together. Use a kitchen fork to mix cooked rice, as this is less likely to damage the grains.

Moulding – cooked rice is sometimes packed into ring moulds (e.g. savarin moulds) or cup-shaped moulds (e.g. dariole moulds). The mould is first lightly oiled. After a short time, the rice can be turned out, forming an attractive shape.

Other ingredients

Rice is the traditional accompaniment to curries and many ethnic dishes. It is an alternative to potatoes for dishes where the food is served in a sauce, as well as grilled dishes such as kebabs.

Rice can also be combined with a wide range of other foods:

- *vegetables* – rice can be mixed with various vegetables to accompany a main course, or as a salad, or to make a main course, e.g. with chopped onion, red and green peppers, chillies, beans, tomatoes, cauliflower or broccoli florets and peas. Cabbage and lettuce (selected large leaves), tomatoes and peppers (top removed and centre scooped out) and aubergines (cut in half, and centre scooped out) can be stuffed with rice-based mixtures

- *stock* – rice is cooked in stock for pilafs, risottos and paellas. The rice absorbs the stock during cooking, and thus gets more flavourful (the colour will also change). Measure recipe quantities accurately, so that the rice is cooked when all the liquid has been absorbed

- *cheese* – some pilafs and risottos have grated cheese added at the last moment

- *herbs and spices* – to add flavour to rice dishes

- *fungi* – sliced or quartered mushrooms can be mixed with rice for a side dish, or in more complex main course dishes including stir fried dishes

- *eggs* – hard-boiled, then chopped or sieved and mixed with cooked rice, or the yolk removed, mixed with rice and replaced as a stuffing. Some fried rice recipes have beaten egg cooked in at the last moment

- *fish and shellfish* – paellas often include shellfish (e.g. prawns, scampi, mussels), kedgeree is made with rice and smoked haddock or, sometimes, salmon or other fish

- *meats* – paellas, pilafs, risottos and stir fried dishes often include meat, e.g. diced ham and cubes of chicken. If the meat is cooked with the rice, it should be tender and cut into small pieces. If it is added at the last moment, it must already be cooked.

Cooking rice dishes

Rice requires moist cooking, so water, steam or a stock is essential. Some rice dishes involve two stages. The rice is first boiled, for example, then stir fried or shallow fried to reheat it and blend in the flavours of the other ingredients.

To test that rice is cooked, lightly squeeze one or two grains between your fingers. Let the rice cool a bit first! The rice should feel tender, and keep its shape. If it squashes, it has overcooked.

Types of dishes and their cooking methods

You will rarely see the description 'boiled rice' on a menu. Boiling is the most common method of cooking rice, so people assume that 'chicken curry and rice' means boiled rice. Besides, 'boiled rice' seems a rather unappetising way of describing a tasty dish.

There are other rice dishes where the cooking method is included in the name, e.g. fried and stir fried rice.

There is also a group of rice dishes where the rice is cooked in stock and vegetables, with perhaps meat and/ or fish added. The name used varies from country to country: braised rice is the English term; risotto is Italian in origin or style; pilau or pilaf (other spellings are pilao, pilaw and pilaff) originates from the East; while paella is the Spanish version.

Boiled

Long grain and brown rice may be cooked in plenty of boiling water. At the end of cooking, the rice is thoroughly drained, then served. Alternatively, the rice is cooled (or *refreshed*) under cold running water. It is then reheated for service. One method is to cover the rice with a clean tea towel and place in a warm oven. It may also be reheated in a microwave oven, a steamer or in a bain-marie.

With the exception of glutinous rice, the aim is to remove excess starch and produce fluffy rice, where the grains are separate.

You should stir the rice as you add it to the boiling water, and two or three times during boiling. This stops the grains from sticking together, or collecting on the bottom of the pan and burning.

Where recipes or packet instructions state the quantity of water to be used for a certain weight or volume of rice, you should follow this. The amount of liquid absorbed varies considerably according to the type of rice.

Absorption method of boiling

In this method the amount of water is measured exactly, so that by the end of cooking it has all been absorbed by the rice.

The absorption method (other names are *poach-steamed* and *boiled dry*) is recommended by The Rice Bureau because it retains all the nutritional goodness of the rice. Nothing is lost into the water.

The packet or recipe instructions will tell you the amount of water to use, whether it is necessary to soak the rice and if so for how long:

- use a saucepan that is big enough to allow the rice to expand, and which has a tight-fitting lid

- put the rice, cold water and seasoning in the pan, and bring to the boil

- stir once, lower the heat to a gentle simmer

- cover and cook for the recommended time

- do not lift the lid during cooking, as it is essential to trap the steam over the rice.

Alternatively, use an ovenproof pan or casserole dish, and transfer the rice to a moderate oven (180°C) after it has come to the boil. The cooking time is at least twice as long as the top of the stove method.

Steamed

Rice can be steamed to reheat it. It should be covered, e.g. with lightly oiled greaseproof paper and kitchen foil. A large, shallow dish is best, so the heat can reach the rice quickly. It will take 20 minutes or longer to get piping hot. So that the rice is not overcooked, time the initial boiling carefully and stop cooking when the rice is just tender but not fully cooked.

Pilaf, pilau or braised rice

In many recipes the first stage is to lightly fry chopped onion, etc. without colouring (called *sweating*). The rice is cooked for a few minutes with the vegetables, and then the stock poured on, other ingredients added, the pan covered with a tight-fitting lid and transferred to the oven.

As the rice cooks it absorbs all the stock. Because the rice is cooked in an oven in liquid (like *braising*), it is often called braised rice.

Other ingredients (already cooked) may be added just before service. Lightly stir through with a fork, so as not to damage the rice.

Risotto

The steps are similar to cooking a pilaf, but by tradition a risotto rice is used and all the cooking takes place on top of the stove. In this respect, it is similar to *stewing*. (You will find exceptions, e.g. recipes that use a long grain rice.)

Usually the stock is added in stages, half to begin with and the remainder during cooking when the mixture gets too dry. Once the first amount of stock has come to the boil, the pan is covered with a tight-fitting lid.

Mixed fried and stir fried

The already cooked rice is fried with the other recipe ingredients. Usually the rice is added towards the end of cooking, so it has time to get piping hot, but not to overcook.

The cooking times for fried and stir fried rice dishes are usually short, to preserve the colours and textures of the different ingredients. The food has to be served at once, otherwise this effect is lost.

Aubergine and courgette risotto
by Dufrais

SERVES 4

350 g	aubergine, trimmed and diced	12 oz
10 ml	salt	2 tsp
45 ml	vegetable oil	3 tbsp
2	small onions, roughly chopped	2
1	clove garlic, crushed and peeled	1
5 ml	dried sage	1 tsp
275 g	arborio (risotto) rice	10 oz
500 ml	vegetable stock	18 fl oz
1 × 230 g	can chopped tomatoes	1 × 8 oz
15 ml	caster sugar	1 tbsp
225 g	courgettes, diced	8 oz
200 ml	red Bistro Chef or red wine	7 fl oz
	sprig of fresh sage (to garnish)	

> This takes away excess moisture from the aubergine.

1 Sprinkle the prepared aubergine with salt. Leave to stand for about 30 minutes in a colander. Rinse well and dry with kitchen paper.

2 Heat the oil in a large frying pan. Fry the onions, garlic and sage until soft. Add the aubergine and continue cooking for a few minutes. Stir in the rice, stock, tomatoes and sugar.

> Stir with a fork not spoon, so as not to crush the grains of rice.

3 Cover and simmer for 12 minutes, stirring occasionally.

4 Add the courgettes and red Bistro Chef or wine. Cook for 4 to 6 minutes, covered, or until tender.

> The extra liquid will absorbed

5 Serve garnished with fresh sage.

Above: *mussel and mixed herb risotto. Fish stock is used in this Forte Crest recipe.*
Left: *vegetable and herb risotto. Made with Japan rice and vegetarian stock the other ingredients include courgette, celery, peas, romaine lettuce, tomato concassé, mange tout, cauliflower.*

> A paellera is traditionally used – a special two-handled shallow pan. Otherwise, you can use a large frying pan.

Paella (seafood rice)

by Nestlé Carnation

SERVES 10

30 ml	oil	2 tbsp
2	garlic, crushed and peeled	2
2	medium onions, sliced	2
60 ml	tomato purée	4 tbsp
450 g	risotto rice	1 lb
850 ml	vegetable stock	1½ pt
15 ml	turmeric	1 tbsp
	seasoning to taste	
15 ml	paprika	1 tbsp
1 × 397 g	can chopped tomatoes	1 × 14 oz
75 g	coconut milk powder	3 oz
1 × 397 g	can evaporated milk	1 × 14 oz
225 g	cooked chicken, sliced	8 oz
100 g	smoked mackerel, flaked	4 oz
450 g	cooked, peeled prawns	1 lb
450 g	fresh, live mussels, cleaned	1 lb
225 g	fresh cod, diced	8 oz
60 ml	fresh parsley, chopped	4 tbsp

See page 217.

1 Fry garlic and onions in the oil for 5 minutes. Stir in tomato purée and rice.

2 Add stock, spices, seasonings and tomatoes, simmer for 10 minutes, stirring occasionally.

3 Blend coconut milk powder with evaporated milk, add to the pan and heat for a further 5 minutes.

4 Add chicken, mackerel, prawns, mussels, cod and parsley. Heat until mussels have opened and cod and rice are thoroughly cooked, about 10 minutes. Serve at once.

Braised rice

SERVES 10

550 g	long grain rice	1¼ lb
100 g	margarine or butter	4 oz
275 g	shallots or onions, finely chopped	10 oz
1 litre	chicken or vegetable stock	2 pt
	seasoning to taste	

> Use a pan with a tight fitting lid, which can go in the oven.

1 Melt half the fat. Add the shallots and cook gently until soft, but not coloured. Add the rice and cook for about 3 minutes, stirring frequently. Stir in the stock and bring to the boil.

2 Cover with a circle of greased greaseproof paper, then put the lid on and transfer to a hot oven at 230°C for about 15 minutes. The rice should have absorbed all the stock.

> For extra flavour, add a bayleaf and some thyme.

3 Stir the remaining margarine or butter through the rice with a fork. Check seasoning and serve as soon as possible.

> Remove the bayleaf!

Peach meringue pudding

by The Rice Bureau

SERVES 8

75 g	short grain rice	3 oz
600 ml	milk	1 pt
125 g	caster sugar	5 oz
2.5 ml	ground nutmeg	½ tsp
2	eggs, size 4, separated	2
40 ml	raspberry conserve	8 tsp
4	ripe peaches, halved and stones removed	4

1 Place rice, milk, nutmeg and 25 g (1 oz) of the caster sugar in a saucepan. Bring to the boil, then simmer very gently, stirring frequently, until the rice is cooked and most of the milk absorbed, about 25 minutes.

> Glass so the dish looks attractive.

2 Beat the egg yolks into the rice, then pour the mixture into a glass soufflé dish.

3 Place a little raspberry conserve in each peach half. Arrange the peaches against the outside of the dish, so the conserve can be seen through the side of the dish.

4 Whisk the egg white until stiff. Whisk in half the remaining sugar, then fold in the rest. Spoon meringue over the rice and peaches.

5 Bake at 190°C for about 5 minutes. Serve hot, or leave to cool then chill before serving.

> Because the pudding is cooked for such a short time, it would be safer to use pasteurised eggs (see checklist on page 166).

Knowledge check
Prepare and cook basic rice dishes
Element 2

NVQ SVQ

Skills check
Prepare and cook basic
rice dishes
Unit 2ND6

lev **2**

For help to answer questions
relating to:

Health and safety

? safe working practices

The main hazards are from using
knives and hot equipment.

Food hygiene

? importance of good hygiene

Rice must be stored and handled as
any other fresh food, to protect it
from sources of harmful bacteria.

? importance of time and temperature

Special precautions must be taken
because of the dangers caused by
Bacillus cereus. The spores of this
bacteria are often present from the
time the rice was harvested. They
are reactivated and multiply to
harmful numbers when rice is boiled
and kept hot for a long time. To
reduce the risk, you should serve rice
immediately after cooking. If this is
not possible:

- cool it quickly (under running
  water, as described in the text),
  then refrigerate until required
- quickly and thoroughly reheat
  and serve at once.

Where rice has to be kept hot for
service (e.g. on a self-service
counter), check the temperature is
above 63°C. At the end of service,
throw any left-over rice away

? main contamination threats

Other food (e.g. raw meat, fresh
vegetables/fruit), food handlers, dirty
equipment/work area, harmful
cleaning substances, foreign bodies
(e.g. pieces of grit), etc.

? products not for immediate use

Keep above 63°C or below 5°C. It is
safer to chill rice and reheat
immediately before service than to
keep it hot (see above).

Product knowledge

? quality points for rice

Look at the packaging, the date
mark and the appearance of the rice.

? quality points for cooked dishes

Describe how the dish should look
(appearance, consistency), smell
(aroma), and taste *(texture, flavour)*.

? preparation methods for rice dishes

These are: washing, draining, mixing
and moulding.

? cooking methods for rice dishes

Many rice dishes involve boiling. If
the rice is then cooled and chilled
before use, it might be steamed to
reheat it. In other dishes, the process
is similar to braising (with pilaf) or
stewing (with risotto). Rice which is
fried or stir fried needs to be cooked
by some other method first (normally
by boiling).

? identifying when dishes are cooked

Most rice dishes should produce
fluffy grains that are soft but not too
soft, have kept their shape and are
separate (i.e. not clumped together in
a soggy mass).

With pilafs, risottos, and boiled rice
using the absorption method, all the
cooking liquid should have been
absorbed by the end of cooking.

Healthy catering practices

? replacing high fat ingredients

One of the advantages of most rice
dishes is that they do not involve the
use of fat. The rice itself contains
virtually no fat. Adding cheese will
increase the fat, so you might
consider using a low-fat cheese or
omitting it. Mixing butter through
the rice before service adds flavour,
but also fat. Meat which is added to
pilafs and risottos should have all
the fat trimmed off first.

? fats/oils for healthy eating

For fried rice dishes, use oils which
are high in polyunsaturates, and low
in saturates.

? increasing fibre content of dishes

Any dish based on rice will be a good
source of fibre, and brown rice
contains about twice the fibre of
white rice. Some vegetables will
further increase the fibre content.

? reducing salt

Rice contains almost no natural salt.
For pilafs, risottos and fried rice
dishes, some of the ingredients
reduce the need to add salt, e.g.
turmeric, saffron, onion, green
pepper, cucumber, mint, vinegar.

Self-check questions

1 When using a knife to prepare the
ingredients for a rice dish, give 3 safe
practices you should follow.

2 Why is it safer to keep cooked rice
chilled, and reheat small quantities as
required, than to keep it hot?

3 If rice is kept hot for service, what
should be done with any that is left at
the end of service? Why?

4 Name three types of rice, and describe
their appearance.

5 Describe three rice dishes, and for
each, state how the rice is cooked.

6 For one of these dishes, give the
points you should look for when
judging the quality of the finished dish.

7 Say what might have gone wrong if
cooked long grain or brown rice is
stodgy. How can this be avoided?

8 If you have to cook a variety of rice
you are not familiar with, what points
should you look out for in the
instructions for use on the packet?

Element 1

Prepare basic rice dishes

Get your preparation areas and
equipment ready for use
PC

Select ingredients of the type,
quality and quantity required
PC

▲ Rices: brown, long grain, short grain, wild
Other ingredients: vegetable, stock, cheese,
herbs/spices, fungi, eggs, fish/shellfish, meats

Identify and report problems with the
freshness or quality of ingredients
PC

Prepare rice and other ingredients
PC

▲ Preparation methods: washing, draining,
mixing, moulding

Correctly store rice dishes not for
immediate use
PC

Clean preparation areas and
equipment after use
PC

Prioritise and carry out your work in an
organised, efficient and safe manner
PC

Element 2

Cook basic rice dishes

Get your cooking areas and
equipment ready for use
PC

Cook rice dishes
PC

▲ Rice dishes: boiled, pilau/pilaf, risotto,
mixed fried/stir fried, steamed
Cooking methods: boiling/steaming, braising,
stewing, stir frying

Finish rice dishes
PC

Correctly store rice dishes
not for immediate use
PC

Clean cooking areas and
equipment after use
PC

Identify and report problems with the
quality of rice dishes
PC

Prioritise and carry out your work in an
organised, efficient and safe manner
PC

Preparing and cooking basic
pasta dishes

Preparing pasta dishes

Pasta is low in fat, high in fibre and a good source of protein. Tasty pasta dishes can be prepared quickly, and fairly easily. Also there is an exciting range of more complex dishes for more creative menus.

Pasta contains complex carbohydrates, which the body digests slowly. This gradual release of energy makes pasta a favourite food for long-distance runners.

Types of pasta

The basic ingredients of pasta are flour and water. Commercially-made pastas use a very finely milled flour, called *durum wheat semolina*, produced from the hard seed at the centre of wheat grain. This gives the pasta its rich amber colour and prevents it from losing shape and becoming mushy in cooking.

Some types of pasta also use oil or egg. Egg pasta is a darker yellow colour.

Green pasta is traditionally made by adding spinach to the mix, red pasta by using tomato. More recent introductions are black pasta, coloured with squid-ink, and tricoloured pasta, packed to give a mixture of green, red and white (*tricolore*). Wholewheat pasta is also available.

Some chefs make their own pasta, using a strong (bread) flour, or wholewheat flour. The commercially-produced pastas are available in two forms:

- *dried* – regarded as the best for straight and simple shapes. It has a firm texture and goes well with the heavier sauces. For people who like their pasta *al dente*, dried pasta cooks up best. An Italian expression, *al dente* translates as 'to the tooth', meaning the food offers slight resistance when bitten into

- *fresh and frozen pasta* (i.e. pre-prepared) – often made with whole egg, giving it a softer, smoother texture which goes well with cream and lighter tasting sauces. These products offer a considerable choice, particularly for stuffed pasta shapes and filled pasta dishes.

For this week, customers of Sutcliffe Catering had a choice of four pastas and five sauces.

Pasta comes in over 200 different shapes, with more than 600 names for these shapes:

- the longish, thin varieties include *spaghetti* (string-like when cooked) and *macaroni* (short tubes, about 25 mm long)

- *lasagne* is in sheet form, mostly used for layered dishes, finished in the oven

- various types come already *stuffed* with a filling, including ravioli (squares or little packets) and tortellini (plump, crescent shaped)

- cannelloni (fat tubes) are ready to be stuffed

- other shapes, used as garnishes in soups or cooked like spaghetti and served with a sauce, include stars, twists, bows, ribbons, wheels, spirals, shells, and even animal shapes.

Quality and storage points

Check the best-before date on dried, frozen and similar long-life pastas, and the use-by date on fresh pastas. The packaging should be in good condition, and you must follow the storage recommendations.

Dried pasta should be kept in a cool, dry room. Use the older stock first, but always check the date stamp. Once a packet has been opened, transfer any which is not used to an airtight container. Write the best-before date on the container.

Fresh pasta should be kept refrigerated, and well wrapped so it does not absorb flavours or smells from other foods. Keep apart from uncooked foods.

Other ingredients

Spaghetti is usually served plain – tossed in a little hot butter and accompanied with grated cheese (traditionally Parmesan) – or with a sauce. There is a vast range of suitable sauces, made from meat, fish, shellfish or vegetable-based, with fresh herbs, spices, wine, stock, cream, cheese, eggs, and combinations of these. Some of these sauces can be quite thick and substantial, e.g. a bolognaise made with minced beef.

Macaroni can also be served with one of these sauces, or combined with a thick sauce, placed in a suitable dish and baked or grilled so that the surface browns.

Lasagne dishes consist of two or more layers of pasta, like a multi-tiered sandwich. The fillings include substantial mixes, e.g. of spinach and ricotta cheese, as well as one or more different sauces, e.g. tomato, mornay and basil.

Stuffed pastas are mostly served with a sauce. Ravioli and tortellini are often pre-prepared with a filling, but you may come across home-made versions.

Because it is larger, the filling in cannelloni can be more robust. The stuffed tubes of cannelloni are placed in a dish and covered in sauce before being baked.

Preparing pasta

Spaghetti and pre-prepared stuffed pastas need no preparation – they have simply to be taken out of the packet and put straight into boiling salted water. The other ingredients for the dish will have to be *chopped* or *sliced* (e.g. vegetables), and possibly *grated* (e.g. cheese), before being *mixed* together.

Dishes which involve layering the pasta (e.g. lasagne) or stuffing it (e.g. cannelloni) may require more time-consuming preparation. If you are using a dried pasta, it will have to be cooked first (to become tender). After boiling, the pasta should be cooled quickly under cold running water, and then *drained* thoroughly.

Some varieties of lasagne and cannelloni are pre-cooked. You can put them straight into the dish, with the sauce, etc. As the pasta will absorb some liquid while cooking, use a thinner sauce than usual (about one-third more liquid). If you do not have enough sauce to do this, boil the pasta in water (see opposite page) for about five minutes, then cool under running water and drain.

Just some of the wide range of pastas available.

1) Vermicelli, 2) lasagne, 3) green tagliatelle, 4) tagliatelle, 5) cannelloni, 6) green and white lasagne, 7) wholewheat spaghetti, 8) spaghetti, 9) green spaghetti, 10) pastine, 11) pasta shells, 12) spaghettini, 13) short macaroni, 14) tortellini, 15) alphabet shapes

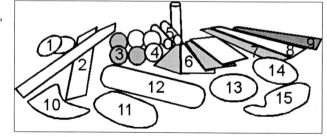

Cooking pasta dishes

Pasta can be sauced, stuffed, layered and baked. There is virtually no limit to the combinations that are possible with vegetables, seafood, pulses, cheeses and meats.

As a general guide, the longer, thin and flat varieties, such as spaghetti, are more suitable for the thinner sauces, while the shapes such as conchiglie and penne are ideal for the thicker sauces which find their way into the holes and folds.

Types of dish, cooking and finishing methods used

The most important cooking method for pasta is *boiling*. This is because pasta is made to be cooked in plenty of water. The exception is the special pre- or partly cooked pasta which can be used for lasagne, cannelloni or macaroni dishes. (Some of these dishes are also available fully prepared, chilled or frozen, to be baked or microwaved to reheat them, see Section 1.)

When pasta dishes are mixed with sauces and various ingredients, to be reheated or grilled in the dish, choose an ovenproof dish or a suitable cooking container. Lightly oil or butter the dish first, so the pasta will not stick. Usually such dishes are covered for the first part of reheating, and the lid removed in time for the surface to brown attractively.

In some dishes, the sauce is mixed with the pasta. In others it is poured over the top of the dish (and perhaps on previous layers, e.g. of lasagne). This is called *saucing*.

Spaghetti

Spaghetti is at its best when served a few moments after it has been boiled and drained. Where this is not possible, the pasta can be boiled in advance, then cooled under cold running water and drained. Keep it chilled and, as required, reheat by plunging it into very hot water for a few moments. Drain and serve at once, with the accompanying sauce or tossed in a little hot butter.

Some spaghetti dishes have raw egg mixed through them, at the last moment. The heat of the pasta cooks the egg.

In others, the spaghetti is mixed in with the sauce. This might be done in a shallow-sided pan, so the pasta, sauce and other ingredients are briefly heated together.

Layering the meat sauce on sheets of cooked lasagne. In the pot on the left is the cheese sauce.

Macaroni

Macaroni can be cooked and served in a similar way to spaghetti. In other macaroni dishes, the pasta is mixed with the sauce, cooked vegetables, meat, etc. Grated cheese is sprinkled over the top, and the dish reheated and browned under the grill or in a very hot oven.

The cooking methods involved are *boiling*, for the initial cooking, and then *grilling*, to reheat and brown the surface. Alternatively, this step can be done using *combination cooking*, e.g. in a microwave oven which has a conventional heating element.

Browning the surface once cheese has been added is called *gratinating with cheese*.

Cannelloni and lasagne

The pasta will have been boiled before the dish is assembled (unless it is the pre-cooked type).

The dish with the layers of sauce, stuffing (for cannelloni) and fillings (for lasagne) is then reheated and, in some cases, the surface browned. If no browning is required, the reheating can be done in a *steamer*. Alternatively, you can use a *combination oven*, which works like a conventional oven, but has the option of introducing steam into the oven. The other type of combination oven uses conventional heat and microwave energy.

Garnishing

Follow your workplace guidelines or recipe suggestions for presenting an attractive-looking pasta dish. The garnish (e.g. a small sprig of fresh basil) can add a contrast of colour. Choose something which is appropriate to the dish ingredients and style, e.g. a whole prawn on top of a seafood pasta.

More on boiling pasta

Good-quality dried pasta will double in size and almost treble in weight when cooked. As a guideline, allow 60 to 75 g uncooked pasta, 75 to 90 g of fresh pasta per person, depending on the thickness and richness of the accompanying sauce.

Always use a large saucepan containing plenty of fast boiling water and a little salt. You will need 1 to 1½ litres of water for every 225 g dry pasta.

Once you have emptied the pasta into the boiling water, stir it occasionally with a plastic spoon. Good-quality pasta should not then stick.

Some chefs add a little oil to the boiling water. They find the oil stops the pasta from sticking together.

If you are boiling spaghetti, and the pan is too small for the lengths of pasta to fit in, feed it in gradually. To do this, take hold of the bunch of spaghetti at one end. Drop the other end into the boiling water, and continue lowering into the water. After a few moments in the water, the spaghetti becomes soft enough to bend around the pan. Let go before the last few centimetres drop into the water.

Many things can affect the required cooking time. Read the packet instructions carefully, but use your own judgement and test the pasta at regular intervals during cooking. The aim is to serve it tender, but still firm. You can test it by removing a small piece from the pan, allowing it to cool sufficiently, then squeezing between your fingers.

Stuffed pastas such as tortellini and ravioli should stand for a minute or two before draining. Otherwise pasta should be drained and tossed as soon as it's cooked. Don't drain it too thoroughly, a little water remaining from the cooking helps the pasta to absorb the sauce.

This dish is high in fibre, low in fat, and suitable for vegetarians.

Spiced courgette and pasta pot

SERVES 10

275 g	wholemeal macaroni	10 oz
10 ml	polyunsaturated oil	2 tsp
550 g	onions, finely chopped	1¼ lb
4	cloves garlic, crushed and peeled	4
1.25 kg	courgettes, sliced into rounds	2½ lb
175 g each	green and red peppers, sliced	6 oz each
550 g	button mushrooms	1¼ oz
5 g	chilli pepper to taste	¼ oz
10 g each	ground cumin and paprika	½ oz each
275 g	haricot beans, cooked	10 oz
7	eggs	7
425 ml	low-fat natural yogurt	15 fl oz
600 ml	skimmed milk	1 pt
	seasoning to taste	
	fresh parsley, chopped (to garnish)	

1 Place the macaroni into boiling salted water. Return to the boil, then simmer for 12 to 15 minutes, stirring from time to time.

2 When the macaroni is cooked, immediately cool under cold running water. Drain thoroughly.

3 Heat the oil, add the onions and garlic, and cook until soft but not coloured, about 4 minutes. Add the courgettes, peppers, mushrooms and spices, and fry until the vegetables are lightly cooked. Lightly mix in the haricot beans and macaroni.

You need a large pan.

4 Place this mixture into a greased casserole dish or portion-size ovenproof dishes.

5 Whisk together the eggs, yogurt, milk and seasoning until well combined. Pour over the vegetables and pasta, just to cover them. Add a little more after the mixture has soaked through.

This dish uses three cooking methods: boiling, frying and baking.

6 Bake until lightly set, about 20 minutes at 200°C. Serve with a sprinkling of chopped parsley.

Cannelloni con spinaci e mandorle

by Buitoni

SERVES 6

350 g	fresh spinach, blanched, chopped finely	12 oz
30 ml	olive oil	2 tbsp
1	large onion, finely chopped	1
1	clove garlic, crushed and peeled	1
1	green pepper, deseeded and finely chopped	1
50 g	ground almonds	2 oz
25 g	whole almonds, finely chopped	1
2.5 ml	nutmeg	½ tsp
20 ml	fresh oregano, chopped	4 tsp
150 ml	vegetable stock	5 fl oz
	seasoning to taste	
12	cannelloni tubes	12

for the sauce

1	medium onion, finely chopped	1
1 x 425 g	can chopped tomatoes	1 x 15 oz
5 ml	sugar	1 tsp
75 g	Mozzarella cheese, grated	3 oz

1 Heat 15 ml (1 tbsp) oil in a pan and fry the onion, garlic and pepper for 3 to 4 minutes until soft. Add the spinach, almonds, nutmeg, 10 ml (2 tsp) oregano, stock and seasoning. Cook for a further 2 to 3 minutes.

2 Fill the cannelloni with this mixture and place in a lightly greased shallow ovenproof dish.

Cannelloni tubes come partly cooked.

3 Heat the remaining oil in a large saucepan and fry the onion for 4 to 5 minutes until browned. Add the tomato, remaining oregano and sugar. Bring to the boil and simmer for 5 minutes.

4 Pour this sauce over the cannelloni. Top with Mozzarella and bake for 30 to 35 minutes at 200°C. Serve immediately.

Spaghetti alla carbonara

by Dufrais

SERVES 4

350 g	spaghetti	12 oz
45 ml	olive oil	3 tbsp
1	medium onion, chopped	1
6	rashers of smoked bacon, derinded and chopped	6
100 ml	white Bistro Chef, or white wine	4 fl oz
4	eggs, size 2	4
75 g	Parmesan cheese, freshly grated	3 oz
30 ml	parsley, freshly chopped	2 tbsp
1	garlic clove, crushed and peeled	1
	seasoning to taste	

1 Drop the spaghetti into plenty of rapidly boiling salted water. Boil for 8 to 10 minutes until tender.

Allow it to curl around the pan as it softens.

2 Meanwhile, fry the onion and bacon in the oil for 4 minutes until golden brown. Add Bistro Chef or white wine and boil until most of the liquid has evaporated.

3 Beat the eggs with the Parmesan, parsley and garlic. Season.

4 Drain the spaghetti. Immediately, stir in the beaten eggs, onion and bacon, so that the heat from the spaghetti cooks the egg. Serve accompanied with more Parmesan.

Lasagne con vegetali

by Buitoni

SERVES 4 to 6

15 ml	olive oil	1 tbsp
2	onions, finely chopped	2
2 each	red and green peppers, deseeded and chopped	2 each
1 x 425 g	can chopped tomatoes	1 x 15 oz
1	clove garlic, crushed and peeled	1
60 ml	tomato purée	4 tbsp
10 ml	fresh basil, chopped	2 tsp
	seasoning to taste	
9 sheets	lasagne verdi	9 sheets
300 ml	mornay (cheese) sauce	½ pt
40 g	Gruyère cheese, grated	1½ oz

1 Heat the oil and fry the onions and peppers for 4 to 5 minutes until softened. Add the tomatoes, garlic, tomato purée, basil and seasoning. Cover and simmer for 30 minutes.

2 Spoon a little of the cooked vegetables into a 28 x 17 cm rectangular ovenproof dish and add a layer of lasagne, without overlapping.

Use pre-cooked lasagne, or cook first.

3 Continue with alternate layers of lasagne and vegetables, finishing with a layer of lasagne. Spread the mornay sauce over the top and sprinkle with the Gruyère.

4 Bake for 25 to 30 minutes at 180°C. Serve with a mixed salad.

For help to answer questions relating to:

Health and safety

? safe working practices

The main hazards are from using hot equipment, lifting large/awkward to handle saucepans, and knives for preparation of other ingredients.

Food hygiene

? importance of good hygiene

Dried pasta is not a particular food safety risk, and it can be kept at room temperature for quite a long time, as you will note from the date stamp on the packet. However, bacteria will be attracted to the cooked pasta dish, and to pre-prepared, stuffed pastas. These must be stored and handled as any other fresh food.

? importance of time and temperature

Bacteria increase rapidly in numbers at temperatures between 5°C and 63°C.

? main contamination threats

Other food (e.g. fresh vegetables/ fruit, raw meat, uncooked fish), food handlers, dirty equipment/work area, harmful cleaning substances and foreign bodies (e.g. pieces of grit).

? products not for immediate use

Store above 63°C or below 5°C. Stuffed pasta dishes can be kept hot for a short time before service, without the quality suffering. Other pasta dishes need to be served immediately after the pasta has been cooked or reheated. Delay will cause the pasta to become sticky and rather solid.

Product knowledge

? quality points for pasta

Look at the packaging, the date mark, and the appearance of the pasta itself.

? quality points for cooked dishes

Describe how the dish should look (*appearance, consistency*), smell (*aroma*), and taste (*texture, flavour*).

? cooking methods for pasta dishes

Most involve boiling, and dishes which are reheated and/or browned on the surface may be grilled or baked in a hot oven. Steaming is sometimes used to reheat dishes.

? identifying when pasta is cooked

The pasta should be tender, but not too soft. Remind yourself of what *al dente* means! The whole dish should be piping hot for service, with sauces and other ingredients properly cooked. Timing is a key skill, in bringing everything together at the right moment.

Healthy catering practices

? replacing high fat ingredients

Pasta is very low in fat. If the dish involves tossing the pasta in butter, or frying some of the ingredients in oil, these steps will obviously add fat. Also the sauce and the accompanying ingredients can make the dish less healthy. Ingredients which are quite high in fat include cheese, cream, milk-based sauces and meat. For some of these, you can substitute low-fat alternatives. All visible fat can be trimmed off meat.

? fats/oils for healthy eating

See page 110.

? increasing fibre content of dishes

Any dish based on pasta will be a good source of fibre, and wholemeal pasta is especially good. Some types of vegetable will further increase the fibre content (see page 138).

? reducing salt

See page 110.

Self-check questions

1 When using a knife to prepare the ingredients for a pasta dish, give 3 safe practices you should follow.

2 Where and how should pre-prepared fresh pasta be stored before use?

3 If cooked pasta is not to be served immediately, how should it be kept? What are the reasons?

4 If the sauce for a pasta dish has been made in advance, where should it be kept?

5 If the cooked pasta for a dish is very soft and sticky, what are the likely causes?

6 Describe how you would cool pasta after boiling.

7 How much water should you use when boiling pasta? What temperature should the water be when the pasta is added?

8 Name a method for reheating each type of pasta dish.

9 Look back to the photograph on page 160. For four of the types of pasta shown, describe briefly a suitable dish, stating the preparation and cooking methods which it uses.

NVQ
SVQ

■ Skills check ■
Prepare and cook basic
pasta dishes
Unit 2ND12

leve
2

Use this to check your progress again
the performance criteria.

Element 1

Prepare basic pasta dishes

Get your preparation areas and equipment ready for use ☐ PC

Select ingredients of the type, quality and quantity required ☐ PC

△ Pastas: prepared fresh/dried spaghetti, macaroni, stuffed pasta, lasagna
Other ingredients: vegetables, meat, stock, cheese, spices, eggs, fish/shellfish, herbs

Identify and report problems with the freshness or quality of ingredients ☐ PC

Prepare pasta ☐ PC

△ Preparation methods: mixing, draining, chopping, grating, slicing

Combine pasta with other ingredients ☐ PC

Correctly store pasta dishes not for immediate use ☐ PC

Clean preparation areas and equipment after use ☐ PC

Prioritise and carry out your work in an organised, efficient and safe manner ☐ PC

Element 2

Cook basic pasta dishes

Get your cooking areas and equipment ready for use ☐ PC1

Cook pasta dishes ☐ PC2

△ Pasta dishes: lasagna, cannelloni, macaroni, spaghetti
Cooking methods: boiling, steaming, combination cooking, grilling

Finish pasta dishes ☐ PC3

△ Finishing methods: garnishing, gratinating with cheese, saucing

Correctly store pasta dishes not for immediate use ☐ PC4

Clean cooking areas and equipment after use ☐ PC5

Identify and report problems with the quality of pasta dishes ☐ PC6

Prioritise and carry out your work in an organised, efficient and safe manner ☐ PC7

Preparing egg dishes

The chicken egg is by far the most common type of egg. When people or recipes refer to eggs, they mean the chicken or hen egg. In recent years, two other types of egg have become better known:

- *duck eggs* – stronger in flavour, sometimes offered as an option for fried eggs and omelettes

- *quail eggs* – tiny, flavourful eggs, mostly used for a starter or as a cocktail snack. They are served hard-boiled, normally in their shell, with sea salt or flavoured salt. Quail eggs can be purchased pre-cooked and chilled, canned or bottled, or uncooked.

There are various types of chicken egg, and the use of descriptions like *free range eggs* and *barn eggs* is controlled by law. They refer to the conditions under which the chickens are kept, such as access to the open air, amount of floor space, etc.

Quality and storage points

An egg should not be used if its shell is damaged. You cannot tell anything more about the quality of the egg until you crack it open to use it. In the case of a boiled egg served in its shell (e.g. for breakfast or a light supper), its quality will not be apparent until the customer opens the egg to eat it.

For these reasons, you have to take special care over the storage of eggs. Check the date stamp on the box or tray. If you have to take the eggs out of their original packaging, write the use-by date on the box or tray you move them to. (This will not be necessary if each egg has been date-stamped by the producer.)

Keep eggs in the refrigerator. Storage in a cool room is no longer recommended, because of the risk of the egg being contaminated with *salmonella*. Another reason for keeping eggs chilled is to protect their freshness.

Eggs pick up foreign flavours quite easily. To reduce this risk, store them away from strong smelling foods.

There should be no need to wash eggs. If you have to do so because something has been spilt on them (e.g. a carton of milk knocked over in the refrigerator), use the eggs as quickly as possible. Washing removes the natural protective coating.

Use very fresh eggs for poaching.

Some customers do not like egg dishes unless they are well cooked.

Baked eggs with prawns, cream and a sprinkling of nutmeg. The white china dishes are ramekins.

Assembling poached eggs florentine for final reheating under the grill or in a very hot oven. The white dishes are the same as those used for eggs sur le plat.

Other ingredients

The favourite accompaniments to eggs as a breakfast dish include bacon (often the smoked type, grilled or fried), sausages (grilled or fried), mushrooms (sliced or quartered and fried), and tomatoes (grilled or fried). Instead of bacon, some people prefer ham (usually sliced and cold).

Speciality breakfast dishes include grilled or sauté kidneys with a side serving of fried, scrambled or poached egg. Smoked haddock (poached) is often enjoyed with a poached egg.

When eggs are served as one of the courses of a meal, poached, or en cocotte, they can be made into a very special dish, perhaps with lobster, crab or prawns.

Hard-boiled eggs can be served cold with mayonnaise as a first course. They can be stuffed: the yolk removed, mixed with seasoning, herbs, etc. and piped into a rosette. They can be pickled, or served with a curry sauce on a bed of rice.

In salads, eggs go well with most meats, poultry and fish (including the smoked varieties), and with most vegetables.

The popular fillings for omelettes include cheese, chopped ham, mushrooms (previously shallow fried), tomato (squares of the tomato flesh) and asparagus (cooked and chopped into short lengths).

For flat omelettes, there is also a very wide range. Examples include onion and peppers (finely chopped and fried), potato (cooked and chopped into small pieces), chopped ham, and herbs.

For a dessert or sweet course, omelettes can be filled with jam and/or fruit.

Preparation methods

For scrambled eggs and omelettes, the eggs are *beaten* lightly. Most chefs use a fork to do this. The aim is to break up the yolks and the whites, and a minute or so of vigorous beating is sufficient to achieve this.

Other chefs prefer to *whisk* the eggs. Do not over-whisk, as this will make the scrambled egg/omelette rather rubbery.

Eggs have other uses in cookery (see Sections 17 and 19). For example, the whites when vigorously *whisked* form a stiff mixture. This can be the basis of a meringue topping for a pie, or meringues (e.g. to be stuffed with cream), or for *folding* into a cake mixture or soufflé, to lighten it.

Part-way through cooking an omelette (but not the flat type), the mixture is *folded* over in the pan to enclose the filling (if there is one) and to form a fat cigar-shape.

A fresh egg has a very thick white. During storage, the natural ageing process causes the white to become thinner. The illustration shows this, with a very fresh egg on the left and a rather old egg on the right. Notice how the egg white in the very fresh egg forms two distinct layers.

Chef's Tip

If you are making many portions of an egg dish (e.g. scrambled), break each egg into a small bowl then transfer to the larger bowl for beating. In this way, if one of the eggs has gone bad (e.g. strong smell, or obviously very stale), you discover the problem before you spoil the eggs you have already put into the bowl.

CHECKlist
Hygiene with eggs

✔ make sure that hands, preparation surfaces, utensils and containers are clean when handling eggs

✔ discard cracked or dirty eggs (e.g. soiled from the chicken farm)

✔ wash your hands after handling eggs, and before handling other food

✔ use pasteurised egg in recipes where the egg is not cooked (e.g. mayonnaise)

✔ serve egg dishes as soon as possible after preparation. If the dish is not going to be eaten immediately, chill quickly and keep in the refrigerator

✔ do not serve lightly cooked eggs (e.g. scrambled eggs, soft-boiled eggs, omelettes) to vulnerable people, e.g. anyone ill or feeling unwell, pregnant women, babies and infants, and the elderly. For these people, the egg should be cooked until the white and the yolk are solid, or use pasteurised egg

Cooking egg dishes

Eggs are one of the most versatile and widely used ingredients in cooking. On their own, they are a favourite breakfast dish, or a quickly prepared and nutritious meal for later in the day. With the addition of a few simple ingredients, eggs make a classic start or finish to a special lunch or dinner.

Take the eggs you require out of the refrigerator 20 to 30 minutes before cooking. This will give them time to come up to room temperature, and they will cook better.

When making scrambled egg or an omelette, add salt (if required) at the last moment before cooking. Salt in contact with the beaten egg mixture for too long will result in a rather runny, watery end product, and turns the colour brown.

Wet and dry cooking methods

The various ways of cooking eggs can be considered as 'wet' or 'dry', to reflect the presence of moisture during cooking. On this basis, the wet processes include:

- *boiling* – the egg is cooked in its shell, in simmering water (more details below)

- *poaching* – the egg is broken into simmering water, and cooked for a few minutes (details below)

- *scrambling* – the beaten eggs (usually 2 or 3 per person) are cooked over a moderate heat, stirring all the while (details below). Often a little butter is used, and perhaps some cream to finish the dish

- *en cocotte* – the egg is cooked in a small, round oven-proof dish (traditionally a cocotte dish, alternatively a ramekin dish). The cocottes are placed in a sauté pan which is partly filled with very hot water – the level of the water should be below the top of the cocottes). The pan is covered with a tight-fitting lid and placed over a high heat so that the water boils for 2 or 3 minutes. The eggs should be lightly set.

  Alternatively, the dish is cooked in the oven, and the individual cocottes placed in a deep-sided baking tray, with a little water. Recipe ingredients may include cream, herbs, etc.

- *moulded* – the egg is broken into a poacher, a shallow-sided pan with a close-fitting lid, holding three or more cup-shaped containers each large enough to take one egg. The pan is filled with water, to reach up to the base of the containers. Once the water is simmering, the eggs are broken into the lightly buttered or oiled containers, the lid put back on, and the pan kept on a medium heat until the eggs are cooked.

  Eggs cooked in this way are sometimes called poached.

The dry processes include:

- *shallow frying* – the egg is broken into a little fat or oil in a frying pan or on a griddle, and cooked over a moderate heat – usually called 'fried eggs' (more details below)

- *sur le plat* – the egg is broken into a flat, shallow-sided dish of that name, which has been lightly buttered or oiled. The dish is placed on top of the stove, or in the oven to cook the egg, and immediately served. It is served in the dish

- *omelettes* – the eggs (usually 2 or 3 per person) are lightly beaten together, then poured into an omelette pan and cooked over a high heat (more details below). Some omelettes are garnished, e.g. chopped herbs or cooked sliced mushrooms are cooked in with the egg. Others are filled or stuffed, e.g. hot jam placed in the centre before it is folded

- *deep frying* – for hard-boiled eggs which are surrounded by sausage meat (as in Scotch eggs) or a non-meat mixture, and breadcrumb coated. Egg croquettes (made with chopped hard-boiled egg, mixed with a thick sauce, shaped then coated in breadcrumbs) can be deep or shallow fried. Eggs are sometimes deep fried in the French style: during cooking, the white is spooned around the yolk, to envelop it completely. This makes it a complex dish.

More on boiling eggs

Most chefs place eggs into water which is already boiling. The other method is to begin with cold water. Whichever you find easier, success depends on exactly how long you cook the egg for. Small eggs need less time than large eggs (see box below). If the egg has just come out of the refrigerator, it will need a little longer.

So even if a customer asks for a 'three-minute egg', you need to use your judgement to get the required result – in this case, a soft-boiled egg, where the white has just lost its transparency.

Time is not quite so critical with hard-boiled eggs, but overcooking causes the yolk to go greenish-black. When hard-boiled eggs are to be served cold (e.g. in egg mayonnaise), stop the cooking quickly by putting the eggs under cold running water.

The water should be simmering, rather than boiling. The ideal temperature is a few degrees less than boiling, so the heat penetrates through the egg more gently. Rapid boiling can produce well cooked white, but the yolk too soft.

If an egg cracks during boiling, sprinkle a little salt on the crack. Salt in the boiling water will also help.

When boiling a number of eggs at the same time, put the eggs in a wire basket, then lower into the water – just as you would chips into the deep fryer. Otherwise, the eggs may bang against each other in the pan, and cracks can appear.

Soft-boiled eggs are a health risk. The temperature at the centre of the egg does not get high enough to kill salmonella bacteria which may be present.

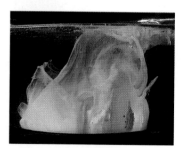

Poaching eggs.
Right: *photographed in a special glass saucepan, to show how the white curls up around the yolk.*
Top and lower: *note the size and shape of the pan, how the eggs are put into the water, and, once cooked, taken out..*

More on poaching eggs

A little white vinegar in the poaching water will help the egg to keep an attractive shape (see photographs above). A shallow-sided, wide-bottomed pan is ideal.

Use absolutely fresh eggs – as an egg ages it becomes more watery and the white will spread out in the water, rather than staying in an attractive shape.

Break each egg into a cup, or on to a saucer, then let it slip over the rim into the water. This avoids the problem that can happen when directly cracking the egg into the water, if the break in the shell is not complete, and the white leaks out before you can remove the yolk. By using a cup or small dish, you can break the eggs open away from the heat of the stove, instead of doing so over a pan of hot water.

If you are poaching only one or two eggs, you can get the white to wrap around the yolk by stirring the water before you add the eggs.

Some recipes suggest cracking the egg into boiling water, explaining that the action of the boiling water will cause the egg white to wrap around the yolk. In fact the convection currents are strong enough just below boiling point to produce this wrapping effect. Also, if you are poaching several eggs at the same time, the fierce heat necessary to keep the liquid boiling while the eggs were added would mean that the first eggs would be cooked too fast and become rubbery.

Use a slotted draining spoon to remove the eggs, and serve immediately. Where the poached egg is part of a more complex dish, e.g. poached eggs florentine (on a bed of spinach, coated with cheese sauce), the eggs can be cooled by placing in a basin of ice-cold water. The egg is reheated at a later stage in the recipe.

Egg boiling times

Method 1: lower eggs into simmering water, sufficient to cover them. Bring water back to simmering point for:

	Soft-boiled	Hard-boiled
Sizes 2 and 3	4 minutes	12 minutes
Sizes 4 and 5	3 minutes	10 minutes

Method 2: place eggs into pan and cover with cold water. For soft-boiled eggs, bring water to the boil, remove pan from heat and leave eggs to stand in the water, 3 minutes for size 2 and 3 eggs, 2 minutes for size 4 and 5 eggs.

For hard-boiled eggs, bring water to the boil, turn down heat and simmer gently, 10 minutes for size 2 and 3 eggs, 8 minutes for size 4 and 5 eggs.

To peel hard-boiled eggs

- gently tap all sides of the egg against a firm surface to crack the shell
- pull away shell carefully, to leave the white surface undamaged
- at the same time, remove the skin (membrane) that lies just beneath the shell.

More on frying eggs

Use a little oil and/or butter to stop the egg from sticking to the pan and to add flavour. When this is hot, but not sizzling, break the eggs, one at a time, into the pan. Do not overfill the pan, or you will find it difficult to remove the eggs without damaging the yolk.

Cook over a moderate heat – a high heat causes the egg white to become leathery, to shrink and brown at the edges.

As the egg white begins to set, spoon oil over the surface to help set the yolk to a translucent film. This is for *sunny side up*, to use the American expression. If the eggs are turned over halfway through cooking so that the yolk is in direct contact with the heat of the pan, this is *over easy*.

Lift the egg out carefully with a perforated slice, allowing excess oil to drain off.

More on scrambling eggs

Break the eggs into a bowl and beat with a fork to combine yolks and white. Season to taste. Add a little milk if you want a softer scrambled egg.

Melt a little butter or margarine in a heavy saucepan over a gentle heat. As soon as the fat melts, pour in the eggs. Stir when large creamy flakes start to form. Too much heat will dry the flakes, too much stirring will break them up.

Once the eggs are set, some chefs add a little cream to give a richer flavour. Scrambled eggs should be served immediately.

More on omelettes

Beat the eggs lightly with a fork, so as to break up the yolks and the white. Add a little cold milk if a softer omelette is preferred.

Heat a little oil and/or butter in the omelette pan over a fairly high heat. Pour in the egg mixture. As the egg begins to set, move it about with a fork to allow more of the liquid egg to come into contact with the base of the pan. Stirring and heating hold the cooked egg together.

Too little heat produces an unevenly cooked omelette. Too much stirring prevents the omelette base from browning. Cooking for too long dries up the egg. Pan size is crucial, as too little egg mixture in a large pan produces a pancake-like result.

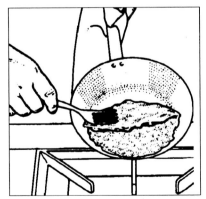

Making an omelette. Above, the finished omelette. Below, folding the omelette into the classic cigar-shape.

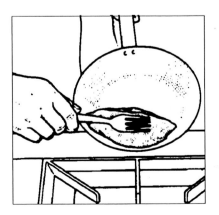

Finishing egg dishes

Some egg dishes are quite colourful in their own right: a breakfast plate which includes grilled tomato, mushrooms, bacon, etc. and fried or scrambled or poached egg needs no further *garnishing*. However, an omelette served on its own will look more colourful with a sprig of parsley on the side, or a neat arrangement of whatever filling is in the omelette (e.g. mushrooms).

Some of the sur le plat egg dishes include a sauce and garnish. For example, the Bercy-style dish is *sauced* (i.e. coated with tomato sauce just before service) and *garnished* with a chipolata sausage on each side of the egg yolk.

Scrambled eggs can be mixed through with herbs, chopped ham, etc. – depending on the dish you are making – or a little of the accompaniment placed on top of the scrambled egg as a garnish.

Dressing has two meanings. It is an alternative term for garnishing a dish. Also, where eggs are part of a salad, then they may be *dressed* with vinaigrette or a similar sauce, shortly before service.

Some dishes with poached eggs and boiled eggs (soft or hard-boiled) are coated with a sauce (this might have cheese in or on top of it, or egg yolk or cream), and then *gratinated* (i.e. placed under a hot grill until the surface has browned). Some chefs call this *glazing* the dish.

Eggs florentine

SERVES 10

10	fresh eggs (size 1 or 2), poached in advance and chilled	10
1.3 kg	spinach	3 lb
50 g	margarine or butter	2 oz
1 litre	mornay sauce	1½ pt
50 g	Parmesan cheese, grated	2 oz
	seasoning to taste	

1 Cook the spinach in a small quantity of boiling salted water (covered) for 3 to 5 minutes.

2 Cool the spinach under cold running water, and drain thoroughly in a conical strainer or sieve. Squeeze dry and form into balls, one ball per portion.

3 Heat the margarine or butter in a sauteuse until it foams. Add the spinach and heat gently. Season to taste.

Or use freshly poached eggs.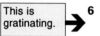

4 Meanwhile, heat the eggs in a saucepan of very hot (but not boiling) salted water for about 1 minute. Drain thoroughly.

5 Neatly arrange the hot spinach on the serving dishes. Place an egg on top. Coat with the hot mornay sauce, and sprinkle with Parmesan and, if required, melted butter.

This is gratinating.

6 Put each dish under the grill until the surface of the sauce turns golden brown. Serve immediately.

This is a sur le plat dish.

Shirred eggs Bercy style

SERVES 6

6	eggs	6
15 g	butter	¾ oz
6	chipolata sausages, twisted in two and grilled	6
150 ml	tomato sauce, hot	5 fl oz
	seasoning to taste	

1 Smear the butter over the inside bases of 6 *sur le plat* dishes and season lightly.

2 Break an egg into each dish.

3 Place the egg dishes over a gentle heat (a solid-top cooking surface is best) until the whites are lightly set.

4 Transfer to the centre shelf of a moderate oven, 170°C to 190°C, and cook until the whites are set, and the yolks soft (3 to 5 minutes) or hard (5 to 8 minutes), according to customer requirements.

5 Place one chipolata sausage on each dish, and pour a band of tomato sauce around the edge of the dish.

Fillings for a folded omelette

Cheese Scatter 25 g (1 oz) grated Cheddar or Cheshire cheese over the omelette just before folding.

Parmesan Mix 15 g (½ oz) grated Parmesan through the beaten egg, then proceed as recipe.

Ham Mix 50 g (2 oz) cooked ham (cut into small even-sized dice) through the beaten egg, then proceed as basic recipe.

Mushroom Shallow fry 25 g (1 oz) sliced mushroom in butter, mix through the beaten egg and proceed as basic recipe. Or cook the mushrooms in the pan, add the egg and continue cooking.

Peppers and onion Gently fry 25 g (1 oz) sliced red pepper and 25 g sliced onion in butter until softened. Add beaten egg with 1 tbsp of single cream, chopped chives, then proceed as basic recipe.

Folded omelette

by The British Egg Information Service

SERVES 1

3	eggs	3
15 ml	cold water	1 tbsp
	seasoning to taste	
15 g	butter or margarine	½ oz

1 Heat a 15 to 18 cm (6 to 7 inch) omelette pan gently. Break eggs into a bowl, add water, seasoning and beat lightly with a fork to break up whites and yolks.

2 Place fat in pan and turn up heat until the fat is sizzling but not brown. Pour in egg mixture.

3 With a fork or spatula, draw cooked egg from the edge of the pan inwards so that the liquid egg runs through to cook on pan base.

4 While the top is still runny, fold over a third of the omelette away from the pan handle. Add chosen filling.

5 Grip the handle of the pan underneath – with palm uppermost – and shake omelette to the edge of the pan away from handle.

6 Tip it over in three folds on to a warm serving plate. Serve immediately.

Most vegetables can be used to add flavour and interest to a flat omelette. Here are a few suggestions:
- thinly sliced green and red peppers added with the onion
- 1 clove crushed garlic added with the potato
- chopped tomato and cooked rice instead of potato
- finely diced cooked ham and good pinch chopped parsley.

Flat omelette

by The British Egg Information Service

SERVES 2

15 ml	olive or vegetable oil	1 tbsp
100 g	onion, finely chopped	4 oz
175 g	potato, cooked, diced	6 oz
4	eggs	4
20 ml	cold water	4 tsp
	seasoning to taste	

1 Heat oil in a 15 to 18 cm (6 to 7 inch) omelette pan. Add onion and cook slowly until soft.

2 Add diced potato and heat through.

3 Beat the eggs, water and seasoning together in a basin, with a fork.

4 When the onion mixture is hot, pour in the egg and cook, drawing egg from edge of pan inwards, so that the liquid egg runs through to cook on the pan base.

5 While the top is slightly runny, place pan under a hot grill until the top is just set. Do not fold the omelette, but slide it out flat.

Knowledge check

Prepare and cook basic egg dishes

NVQ SVQ

Skills check
Prepare and cook basic egg dishes
Unit 2ND10

lev **2**

For help to answer questions relating to:

Health and safety

P safe working practices

Shallow frying and deep frying eggs involve the use of oil. If this gets too hot or spills on to the stove, you might start a fire (see Section 2).

Food hygiene

P importance of good hygiene

Eggs may be contaminated with the salmonella bacteria when they come into the kitchen. To reduce the risk of food poisoning, special care should be taken when handling and preparing eggs (see checklist on page 166).

P importance of time and temperature

Bacteria increase rapidly in numbers at temperatures between 5°C and 63°C.

P main contamination threats

Other food (e.g. fresh vegetables, uncooked meat and fish), food handlers, dirty equipment, harmful cleaning substances, and foreign bodies (e.g. soil on the egg shell).

P products not for immediate use

Store above 63°C or below 5°C. There is a particular risk with egg dishes which have been lightly cooked (the temperature reached will not have been high enough to kill any salmonella). Many egg dishes have to be served at once for reasons of quality.

Product knowledge

P quality points for eggs

Look at the egg shell (no cracking or dirt), at the date mark.

P quality points for cooked dishes

Describe how the dish should look (*appearance, consistency*), smell (*aroma*) and taste (*texture, flavour*). Using too high a temperature when frying or scrambling eggs can cause the white to become rubbery.

P preparation methods for egg dishes

Beating, whisking and folding.

P cooking methods for egg dishes

These can be put into two groups: dry and wet cooking methods.

P identifying when dishes are cooked

Getting the right texture and appearance are important, e.g. scrambled eggs creamy. Some people like the yolk of a fried egg to be cooked solid, or the egg fried on both sides. There are also preferences about boiled eggs when served as a breakfast dish or snack. Lightly cooked eggs are not safe for the elderly, very young, or ill.

Healthy catering practices

P replacing high fat ingredients

Eggs contain some fat and cholesterol (in the yolk). This is why people should restrict the number of eggs they eat per week. When eggs are combined with butter and cream (e.g. in scrambled eggs) or cheese (e.g. in an omelette) or served with bacon, the fat content of the dish is further increased. The difficulty for chefs is that customers like the flavour and richness of these ingredients. Lean bacon, carefully trimmed, has less fat than streaky bacon.

P fats/oils for healthy eating

See page 110. For this reason, it is better to fry eggs in oil high in polyunsaturates rather than butter.

P cooking methods etc. to reduce fat

No fat is added to boiled or poached eggs. All the other methods use fat.

P increasing fibre content of dishes

The best sources of fibre (e.g. pulses and brown rice) are unlikely combinations with popular egg dishes. Scrambled or poached eggs on brown toast offer a way around the problem. Eggs in salads with brown rice and/or pulses would produce a high-fibre dish.

P reducing salt

See page 110.

P reducing sugar

Egg dishes likely to have sugar are dealt with in Sections 17 and 19. Omelettes served with jam and sugar as a sweet dish or dessert course are not a good choice for people wishing to cut down on their sugar intake.

Self-check questions

1 When frying eggs, what precautions should you take to avoid the oil smoking or catching fire?

2 How can you prevent burns when working at the stove (e.g. making scrambled egg/omelettes)?

3 Name the bacteria which is sometimes found in eggs.

4 Describe how eggs should be stored before cooking.

5 Why are eggs beaten before scrambling them or making an omelette? What equipment is used?

6 What can happen if too much heat is used when frying eggs?

7 What causes hard-boiled eggs to discolour? How can this be prevented?

8 What egg dishes should be avoided when cooking for the elderly, very young, ill, pregnant women, etc.?

Use this to check your progress against the performance criteria.

Element 1

Prepare basic egg dishes

Get your preparation areas and equipment ready for use — PC

Select ingredients of the type, quality and quantity required — PC

▲ Eggs: chicken, duck, quail
Other ingredients: vegetables, ham/bacon, cooked/smoked fish/shellfish, cooked/smoked meat/poultry/offal, rice, herbs, fungi, spices

Identify and report problems with the freshness or quality of ingredients — PC

Combine eggs with other ingredients — PC

Prepare eggs — PC

▲ Preparation methods: beating, whisking, folding

Clean preparation areas and equipment after use — PC

Prioritise and carry out your work in an organised, efficient and safe manner — PC

Element 2

Cook basic egg dishes

Get your cooking areas and equipment ready for use — PC

Identify and report problems with the quantity or quality of ingredients — PC

Cook egg dishes — PC

▲ Wet cooking methods: boiled, poached/moulded, scrambled, en cocotte
Dry cooking methods: shallow fried/sur le plat, omelettes garnished and filled/stuffed, deep fried

Finish egg dishes — PC

▲ Finishing methods: garnishing, dressing, glazing, saucing, gratinating

Correctly store egg dishes not for immediate use — PC

Clean cooking areas and equipment after use — PC

Prioritise and carry out your work in an organised, efficient and safe manner — PC

Preparing and cooking basic
desserts

Preparing, cooking and finishing cold desserts

For many people, the dessert is the highlight of an enjoyable meal. When it is the final course, it plays a large part in the overall impression formed of the meal.

The majority of desserts are sweet in flavour. Some people use the word 'sweets' instead of 'desserts'. Even if the flavour is not especially sweet, it should provide a contrast, and complement to, the previous dishes of the meal. If the first course is fruit-based, for example, it would not be good menu planning to serve another fruit-based dish as the dessert. Similarly, a flan or tartlet for dessert after a meat or fish pie would be too much of pastry.

Lemon meringue flan. The stiffly beaten meringue mixture, and the finished dish.

Types of cold dessert

Trifle – sponge, jelly and fruit base (usually a mixture of fresh fruits, cut into bite-sized pieces), perhaps with jam and/or sherry, covered in custard and/or whipped cream.

Egg custard – a paler colour, more delicate flavour and not quite as thick as the commercially-made product (from powder, or ready-made out of a can). Sometimes the eggs and milk (with a little sugar) are cooked on top of the stove, and a little cornflour or potato flour added to give a slightly thicker result, making *crème anglaise* or custard sauce. When the mixture is baked in the oven, it will set to the consistency of a soft jelly.

Crème caramel – egg custard cooked over a caramel (melted sugar) base. When the custard is turned out for service, the caramel gives an attractive toffee-brown top, and runs down the sides to form a sauce.

Cold rice desserts – made with a dessert-type rice, as the name implies, which has been boiled (usually with milk), cooled, then made into a base for fruit (e.g. pear, peach, banana or pineapple). Condés and créoles (names for two dishes of this sort) are finished with apricot glaze, which gives an attractive appearance, and adds flavour.

Jellies – flavoured with fruit, sometimes with wine, and set with gelatin or agar agar (suitable for vegetarians, see page 144). There is a wide range of commercially-made jelly powders and cubes, to which water is added and the mixture chilled until it has set.

Flans and tartlets – made of short pastry or sweet pastry (like short pastry, but with sugar and sometimes egg in place of water, see Section 18). Essentially a shell or base of pastry filled with custard and/or fruit, or various other ingredients, e.g. treacle. Tartlets are smaller than flans, usually the size of a single portion. A flan might be cut into 4, 6, 8 or more wedge-shaped pieces. The flan base can also be sponge cake.

Meringue shells and nests – egg whites whisked into a very white, very stiff mixture, sweetened with sugar, piped into a shape (e.g. nest) then baked in a low heat. Two shells are sandwiched together, e.g. with whipped cream and fresh fruit. The centre of a nest can be filled in a similar way.

Moulded creams – mousses, bavarois and similar cream-based mixtures set with gelatin or a vegetarian jelly, and turned out for service. In some recipes, egg (cooked like an egg custard) provides the strength to hold the mixture's shape.

Fruit-based – baked and stewed fruit. Cooking varieties of apple (e.g. Bramley) are baked in their skin in the oven, perhaps the centre filled with honey and nuts or another mixture, and served hot (sometimes cold). Stewed fruit is dried fruit (e.g. prunes and apricots), gently simmered in a little water and sugar until soft, then served hot or cold as a *composte*. Apples and plums cooked in this way and served plain with custard or cream are usually called 'stewed'. But when pears and peaches are cooked like this (sometimes in red or white wine), they are usually called poached.

Preparing, cooking and finishing cold desserts

As you might expect with such a range of desserts, the various methods involved in their preparation, cooking and finishing make quite a long list. But most basic desserts use one or two only. Here is a brief introduction to each method and examples of when it is used.

Preparation methods

Piping – egg white, beaten stiffly with caster sugar to make a meringue mixture, is piped to form attractive shapes (e.g. shells or nests). The mixture is stiff enough to hold its shape as it is forced out the nozzle of the piping bag (see photograph on previous page). This is easier than trying to shape the (very sticky) mixture with a spoon or palette knife.

Aeration – this means incorporating air into the mixture. Whipping double cream produces a considerable increase in volume, because of the amount of air beaten in, and a light, fairly stiff mixture. Whipping egg white results in an even greater increase in volume.

Mixing – most recipes require you to combine or mix the ingredients, so that they are blended together. The instruction sometimes says 'lightly' mix, when you should use a gentle action. This may be to avoid beating out the air, incorporated with much effort at an earlier stage. Or it may be to avoid damaging the texture of some of the ingredients (e.g. pieces of delicate fruit, or squares of sponge).

Combining – this is used in a similar way to 'mixing', e.g. 'combine all the ingredients'. The instruction may add 'thoroughly' or 'gently', depending on the intended result.

Puréeing – this means producing a smooth pulp-like mixture (e.g. of fruit for a fruit-flavoured mousse). Usually the recipe intends you to use a food processor, blender or liquidiser. A more time-consuming way is to force the fruit etc. through a sieve.

Addition of flavours/colours – this refers to the mixing in of small quantities of vanilla essence, cochineal colouring, peppermint flavouring, etc. These are commercially-produced products, sold in concentrated liquid form. Be careful, because even a few drops too much can turn the flavour/colour into an unpleasant extreme. Some recipes leave it to you to decide what flavours or colours to use, or suggest vanilla pods or fruit juices which give more subtle flavours.

Chef's Tip

To soak stewed fruit, cover in water at 80°C and leave for about two hours. This produces a better texture and flavour than soaking for 12 hours in cold water, the usual practice.

For a more delicate vanilla flavour than the essence, place some vanilla pods in a jar filled with caster sugar. Use this sugar in place of the recipe sugar and the vanilla essence.

Cooking methods

Boiling – the rice for a rice pudding is boiled, as is the sugar for a caramel sauce. Some fruit sauces involve boiling the fruit, to make it a soft pulp. The thinly cut rind of orange or lemon is sometimes boiled for a minute or less to take away the bitterness, before it is used to flavour a mousse or sauce, or for decoration.

Poaching – you are most likely to be doing this with a cooked fruit dish, or a rice or jelly which includes freshly-cooked fruit (e.g. peaches or pears). The gentle cooking action helps keep the shape of the fruit.

Stewing – by tradition, when dried fruit (e.g. prunes, apricots and peaches) is boiled, this is described as stewing. Like a stew, the cooking juice usually forms part of the finished dish. The fruit is soaked before cooking, to replace the water content. Drain away the soaking water, just cover the fruit with cold water (the fruit will release its own juices as it cooks) and bring to a gentle boil for the recipe time.

Baking – egg custards and crème caramels are baked, often in a larger dish partly filled with water. This provides a gentler heat. Flans and tartlets are baked. This is necessary to cook the pastry (see Section 18), and sometimes to cook all or some of the filling. Meringue shells and nests have to be baked, in a cool oven (some chefs use a hot cupboard), to set the egg white hard and brittle, but not to colour it. On the other hand, the meringue topping for a lemon meringue pie is baked at a higher temperature and for a shorter time, to produce a soft meringue.

Autumn fruit trifle

by Peter Gladwin, Party Ingredients, Nine Elms, London

SERVES 6

450 g	sponge cake (e.g. Génoise)	1 lb
225 g	raspberry jam	8 oz
300 ml	double cream	½ pt
125 ml	Muscat-de-Beaumes-de-Venise	4 fl oz
675 g	autumn fruits: plums (at least 3), blackberries, raspberries, blueberries, grapes	1½ lb
100 g	sugar	4 oz
600 ml	fresh egg custard	1 pt

1 Select an attractive glass bowl. Place a small piece of the sponge in the base (as a support for the plum decoration in step 2).

2 Cut around the plums to form discs. Put aside the ends. Place the best pieces in fairly widely spaced rows up the sides of the serving dish.

3 Roughly chop the remainder of the plums, and remove the stones.

Place them in a saucepan with a little water and the sugar. Bring to the boil, stirring continuously. Turn the heat off, then gently stir in the blueberries and raspberries (to cook in the residual heat).

4 Line the sides of the bowl (between the rows of plum discs) with slices of sponge (spread with jam on the side that faces into the centre of the bowl). Carefully lift these aside, and trickle custard down the side of the dish, between the sponge and the glass surface. Try to avoid the custard running in front of the plum discs.

5 Pour the Beaumes-de-Venise wine over the sponge. ← For a less expensive alternative to Beaumes-de-Venise, use a sweet dessert wine, or sherry.

6 Assemble the centre of trifle with alternating layers of sponge (spread with jam), stewed fruit and custard, ending up with a layer of custard.

7 Whip the cream. Spread some of it over the surface of the trifle. Then pipe parallel rows across the surface.

8 Slice the bottom off the grapes, and cut carefully up from this to remove the pips.

9 Fill the space between the rows of cream with blackberries and grapes (alternating).

Crème caramel

SERVES 20

Caramel

450 g	granulated sugar	1 lb
200 ml	cold water	7 fl oz
150 ml	hot water	5 fl oz

Egg custard

2 litres	milk	4 pts
12	eggs	12
225 g	caster sugar	8 oz
5 ml	vanilla essence	1 tsp

1 Place the sugar and cold water into a sugar boiling pan.

2 Bring to the boil and continue boiling until golden brown. During cooking, remove any splashes from the sides of the pan with a clean brush dipped in water. This will take about 8 minutes and the syrup will suddenly start changing colour, so be careful not to let it burn.

3 Remove the pan from the heat and dip into cold water for 5 seconds – this will stop further cooking.

4 Carefully add the hot water and gently shake the pan so that the water combines with the caramel. The water will cause the caramel to bubble violently, so keep your wrists and arms well covered.

5 Pour the hot caramel into 20 dariole moulds and allow to cool and set.

Egg custard

1 Warm the milk in a saucepan.

2 Whisk together the eggs, sugar and vanilla essence. Pour the milk on the egg mixture, whisk together.

3 Place the moulds into a deep oven tray. Strain the custard, then pour it into the moulds. Add enough cold water to half fill the tray.

4 Place in the oven at 160°C and cook until set, which will take 1 to 1½ hours. Alternatively, cook in a bain-marie with hot water for 45 minutes.

5 Remove the moulds from the tray, allow to cool, then place in a refrigerator to chill.

6 To serve: loosen the edges of the custard by gently pressing around the rim of the mould with the fingers and lightly shake the mould to free the custard at the sides. Turn out on to the cold serving dish. Pour over any caramel remaining in the moulds.

Finishing methods

Cooling – this applies to any dessert which has been cooked and is then served cold. Crème caramel, for example, should be taken out of the cooking water, left in a cool part of the kitchen, covered and, when cool – this should not take too long, between 30 minutes to an hour – served or put in the refrigerator until required.

If there is a blast chiller in your workplace, this will make the cooling process far quicker.

Jellies have to be cooled before they can be put in the refrigerator to set. This can be done quite quickly after making if you use some boiling water to dissolve the jelly powder or cube, then make up the rest of the recipe liquid with cold water.

In some recipes, the mixture has to be cooled part-way through. Mousses are an example. After cooking the basic custard, gelatin is added and the mixture allowed to cool (perhaps over a basin of iced-water) until it is just beginning to set. At that stage the whipped cream and/or stiffly beaten egg white is carefully folded in. The mixture is then poured into the mould or serving dish and chilled.

With rice-based puddings (e.g. fruit condé: half a poached pear on a bed of rice) the rice is cooled before the dish is assembled.

Chilling – this is done in the refrigerator or cold room, to take the temperature of the dessert right down. Recipes using gelatin need a very low temperature to set. In any case, unless a cold dessert is served within a few hours of being made, at room temperature, it should always be chilled to 5°C or below. This is to prevent harmful bacteria from multiplying and causing food poisoning.

Filling – meringue shells and nests are filled, typically with fruit and whipped cream, perhaps with nuts and chestnut purée. Flans and tartlets are filled, often with *pastry cream* or *crème pâtissière* (egg custard with a little flour added to the eggs and sugar), then a layer of fruit.

Demoulding – turning out of a mould. You will need to do this with jellies, mousses and similar desserts when they are set in a decorative mould. Sometimes recipes suggest you lightly oil the mould first, so that the mixture will turn out easily. Sometimes it helps to wrap the mould for a minute or so in a clean tea towel soaked in very hot water. Or you can dip the mould in a basin of very hot water. The trick is to release the mixture from the mould, but not heat it so much that it starts to melt. It sometimes helps to press the mixture gently all round the top of the mould (or cut around it with a thinly-bladed knife), before you heat it or turn it over. When you do shake the mould (having upturned it over the serving dish), do not be over-vigorous or you could damage the more delicate mixtures.

Crème caramel has to be turned out of its cooking container before service. Usually a vigorous shake is sufficient, but if this is not the case, push around the top first, with your fingers. This breaks the seal which the egg custard sometimes forms against the edges of the container.

Glazing – this produces an attractive shiny surface. Fruit-filled flans and tartlets are usually glazed. This can be done by brushing with or pouring over a suitable jam (e.g. apricot), which has been boiled with a little water, or using fruit juice thickened with a little arrowroot. There are ready-to-use glazes available.

Pastry is glazed just before baking, so that the finished dish has an attractive brown surface. Egg beaten with a little milk gives a rich glaze. Water can be used in place of milk, or egg yolk with a pinch of salt. (These are all variations on what chefs call eggwash.)

Piping – as in the preparation method (see above), often done to decorate the finished dish with whipped cream. Sometimes thin lines of chocolate are piped over the top or around the dish, to introduce a more colourful decoration.

Dusting – sprinkling a fine layer of icing, caster sugar or cocoa powder over the surface. Put the sugar or powder in a sieve and shake over the surface (for example. of trifle).

Icing sugar has been dusted on this pastry, providing an attractive contrast with the strawberry sauce.

Attractively presented desserts are good for sales.

With thanks to Forte Crest (top photo), De Vere Hotels (lower photo).

Preparing, cooking and finishing hot desserts

In situations where customers order most items from a menu, or choose their food from a self-service counter, hot desserts can be very popular. Indeed, there is something special about a hot pudding, especially on a cold day, or when you are feeling particularly hungry.

Types of hot dessert

Pancakes – pancake batter is simple to make (flour, eggs and milk), the skill being in the cooking. The pan must be a good-quality one that will not stick. Heat the pan up with a little oil, pour off the excess oil then add some batter, just sufficient to coat the base of the pan. When the bubbles show through, toss the pancake to turn it over neatly. If you find it easier, use a fish slice or palette knife to lift and turn the pancake. Stack the cooked pancakes (flat not folded) on a plate and put in a hot cupboard until required. Sprinkle a little sugar between each one to stop them sticking together.

Crêpes – this is the French word for pancakes, which has become part of the English language. Many of the restaurants which specialise in pancakes prefer to use the word crêpe.

Sponge-based, steamed and baked – as the name says, these use similar ingredients to a sponge cake (i.e. flour, eggs and fat). During baking or steaming, the air in the mixture expands to give it a lighter texture. In place of, or in addition to eggs, some recipes use baking powder, others self-raising flour. Some use suet, when the pudding is always steamed (suet requires a slow, moist cooking). Other popular ingredients are dried fruit (e.g. currants and sultanas), syrup or treacle, lemon or orange, chocolate or other flavours such as vanilla.

Eve's pudding is a baked sponge, over a base of apple. There are variations on this, including one where a chocolate sauce is poured over the uncooked sponge, During baking, the sauce sinks. When the pudding is cut, a rich sauce floats up from the bottom.

Egg-based set – these are made with egg custard (milk, eggs and sugar), which sets the mixture during baking. Examples are bread and butter pudding (buttered slices of bread layered with dried fruit) and cabinet pudding (squares of sponge with cherries, sultanas and currants).

Right: *preparing a pancake mix. Whisk from the centre outwards to gradually incorporate the flour.* Below: *checking the consistency of egg custard. It should just coat the back of the spoon, as shown here.*

Cereal-based milk puddings – these include rice pudding (a dessert rice, see page 154, baked in the oven with milk). Sometimes the rice is boiled with the milk, placed in a pie dish and then lightly browned under the grill. Semolina, sago, tapioca and ground rice puddings are cooked in this way.

Fruit-based – baked apple, as mentioned at the beginning of this section, is often served hot. Sometimes stewed or poached fruit is served hot, e.g. hot plums with custard. Fruit can also be wrapped in pastry and baked, or dipped in batter and deep fried.

Pies and tarts, sweet and short pastry – fruit fillings for pies include apple, rhubarb, apricots, plums and the various berries, but not strawberries which would be overwhelmed by the pastry. Pies have a pastry top. With tarts the filling is enclosed in the pastry. Besides fruit, other popular fillings include jams, lemon curd, treacle, syrup and minced meat (of the type made with currants, sultanas, suet, etc.).

Preparing, cooking and finishing hot desserts

As before, here is a brief introduction with examples of their use. As you will note, some methods are similar to those used for cold desserts.

Preparation methods

Peeling – some of the fresh fruits used for a pie or tart, or in a sponge pudding, may have to be peeled, e.g. apples, pears and pineapple. Apricots and plums are not usually peeled.

Slicing – apples are usually sliced before being put in a pie. Apricots are cut in half or sliced.

Creaming – in making sponge-based puddings, vigorously beating the fat and sugar until the mixture is creamy in colour and fluffy in texture.

Folding – carefully blending ingredients into a mixture, by gently turning or folding one part over the other with a spatula or spoon. Flour is folded into the creamed fat and sugar mixture for a sponge, to preserve the lightness of the mix.

Mixing – combining ingredients. The instructions may tell you to 'lightly mix', or 'thoroughly mix', for example.

Aeration – getting air into the mixture, usually by whisking.

Moulding – putting the mixture into a particular shape of container. Sometimes boat-shaped baking tins are used to give small tarts an interesting shape.

Filling – pies and tarts are filled with the fruit or other mixture.

Portioning – if you are making a number of puddings having made a big quantity of the mixture, it is important to divide or portion the mixture accurately, so that each pudding is the same size.

Left: *tossing a pancake.*
Below: *the more cautious approach!*

Cooking methods

Boiling – the rice, semolina, etc. in a cereal-based pudding is boiled or simmered with the milk.

Poaching – for a hot fruit dessert, the fruit might be poached, i.e. gently cooked at a few degrees below boiling.

Baking – pies and tarts, egg-based puddings and some sponge puddings are baked in the oven.

Combination cooking – this uses two heat sources. One type works like a conventional oven, but steam can be let into the oven to produce the moist heat some chefs prefer for egg-based puddings. The other type uses microwave energy, with electric heating elements to provide the second heat source. This means dishes normally baked in an oven can be cooked more quickly (because of the microwaves) and brown attractively (because of the conventional heat).

Steaming – sponge puddings made with suet are steamed (suet requires a moist heat), and so are some non-suet sponge recipes. The pudding basin must be oiled or greased before the mixture is put in (to prevent sticking). Do not overfill the basin, as the pudding will expand a little during cooking. Cover securely with greased greaseproof paper before steaming.

Bain-marie – baked egg custard is placed in a larger baking tray half full of water (sometimes called a bain-marie) for cooking in the oven. This allows the custard to cook very gently.

Frying – pancakes are shallow fried in a special pancake pan (with very low sides and a heavy bottom). Alternatively a griddle, or a purpose-made pancake cooker, can be used.

Lemon pancakes

SERVES 4

75 g	plain flour	3 oz
1	egg	1
225 ml	milk	8 fl oz
15 g	butter	½ oz
30 ml	oil for cooking	2 tbsp
50 g	caster sugar	2 oz
4	lemon segments	4
	pinch of salt	

1 Sieve together the flour and salt. Make a well in the centre. Add the egg and half the milk. Whisk to a smooth thick batter, starting from the centre and working outwards gradually incorporating all the flour. Whisk in the remaining milk to produce a thin batter. Strain into clean bowl.

2 Melt the butter and blend it in. Cover the mixture and put it aside in a cool place to rest for about 1 hour.

3 Heat the pancake pan and add a little oil. When hot, pour off the surplus oil, then pour in enough batter to cover the bottom of the pan, tilting the pan to ensure that the batter spreads evenly across it.

4 Cook the batter quickly until it turns golden brown. Toss the crêpe or turn it over with a palette knife and cook the other side.

5 Turn the crêpe out on to a warm plate, then cover with an upturned plate and keep hot in a warm oven or hot cupboard.

6 Repeat the procedure, piling the pancakes one on top of the other between the plates, until you have produced 12 small crêpes (3 per portion). ⬅ The pancakes should not stick together, but if they start to do so, place a small square of grease-proof paper between each one.

7 Sprinkle each crêpe with caster sugar then fold in half and half again to form a triangular shape.

8 Place the crêpes on a hot serving dish, in one long row or 4 small rows, each slightly overlapping the next. Sprinkle with caster sugar and garnish with the lemon.

If pancakes stick to pan/griddle:

1 The equipment was dirty: it should be thoroughly wiped with absorbent paper before the next pancake is cooked.

2 The equipment was cleaned incorrectly, e.g. washed in water. If this has happened, switch to another pan so that the one which sticks can be prepared properly again (see page 73).

3 Too much or too little oil was used in the pan.

4 The pancake mixture was too light. In this case the rest of the mixture can be improved by adding in a little more flour, either by blending it in with a liquidiser or by hand whisking (and then straining it before use to remove any lumps).

Apple and raisin pancakes with rum butter sauce

by The Butter Council

SERVES 4

100 g	plain flour	4 oz
	pinch of salt	
5 ml	finely grated lemon rind	1 tsp
1	egg	1
300 ml	milk	½ pt
75 g	butter	3 oz
225 g	cooking apples, peeled, cored and sliced	8 oz
25 g	raisins	1 oz
50 g	brown sugar	2 oz
15 ml	rum or brandy	1 tbsp
15 ml	lemon juice	1 tbsp

Baked egg custard

by The British Egg Information Service

SERVES 4

600 ml	milk, warmed until it 'steams'	1 pt
3	eggs, beaten together	3
25 g	caster sugar	1 oz
	few drops vanilla essence and/or a little freshly grated nutmeg	

1 Whisk the eggs and sugar lightly in a bowl. Gradually stir in the hot milk.

2 Pour the mixture through a conical strainer into a 900 ml (1½ pint) very lightly buttered ovenproof dish. Add the essence or sprinkle on the nutmeg.

3 Stand the dish in a roasting tin in the oven, filled with warm water to come half-way up the sides of the dish. ⬅ Like the type of bain-marie used on top of the stove, and in hot cupboards, the water gives a gentler heating.

4 Bake at 160°C for about 45 to 50 minutes, or until just set and firm to the touch. Serve hot or cold.

---

1 Sift the flour into a bowl, add the salt, lemon rind, egg and milk, and whisk together to make a smooth batter.

2 Using a tiny knob of butter for each, make 8 small pancakes and keep warm in a low oven (steps 3 to 6 as in lemon pancakes).

3 Cook the apples with the raisins in a little water until soft.

4 Melt the remaining butter and sugar together in a saucepan and stir well. Add the brandy and lemon juice.

5 Divide the apple mixture between the pancakes and roll up or fold into triangles. Place on warm serving dishes, pour over the sauce and serve.

179

For help to answer questions relating to:

Health and safety

? safe working practices

The hazards will be the usual ones involved in preparing and cooking food, and using equipment (especially if you are using a food mixer or liquidiser).

Food hygiene

? importance of good hygiene

Dishes which involve cream, eggs and rice are high risk. They provide ideal conditions for the growth of harmful bacteria, but the dangers can be avoided by careful attention to hygiene, and keeping such dishes out of the temperature danger zone.

? importance of time and temperature

Bacteria increase rapidly in numbers at temperatures between 5°C and 63°C (the danger zone).

? main contamination threats

Other food (e.g. fresh fruit), food handlers, dirty equipment/work area, harmful cleaning substances, foreign bodies (e.g. piece of broken glass), etc.

? products not for immediate use

Store above 63°C or below 5°C.

Product knowledge

? quality points

Describe how the dish should look (appearance, consistency), smell (aroma) and taste (texture, flavour).

? preparation methods

For cold desserts, these are: piping, aeration, mixing, combining, puréeing, and addition of flavours/colours. For hot: creaming, moulding, mixing, portioning, filling, aeration, folding, peeling, and slicing.

? cooking methods

For cold desserts, these are: boiling/poaching, baking, and stewing. For hot: boiling/poaching, baking, combination cooking, steaming, and bain-marie.

? identifying when desserts are cooked

Fruit should be soft, but not too soft (unless you are cooking it to a pulp). A cocktail stick pushed into a baked egg custard, crème caramel, sponge or egg-based dessert should come out clean. Meringues should be firm enough to hold their shape once they have cooled. Pastry should be nicely coloured, firm and with no sign of moistness. Rice should be tender.

Healthy catering practices

? replacing high fat ingredients

Remind yourself of some of the tips on page 130 for replacing cream, butter, etc. There are low-fat recipes for sponges and pastries. Skimmed milk may be acceptable for a custard.

? fats/oils for healthy eating

See page 110.

? increasing fibre content of dishes

Any dish using wholegrain flour will be a good source of fibre. Apples and pears are quite a good source of fibre, and blackberries more so.

? reducing sugar

You may find that the amount of sugar added to fruit dishes can be reduced. Using a short pastry, in place of a sweet short pastry for flans, tarts and pies, means less sugar in the final dish.

Self-check questions

1 When cooking fruit or a sauce at the stove, what steps can you take to avoid burns?

2 Describe how piping bags and nozzles should be cleaned, and why it is important that they are absolutely clean before use.

3 Name another item of equipment used for making desserts which requires particular care to keep clean, and describe what you should do to ensure this.

4 For each of the preparation methods (see left column), name one dessert which uses that method.

5 State where a dessert can be left to cool in your kitchen, and describe the precautions to prevent contamination.

6 For two cold desserts, and two hot desserts, describe what the finished dish should look and taste like, and give any other relevant points on which you can judge its quality.

7 If you have trouble turning a jelly, mousse or similar dessert out of its mould, what can you do to solve the problem?

8 Name a dessert which is glazed. Explain how this is done and what the purpose is.

Use this to check your progress against the performance criteria.

Element 1
Prepare, cook and finish basic cold desserts

Get your preparation and cooking areas and equipment ready for use ☐ PC

Select ingredients of the type, quality and quantity required ☐ PC

△ Desserts: trifle, egg custard, crème caramel, cold rice desserts, jellies, flans, tartlets (sweet and short pastry), basic meringue (shells and nests), moulded creams, fruit-based (basic baked and stewed fruit)

Identify and report problems with the quality of ingredients ☐ PC

Prepare and cook desserts ☐ PC

△ Preparation methods: piping, mixing, aeration, combining, addition of flavours/colours, puréeing
Cooking methods: boiling/poaching, stewing, baking

Finish desserts ☐ PC

△ Finishing methods: cooling, glazing, filling, piping, demoulding, dusting, chilling

Store desserts not for immediate use ☐ PC

Clean preparation areas and equipment after use ☐ PC

Prioritise and carry out your work in an organised, efficient and safe manner ☐ PC8

Element 2
Prepare, cook and finish basic hot desserts

Get your preparation and cooking areas and equipment ready for use ☐ PC1

Select ingredients of the type, quality and quantity required ☐ PC2

△ Desserts: pancakes/crêpes, sponge-based (steamed and baked), egg-based set, basic cereal-based milk puddings, fruit-based, pies and tarts (sweet and short pastry)

Identify and report problems with the quality of ingredients ☐ PC3

Prepare and cook desserts ☐ PC4

△ Preparation methods: creaming, moulding, mixing, aeration, folding, peeling, portioning, slicing, filling
Cooking methods: boiling/poaching, steaming, baking, bain-marie, combination cooking

Finish desserts ☐ PC5

△ Finishing methods: glazing, filling, demoulding, dusting, portioning

Store desserts not for immediate use ☐ PC6

Clean preparation areas and equipment after use ☐ PC7

Prioritise and carry out your work in an organised, efficient and safe manner ☐ PC8

Preparing and cooking basic
pastry dishes

Unit 2ND8, Element 1
Preparing basic pastry

To make good pastry, you need to be familiar with the basic techniques and rules, and of course to follow the recipe carefully. But much of the success is down to lightness of touch. This may come easily to you. If not, watch more experienced colleagues to see what they do. Ask their help, and practise at every opportunity.

Types of pastry

The four main types dealt with in this section are short, sweet, suet and choux pastry. All use flour. The differences are in the other ingredients – the names give a strong clue to what these are:

- *short* pastry is made from blending flour with half its weight of fat (butter or pastry margarine), then adding just enough water to produce a paste which can be rolled

- *sweet* pastry adds sugar to the ingredient list, and uses an egg in place of the water. This produces a richer taste. The paste is slightly more difficult to handle than a short pastry, as it tends to fall apart

- *suet* pastry uses chopped beef suet (vegetarian equivalents are available) as the fat, with a little baking powder (to give the pastry lightness) and enough water to produce a manageable paste

- *choux* pastry uses more water than the other types, and eggs. The mixture is vigorously beaten together, which gives the pastry the strength elasticity it needs to expand, as all the recipe water turns to steam. When cooked, the paste more than doubles in size, with a soft, hollow centre – compare profiteroles (which are made with choux pastry) to the pastry used for a savoury flan (e.g. a quiche).

Left: *apple pie (sweet short pastry)*
Below: *Quiche lorraine (short pastry).*

Above: *Cornish pasty (short pastry) and sausage roll (puff pastry)*
Right: *steak and kidney pudding (suet pastry)*
Below: *chocolate profiteroles (choux pastry).*

There are two other types of pastry that you might be expected to cook, but not prepare, as most caterers buy in the ready-prepared product, chilled or frozen. These are:

- *puff* pastry which uses an intricate rolling and folding process to make hundreds of well-risen, wafer-thin leaves (you can see these in vols-au-vent). Layers of fat are sandwiched between paste. During baking, the fat melts and steam from water in the paste puffs the layers apart

- *rough puff* or *flaky* pastry which has a similar light texture to puff pastry, but rises in a more random way – if it was used to make a vol-au-vent, the end result would be rather topsy-turvy. The paste has small lumps of fat in it, rather than whole layers.

Preparing pastry

With any type of pastry, you should sieve the flour first. This helps get air into the flour – compare the feel of the flour before and after sifting, to see how much flour can settle during transport and storage.

Here are some other points that will help you make good short and sweet pastry:

- use a cool area of the kitchen, or plan your time so that you can make the pastry when the kitchen is cool

- take the pastry fat, butter or margarine out of the refrigerator half an hour or so in advance. This lets it soften, but not so much that it becomes oily during the mixing

- use the tips of your fingers, held well above the surface, so that the flour falls back into the bowl, and traps more air in the mixture. Using the tips of your fingers also helps keep the fat away from the warmth of your hands

- you should end up with a sandy-textured mixture rather like breadcrumbs. There should be no loose flour left

- do not mix any more than necessary. The pastry will get another chance to blend together when it is rolled

- do not add too much water to short pastry, or be tempted to use extra egg with sweet pastry, or you will get a sticky mess. What seems a dry, very sandy mixture will blend into a smooth paste when it is rolled

- place the paste in a refrigerator to rest – before rolling, before cutting or shaping and before baking. Around 10 minutes at each stage is usually sufficient. The pastry should be covered, as a hygiene precaution and to stop it drying out. Some chefs transfer the pastry to a food-quality plastic bag.

With suet pastry, the baking powder is sieved with the flour and salt. Mix the suet in well, add the water and lightly mix to form a paste. This takes less time than the equivalent stage of short and sweet pastries, and it is much less tricky.

With choux pastry, your arm will feel as if it is dropping off before you are in danger of over-mixing the paste!

Sweet short pastry

MAKES 350 g (12 oz)

225 g	plain (soft) flour	8 oz
100 g	butter or margarine	4 oz
50 g	caster sugar	2 oz
½	egg (size 3)	½
pinch	grated lemon zest (optional)	pinch

> For short pastry, replace sugar with pinch of salt, and replace egg with 40 ml of water.

1 Sieve the flour.

2 Blend the fat lightly into the flour to produce a sandy texture.

3 If you have to use a whole egg, beat it lightly first so that half can be measured off. Mix this half with the sugar and lemon zest.

> Make a hollow in the centre of the pastry, and pour the egg into it. Blend carefully, working from the centre outwards until the mixture just holds together.

4 Add the egg and sugar mixture to the fat and flour, and mix to a smooth paste. Rest before using.

Overview of the preparation methods

Rubbing in – this describes the process of blending the fat and flour to get a sandy mixture for short and sweet pastry.

Mixing – this is the simpler process of mixing the chopped suet with the flour.

Relaxing or *resting* – leaving short and sweet pastry paste in a cool place before and after rolling. This gives the starch in the flour time to absorb the liquids more evenly. It also helps the fat firm up so the pastry keeps a better texture, shapes and cuts more easily, and shrinks less when cooking.

Kneading – this is working the paste into a properly blended mixture. With short and sweet pastry it is a rather misleading term, because of the likelihood of producing a tough end-result if you over-mix the paste. It is more widely used in the making of bread and pizza dough (see Section 20).

Some chefs prefer to make short and sweet pastry using the *creaming* method:

- for short pastry, half the flour and all the fat are creamed together until light and soft. The water is mixed in, the remaining flour added and mixed to a smooth paste

- for sweet pastry, the egg and sugar are creamed together, the fat mixed in, and then the flour.

Chef's Tip

If you have hot hands, hold your wrists under a running cold tap for a few minutes before starting to mix pastry.

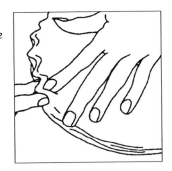

Crimping the edge of a pie to give an attractive finish.

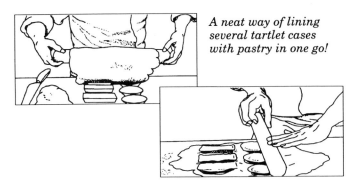

A neat way of lining several tartlet cases with pastry in one go!

Processing methods

Choux pastry is usually *piped* into the desired shape before baking, e.g. small balls for profiteroles, larger balls for choux buns, and short lengths like sausages for éclairs. Don't overfill the piping bag (two-thirds is sufficient).

Other pastries are *rolled* (see below). This helps the flour and fat knead together and gets the paste into thin sheets, for *lining* the baking tin or basin, or *cutting* into circles or squares, or *shaping* in a decorative way, e.g. as twisted lengths, or to enclose an apple or a pear for cooking.

Once the baking container has been lined, or the top of a pie or tart put into position, *trim* off untidy pieces of pastry with a knife.

Brush a little eggwash (beaten egg, perhaps with a little milk or water), between two layers of pastry when you want a good seal. Brushing the top of pastry with eggwash just before baking will give a golden, shiny finish. This is called *glazing* (see page 176).

With puff and rough puff pastries, do not let the eggwash run down the sides. If it does it will stop the pastry layers rising evenly (by sticking the edges together).

Dessert pies can be brushed with lightly beaten egg white and sprinkled with caster sugar, or water and sugar.

Preparing the baking tray

It is best to use a white fat such as pastry margarine for greasing containers. Butter or yellow margarine will stick or even burn (because of the milk solids in butter and the water in yellow margarine).

Rub a lump of the fat over the whole surface. This is less messy if you hold the fat in a small piece of greaseproof paper. If the fat is soft, it may be easier to use a pastry brush.

Dust with flour, where the recipe specifies. Tip the tray in all directions to spread the flour evenly. Bang the back of the sheet to shake off excess flour – the finished coating should be light and uniform.

For puff and rough puff pastry items, dampen the baking tray with cold water after greasing. This helps prevent the pastry from burning on the underside in the very hot oven.

More on rolling pastry

1 Shape the paste to a small version of the shape you intend to roll it. This cuts down waste, and reduces the amount of rolling required.

2 Use a firm even stroke, with equal pressure over the length of the rolling pin. Keep your fingers well clear of the pastry.

3 Stop rolling just short of the edge. If you roll over the edge, the pastry will not keep an even thickness.

4 Roll the pastry in one direction only: away from your body. Rolling in all sorts of different directions will distort the pastry.

5 As soon as there is any danger of the paste sticking, sprinkle flour over the surface of the rolling pin. Lift the pastry up with the rolling pin, dust the work surface with flour and put the pastry back. (It is usually turned at this stage, see point 9.) Some chefs also flour the surface of the pastry. If you find this helps, use the lightest dusting otherwise the pastry will end up with too much flour in it.

6 Use a flour dredger to dust surfaces. Too much extra flour will only make the pastry hard.

7 If, in spite of flouring, the paste starts sticking too much, and becoming unmanageable, transfer to a tray or bowl, cover and place in the refrigerator for 10 to 15 minutes to recover.

8 If you have chilled the paste for longer than 30 minutes, allow it to stand for a few minutes at room temperature to soften slightly before rolling again.

9 When the shape begins to get too elongated, lift the pastry up with the rolling pin, dust the work surface with flour and put the pastry back. As you do so, turn it by 90° if you are rolling an oblong shape, a few degrees for a circle – in this way, you continue to roll away from you.

Rolling puff pastry

Remember that puff pastry has been carefully made to have many layers of paste interleaved by layers of fat. It comes as a fat oblong piece, so that you can roll it into thinner sheets quite easily, and without distorting the layers of fat and paste. Be careful not to roll right up to the edge (point 3 above).

Do not crunch the trimmings up into a ball (as you might with short or sweet pastry), but pile them one on top of the other. Roll out and use as rough puff pastry.

More on cutting and shaping

To lift the rolled pastry on to the baking tray, flan ring, etc., partly wrap it around the floured rolling pin. Alternatively, fold the pastry in half, and if necessary in half again. Lift by hand, place in position, and unfold.

Pastry should be cut cleanly. This is particularly important for puff and flaky pastry, so that you free the layers, and the pastry rises neatly during baking:

- use a pastry cutter (a metal one is best) when you require a particular shape
- dip the edge of the cutter in flour
- press the cutter into the paste firmly, don't twist.

For cutting puff pastry shapes and vols-au-vent, some chefs prefer to dip the cutter in hot oil, others to grease it lightly with pastry margarine or white fat.

After you have cut shapes for pie tops, or the top ring for a vol-au-vent or bouchée, turn the pastry over. The underside (which was next to the work surface) is smooth and the pastry will rise evenly.

Keep trimmings for making decorations. Trimmings of puff pastry can be used for cheese straws and other dishes where it is not so important for the pastry to rise evenly.

Lining tart and flan cases

1 Shape the pastry into a ball. Lightly flatten the ball to form a fat pancake shape.

2 Roll it out into a circle larger than the tart or flan case (so that you have enough to go up the sides), 3 to 4 mm thick. To check the size, place the case on top of the pastry.

3 Lift the pastry on to the case. If you are using a flan ring, first place the ring on a floured baking tray.

4 Work the edges of the pastry gently down the inside of the case, so that the sides are well covered. Avoid stretching the pastry, otherwise the sides will drop during cooking.

5 Roll the rolling pin across the top of the case to trim the top. Put the trimmings aside.

6 Lightly press up the top edges of the pastry, so they are even, and just higher than the top of the case. At this stage, you can decorate the edges, by crimping between your fingers or using a pastry wheel.

Lining tartlet cases

Roll out a square or oblong sheet of pastry, 3 to 4 mm thick. Cut circles larger than the tartlet cases with a pastry cutter. Line and decorate the cases as above.

See illustration for a quick way of lining pastry boats, tartlet and patty tins of various shapes and sizes.

Make the pastry for a flan. Left: rubbing in, below: cover the pastry to rest it.

Rolling out the pastry. Above: shaping the paste; left: rolling it into the shape of the flan ring; below: shaping the paste into the ring.

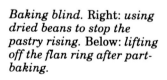

Baking blind. Right: using dried beans to stop the pastry rising. Below: lifting off the flan ring after part-baking.

Filling pies and tarts (before cooking)

Dishes which have some liquid in them (e.g. the stock in a steak pudding) create steam as they cook. Cut a small hole in the top of the pie or use a pie funnel to let the steam escape.

Do not add too much liquid to a fruit pie, or the contents will bubble out. For a pie serving six people, a few tablespoons of water will be sufficient. The fruit supplies extra juices.

With a fruit tart (where the top and bottom are pastry), a good seal around the rim will hold in the juices. Dampen only the bottom crust with eggwash (or fruit juice), and press together firmly. (When both edges are dampened it is more difficult to make a good seal.)

Sugar directly under the crust of a pie can make the underneath of the pastry soggy. If sugar is to be added, mix this with the filling, or place over the centre layers (e.g. of fruit).

For tarts and flans which are filled with egg custard or similar mixture, you may find it easier to do this once the dish is in the oven. Carrying a flan filled to the brim requires a very steady hand to avoid spills.

Lining a pudding basin with suet pastry

1 Roll out about three-quarters of the pastry 8 to 10 mm thick, in a circle big enough to line the basin. You can judge this by eye, otherwise experiment with a circle of greaseproof paper. Allow for the pastry to overlap the sides of the basin.

2 With the rolling pin, lift the pastry up on to the basin.

3 Press the pastry well into the basin. Leave the edges overlapping the side of the basin for the time being.

4 Almost fill the basin with the mixture.

5 Dampen the pastry edges with water.

6 Roll out the remaining pastry into a circle.

7 Cover the top of the pudding. Seal the edges. Trim off the excess pastry.

Wrapping a pudding for steaming

1 Cover the pudding with a circle of lightly greased greaseproof paper, folded in the middle with a pleat about 25 mm wide, to allow for expansion during cooking.

2 Over the greaseproof paper, place a pudding cloth (such as an old, clean tea towel or table napkin), also pleated in the middle.

3 Twist a piece of string twice round the basin below the rim and tie the paper and cloth securely.

4 Tie the opposite ends of the pudding cloth together. This makes a convenient handle for lifting the pudding in and out of the steamer.

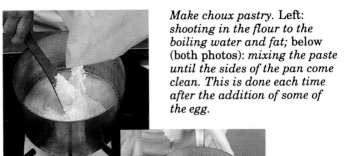

Make choux pastry. Left: shooting in the flour to the boiling water and fat; below (both photos): mixing the paste until the sides of the pan come clean. This is done each time after the addition of some of the egg.

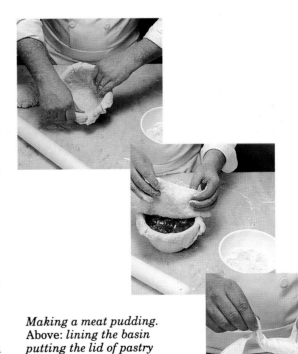

Making a meat pudding. Above: lining the basin putting the lid of pastry over the filling. Right: wrapping the pudding for steaming. Note how the ends of the cloth are being tied to make it easy to lift the pudding in and out of the steamer.

185

Cooking pastry dishes

Follow recipe instructions on temperatures and times, and you should get good results. The faults that most often occur with pastry – solid or dense, tough or chewy texture, shrinking or uneven shape – can happen because the oven temperature is too low. But the more likely reason is that the pastry was over-mixed, or not rested sufficiently, or an error was made in measuring the ingredients – in other words, in the preparation stage.

Types of pastry dish

Four of the types of pastry dish you will come across are:

- *pies* – the filling is cooked under a pastry top in a suitable pie dish. The pastry seals in the cooking juices and flavours. Steak and mushroom, chicken and ham, potato and spinach are examples of savoury pie fillings. Fruit is a popular filling for dessert pies, e.g. plums, apples, gooseberries and damsons

- *tarts* – the filling is sandwiched between layers of pastry (a closed tart), or the filling is put into a pastry case (an open tart). Open tarts are often called *flans*

- *tartlets* – a single-portion size, open tart

- *puddings* – the filling is cooked in a pudding basin, bottom and sides lined with suet pastry, filling added, and top sealed with pastry.

The terms pie and tart are not strictly used. You will find recipes for pies which have a top and bottom of pastry, so that the filling is enclosed.

Some chefs find it easier to cook the pie filling in advance. It is reheated during the time the pastry is baked.

Cooking methods

Suet pastry is *steamed*. This is because suet needs a moist heat to melt into the surrounding mixture.

Other pastries are *baked*.

A very hot oven – 200°C to 220°C – is used for puff and rough puff pastry. It forces the pastry to rise in layers. The heat also enables the flour to absorb the fat as it melts: too cool an oven, and you'll find the fat runs out on to the baking sheet.

With those dishes where the pastry is cooked at the same time as the filling (e.g. a quiche lorraine), there is a tendency for the base of the case to remain slightly soggy. Use a thin black baking tray. This will not reflect the heat, but instead transfer it more efficiently to the pastry base, offsetting the cooling effect of the custard. Also, if possible, use an oven which can be set to produce substantial bottom heat to cook the pastry from beneath.

Baking blind

With some recipes, the problem of a soggy base can be overcome by baking the pastry case empty. This is known as *baking blind*.

The pastry tends to rise during cooking, which means that not much room is left for the filling. Pricking the base of the pastry all over with a fork will help.

A more reliable way is to line the pastry case with greaseproof paper, cut neatly to size (called a *cartouche*). Fill the centre with dry beans, rice or balls made from the left over trimmings of paste.

Bake the lined pastry at about 200°C until the edges are set (20 minutes or so). Remove the beans and paper, and continue baking the flan case until it is evenly coloured, a further 10 minutes. You can brush the pastry base with eggwash before returning to the oven, as an added precaution.

If you are using a flan ring, remove it from the pastry after you have taken the beans and paper away. This helps the outside edges colour nicely.

Completing the dish

With experience, you will be able to judge from the appearance when pastry is cooked:

- good colour – not pale, not too dark or burnt
- dry texture – not soggy, not over-dry or too biscuity.

Ovens vary in efficiency. There can be several degrees difference in the temperature of a conventional oven, depending on where you place the pastry dish. Open the oven carefully towards the end of cooking to see whether you need to cut short the cooking time, or turn the heat down a little.

With meat pies that take a few hours to cook (assuming the meat is not pre-cooked), cover the top with kitchen foil when the pastry is brown. Remove the foil just before the end of cooking, so the pastry can dry out again.

Cooked pastry is delicate. Remove it from the baking tray or container carefully. If it has stuck, gently push a palette knife backwards and forwards underneath.

When pastry is to be cooled before service, place it on a wire mesh tray. This allows air to circulate around the base of the pastry, helping to keep it dry.

With suet pastry, you have to rely on recipe timing as the pastry is hidden by the wrapping. Nor will you be able to tell whether the filling is cooked (meat fillings take 2 to 3 hours or more), until the dish is served. Such dishes should be served within a short time of being cooked, piping hot.

Finishing methods

Some open tarts and flans are *filled* after baking (and cooling). The filling is already cooked (e.g. poached peaches), or does not need cooking (e.g. raspberries). These dishes are usually *glazed*, with thinned jam, thickened fruit juice or a jelly (see page 176).

Sometimes the pastry is partly baked, filled and then returned to the oven.

For a meringue top, the stiffly beaten egg white is *piped* on to the tart or flan. The dish is baked until the meringue is a light brown colour, and still quite soft.

Another use for piping is to decorate the dish with whipped cream – rosettes or a border, perhaps. Choux buns and profiteroles are usually filled with whipped cream or an egg-custard type mix: make a small hole in the bottom or at one end, and pipe the filling in. The pastry can be dipped into hot chocolate, or stripes of chocolate piped over the top.

Hot dishes can be decorated with piped cream. Do this at the time of service so the cream does not melt too much. Other pastries must be well cooled before cream is added.

Suet pastry

MAKES 900 g (2 lb)

450 g	plain flour	1 lb
25 g	baking powder	1 oz
225 g	chopped beef suet	8 oz
300 ml	cold water	10 fl oz
	pinch salt	

1 Sieve the flour, baking powder and salt into a bowl, add the suet and thoroughly mix together.

> Some chefs use a small palette knife to mix the ingredients.

2 Add the water and lightly mix to form a paste.

Choux pastry

MAKES 12 ECLAIRS

150 ml	water	5 fl oz
100 g	butter or margarine	4 oz
125 g	strong flour	5 oz
4 eggs	beaten lightly	4 eggs
	pinch sugar	

1 Sieve the flour and sugar.

2 Place the water and fat in a small saucepan and bring to the boil.

3 Add all the flour in one go and mix thoroughly.

4 Stir over a low heat for about 1 minute. The mixture should leave the sides of the pan cleanly.

> If the mixture is too hot for the next stage, the egg will start cooking too soon.

5 Allow to cool for a few minutes.

6 Add the beaten egg a little at a time, mixing the paste vigorously. Scrape down the bowl occasionally to ensure even mixing.

> The mixture should just be able to hold its shape when piped.

7 Continue adding the egg until you get a soft consistency.

8 Place the mixture into a piping bag with a plain nozzle of the appropriate diameter. Pipe on to a greased baking sheet.

> There are no set rules, but here are some guidelines. Using a 10 mm plain nozzle pipe 60 mm length for éclairs, 25 mm diameter balls for choux buns (the quantities in this recipe will make 8), and 10 mm diameter balls for profiteroles (makes 16).

9 Bake at 200°C to 220°C until crisp and golden brown, about 25 to 30 minutes.

For help to answer questions relating to:

Health and safety

safe working practices

The main hazards are from handling hot and heavy equipment, catching your arm on the hot oven shelf, etc. If you use a mixer or other mechanical equipment for preparing pastry, remind yourself what was covered in the training session.

Food hygiene

importance of good hygiene

Pastry must be stored and handled carefully to protect it from sources of harmful bacteria. Pastries with meat, fish, cream and similar fillings are particularly at risk.

importance of time and temperature

Bacteria increase rapidly in numbers at temperatures between 5°C and 63°C. Some pastries do not have to be kept hot or cold, providing they are served within a few hours.

main contamination threats

Other food (e.g. raw meat, fresh vegetables/fruit), food handlers, dirty equipment/work area, harmful cleaning substances, foreign bodies (e.g. pieces of broken glass or china).

products not for immediate use

While pastry is resting, and if there is any delay between making the paste and cooking, it must be kept covered and chilled.

Some dishes are served after cooking, or kept hot for service (above 63°C). With other dishes, the pastry needs to cool before the filling is added, or if the whole dish is served cold. While cooling, the pastry should not be covered (or it will become soggy) – place it where there is minimum risk of contamination.

After filling, cold pastry dishes should be served at once, or covered and put in the refrigerator.

Product knowledge

quality points for pastry

Not over-mixing the paste is largely a matter of experience. The paste for short and sweet pastry should feel soft and break easily. Choux paste should not cling to the sides of the pan. It should just be able to hold its shape when piped.

quality points for cooked dishes

Describe how the dish should look, e.g. even shape, good colour *(appearance)*, smell *(aroma)*, and taste, e.g. not tough or chewy, not greasy, not soggy *(texture, flavour)*.

preparation methods for pastry

These are: rubbing in, mixing, relaxing, and kneading.

cooking methods for pastry dishes

Only suet pastry dishes are steamed. All others are baked.

identifying when dishes are cooked

The appearance of the pastry is a good guide: its colour, whether it has dried sufficiently, and whether it has risen. It is important to follow recipe timings, especially with pies, closed tarts and puddings, where you cannot see what is happening to the filling.

Healthy catering practices

replacing high fat ingredients

Fat is an essential part of the pastry. You might be able to do something about the filling, e.g. using very lean meat, and trimming off all visible fat.

fats/oils for healthy eating

Use products low in saturates and high in polyunsaturates.

increasing fibre content of dishes

Wholemeal flour has twice the fibre content of white flour. It absorbs more liquid, so the recipe has to be adjusted. It is more difficult to handle, so practise first with a recipe that uses half white, half wholemeal flour.

reducing sugar

Some chefs use short pastry instead of sweet pastry for dessert flans, tarts and pies, to provide a less sweet dish (short pastry uses no sugar). Choux pastry has only a pinch of sugar.

Self-check questions

1 What can happen if you use an oven cloth which is wet or greasy?

2 Describe how and where pastry should be left to rest.

3 State the chopping board and knife to use if you are preparing the raw filling for: a) steak pie, b) fruit pie, c) fish pie.

4 Describe how to prepare a working surface for rolling pastry.

5 If there is cream left in the piping bag after you have completed the task it was made for, describe how you would store it.

6 Give some reasons why short pastry when cooked might be tough and chewy.

7 If puff pastry rises in an uneven way, what might have caused this?

8 If the filling in a suet pudding has not cooked sufficiently, what are the possible reasons?

Use this to check your progress again the performance criteria.

Element 1
Prepare basic pastry

Get your preparation areas and equipment ready for use	PC
Select ingredients of the type, quality and quantity required	PC
▲ Pastry: short, sweet, suet, choux	
Identify and report problems with the freshness or quantity of ingredients	PC
Prepare and process pastry	PC
▲ Preparation methods: rubbing in, mixing, relaxing, kneading. Processing methods: cutting, rolling, shaping, lining	
Correctly store pastry not for immediate use	PC
Clean preparation areas and equipment after use	PC
Prioritise and carry out your work in an organised, efficient and safe manner	PC

Element 2
Cook basic pastry dishes

Get your cooking areas and equipment ready for use	PC
Select ingredients of the type, quality and quantity required	PC
▲ Pastry: short, sweet, suet, choux, frozen/ convenience/puff/flaky	
Identify and report problems with the freshness or quantity of ingredients	PC
Combine pastry with other ingredients ready for cooking	PC
Cook pastry dishes	PC
▲ Cooking methods: baking, steaming	
Finish pastry dishes	PC
▲ Finishing methods: dusting, filling, piping	
Correctly store pastry dishes not for immediate use	PC
Clean cooking areas and equipment after use	PC
Prioritise and carry out your work in an organised, efficient and safe manner	PC

Preparing, cooking and finishing basic
cakes, sponges and
scones

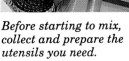

Before starting to mix, collect and prepare the utensils you need.

The preparation and cooking of cakes, sponges and scones gives great scope for the enthusiastic food scientist, as well as the creative pastry chef. The wide range of textures and flavours – from very light golden sponges to moist, fruit-rich cakes are caused by complex chemical and physical changes.

You don't need the knowledge or understanding of a scientist to make good cakes, but you do need rigorous attention to detail. For the result to be right:

- the ingredients must be measured exactly – with scales that are accurate even for very small quantities. Use either metric or imperial measures (when a recipe gives both) – not a mixture

- the order, and the way in which ingredients are combined, must be correct – get the advice of a colleague if you are uncertain what the recipe instructions require

- the temperature of the ingredients when they are mixed has to be suitable for the preparation method – if the fat is too cold in a creaming recipe, for example, it is likely to curdle when the eggs are added

- the time and the temperature at which the ingredients cook must be carefully controlled – get to know your oven, the settings and positions that work best for different products.

Planning in advance

Read the recipe through, to get a good idea of what must be done. Often you have to do something straight away, e.g. 'pour the mixture into the greased baking tin and immediately place in the oven at 220°C'. It is frustrating if you don't realise until that point that:

- you require a baking tin

- the tin has to be greased

- the oven has to be pre-warmed.

To avoid such situations, plan ahead. Collect and prepare all the equipment you will want. Get all the ingredients listed in the recipe. Where it will save time later, measure and prepare them in advance. Let them reach the recommended temperature.

Flour, spices and similar dry ingredients can be weighed and sieved as one of the first steps, even if they are not added until later in the recipe.

Flour settles during handling and storage. Sieving gets some air back into it. It also breaks down any lumps (unlikely in flour, more likely in spices, ground almonds, etc.). Sieving is a good way of mixing dry ingredients (e.g. flour, salt, baking powder and spices) – two or three times may be recommended.

Remove eggs from the refrigerator about half an hour before use.

With some ingredients, e.g. adding a few drops of vanilla essence, there is little point in measuring them in advance. But it may be possible and sensible to add the essence to another recipe liquid, e.g. ½ litre of milk.

If you need to wash dried fruit, and the fruit is very dry, use hot water to make it plumper. Otherwise use cold water. To dry, spread out on trays (covered with a clean tea towel) and leave in a hot cupboard for 2 to 3 hours.

Rinse sugared or glacé fruits in warm water and pat dry with kitchen paper. Otherwise the sugary coating may cause the fruit to sink.

An array of baking utensils and containers. For a key identifying some of those used for cakes, see page 197.

Preparation methods

Some preparation methods have a special significance in making cakes, sponges and scones, because they describe the particular style in which they are made. Most recipes have flour, fat, sugar and eggs as the principal ingredients. It is how they are combined which differs:

- a Victoria sandwich is traditionally made by the *creaming method* – the fat and sugar are *beaten* together until they make a light, fluffy, creamy mixture. The eggs (with a little of the flour) are beaten in – with care, otherwise the mixture loses its smoothness and separates (becomes grainy). The rest of the flour is *folded in* (see page 178). This is also known as the *sugar batter method*

- genoise sponge and Swiss rolls are traditionally made by the *whisking method* – the eggs and sugar are whisked over hot water until they become light and creamy, and double in volume. Take great care not to over-heat the mixture (or you get a sweet type of scrambled eggs). Fold in the flour very gently, or you knock the air out again

- many recipes for small cakes and scones use the *rubbing-in method* – the fat is rubbed into the flour to produce a sandy mixture, before the other ingredients are mixed in (this is similar to making short pastry, see Section 18)

- some modern recipes are formulated to use the *one-stage method* – all the ingredients are put in the bowl and mixed together.

The other three preparation methods you will come across are:

- *greasing* – preparing the baking container, see box

- *glazing* – scones can be brushed with eggwash before cooking, to produce a golden finish after cooking (see page 176). Some small cakes or buns are sprinkled with sugar, which melts during baking to help the surface colour and form a crust

- *portioning* – in bulk preparation, when you make enough for many portions, you need to divide the mixture accurately between baking containers. With sponges and cakes which rise a lot during cooking, tiny differences in the amount of mixture can lead to a quite noticeable variation in the sizes of the finished product.

Preparing baking containers

Use a white fat, such as pastry margarine, to grease baking tins, not butter or yellow margarine (see page 183). For:

- *light cakes with little or no fat* – grease the base
- *other light cakes* – grease base and sides, then sprinkle with flour. As an added precaution against sticking, many chefs also line the base of the cake tin with greased, greaseproof paper. Sometimes this is called *base line*
- *medium to heavy cakes* (e.g. Madeira and light fruit cake) – grease base and sides, then line base and sides with greased greaseproof paper
- *dense cakes* (e.g. rich fruit cake) – grease base and sides, then line base with a cardboard circle and three or four thicknesses of greased paper.

To line square and oblong tins:

- place the tin on a sheet of greaseproof paper, and pencil around the base
- trim the size of the paper, so that it will cover the base and the sides of the tin
- cut along each corner, so that when the paper is placed in the tin, you can fold and overlap the side pieces.

To line round tins:

- cut a strip of paper equal to the depth of the tin plus an overlapping margin of about 6 cm (this will go under the lining for the bottom of the tin)
- cut this paper so it is long enough to wrap completely around the tin and overlap by about 2 cm
- fold the paper along its length, to get a strip the same width as the depth of the tin
- make a series of parallel cuts on the overlapping (6 cm) strip, up to the fold
- place inside the greased tin, so that the cut edge fits around the base
- place the tin on another sheet of paper and pencil around the base
- cut out a circle of paper, and fit into the base of the tin.

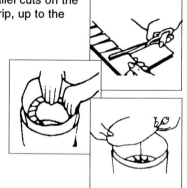

This recipe is fibre-rich, thanks to the wholemeal flour. The topping is lower in fat than butter cream would be.

Passion cake

by McDougalls (RHM Foods)

SERVES 10 to 12

450 g	plain 100% wholemeal flour	1 lb
2.5 ml	bicarbonate of soda	½ tsp
10 ml	mixed spice	2 tsp
60 ml	cooking oil	4 tbsp
60 ml	honey	4 tbsp
2	eggs	2
450 g	carrots, finely grated	1 lb
2	bananas, mashed	2
100 g	soft brown sugar	4 oz

Topping

100 g	cream cheese	4 oz
100 g	icing sugar	4 oz
5 ml	orange juice	1 tsp

1 Grease and line the base of a 20 cm round cake tin.

2 Place all the cake ingredients in a bowl and beat thoroughly to a stiff consistency.

3 Turn into the prepared tin, smooth level and bake for 1¼ hours at 190°C. Cool.

4 Beat topping ingredients until smooth and creamy. Spread on top of cake and decorate (e.g. with curls of orange peel).

Another fibre-rich, low fat recipe.

Wholemeal yogurt scones

by The Flour Advisory Bureau

MAKES 12 to 15

225 g	wholemeal flour	8 oz
5 ml	salt	1 tsp
5 ml	bicarbonate of soda	1 tsp
25 g	margarine	1 oz
150 ml	natural yogurt	5 fl oz

1 Place flour, salt and bicarbonate of soda in bowl. Rub in margarine and stir in yogurt to make a soft dough.

2 Roll out to 1 cm thick and cut into rounds, using a 5 cm plain cutter.

3 Place on baking sheet and brush with a little milk. Bake at 220°C for 7 to 10 minutes until well risen and golden brown.

Whisked sponge

by The British Egg Information Service

MAKES 15 cm CAKE

2	eggs	2
50 g	caster sugar	2 oz
50 g	plain flour, sieved twice	2 oz
¼ tsp	vanilla essence	¼ tsp

1 Very lightly grease and line base and sides of two 15 cm sandwich tins.

2 Place the eggs and sugar in a bowl over a pan of hot, not boiling, water. If using a table model electric mixer, do not whisk over hot water.

Scald the bowl with boiling water to remove any trace of grease or oil, otherwise eggs will not whisk successfully ←

3 Whisk the mixture using a rotary or electric hand whisk for 5 to 10 minutes or until the mixture is light in colour and very thick. It increases in volume by about two-thirds. When the whisk is lifted up it should leave a trail in the mixture for at least 5 seconds.

This is the whisking method. →

4 Remove the bowl from the saucepan and continue to whisk for a further 3 minutes until cooled.

5 With a metal teaspoon, fold the flour and vanilla essence into the foam by cutting and folding the mixture until the flour is evenly mixed in.

6 Divide the mixture evenly into the sandwich tins.

7 Gently shake the tins to level the mixture before baking at 180°C for 20 to 25 minutes or until well risen and golden brown.

8 When cooled a little, turn out the cakes on to a wire cooling tray.

9 Just before filling, peel off the lining paper.

Filling suggestions: jam, cream or butter icing.

Victoria sandwich

SERVES 16

275 g	butter or margarine	10 oz
275 g	caster sugar	10 oz
10 ml	glycerine	2 tsp
275 ml	eggs (probably 6 or 7)	10 fl oz
275 g	plain flour	10 oz
5 ml	baking powder	1 tsp
100 g	raspberry jam	4 oz

icing or caster sugar to decorate

1 Lightly grease and flour two 25 cm diameter, 4 cm deep cake tins. Make sure the ingredients for the cake mixture are at room temperature (21°C to 22°C).

2 Sieve together the flour and baking powder. ←

On to a sheet of greaseproof paper or into a bowl.

3 Place the butter, sugar and glycerine into a mixing bowl and beat until light and creamy. Occasionally scrape down the sides of the bowl to ensure that all the mixture is beaten evenly.

This is the creaming method. →

4 Add the eggs a little at a time, thoroughly beating with each addition. From time to time, scrape the mixture down off the sides of the bowl.

5 Lightly mix in the flour with as gentle a movement as possible until it is evenly distributed.

6 Divide the mixture equally between the cake tins. Smooth the surface carefully. Immediately place the tins on a baking tray and bake at 185°C until cooked – about 30 minutes.

7 Allow to cool slightly, then turn the cakes the right way up on to a wire cooling tray. Leave until cool.

8 Spread a good layer of jam on top of one cake, then place the other on top of it, flat side down.

9 Dredge over the surface with icing sugar and serve on a round dish or salver lined with a doily.

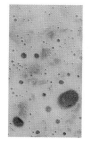

Before and after.

During baking, four main things happen:

- *the air and/or gas expand* – air from beating, creaming, etc., carbon dioxide gas produced by baking powder (when used) or self-raising flour (which contains baking powder)

- *the mixture sets* – flours, eggs and milk all contain protein. When the proteins in the baking mixture reach a temperature of about 70°C they set (or *coagulate*). This is what gives structure to the final product

- *the surface browns* – from the high temperatures, presence of sugar, milk, eggs and similar ingredients which contain substances that encourage browning

- *a crust forms* – water evaporates from the surface, leaving it dry. To prevent the crust forming too soon – which will stop the cake rising fully – some recipes suggest that a pan of water is placed in the oven with the cake. If you have a combination oven, the steam setting will provide the moist atmosphere.

The timing and cooking temperatures given in recipes are worked out to achieve the right balance between these various changes. The mixture should set at the moment expansion reaches the intended level, with surface browning and crust formation happening before the interior of the cake or scone has become too dry.

Planning in advance

The oven should be turned on 15 to 20 minutes before the mixture is ready, to reach the right temperature. Don't turn the oven on too soon, as this wastes energy.

Check that colleagues will not be needing the oven. If oven space is a problem, you may have to replan your work, so that baking can be done earlier or later in the day. Many cakes and sponges have to be left undisturbed in the oven, for most of the cooking time.

Put cake mixtures made with baking powder in the oven without delay, otherwise much of the raising ability of the powder will be wasted.

Use the correct size of baking container. If the tin is too small for a cake that expands in size as it cooks, the mixture will spill over the edges. You will then have a mess in the oven, and a cake that perhaps has to be thrown away, or used for trifle.

What part of the oven to use

Fan-assisted ovens keep an even temperature throughout the compartment. Specialist baking ovens are low in height, so there is little temperature difference between top and bottom.

In a conventional oven, there is temperature variation. The best positions are:

- *Swiss rolls* – at the top, where the oven is hottest

- *small cakes and sponges, scones* – just above centre to get more top heat

- *Madeira cakes* – centre, for an even heat

- *very rich fruit cakes* – near the bottom, so there is least risk of burning the base of the cake.

Checking cooking progress

Keep the oven door closed while cakes are cooking, or the influx of cold air as the door opens will cause the cake to collapse.

If you have to open the oven door during the last few minutes of cooking to check progress, this will not usually cause a problem. Open the door slowly, by the minimum amount. Keep it open for as short a time as possible, and then close it gently.

If the cake is cooked it will:

- feel firm and spongy when touched gently in the centre

- have shrunk slightly from the sides of the tin

- have set throughout: a skewer or cocktail stick pushed in the centre comes out clean. Warm the skewer first, by pushing it between the baking paper and the tin.

The skewer method will not work with fruit-rich cakes (since it is bound to pierce moist fruit). A bubbling sound indicates that the cake is not yet cooked.

With Swiss rolls, you should be able to draw your fingers lightly across the surface without leaving a mark.

Scones should be a good colour, risen sufficiently, and not too moist nor dry.

Overview of the preparation methods

Portioning – dividing the mixture equally, so that each scone or cake is a similar size and weight when cooked.

Shaping – arranging the mixture to make a particular shape when baked. Some types of buns are shaped into balls. Scones can be shaped into a very thick pancake, then cut in an X-shape to produce four wedges.

Spreading – arranging the mixture in the baking container so that it is even in thickness, and the top is smooth.

Filling – putting the mixture into the baking container or individual cake papers. Sometimes it is easier and neater to *pipe* the mixture into small containers.

Rolling – scone mixtures are usually rolled, so they are even in thickness and can be easily cut into rounds.

Lining – fitting greased greaseproof paper (usually) around the sides and on the bottom of the baking container, as an additional precaution against sticking (see box on page 190).

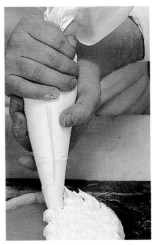

Note how the piping bag is held closed at the top with one hand, and its movement controlled with the other hand.

Finishing methods

Handle cakes and scones gently when you take them out of the oven. Sudden movement, banging the baking container down, etc. may harm the shape or texture of the more delicate types.

Cooling and turning out

Check the recipe instructions. Some cakes are left to cool for two or three minutes, then turned out of the baking container. Others are left to cool completely in the tin (e.g. fruit cakes). Choose a cool area of the kitchen, but not in a direct breeze.

Once the cake has cooled, decorate and serve, or leave covered (e.g. with a clean, dry teacloth) or in an airtight container for longer storage (more than a day). Put in a cool room.

To turn out a cake, place a rack over the top of the cake. Turn upside down, then carefully lift off the cake tin. So that the cake top is not marked with indentations from the rack, invert it on to a second rack, or turn over very carefully by hand.

Remove any lining paper.

Swiss roll is turned out on to lightly sugared greaseproof paper (some chefs first place the paper on a cloth, to make it easier to roll the sponge up).

Cakes cooked in single-portion size moulds can be picked out individually, or the whole tray turned upside down. Cakes cooked in paper cases are usually left in the case for service.

Filling

Just as sandwiches are filled, so are some cakes and scones. Cakes may have two or three layers, perhaps with different fillings, e.g. cherries in thickened syrup on one layer, whipped cream on another.

When cutting a cake into layers, keep the cake flat on the work surface. Use a long-bladed knife, sawing rather than pushing, as you keep the knife horizontal. Never stand delicate cakes on their sides to cut.

If you are splitting a number of cakes, keep the layers of each cake together so that you can match them when you assemble the cake.

Glazing

The surface of the cake is coated with fondant icing, to give it a very glossy or shiny look. Small cakes can be dipped into the icing. With larger ones, the icing is spooned over.

Piping

This is mostly used in decorating cakes (see overleaf). Cream may be piped on to scones, perhaps with a spoon of jam in the centre.

Spreading

Many fillings (e.g. jam, whipped cream, butter icing) are spread on cakes and scones, using a palette knife.

The filling may be the sandwich-type described above, between layers of cake (baked separately or cut in half), or a finish for the top, or both these. For attractive finishes, a serrated spreader can be used.

Rolling

The mixture for Swiss rolls is rolled up while the sponge is still warm from cooking. If jam is being used as a filling, this is spread before rolling. If the filling is whipped cream or buttercream, the sponge is rolled (with the paper inside), allowed to cool, unrolled, paper removed, spread, then rolled again.

Trimming

To prevent cracking when it is rolled, first trim off any crisp edges on a Swiss roll.

Before icing cakes, it is sometimes necessary to trim off uneven edges, or the top so that you have a flat surface.

Trimming is also used to produce special shapes, e.g. the wings for angel cakes, or so that the cake can stand on one edge.

Always use a very sharp knife for trimming cakes. One with a serrated edge may do the neatest cut.

Sprinkling, dusting or dredging

This is often done with caster or icing sugar, sometimes with cocoa powder. For a fine, even coating (or dusting) put the sugar or powder in a sieve and shake over the top of the cake.

Alternatively you can use a dredger – this is like a large pepper pot, but filled with sugar.

Or else sprinkle the sugar over by hand, or shake from a large spoon – this might be the easiest way if you are creating a special pattern.

Rolling up the sponge for a Swiss roll. In this illustration it has been spread with jam first, and a tea cloth is being used to help roll the sponge.

Decorating cakes and sponges

Start with the simplest ideas, until you gain the experience to be more ambitious. A simple decoration well done can be very effective. A complex decoration is ruined by even a minor flaw.

Using the different types of decoration, filling and topping

These should suit the:

- texture, flavour and colours of the cake – contrasts as well as complementary themes are effective, but your choice should be appropriate – passion fruit-flavoured icing on a walnut cake would get the thumbs down from most customers!

- occasion on which it is to be served – royal icing is traditional for special celebration cakes, fresh cream is unsuitable for a cake which cannot be kept chilled

- preferences of your customers (where known) – some people do not like hard icings, or cannot eat certain foods, e.g. chocolate, nuts or fresh cream.

Jam

Jam fillings and toppings should be reasonably thin and even, otherwise you will find them dragging up the surface of the cake. Remove any large lumps of fruit before using and, if necessary, warm to get a better spreading consistency.

Fruit filling and fresh fruit

Choose the best quality fruit, and use only perfect pieces for decorations. Cut into neat pieces, and remove any pips or seeds. Use pitted cherries, or take the stones out individually.

Brush the fruit with a glaze (e.g. apricot jam) to give it an attractive gloss and to stop it from drying out. Dip or brush banana and apple with lemon juice to stop browning – even then, these fruits are not suitable for cakes that might not be served for a few hours.

Chocolate

Plain chocolate – because it sets hard, and has an attractive deep colour – is usually more suitable than milk chocolate for coatings and decorations.

Do not melt chocolate over direct heat as it scorches easily. Break into a bowl set over hot (not boiling) water and stir occasionally until the chocolate melts. Avoid drops of water getting into the chocolate, as this will cause it to become grainy.

Water icing

This is made by mixing sieved icing sugar with a few drops of vanilla essence and sufficient warm water to achieve the right consistency.

Use colourings and essences sparingly. Pour a few drops into a spoon, then add to the icing. Repeat until you have got the right effect.

Butter cream

Butter creams (made by creaming icing sugar and butter) tend to separate. To avoid this, whisk in a few drops at a time of essences and other liquid ingredients.

If you are using chocolate as the flavouring, let it cool to room temperature after melting, then add the butter cream.

Water icing
Covers 18 cm cake

100 g	icing sugar, sieved	4 oz
15 ml	water	1 tbsp
	few drops food colouring	

1 Mix icing sugar with water in a basin. Beat until smooth. Colour as required.

Variations

Orange – replace water with strained orange juice or undiluted orange squash.

Chocolate – sieve 10 ml (2 tsp) cocoa powder with icing sugar before mixing with water.

Butter cream
To fill/decorate 18 cm cake

50 g	butter (unsalted)	2 oz
100 g	icing sugar, sieved	4 oz
2–3 drops	food essence/flavouring	2–3 drops

1 Cream butter until soft. Gradually add icing sugar and cream together. Add flavouring to taste and beat well.

Variations

Lemon – add finely grated zest of 1 lemon and 1 tbsp lemon juice.

Mocha – add 1 tsp cocoa powder and 1 tsp coffee essence.

Chantilly cream
SERVES 4 to 6

150 ml	double or whipping cream	5 fl oz
25 g	caster sugar	1 oz
	few drops vanilla essence	

Use a stainless steel (preferably), glass or china basin, not plastic. The basin should be cold.

1 Whisk the ingredients until the cream stands in soft peaks. Chill until required.

Whipped cream

Chill equipment, including piping bags and nozzles. Work in a cool area of the kitchen.

Only half-fill the bowl in which the cream is to be whipped. Whip quickly until the cream takes on a matt finish. Continue more slowly, until the cream stands in soft peaks, clings to the whisk and holds its shape:

- avoid over-whipping, as this will turn the cream into butter

- do not whip cream too stiffly for piping. It will thicken more as you pipe it (because of the pressure needed to force it through the piping nozzle)

- sugar increases whipping time, and large amounts of sugar can reduce the stiffness and stability of cream. Add sugar after the cream has been whipped.

Cover and keep chilled any cream not required immediately. Whip small amounts when you need them, rather than a large amount at once.

Using a piping bag

1 Select the nozzle of the right size for the piping bag, with a plain or shaped end, as needed.

2 Push the nozzle right down to the pointed end of the piping bag, so it shows through the opening. It should make a tight fit with the bag, otherwise the mixture will ooze out, or the nozzle will shoot out of the bag.

3 If you are piping a rather soft mixture, there is a danger the mixture will run out of the bag while you are filling it. To avoid this, twist the bag a couple of times just above the nozzle, and firmly push the twisted part of the bag inside the nozzle. A clothes peg will do the job just as well – even if it looks unprofessional!

4 Turn the top one-third of the bag inside out. This makes it easier to fill.

5 Holding the bag under the fold you have just made, spoon some of the mixture down into the bag. Do not fill more than halfway.

6 Unfold the top of the bag, then close it up neatly.

7 Take hold of the bag above the mixture. Pull the bag up between your thumb and forefinger until the palm of your hand is against the mixture.

8 Keep the top of the bag closed with your thumb and forefinger. Squeeze the contents of the bag, using the palm of your hand and the tips of your fingers. The other hand can be used a) to control the direction of the bag, or b) to hold the item being decorated.

9 Before starting a complicated decoration, make sure there is no air in the bag by squeezing some of the mixture out on to a plate, or back into the bowl.

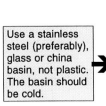

Decorating methods

When decorating fairly solid cakes, turn the cake over so that the flat base becomes the top. If what was the top is rounded, slice off so that it sits flat.

If you don't have access to a cake turntable, sit the cake on its board or on an upturned plate, on top of a basin. The basin acts as a turntable.

Trimming

This is done to neaten the appearance, to make flat surfaces, or special shapes. Use a sharp knife.

Filling

When cakes are decorated, the filling is usually done at the same time. For gâteaux, the range of fillings is extensive – fruit, jam, whipped cream, butter cream of various flavours, icing, etc. For plainer cakes, jam and/or butter cream are popular fillings.

Spreading and smoothing

Fillings need to be spread, so that they coat the surface fairly evenly. Take care not to harm the surface of delicate cakes – you may find crumbs form and get caught up in the filling, as you spread it.

It takes practice to get an absolutely smooth finish for icing. A palette knife makes the task easier. From time to time, dip the blade in hot water. Be careful not to flood the surface.

For a rougher finish, use a serrated scraper or a fork.

Sprinkling, dusting or dredging

A sprinkling of icing or caster sugar, cocoa powder, grated chocolate, crushed nuts, hundreds and thousands, etc. will make a simple, but effective decoration. A sieve or sugar shaker is easier to use when you want a fine, even layer.

You can get a very decorative effect using a cake doily. Place the doily on top of the cake, shake the sugar over, then carefully remove the doily and the sugar which has been caught on it. You are left with the pattern of the doily on the cake.

Topping

Fruit makes a colourful, interesting topping, perhaps in combination with whipped cream. Drain the fruit thoroughly first. Flaked or nibbed almonds or grated chocolate can be sprinkled over butter icing or cream.

A tempting selection of cakes and pastries.

Coating

To coat the sides of a cake, spread the coating (e.g. chocolate vermicelli) on a sheet of greaseproof paper. Holding the cake between the palms of your hands, gently roll it over the coating.

Some cakes are too delicate to be picked up in this way. Press the coating against the side using a palette knife or your hands.

If the cake is to be covered with a thin coating, stand it on a wire rack resting on a tray. The tray will then catch the excess coating as it drips off the cake.

Some cakes are moistened with fruit juice, stock syrup or liqueurs. Don't overdo this, or the cake will fall apart.

Piping with icing and chocolate

Practise piping decorations on a tray or board, before piping on to the cake (see boxes on using and making a piping bag, page 198). You can scrape the icing off the tray before it hardens and return it to the bowl to use again.

Allow icing to dry before adding a different colour icing. If you don't, the colours will run into each other.

Piping with cream

Use a larger tube than you would for icing, and a cloth/plastic piping bag. Otherwise, the technique is similar to piping icing or chocolate (see box, page 195).

For help to answer questions relating to:

Health and safety

? **safe working practices**

Most of the safety risks in baking arise from using ovens, other equipment and food – these are often very hot, may be difficult to handle, and can be dangerous because they involve moving parts, cutting equipment, or the use of electricity or gas.

Food hygiene

? **importance of good hygiene**

The ingredients for cakes, etc., and the finished products, must be stored and handled as any other fresh food, to protect them from sources of harmful bacteria.

? **importance of time and temperature**

Bacteria increase rapidly in numbers at temperatures between 5°C and 63°C.

? **main contamination threats**

Other food (e.g. fresh fruit), food handlers, dirty equipment/work area, harmful cleaning substances, foreign bodies (e.g. pieces of grit in dried fruit), etc.

? **products not for immediate use**

Many cake and sponge mixes have to be cooked within a short time of preparation. If advance preparation is possible (e.g. measuring and combining of some of the ingredients), these ingredients must be kept covered. Some may need to be kept chilled, but check with the recipe on the temperature they should be when ready for use.

Once cooked, most cakes, etc. are best kept at room temperature. If they contain cream or similar fillings or decorations which are high risk in hygiene terms, then storage should be below 5°C.

Scones are best served on the day they were cooked. Some sponges will keep for a few days, others get stale quickly. Rich fruit cakes benefit from keeping.

Product knowledge

? **quality points for baking mixtures**

The main problems are curdling, inadequate mixing of the ingredients, or some fault with an ingredient (e.g. an egg with a cracked shell, dried fruit containing pieces of grit).

? **quality points for cooked cakes, etc.**

A lot can be judged from the appearance – not coarse and open, not too solid nor dense, crust good colour and not cracked or over-risen, not sunken in the centre.

If it is possible to taste a sample, then you can examine the flavour and texture (not tough or chewy, not uneven with large holes). The fruit, when used, should be evenly distributed, not sunk to the bottom.

? **quality points for decorated cakes, etc.**

Appearance is the main test, but the consistency and flavour of icing and other coverings should be right (e.g. icing very smooth).

? **preparation methods**

These are: creaming and beating, whisking, folding, rubbing in, greasing, glazing and portioning.

? **preparation and finishing methods**

These are: portioning, shaping, spreading, filling, rolling, lining (preparation for cooking); and: spreading, turning out, cooling, glazing, trimming, basic piping, sprinkling, dusting or dredging, rolling and filling (finishing methods).

? **decorating methods**

These are: trimming, filling, spreading and smoothing, piping with icing and chocolate, piping with cream, dusting, dredging or sprinkling, coating and topping.

? **identifying when cooked**

By touch: firm and spongy in the centre; by appearance: shrunken slightly from the sides of the tin, well coloured, and a skewer comes out clean.

Healthy catering practices

? **replacing high fat ingredients**

There is little scope for changing the ingredients of cakes, sponges and scones because the recipes are very carefully balanced. You may have more choice with the fillings and decorations, e.g. to avoid cream and butter icing.

? **fats/oils for healthy eating**

See page 110.

? **increasing fibre content**

Wholemeal flour has twice the fibre content of white flour, and there are some recipes available for wholemeal cakes and scones.

? **reducing sugar**

Sugar is essential in many recipes, but some have been developed which reduce the amount of sugar, or use sugar substitutes. You may be able to avoid sugar-rich fillings and decorations, e.g. by using fruit.

Self-check questions

1 When lighting a gas oven, what precautions should you take?

2 How long in advance do you need to turn on the ovens which are used for baking in your workplace?

3 Give the main steps in preparing a cake by a) the whisking method, and b) the creaming method.

4 Describe how you would prepare the baking container for three different types of cake/sponge/scone.

5 For the examples used in the previous question, state how you can tell when cooking is complete.

6 Now describe some methods of decoration for each of your examples.

7 Say how the following should be stored if they are not going to be served immediately: a) cake or scone decorated with fresh cream, b) plain scone and c) fruit cake.

8 If a cake or its filling contains nuts, but this is not apparent from its appearance or the name, why is it important that customers are told (or given an accurate answer if they ask)?

On left: *more baking containers and utensils. The thermometer (centre of photo) is for sugar work. The sifter (foreground) is for dusting with sugar or flour.*

Some of the equipment and utensils used in cake-making and baking (see photo on page 189): 1) non-stick cake tin, 2) flour scoop, 3) measuring jug, 4) mixing spoon (plastic spoons are considered more hygienic than wooden ones), 5) flan rings, 6) tartlet tin, 7) boat-shaped tartlet tin, 8) piping tubes, 9) cutters for fancy shapes, 10) brush for glazing, 11) rolling pin (plastic, like the spoons), 12) flour sifter.

To make a paper piping bag

1 Cut a triangle from a sheet of greaseproof or waxed paper. To get the shape and mark the cutting line, fold over one corner to meet the opposite edge.

2 With the longest side facing away from you, roll the paper up to form a cone.

3 If necessary, tighten the cone, so that the point is needle sharp.

4 Holding the cone firmly together, tuck the ends down inside to stop the cone unravelling.

5 Fill the piping bag – but not more than one-third full.

6 Flatten the cone above the filling. Fold over one side, then the other side. Finally, fold the centre over on to itself twice.

7 Cut off the tip of the piping bag with sharp scissors: the smaller the opening, the finer the decoration.

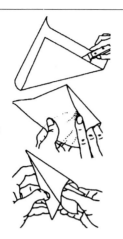

Using the bag

- keep the point of the bag 1 to 3 cm above the surface
- move faster over the surface for thinner lines

Feathered icing

Use fondant icing or glacé icing, thinned so that it pipes easily:

- pipe parallel lines a short distance apart
- turn the cake through 90° and run a long, thin bladed knife dragging the lines towards you – the knife should barely touch the cake surface. These lines should be quite well spaced, to allow for the lines going in the opposite direction (next step). Wipe the knife blade clean after each line
- turn the cake through 180°, so that you pull the icing in the opposite direction. Drag the knife across the lines as before.

NVQ SVQ

Skills check
Prepare, cook and finish basic cakes, sponges and scones
Unit 2ND9

level 2

Use this to check your progress against the performance criteria.

Element 1

Prepare basic cakes, sponges and scones

Get your preparation areas and equipment ready for use	☐ PC1
Select ingredients of the type, quality and quantity required	☐ PC2
Identify and report problems with the quality of ingredients	☐ PC3
Prepare cakes, sponges and scones	☐ PC4

▲ Preparation methods: creaming/beating, whisking, folding, rubbing in, greasing, glazing, portioning

Correctly store mixtures not for immediate use	☐ PC5
Clean preparation areas and equipment after use	☐ PC6
Prioritise/carry out your work in an organised, efficient & safe manner	☐ PC7

Element 2

Cook and finish basic cakes, sponges and scones

Get your preparation and cooking areas and equipment ready for use	☐ PC1
Check mixtures are of the type, quality and quantity required	☐ PC2
Identify and report problems with the quality of ingredients	☐ PC3
Prepare mixture for cooking	☐ PC4

▲ Preparation methods: portioning, shaping, spreading, filling, rolling, lining

Cook and finish cakes, sponges and scones	☐ PC5

▲ Finishing methods: spreading, turning out, cooling, glazing, trimming, basic piping, sprinkling/dusting/dredging, filling, rolling

Store finished cakes, sponges and scones not for immediate use	☐ PC6
Clean preparation/cooking areas and equipment after use	☐ PC7
Prioritise/carry out your work in an organised, efficient & safe manner	☐ PC8

Element 3

Decorate basic cakes and sponges

Get your preparation areas and equipment ready for use	☐ PC1
Select ingredients of the type, quality and quantity required	☐ PC2

▲ Decorations, fillings or toppings: water icing, butter cream, whipped cream, jam, fruit filling/ fresh fruit, chocolate

Identify & report problems with freshness/ quantity of ingredients	☐ PC3
Prepare decorations, fillings or toppings	☐ PC4
Decorate, top or fill cakes and sponges	☐ PC5

▲ Decorating methods: trimming, filling, spreading and smoothing, piping with icing/ chocolate, piping with cream, sprinkling/ dusting/dredging, coating, topping

Store decorated cakes and sponges not for immediate use	☐ PC6
Clean preparation areas and equipment after use	☐ PC7
Prioritise/carry out your work in an organised, efficient & safe manner	☐ PC8

Preparing and cooking basic
dough products

Preparing dough products

The simplest kind of bread, flat bread, is just a baked dough of flour and water. This is sometimes called unleavened bread, meaning that it has not risen. Leavened or raised breads are the kind that most people are familiar with, and enjoy regularly. They use yeast to give lightness and flavour.

For any type of bread, the final texture is extremely important. For yeast to develop the best texture, great care has to be taken that the ingredients are combined, and treated in the right way.

There is a fairly lengthy process before baking can begin, of mixing, fermenting (when the yeast does its work by producing carbon dioxide), knocking back and the final proving.

About the ingredients

There are many hundreds of variations on the basic recipe: milk can be used instead of water, fat can be added, as can salt, sugar and eggs. These all interact with each other and with the yeast in particular ways.

Then there are the ingredients which mostly give flavour: spices, dried fruit, butter as the fat, and yogurt.

Flour

White flour comes in various strengths according to how much protein the flour contains and therefore how much gluten it will make.

Strong or *hard flours* are suitable for bread because they develop a lot of gluten. Strong white flour is creamy white, feels slightly coarse when rubbed between the fingers and, if squeezed into a lump, will quickly fall apart again.

Stoneground bread is still made by the traditional process. The grain is fed between two circular millstones, the top one revolving, crushing the grain and pushing it outwards. As it passes across the stone, the grain gets more and more finely ground, eventually to become flour.

Other cereals such as oats, barley, maize and rye can be used in combination with wheat flour to introduce their own distinctive flavours.

Wheat

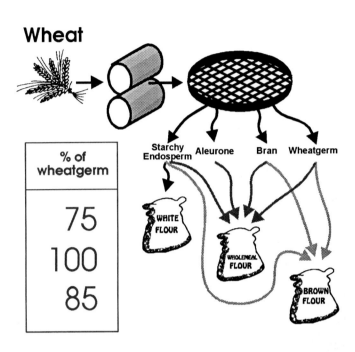

% of wheatgerm
75
100
85

Most flour is produced by roller milling. After thorough cleaning, the wheat grains pass through a succession of rollers and sieves to be separated into their various components. These are then kept apart, for the production of white flour, or blended back together to produce wholemeal (100% of the original grain) and brown flours (about 85% of the original grain).

Fresh yeast

Fresh or compressed yeast should be:

- almost odourless (hint of sweet fruitiness)
- firm, plastic texture
- creamy colour

and dissolve easily in water, without forming lumps.

A sour, unpleasant smell, sticky texture and browning on the surface are signs that the yeast is dying or dead.

The yeast will die at temperatures above 50°C. Salt destroys yeast, and should never be in contact with it.

The ideal storage temperature for yeast is between 4°C and 6°C. Keep it in its original packaging, or wrapped in foil, clingfilm or waxed paper. Do not use beyond the best-before date.

Fast action yeast is a super-speed version of compressed yeast. Doughs made from it only need to rise once.

Dried yeast

This has a longer storage life, making it a good stand-by for caterers who bake occasionally. Keep in a moisture-free sealed container, in a cool, dry place.

Before use, dissolve in warm water, following the instructions on the packet. Pay attention to the temperature of the water – if it is too high or too low, the yeast is likely to lose most of its fermenting power.

Doughs made with dried yeast must be kneaded and left to rise twice.

Fat and oil

Fats are traditionally known as shortening agents. This name comes from the tenderising effect they have as a result of 'shortening' or cutting up the gluten.

Oils have a limited use in baking, because they cannot hold any air.

Eggs

Eggs add richness, flavour and colour to doughs.

Sugar

Sugar is sometimes used to sweeten doughs, but the main reasons are the contributions it makes to:

- *tenderness and moistness* – this comes from sugar's ability to absorb liquid in the mixture, so preventing some of the proteins in the flour from forming gluten and reducing evaporation of moisture
- *lightness* – yeast needs sugar so that it can ferment and create gas bubbles in the dough. But too much sugar uses up some of the liquid needed by the yeast
- *browning* – this happens very effectively in high-temperature cooking when sugar is in the mixture.

Water and milk

Yeast needs water or a liquid containing water, to do its task. For some breads and many of the sweeter dough products, the liquid is milk, or milk and water (or, for convenience, water and dried milk powder). The milk adds flavour.

Salt

Salt plays three important roles in yeast doughs, besides adding flavour. It strengthens the gluten, helps colour the crust, and improves the keeping quality of the cooked product. However it does slow down the action of the yeast, so too much salt may mean that the dough does not rise properly. If you are concerned about using salt on health grounds, use low sodium salt instead.

Preparation methods

The dry ingredients (flour, sugar, salt, milk powder, spices, etc.) are usually sieved together. This helps them mix and removes any lumps.

In some recipes, the flour and fat are rubbed together, before the other ingredients are added, to produce a sandy texture (as in making short pastry, see page 182).

Preparing the baking container

Always brush tins with white cooking fat (see page 183), so the bread won't stick. If bread tins are cold, warm them slightly before putting the dough in.

Mixing

The first stage, of combining the dry ingredients with the liquid, eggs, if used, and yeast is done by mixing (often by machine).

Kneading

This is mixing the dough vigorously, often with the hands. Continue until the dough is no longer sticky to the touch and has a shiny surface. Kneading is done to:

- squeeze the gas pockets (formed by the action of the yeast) and split them into more, smaller pockets
- develop the gluten.

After proving (see below), the dough is kneaded again, or knocked back to its original size. This divides the gas pockets once again, which improves the texture as well as taking the strain off the dough. It also allows the dough to cool down (heat is produced by fermentation).

Kneading should be done in a warm place, free from draughts.

Proving

The dough is set aside after kneading to prove or ferment. The recipe will indicate what temperature the dough needs to be during this stage, so that the yeast works properly. The gas-pockets stretch the dough (usually to double its size) to its limit before it breaks.

While proving, the surface of the dough should be covered with polythene, lightly oiled, to keep it moist, and to prevent a skin forming. Covering the dough also protects it from dust (and that includes bacteria).

To test whether the dough has expanded to its fullest extent, press it – it should not spring back.

There is usually a second proving, before baking. This allows the yeast to produce more gas, enlarging the many pockets that have now been created in the dough. The dough should double in size.

Rolling

Bun-shapes and round loaves can be achieved by working the dough with your hands. For most other shapes, the dough is rolled like pastry to produce a flat sheet, thick or thin depending on what is being made. It is then cut and/or shaped.

Folding

This is part of the kneading process – folding and pushing the dough down to get air into the dough.

In bread-making, the dough for loaves is rolled, then folded to go into the bread tin. This gives it a good depth and the right shape.

Shaping

Rolls and loaves are made into many different shapes by cutting, folding and rolling the dough (see illustration on page 207), and weaving together lengths of dough (plaiting).

Portioning

For rolls, buns or pizzas, or for large mixes making several loaves, the dough has to be divided up – all but the most experienced bakers do this by weighing each portion. This is why it is sometimes called *dividing and scaling*.

Don't risk doing this by eye, because, as the dough is expanding all the time, it is difficult to judge.

Glazing

Glazing helps the surface to brown. It can be done by brushing the surface with eggwash (egg beaten with water or milk). For a sweeter, golden finish, use warmed honey or sugar syrup (sugar dissolved in a little water).

Some glazes are added after baking.

The presence of moisture during baking plays a key role in developing the crust. Breads are often sprayed with steam during the first 10 minutes or so of cooking to produce a hard, glossy brown crust. Other options are to place a pan of hot water at the bottom of the oven, or to inject steam into the oven.

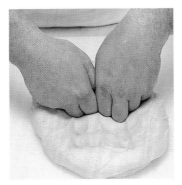

Left: *kneading the dough.*
Below: *portioning or scaling the dough.*

Above: *a proving oven.*
Below: *glazing buns after cooking.*

This makes between 16 and 20 rolls.

Traditional bread and rolls

by McDougalls (RHM Foods)

MAKES 2 loaves

675 g	flour: strong white or plain 100% wholemeal	1½ lb
10 ml	salt	2 tsp
25 g	lard or vegetable fat	1 oz
1	sachet fast action dried yeast	1
425 ml	warm water	¾ pt

1 Mix together the flour and salt, rub in fat, then stir in dried yeast.

2 Add the water and mix to a dough.

3 Turn out on to a lightly floured surface and knead for 10 minutes.

4 Divide and shape the dough, as required, and place in greased tins.

5 Cover with oiled polythene and leave in a warm place until doubled in size.

6 Uncover and bake in an oven preheated to 230°C: ½ kg (1 lb) loaves approximately 25 minutes, 1 kg (2 lb) loaf approximately 35 minutes, rolls approximately 15 minutes.

If you are using normal compressed yeast, the recipe should be adjusted:

1 Allow 15 g (½ oz) fresh yeast for quantities up to 450 g (1 lb), and 25 g (1 oz) for quantities up to 1½ kg (3 lb).

2 Blend the fresh yeast into the warm liquid from the recipe and leave to stand until the surface froths, about 10 minutes.

3 Make up dough as normal, knead well, cover lightly with oiled polythene and leave in a warm place to double in size.

4 Knead again, shape as required, cover, allow to rise again, and cook as for recipe.

Oaten bread and rolls

by Mornflake Oats

MAKES 2 loaves

450 g	strong plain flour	1 lb
10 ml	salt	2 tsp
225 g	oats	8 oz
15 ml	dried yeast	1 tbsp
10 ml	sugar	2 tsp
	water to mix	
	beaten egg to glaze	

1 Mix together the sifted flour, salt and oats.

2 Measure yeast and sugar into a measuring jug and fill up to 425 ml (¾ pt) with hand-hot water. Stir well and leave in a warm place for about 10 minutes until frothy.

3 Stir yeast mixture into flour, etc. to give a soft dough. Knead on a floured surface for 5 minutes until smooth and elastic. Place in a floured bowl and cover lightly with greased polythene. Prove until double in size.

4 Knead the dough again and shape.

5 Halve the dough and shape each piece to fit into a greased 850 ml (1½ pt) loaf tin. Cover and prove until double in size. Brush with beaten egg and bake at 230°C for 20 minutes, then at 190°C for a further 45 minutes, or until the loaf sounds hollow when tapped.

6 Cool the bread on a wire rack. Serve the same day.

For rolls, shape dough into 12 rounded rolls and make a 1 cm (½ inch) cut across the top of each. Arrange on two greased baking sheets. Cover and prove until doubled in size. Brush with beaten egg and bake at 230°C for 10 to 15 minutes, or until they sound hollow when tapped.

This is an enriched dough for buns

Wholemeal Chelsea buns

by McDougalls (RHM Foods)

MAKES 16 slices

450 g	wholemeal flour	1 lb
5 ml	salt	1 tsp
50 g	margarine	2 oz
50 g	soft brown sugar	2 oz
1	sachet fast action dried yeast	1
150 ml	milk, warmed	5 fl oz
2	eggs, size 3, beaten	2

Filling

25 g	butter or margarine, melted	1 oz
50 g	soft brown sugar	2 oz
5 ml	cinnamon	1 tsp
50 g	dried apricots, finely chopped	2 oz
50 g	dates, finely chopped	2 oz
25 g	almonds, finely chopped	1 oz

Sugar glaze

30 ml each	milk, sugar, water	2 tbsp each

1 For the dough, rub the margarine into the flour and salt. Stir in sugar and yeast. Add milk and eggs, mix well and knead on a floured surface for 10 minutes until smooth.

2 Place dough in a bowl, cover with lightly oiled polythene and leave in a warm place until doubled in size (50 to 60 minutes).

3 Roll out the dough to a 35 cm (14 inch) square and brush with the melted butter. Mix together the sugar, cinnamon, apricots, dates and almonds, and sprinkle over the dough. Roll up Swiss roll style and cut into 16 slices. See page 194.

4 Arrange cut side down on a greased baking tray. Cover and leave in a warm place until double in size. Bake at 200°C for 25 minutes.

5 Meanwhile heat the milk, sugar and water for the glaze until the sugar has dissolved. Simmer for 2 minutes. Brush over the buns while they are still hot. Remove to a wire rack and cool.

Pizza romana

SERVES 10

Pizza dough

675 g	plain (soft) flour	1½ lb
5 ml	salt	1 tsp
75 ml	oil	3 fl oz
30 g	compressed yeast (fresh)	1¼ oz
400 ml	cold water at 18°C	14 fl oz

Topping

100 g	onions, finely chopped	4 oz
1	clove of garlic, peeled and crushed	1
50 ml	oil	2 fl oz
1 × 900 g	can chopped tomatoes	1 × 2 lb
25 g	tomato purée	1 oz
5 ml	fresh oregano, chopped	1 tsp
10 ml	fresh basil, chopped	2 tsp
20	anchovy fillets	20
150 g	Mozzarella cheese	6 oz
100 g	Parmesan cheese, grated	4 oz
	seasoning to taste	
	oil for brushing over the pizza bases	

1 Prepare the topping:

a) gently shallow fry the onions and garlic in the oil without browning for 2 to 3 minutes

b) add the oregano and basil and cook for a further 2 minutes

c) add the canned tomatoes and tomato purée and simmer until the mixture becomes quite thick (about 20 minutes)

d) check the seasoning, then allow the mixture to cool

e) cut the anchovy fillets in half lengthways

f) cut the Mozzarella into pieces.

2 Prepare the dough:

a) sieve the flour and salt together into a mixing bowl

b) make a hollow in the centre and add the oil

c) place the yeast into a small bowl, add some of the water, mix until combined, then add the yeast and water mixture to the flour

d) add most of the remaining water and mix together until a smooth, pliable, soft dough is produced. Add the remainder of the water if the dough is too stiff to work easily

e) cover and set aside for 15 minutes at room temperature (this will allow the yeast to ferment).

3 Divide the dough into 10 pieces of equal weight, then mould these into balls.

4 Roll out the balls of dough into thin rounds and place them on greased baking trays.

5 Lightly brush over the surfaces of the dough bases with oil.

6 Add the topping, leaving a 10 mm border uncovered round each base.

7 Decorate the topping with the anchovy fillets, then add the Mozzarella and Parmesan.

8 Allow the pizzas to sit at room temperature for 30 to 40 minutes.

9 Bake at 225°C until cooked, about 15 to 20 minutes.

> There is more information on preparing and cooking pizzas, and ideas for pizza toppings in Section 24.

Hot cross buns

by McDougalls (RHM Foods)

MAKES 12 BUNS

450 g	flour: strong white	1 lb
2.5 ml	salt	1 tsp
50 g	butter	2 oz
1	sachet fast action dried yeast	1
50 g	caster sugar	2 oz
10 ml	mixed spice	2 tsp
10 ml	ground cinnamon	2 tsp
75 g	sultanas	3 oz
50 g	currants	2 oz
1	egg, size 3 beaten with enough milk to make 150 ml (¼ pt)	1
150 ml	warm water	¼ pt

Glaze

15 ml	sugar	1 tbsp
15 ml	milk	1 tbsp
15 ml	water	1 tbs

1 Mix together the flour and salt, rub in the fat. Stir in the yeast, sugar, spices and dried fruit.

2 Stir in the egg mixture and warm water and mix to a dough.

3 Knead on a lightly floured surface for 10 minutes.

4 Divide dough into 12 pieces and shape into buns.

5 Place on a greased baking sheet, cover with a polythene bag brushed with oil and leave in a warm place until almost doubled in size.

6 Uncover and place pastry strips on to the top of the buns, to form crosses.

7 Bake in an oven preheated to 200°C for about 15 minutes.

8 While the buns are baking, boil together the ingredients for the glaze. Brush over the buns as soon as they come out of the oven.

> If you do not have suitable strips of leftover short or sweet pastry, use marzipan and place on the buns 5 minutes before the end of baking.

Cooking dough products

During cooking the pockets of gas created by the yeast during proving expand as they heat up, and the yeast has a final burst of activity (sometimes called *oven spring*). This is why the last stage of knocking back is important in recipes using compressed yeast – if the dough has been allowed to stretch as far it could, it might burst at this stage.

Once the centre of the dough has reached about 60°C, the yeast is killed, the starch in the flour begins to gelatinise (how much will depend on the water content) and the gluten proteins coagulate (i.e. set). Both of these actions firm up the structure of the dough and the final stage then occurs: surface browning and crust formation.

Checking that the rolls are cooked.

Introducing the dough products

One way of classifying dough products is by the type of dough they are made from:

- *white dough* – made from white flour (contains about 75% of the wheat grain) of the strong variety – with high protein content, to produce large volume, open texture and light colour

- *wholemeal/wheatmeal dough* – made from flour which contains the whole of the wheat grain, with nothing added or taken away. Closer texture than white doughs, more fibre and greater variety of flavours and colours

- *bun dough* – more fat than white dough, sometimes eggs, spices, etc.

- *enriched dough* – as the name suggests, a richer recipe with eggs, milk, butter, extra sugar, dried fruit, etc. Babas (sweet buns usually soaked in rum to make a dessert), savarins (similar to babas, but without dried fruit and ring shaped) and brioches (sweet rolls sometimes offered as an alternative to bread rolls, or served as a pastry) are made from enriched dough.

Then there are the group names for the different types of product made from these doughs:

- *bread loaves* – there is a great variety of loaf shapes and names, e.g. sliced, split tin, plait, bloomer, cob, farmhouse, coburg, Vienna and Danish. The tops can be crusty, soft, shaped or cut in a particular way, and coated with cracked wheat, sesame seeds, poppy seeds or nuts. Some loaves are sweet, with dried fruit, fruit peel, etc. in them

- *bread rolls* – some have soft special names, e.g. bridge rolls, baps or burger buns. Some are soft, some crusty, and they can be made with white or wholemeal dough, or other types of flour such as Granary

- *buns and doughnuts* – these are usually the sweeter sort, because they are coated with a sugar glaze (called *bun wash*), icing, etc. after cooking, and/or have additions to the dough such as dried fruit, spices or milk. Doughnuts have jam in the centre.

The last three each use a particular type of dough:

- *pizza bases* – pizza dough is made with soft flour, and involves one, quite short, period of proving

- *pitta* – made from a plain dough, shaped into long ovals. Baking time is only a few minutes. After cooling, with some recipes the pittas are flattened (gently, so that they do not burst)

- *nan* – Indian in origin, traditionally cooked in a tandoor oven – pressed against the side or on a special pad. Some recipes have no yeast, using baking powder as the raising agent. If you do not have access to a tandoor oven, recipes are available which can be partly cooked in a frying pan, then finished under the grill.

Doughnuts, before and after deep frying.

Baking ovens: note that each oven is quite low in height. This ensures an even heat.

How they are cooked

Doughnuts are *deep fried*. Use a good-quality oil, which is reserved for cooking doughnuts (otherwise they will absorb flavours of fish, etc. from the oil). The doughnuts do not take long to cook, typically about 6 minutes. As they float in the oil, turn them over halfway through cooking.

Nan bread is cooked on the wall of a tandoor oven, a variation on baking. A similar effect can be produced by shallow frying the bottom of the nan and grilling the top.

Other dough products are *baked*.

More on baking

The recipe should give an exact oven temperature. As a rule it should be set at between 200°C and 245°C for ordinary doughs and 175°C to 195°C for sweetened doughs (this lower temperature prevents the surface browning before the inside has set).

If you are using a conventional oven, the heat may vary by as much as 20°C from shelf to shelf. With such equipment the best position for bread loaves is the centre, and for rolls, just above centre.

Allow room for the dough to expand in the oven – do not position directly under a shelf.

How long baking takes depends on the ingredients used and the size of the product. When a golden brown crust has formed, it usually means that the bread is cooked. Loaves and rolls should sound hollow when tapped – if they sound dense and feel heavy, it means that there is still liquid inside.

Cooling

After baking, remove yeast products from the baking containers as soon as possible. Put on racks to cool, with plenty of space around them so that air can circulate.

When bread leaves the oven, its surface is very dry and hot – over 200°C – while the interior is moist and only about 93°C.

As the bread cools, the moisture works its way out and the temperature evens out. Although the starch solidifies as the temperature goes down, it still lets air and gases through it. This is just as well because the gas left in pockets starts to get smaller and air has to get in to fill the holes – otherwise the bread would collapse.

Faults in bread making

Bread heavy and close in texture
- plain flour used rather than a strong white or wholemeal plain flour
- too much salt
- insufficient kneading or proving – remember to knead the dough until it is soft and smooth
- yeast killed by too much heat
- stale fresh yeast

Surface cracked
- bread allowed to dry out while rising – keep well covered with oiled polythene
- oven too hot, or loaf placed to one side against the heat – place loaf in centre of oven

Loaf collapses or has sour flavour
- allowed to over-rise – do not be over-ambitious
- oven was too cool when bread was cooked – a hot oven stops the yeast working, and therefore the bread from over-rising

Wholemeal bread heavy
- too little water – wholemeal flour requires more water to give the same textured dough as strong white flour

Uneven texture with large holes
- dough not thoroughly kneaded or left uncovered during rising

Bread stales quickly and is crumbly
- too much yeast used
- strong bread flour not used
- bread rose too quickly in too warm a place

With thanks to McDougalls (RHM Foods).

Storing

Store bread in a cool, well-ventilated room, and covered with a clean tea towel or kitchen paper. Do not refrigerate (bread gets stale more quickly if kept in the refrigerator). A humid atmosphere gives bread a leathery crust, and mould may develop.

As a general rule:

- white crust breads have the shortest shelf life

- brown breads keep better than their white equivalents. Seed breads and breads containing rye stay moist even after they have been part-sliced

- bread containing a little fat is more moist

- wholemeal loaves become more crumbly after a day

- enriched breads, teacakes and brioches are best eaten the day after baking

- the larger the loaf, the longer it stays fresh.

For help to answer questions
relating to:

Health and safety

🖋 **safe working practices**

The main hazards are from hot
equipment, difficult manual handling
tasks (e.g. large baking trays), use of
mixing, cutting and other dangerous
equipment, and deep frying (of
doughnuts).

Food hygiene

🖋 **importance of good hygiene**

Dough products must be stored and
handled as any other fresh food, to
protect them from sources of harmful
bacteria.

🖋 **importance of time and temperature**

Bacteria increase rapidly in numbers
at temperatures between 5°C and
63°C. Plain breads, rolls, etc. are not
high risk foods, and are best stored
in a cool, dry room (refrigerating
them makes them go stale more
quickly). Any that are decorated or
filled with cream (e.g. babas and
savarins) are high risk, and should
be kept chilled.

🖋 **main contamination threats**

Other food (e.g. raw meat or fish),
dirty equipment/work area, harmful
cleaning substances, foreign bodies
(e.g. pieces of grit), etc.

🖋 **products not for immediate use**

For the yeast to do its work, the
temperature during mixing and
proving is very important: not too
hot, nor too cold. For storage after
baking, see notes above on time and
temperature.

Product knowledge

🖋 **quality points for doughs**

At the end of kneading, the dough
should have a shiny surface and no
longer be sticky to the touch. After
the first proving, the dough should
not spring back when pressed. At the
end of the second proving, it should
be double in size.

🖋 **quality points for cooked products**

Describe how the item should look
(*appearance, consistency*), smell
(*aroma*), and taste (*texture, flavour*).

🖋 **cooking methods for dough products**

All are baked, with the exception of
doughnuts which are deep fried (nan
bread is also slightly different).

🖋 **identifying when doughs are cooked**

The appearance is a good guide.
Loaves and rolls should sound hollow
when tapped.

Healthy catering practices

🖋 **replacing high fat ingredients**

The recipes for dough products are
very sensitive to any changes.
However the amount of fat between
recipes does vary, giving you some
choice.

🖋 **fats/oils for healthy eating**

See page 110.

🖋 **increasing fibre content**

All dough products are quite a good
source of fibre, those made from
wholewheat and brown flours
especially so.

🖋 **reducing sugar**

As with fat, there is little scope for
changing recipes, because sugar
plays such an important role. But
some recipes use less sugar than
others, and you can certainly avoid
those with sugar coatings.

Self-check questions

1 State some of the things you do to
prevent accidents when lifting
equipment, trays of dough, etc.

2 Describe some of the safety
procedures for using mixing machines
(or similar equipment).

3 Give two reasons why dough must be
covered during proving. What sort of
covering can be used?

4 What are some of the reasons why
yeast might not work properly?

5 Describe the storage of a) fresh yeast,
b) dried yeast.

6 Besides yeast, what are the main
ingredients of dough? What other
ingredients are used in enriched
dough?

7 Why is dough left to prove? What are
the reasons for kneading it?

8 Describe how bread should be stored
after baking. When is it essential that
a dough product be served
immediately, or kept chilled until
required?

NVQ SVQ

Skills check
Prepare and cook basic
dough products
Unit 2ND7

leve **2**

Use this to check your progress again
the performance criteria.

Element 1

Prepare basic dough products for cooking

Get your preparation areas and
equipment ready for use ☐ PC

Select ingredients of the type,
quality and quantity required ☐ PC

▲ white/wheatmeal/wholemeal flour, fresh yeast,
dried yeast, fat/oil, eggs, sugar, milk/water

Identify and report problems with the
freshness or quality of ingredients ☐ PC

Prepare doughs ☐ PC

▲ Doughs: white, wholemeal/wheatmeal,
bun/enriched
Preparation methods: mixing, kneading, proving,
folding, glazing, shaping, rolling, portioning

Correctly store doughs not for
immediate use ☐ PC

Clean preparation areas and
equipment after use ☐ PC

Prioritise and carry out your work in an
organised, efficient and safe manner ☐ PC

Element 2

Cook basic dough products

Get your cooking areas and
equipment ready for use ☐ PC

Cook dough products ☐ PC2

▲ Dough products: white, wholemeal/wheatmeal,
bun/enriched, bread loaves, bread rolls,
buns/doughnuts, pizza bases, pitta/nan
Cooking methods: baking deep frying

Correctly store products
not for immediate use ☐ PC3

Clean cooking areas and
equipment after use ☐ PC4

Identify and report problems with the
quality of dough products ☐ PC5

Prioritise and carry out your work in an
organised, efficient and safe manner ☐ PC6

Preparing and presenting food for
cold presentation

Preparing and presenting sandwiches and canapés

There is enormous scope for being creative. But in making your choice you need to be aware of the cost of ingredients, and how much time you have available.

This is why you will usually have to work to tight guidelines. If display panels or menus advertise sandwiches and what is in them, then that is precisely what you must give customers. And when customers are paying a price for a tray of assorted sandwiches, or a selection of canapés, you must keep within the food cost budget.

Some of the many varieties of bread.

Types of bread

Good-quality, very fresh bread is the only acceptable choice for a sandwich. The most interesting fillings will not make up for bread that is too old, or has dried out through poor storage.

Some breads keep fresh for two days or so. Others only last for a few hours, and are often bought in frozen or partly-baked so they can be served at their best.

Bread for the base of canapés is toasted, so absolute freshness is not necessary. Nevertheless, no bread should be used if has passed its best-before date, or if it has gone mouldy.

Sliced and unsliced

White, brown, wholemeal or some of the speciality types such as:

- *soft grain* – white bread flours with added softened kibbled grains

- traditional *wheatgerm* – with extra wheatgerm added

- *malted wheatgrain* – brown flour with added malted grains

- *bran enriched* – brown or wholemeal flour with added bran

- *organic* – milled from a wheat grown and processed naturally without the use of chemicals.

Many bakers who supply caterers offer sliced bread in extra large loaf size (see box on page 209), and cut to the thickness preferred. Some will slice the bread along its length, so that two pieces (or planks as they are sometimes called) make three or four sandwiches instead of the one you get from loaves of sliced bread sold in supermarkets and high street bakers.

Unsliced bread gives you the scope to make chunky sandwiches, or to cut the bread lengthwise (see diagram on page 210).

French stick

This is traditionally a white bread, long, thin and very crusty. When made as the French do, it stays fresh for a few hours only.

Cut the stick in half or in three or four chunks – depending on the portion size. Then cut horizontally into each chunk, but not right through the bread, so the two sides are hinged together and can be opened to take the filling. Or make two parallel cuts running the length of the chunk, for a double filling.

Rolls

Rolls are made from a similar range of flours to bread. Some white and brown rolls are soft – the Scottish bap is very soft, floury and white. The top of soft rolls may have been sprinkled before baking with sesame seeds, cracked wheat, etc. White rolls may have a hard crust.

Filled bridge rolls (small, soft crust) are sometimes offered alongside canapés for a slightly more substantial dish.

Pitta bread

Pitta bread is thin and oval shaped. It has become more widely known through Greek restaurants (where it is served warm to accompany taramasalata, humus, etc.) and the take-away speciality *doner kebab* (filled with sliced hot lamb and salad).

Cut the pitta bread along one side, and through to the centre. This creates a cavity which can be filled. Pitta is not buttered – fillings usually include a salad of some sort to provide moistness. For a smaller portion, pittas can be cut in half. Or use the mini-pitta bread version.

Rye bread

This is made partly or entirely of rye flour. The light types (part-rye flour, part-wheat flour) are popular for sandwiches. The denser, very dark type (all-rye flour) with its thick, hard crust is good for open sandwiches.

Crisp bread

These are the various products you can buy in supermarkets and through catering suppliers. They are a cross between bread – some even look like a mini-slice of very dry bread, as if it had been deep fried without oil – and savoury biscuits. They make good bases for canapés.

Toasted bread

Toasted sandwiches are popular in situations where they can be made to order, and served warm. Club sandwiches are made with freshly toasted bread, filled with hot meat (e.g. thin steak) and/or cold meats (e.g. ham), as well as salad, cheeses, etc., in three or more layers. Both types of sandwich are usually made with white, brown or wholemeal bread.

Bread for canapé bases is toasted. The toasting gives the base more strength than a slice of plain bread would have.

The easiest method for making a quantity of canapés is to use bread sliced along its length (planks). After toasting both sides, stack the slices and press down. This stops the toast curling. After a few minutes, unstack to use (if left too long, the toast may go soggy).

Ingredients for sandwiches and canapés

The main groups are as follows, and further ideas are given in the rest of this section:

- *fats and spreads* – bread for sandwiches and toast for canapés are usually spread with butter or one of the various margarines or butter-type spreads available. Without these, the sandwich would be too dry and characterless for most people, and the filling would tend to spread into the bread

- *cooked and cured meats and poultry* – the meat has to be tender, e.g. roast beef, pork and lamb, chicken and turkey, grilled bacon, and the various speciality sausages (e.g. salami and garlic). Meat is cured by smoking (e.g. speciality hams, chicken and turkey), dry salting (e.g. York ham) or soaking (pickling) in brine (e.g. ham or silverside of beef). Most cured meats have to be cooked (e.g. hams boiled and/or baked). Some are eaten uncooked (e.g. Parma ham) – these tend to be expensive, and are more likely to be used for canapés than sandwiches

- *cooked and cured fish and shellfish* – salmon, tuna, smoked mackerel, prawns and crab are good sandwich fillings. Smoked salmon is considered by many to make the finest sandwiches and canapés. Anchovies, prawns, crab, lobster and caviar are used for canapés, also smoked eel and smoked cod's roe (which makes taramasalata)

- *fresh vegetables and fruit* – lettuce, cucumber, spring onions, watercress, mustard and cress, tomatoes and celery (chopped finely) are much used as sandwich fillings. Avocado makes a more luxurious sandwich – with prawns or bacon. Grapes go well with brie or cream cheese. Bananas (sliced with lemon juice) and apple (grated with lemon juice and perhaps sultanas) are more unusual sandwich fillings. Sliced cucumber and short lengths of celery make canapé bases, and various salad vegetables and fruit (including pineapple and cherries) are used for colour and contrast in canapés

- *eggs* – hard-boiled and sliced as a sandwich filling, or finely chopped and mixed with mayonnaise. For a canapé base, cut the hard-boiled egg in half, remove the yolk, blend with various ingredients and pipe back into the space left by the yolk

- *cheese* – cheddar is the great standby for sandwiches. Many people like a more adventurous choice from the many types of soft cheese through to the continental varieties (e.g. Brie, Roquefort, Emmental) and regional British cheeses such as Double Gloucester and Stilton. Squares of cheese are served as canapés, and cream cheeses make canapés spreads.

Preparing sandwiches

You must work to the very highest standards of hygiene. Sandwiches – like any other food which is served cold (see page 212) – provide ideal conditions for bacteria to multiply. Any time the sandwich spends above 5°C greatly increases the risk. This is why there are strict workplace rules on how long and where sandwiches can be kept (see industry example overleaf).

Whether you have a few or many sandwiches to make, you will find it helps to break the task down into stages, e.g. spreading all the bread, laying out slices which will take the same filling side by side, and doing one type of filling at a time (see page 5). Use a round-bladed or palette knife to get an even layer of spreading, and take the spreading right to the edges.

Salad fillings need to be well dried. Use a salad spinner or lay lettuce leaves, etc. between sheets of kitchen paper to absorb remaining water after you have shaken them dry as much as possible.

For sandwiches that will be cut into two, arrange the filling so that each half has an equal number of slices of egg, a piece of cheese, etc. Consider what the sandwich will look like when cut – a thick piece of prime beef at the centre, not the outer edge or some gristle, the creamy centre of Brie, not the rind.

When assorted sandwiches are going on a serving dish, arrange them so that the fillings can be seen by customers as they make their choice. One way is to cut small shapes which can be stood on their side.

Sandwiches not covered are a hygiene risk. They also dry out. When prepared in advance, they must be covered with an airtight wrapping and kept chilled. Don't squash the sandwich into its wrapper, or you will distort its shape and encourage sogginess. How long sandwiches can be kept chilled without the quality spoiling depends on the bread and the filling. Your workplace will have rules about this.

Quantity guidelines

A sandwich loaf (800 g) yields 22 slices and requires 100 g creamed butter.

Catering sandwich loaf (1.6 kg) yields 48 to 50 slices and requires 200 g creamed butter.

Unsliced bloomer loaf yields 16 slices on average, and requires 100 g creamed butter.

French stick (27 cm) yields 20 slices or 5 chunks and requires about 150 g creamed butter.

24 bread rolls require 200 g creamed butter.

With thanks to The Flour Advisory Bureau.

Preparation and quality standards

How to judge quality standards of finished product
- freshly made
- quality ingredients
- well filled/correctly filled
- presented well and looking appetising

How to ensure quality of ingredients
- use on the day of delivery and never beyond use-by date
- handle loaves with care – don't squash them
- keep the package airtight when storing loaves

Why guidelines on quantities of ingredients are important
- effective portion control protects our profits
- to ensure customer satisfaction with the amount
- over-portioning does not necessarily improve the taste for the customer
- to ensure value for money
- to provide consistency of product

How to ensure portions are correct
- use the electronic scales to check weights at random
- use correct amount of pre-portioned ingredients
- work as trained

How to fill sandwiches correctly
- ingredients cover base of the bread evenly – so that customers get a full taste every mouthful
- when closed all fillings are visible – for good presentation

Why time labelling
- products not sold within a specified time of filling must be wasted
- to ensure freshness and food safety
- to comply with food hygiene regulations

How do we know how many of each product to prepare
- depends on level of business, day of week, time of day
- orders from till staff or check the display
- experience of what sells the best
- sales reports detailing how many of each have been sold

With thanks to the Retail Catering Division of the Compass Group

---

Open sandwiches

With open sandwiches, the emphasis is on attractive display of the ingredients. You can be less concerned about the practicalities of how the sandwich is eaten – open sandwiches are eaten off the plate, using a knife and fork. This means, for example, that:

- slices of meat or smoked fish can be rolled

- thick dressings like mayonnaise can be piped to form part of the final decoration, perhaps with a stuffed olive placed in the centre, or a little caviar

- fine, delicate vegetables like asparagus can add impact to the presentation, as well as contributing to the flavour.

Open sandwiches should be made as required. They quickly dry out, and it is difficult to wrap or cover them without harming the appearance.

Assembly and quality points

Brie, Tomato and cucumber baguette

1 Spread baguette with Bodyline:
   - spread evenly over the length of the baguette both sides
   - use a palette knife
   - baguette should be cooled for 30 minutes after baking, and before use.

2 Place Brie in baguette:
   - Brie should be laid evenly along length of baguette
   - Brie should be stored at 1°C to –5°C.

   3 Place tomato and cucumber on top of Brie:
   - tomato and cucumber slices should be placed alternatively along length of baguette
   - tomato and cucumber washed before hand and stored at 1°C to –5°C.

4 Wrap with collar:
   - place collar at centre of baguette with the logo centred over filling
   - filling and logo facing customer.

5 Time label:
   - label the collar in space provided with the correct time of preparation
   - 3-hour shelf-life.

Ham salad sandwich

1 Spread Bodyline on each slice of bread:
   - cover bread evenly.

2 Place lettuce on base of sandwich:
   - lettuce to be properly washed and drained
   - check for freshness
   - covers bread slice.

3 Place ham on top of lettuce:
   - store in fridge at 1°C to –5°C and check date
   - place on centrally.

4 Place tomato slices at top of sandwich and cucumber at the base:
   - ensure crisp and fresh
   - each half must have tomato and cucumber.

5 Place top slice of bread on to complete sandwich:
   - Bodylined slice down.

6 Cut in half vertically:
   - on chopping board
   - ensure equal halves
   - all fillings should be visible.

7 See specification for wrapping and time labelling of sandwiches:
   - 24-hour shelf-life when refrigerated
   - 4-hour shelf-life when displayed.

With thanks to the Retail Catering Division of the Compass Group

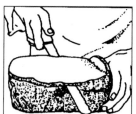

Left: *slicing a loaf of bread along its length to form 'planks'. Note how the heel of bread has been left – to cut right along the loaf would be dangerous.*
Below: *cutting triangle shapes of toasted bread for canapés.*

Preparing canapés

Canapés are usually eaten with the fingers, lifted one at a time from a large serving dish on which a selection has been arranged. They should be:

- firm enough to be lifted, yet easy to chew
- small enough to be popped into the mouth in one go – bigger ones requiring two mouthfuls may be acceptable.

Pastry, bread and biscuit are good bases for caviar, pâté, sliced meats, smoked fish, cream cheese, etc. Bread is generally toasted and cut into shapes: rounds, squares, rectangles or triangles. Some chefs deep fry the bread. There is no need to toast the bread if it has the support of its crust (as with French bread), or if it is quite dense in texture (as with pumpernickel or rye bread).

Some foods are firm enough to make a canapé on their own, or when combined with other ingredients. With large prawns, smoked oysters and squares of cheese, cocktail sticks should be available so they can be picked up. Quail eggs and stuffed hard-boiled eggs can easily be picked up, so can the various rolled canapés, e.g. asparagus rolled up in slices of smoked trout. Hot canapés require a cocktail stick, e.g. cocktail sausages, prunes stuffed with chutney and wrapped in bacon.

You may see cold canapés coated with aspic – to give a glossy appearance and improve their keeping quality by sealing in the moistness. Getting an even layer of aspic of the right thickness is quite a skill. You need to be especially careful about hygiene, because of the dangers of heating and chilling the aspic several times.

Canapés cannot be prepared more than a few hours in advance without spoiling in quality. The base is likely to go soggy. Others dry out. Many are difficult to cover without damaging the presentation.

Preparing and presenting cooked, cured and prepared foods

Elaborate cold buffets where each dish takes skilled chefs many hours to decorate are unusual nowadays. This is because of the cost, because of concerns about hygiene, and because customers' preferences are for simpler presentations.

Nevertheless, as the food is served cold, you have a lot of scope for creativity. And there are fewer expectations and traditions than there are with hot food, so you have greater freedom. For example, people expect hot roast beef to come with Yorkshire pudding, although you might add watercress or parsley to the dish for colour. With cold roast beef, you could decorate the dish with olives perhaps, or peach halves filled with chutney, or tomatoes filled with horseradish.

Creating visual appeal

Many chefs can arrange food attractively without being able to explain why it is that they are selecting particular colours and shapes, or why they are positioning items in one place rather than another.

But there are some rules which provide a starting point if you have not had much experience of doing this:

- *keep arrangements simple* – elaborate designs are rarely worth the long time they take. While food is being handled in a warm kitchen, conditions are ideal for the growth of harmful bacteria

- *plan your arrangement in advance* – a good idea is to sketch the effect you want on a piece of paper. Try a central feature, that the rest of the design leads into. It is poor hygiene practice to keep taking the food on and off the plate until you have a satisfactory design

- *trim, prepare or cut food carefully* – ragged cuts and uneven edges or mixtures of shapes look untidy. Try to keep everything roughly the same size

- *make the food easy to recognise* – using cuts and arrangements that improve the appearance of the food, but not disguise or hide it. Ingredients should not be chopped or minced so finely that they cannot be told apart (unless they are foods being used as a flavouring, such as garlic and onion)

- *consider how the food is to be eaten* – sitting at a table (when it is easy to use both hands), moving about with a plate in one hand, a fork or spoon and perhaps a drink (a fork buffet), or with the fingers only (a finger buffet)

- *consider how the food is to be served* – on the customer's plate, on a dish presented at the table, on a large dish which many people help themselves to. In the last example – which happens in buffet and counter service – dishes need to look good even when some portions have been take from them

- *make the most of the service dish* – so that the shape and design of dish and food work to each other's advantage. Doilies and napkins folded in special ways (e.g. boats, petals or fans) can add interest

- *select the right-sized dish* – for the portion sizes, for the customer to hold comfortably, for the buffet table or display counter. A large buffet filled with small dishes looks messy. If a single-portion dish is too large, the food will look lost or too much will have to be used

- *don't overload the serving dish* – it should look full but not crowded. Over-filled dishes are difficult to serve – some food may get spilt as the first portions are taken. The rim should be left clear so that the dish can be handled without any danger of the food being touched, and the food is not likely to fall off

- *use different colours* – but not more than three as a rule, because too many colours can create a messy effect. Sometimes two or three shades of the same colour can be very effective

- *give variation to the height* – food lying flat on the plate tends to look dull. Piling up or overlapping some of the ingredients, or using one as a container for others (e.g. a lettuce leaf holding finely sliced tomato) are some ways to provide contrast

- *provide a focal point* – something to catch the eye. This could be the main ingredient, placed in a prominent position, or a related ingredient introduced because of its attractiveness (e.g. an edible flower such as a nasturtium). On a large food display, one dish can be the focal point, or an arrangement of flowers, an ice carving, etc.

Displaying food and hygiene

Hygiene is a big concern when cold food is displayed for service, e.g. on buffet tables or self-service counters. The greatest risks are when:

- the food is at room temperature – which means any bacteria present rapidly multiply

- customers serve themselves – you cannot control what customers do, e.g. picking up food with their fingers and returning it to the dish

- the food is uncovered – any flies in the area will be attracted to it, or customers might sneeze over it.

These risks can be reduced by:

- limiting the time any item of food is on display to not more than four hours

- throwing out food which has been displayed for the maximum time limit

- not displaying food a second time, even if the first occasion was less than four hours before

- not displaying more food than necessary by using small dishes and replacing them regularly.

If members of staff are not helping to serve the food, then the display should be checked regularly to keep it tidy, replace serving spoons (e.g. if these drop in the food), refill dishes, etc.

The ideal situation is when the food is kept in an enclosed refrigerated display cabinet. This has glass sliding doors at the back so that staff can replace dishes. For a self-service situation, glass panels at the front allow customers to remove the dishes they want.

Some models have an open back, but no access for customers – staff serve dishes as requested by customers. Another variation has open access from both sides – a glass 'sneeze' screen on the customer side gives some protection. There are also refrigerated buffet tables and even refrigerated dessert and cheese trolleys.

Attractive buffet displays encourage food sales. They also provide a convenient way of serving a large number of people quickly.

CHECK ☑ **list**

Good hygiene in cold preparation

✔ use a suitable implement, such as tongs, to avoid touching the food – in many kitchens, it is the rule that disposable gloves are worn

✔ use knives and chopping boards that are specifically reserved (e.g. colour coded) for preparing cooked foods

✔ store and handle cooked food well away from raw food

✔ clean or sanitise all cans of meat, fish, etc., before opening

✔ wash equipment and work surfaces down regularly, and use an approved sanitising cloth or solution

✔ use one surface for one purpose only

✔ ensure slicing machines and other equipment are thoroughly cleaned and sanitised before use

✔ prepare food as close to service time as practicable

✔ keep preparation time (when the food is exposed to room temperature) down to the minimum

✔ keep the food chilled – 5°C or lower – for as much of the time as possible

Very high standards of personal hygiene are essential for cold presentation.

Range of cold dishes, their preparation and garnishing

The foods you prepare and present will include the following:

- *salads* – those already made (in your workplace or bought in). Some may require *dressing* – mixing with mayonnaise, vinaigrette or a similar cold sauce. You may have to *portion* the salad, placing a measured amount in each serving dish for one person, two people, or whatever. You will usually have to *garnish* or decorate the dish – adding some lettuce leaves, a sprig of parsley, slices of cucumber and tomato, segments of orange, slices of lemon, chopped chives – or other appropriate *vegetables, fruit* or *herbs*. Do not overdo salad garnishes

- *pies* – pork pies and Melton Mowbray pies are widely known. These are made to serve cold, with special pastry and jelly or aspic to set the contents. Other cold pie fillings include chicken (on its own or with ham), veal and ham (sometimes with egg), and game (of one type, e.g. grouse, or a mixture). Smaller pies are left whole, but in a display of pies you might cut one open so that customers can see the contents. The larger ones are usually portioned – cut into wedges (the round ones), or sliced (the oblong-shaped ones)

- *cooked meats and poultry* – mostly the joints that are roasted or boiled, or good quality, with none or very little visible fat and gristle (which would spoil the appearance). Chicken breasts are served whole, or sliced or cut into small pieces which are then mixed with vegetables and/or fruit to make a salad (e.g. chopped celery, sliced apple, halved grapes and a mayonnaise dressing). Other meats are usually *sliced* or carved thinly for basic salads

- *fish* – salmon and salmon trout are deep poached (see Section 9) and served cold, either as fillets or presented whole, when they can make a very attractive centre piece of a cold display. Smoked salmon, sliced very thinly, is the all-time favourite as a special starter, or a luxury choice on a buffet. Speciality dishes include gravadlax (salmon pickled with dill, sugar, salt, peppercorns and sometimes brandy) and rollmops (herrings, boned, rolled and pickled in spiced vinegar)

- *terrines* and *pâtés* – many types and combinations including vegetarian, fish (e.g. tuna, salmon and trout), meat (e.g. chicken, pork and turkey), game (e.g. rabbit, venison and pheasant) and liver (chicken, geese, duck, pork, calves, lamb etc.). There is no significant difference between pâtés and terrines. Both can have a range of textures, from very smooth to coarse. Both are cooked in deep, oval-shaped dishes called terrines. Sometimes pâtés are served from the terrine (e.g. at the cold food counter in a pub). Terrines traditionally are, except when slices are presented and garnished on the customer's plate. When slicing pâtés and terrines, especially the smooth-textured ones, you may find that warming the knife blade in very hot water gives a cleaner cut

- *cured meats* – these include hams (salted and/or smoked, or cured, e.g. in molasses), pickled pork or beef (e.g. pastrami), smoked chicken and turkey, and smoked mutton. All are sliced thinly. Parma ham (lightly salted and air-cured for many months, but unlike most other hams not cooked after curing) is cut into transparently thin slices

- *shellfish* – freshly cooked shellfish served cold includes lobster, crab, crawfish, crayfish, Dublin Bay prawns (scampi), shrimps, prawns, mussels, cockles (cockles can also be eaten raw), winkles and whelks (see Section 22).

Arrangements of food do not have to be elaborate to be effective.

Top: *charcuterie (Parma ham, speck Napoli and Coppa) with mustard fruit and dressed salad*
Centre: *pork and goose liver terrine with hot pepper jelly*
Lower: *seafood salad (dill herring, Green Lip mussel, king prawn, smoked salmon, and gravadlax).*

With thanks to Forte Crest.

For help to answer questions relating to:

Health and safety

? safe working practices

The main hazards are: using knives, slicing and chopping equipment, and difficult lifting or handling tasks.

Food hygiene

? importance of good hygiene

Any bacteria present on the food will multiply rapidly once the temperature is above 5°C. Therefore it is essential to a) prevent bacteria getting on to the food, and b) keep the food well chilled.

? importance of time and temperature

Since it is not always possible to keep the food below 5°C (e.g. when preparing or garnishing it, and during display on a buffet table or counter which is not refrigerated), the time it is most at risk must be carefully controlled.

? main contamination threats

Other food (e.g. fresh vegetables/fruit), food handlers, dirty equipment/work area, harmful cleaning substances, foreign bodies (e.g. pieces of broken china), customers handling it unhygienically, flies and other insects

? products not for immediate use

Below 5°C.

Product knowledge

? quality points

Good *appearance* or presentation of sandwiches, canapés and cold foods is important, but this should not put at risk the *texture* or *flavour* of the food, nor harm its *aroma*.

Healthy catering practices

? substitutes for high-fat ingredients

Remind yourself of some of the tips on page 6 for replacing butter, etc. Some dressings are high in fat or oil because that is how they are expected to be (e.g. vinaigrette and mayonnaise). In their place you might consider simpler dressings, e.g. lemon juice, or a blend of low-fat soft cheese and fresh herbs.

? fats/oils for healthy eating

See page 110.

increasing fibre content of dishes

Sandwiches made with brown or wholemeal bread will be a good source of fibre. So will salads which include brown rice, wholemeal pasta, unpeeled new potatoes, cabbage and carrots.

? reducing salt

See page 110.

Self-check questions

1 Give some safe practices you should follow when a) using a slicing machine to cut meat or bread, b) lifting a large tray of bread (or other food).

2 Why is it so important to follow good hygiene practices when preparing cold food?

3 Identify the knives and chopping boards you should use for cold foods.

4 Why would it be dangerous if you sliced cold meat with a knife or machine which had previously been used to cut raw meat? What can you do to avoid such risks?

5 What is the maximum time cold food can be left on display for service, if it is not kept refrigerated?

6 If food is left over from a cold buffet, etc. where it has not been kept chilled, what should be done with it?

7 What are the dangers of spending a long time garnishing or decorating food for cold service?

8 How should sandwiches be kept if they have been prepared in advance?

Use this to check your progress against the performance criteria.

Element 1

Prepare & present sandwiches and canapés

Get your preparation areas and equipment ready for use	☐ PC
Select ingredients of the type, quality and quantity required	☐ PC2

▲ Bread: sliced/unsliced, French stick, rolls, pitta, rye bread, crisp bread, toasted bread
Other: cooked/cured meat/poultry, fish/shellfish, fresh fruit/vegetables, cheese, eggs, fats

Identify and report problems with the freshness or quantity of ingredients	☐ PC3
Prepare bread and other ingredients	☐ PC4
Prepare and finish canapés and sandwiches	☐ PC5
Correctly store canapés and sandwiches not for immediate use	☐ PC6
Clean preparation areas and equipment after use	☐ PC7
Prioritise and carry out your work in an organised, efficient and safe manner	☐ PC8

Element 2

Prepare and present cooked, cured and prepared foods

Get your preparation areas and equipment ready for use	☐ PC1
Select products and ingredients of the type, quality and quantity required	☐ PC2

▲ Products: salads, pies, cooked/cured meats/poultry, cooked fish/shellfish, terrines, pâtés
Garnish ingredients: fruit, vegetables, herbs

Identify and report problems with the freshness or quantity of ingredients	☐ PC3
Prepare garnish ingredients	☐ PC4

▲ Slicing, dressing, garnishing, portioning

Prepare and garnish food products (methods as for garnishes)	☐ PC5
Correctly store prepared food not for immediate use	☐ PC6
Display food under hygienic conditions	☐ PC7
Correctly store or dispose of returned, unused food	☐ PC8
Clean preparation areas and equipment after use	☐ PC9
Prioritise and carry out your work in an organised, efficient and safe manner	☐ PC10

Preparing and cooking basic
shellfish dishes

Preparing shellfish dishes

Shellfish has to be absolutely fresh. There are two reasons:

- *the eating quality* – shellfish spoils very quickly, losing flavour and texture. Although you can use less-than-perfect vegetables, for example, to make a soup, there is nothing that can be done with shellfish that is not known to be fresh

- *the dangers of food poisoning* – shellfish is a high risk food, attractive to bacteria. Although there are strict government controls to prevent shellfish from polluted areas of the sea reaching the market, contamination can happen very easily at any subsequent stage. As some types are eaten raw (e.g. oysters) and others are usually bought in pre-cooked (shrimps and prawns), suppliers and caterers have to be especially careful.

Many of the caterers that specialise in shellfish buy daily from one of the large wholesale fish markets (e.g. Billingsgate in London). Or they use reliable suppliers with the purchasing strength and the chilled distribution network necessary to get top-quality shellfish delivered when required.

This is why you do not see fresh shellfish like lobster, crab and oysters for sale in many places. It is also one reason why much shellfish is expensive. Other reasons are that demand exceeds supply, and maintaining oyster beds, lobster and crab pots, etc. is a costly business.

Although the focus of this section (like the NVQ/SVQ unit) is the preparation and cooking of *fresh* shellfish, much of the information will be helpful if you are cooking or presenting shellfish which is raw or cooked and supplied frozen or vacuum packed. The frozen and vacuum packed products, with quite a long storage life, offer greater flexibility when supplies of live shellfish are difficult to come by.

Storage, quality points and types of shellfish

Fresh shellfish should be kept moist and cool so that it stays alive until the moment of cooking – any which die during storage must be thrown away.

Some speciality seafood restaurants let customers choose which shellfish they want from tanks in which the creatures are swimming or crawling around. The more usual practice is to keep the shellfish in the special packaging in which it was delivered, in a cold room or its own refrigerator, at a temperature between 2°C and 8°C.

Mussels and oysters should be kept packed in crushed ice. The round side of the shell should face downwards to help collect and retain the natural juices.

Scampi and the largest prawns are sometimes purchased alive or frozen raw in their shells. Most caterers obtain these and shrimps ready-prepared (since only the tail is eaten), chilled, frozen or canned. Shrimps and prawns are ready-cooked, so they can be served cold (e.g. in a seafood salad or prawn cocktail), or reheated (e.g. in a paella or seafood pie). A lot of the scampi served by caterers is purchased ready-breadcrumbed for deep frying.

Quality points

All live shellfish should have:

- a fresh, salty sea smell
- a clear, fresh colour
- a heavy and full sound when tapped lightly.

Crabs and prawns should:

- feel heavy in proportion to their size
- show obvious signs of movement (e.g. flexing their claws/legs)
- have no claws missing.

The shells of mussels and oysters should be tightly closed or shut rapidly when tapped. If the shells are open or close slowly then it is likely that the creature is dead or dying and the flesh is deteriorating, so they must not be used.

Crab

The brown crab is the easiest to find fresh in British shops (in the months of April to December). The velvet crab and spider crab, also found around the coasts of Britain, are mostly sent to Europe where they are very much prized.

Once cooked, the crab flesh (called meat) from the legs and claws is flaky and white. That from the body is brown, creamy in texture, and stronger in flavour.

Male (cock) crabs have bigger claws than the females (hen crabs), and so give more white meat. Hen crabs make up for this with more brown meat for their size, of superior quality to the male. And during the summer months, the hen's shell is lined with delicious pink coral.

Shrimps and prawns

There are over 100 species of shrimps and prawns. Brown shrimps are the smallest of the group. These turn browner when cooked – which is how all shrimps are sold. Pink shrimps become that colour after cooking.

Prawns are larger. Cold water prawns come mostly from Greenland, Iceland and Norway, and the seas north of Scotland. They are a delicate pink and white colour when cooked.

From the Middle and Far East come small warm water prawns; from the Far East the larger 'tiger' prawns. Mediterranean prawns (from the sea of that name) are also large.

Scampi

Scampi look like small lobsters, although the claws are not large enough to break open for their meat. They keep their attractive peach and coral colours after cooking.

Scampi are also called *Dublin Bay prawns* (available fresh in the months of April to November), *Norway lobsters* or *langoustines*.

Mussels

Mussels cling to the seabed or hang on to rocks, ropes or the metal structure of piers, etc. Their shells range in colour from blue-black to golden tortoiseshell. They take about two years to reach maturity, and have an excellent, slightly sweet flavour. Farmed mussels are available throughout the year.

Some freshly-cooked shellfish.

Above: *crab.*
Right top: *scampi (or Dublin Bay prawns).*

Right lower: *prawns*
Below: *King prawns.*

Oysters

Over-fishing has affected some of the coastal waters where top-quality oysters once flourished. Farmed oysters (available throughout the year) have partly filled the gap. And for cooked dishes requiring oysters, there are reliable suppliers of canned or frozen ones.

Native oysters (from the shores of Britain) are traditionally only eaten when there is an R in the month: September through to April. Pacific oysters are available fresh throughout the year. Canned and frozen oysters can be used at any time for cooked dishes.

Preparation methods

The methods you will come across are:

- *cleaning* – most fresh shellfish have to be washed thoroughly before cooking. This is because any slime or dirt on their shells would go into the cooking liquid, and spoil the delicate flavour

- *scraping* – to remove barnacles from the outer shells of mussels

- *debearding* and *trimming* – to remove, from the hinged side of mussel shells, the tufts of hair or beard (it's this that the mussel uses to cling to the rocks or seabed)

- *coating* – for deep fried scampi, the pieces are coated in flour, eggwash and breadcrumbs. The method is the same as that used for meat (page 95) and fish (page 114)

- *shelling* – oyster shells are opened to cook and to serve raw (when they are presented on the deeper half of the shell). Fresh prawns and scampi are sometimes shelled before shallow or deep frying (with scampi it is more usual to buy the prepared product, already shelled).

Crab and mussels are cooked in their shell – although there are some complex crab dishes which require the raw crab to be cut into pieces before stewing or frying.

Preparing crab

If live crabs are put straight into boiling water, they tend to throw or shed their legs (with the shock). The best practice (approved by welfare organisations and the RSPCA) is to leave the crabs in cold, unsalted water for a few hours before cooking. This sedates them.

Preparing mussels

Thoroughly scrub mussels under cold running water to remove slime and mud on the outer shells. The juices released by mussels as they open during cooking adds to the flavour of the cooking liquid. Traces of dirt left on the shell through inadequate preparation would spoil this.

Scrape off any barnacles, and pull away or trim off the tuft of hair (beard) which sprouts between each shell.

Soaking the mussels in cold, salty water has no useful purpose (it is sometimes said that this encourages the mussel to expel sand from inside the shell).

Preparing fresh prawns and scampi

Wash thoroughly before boiling in the shell.

To remove scampi from the shell before cooking:

- twist the middle tail flap from side to side, then pull carefully away so that the dirt tract is drawn out from the tail in one piece

- twist off the head and pull off the claws (these can be used for sauces and soups)

- peel the shell off from the tail, working from the underside – some chefs give the tail a blow with the hand first, to break the connecting bones on the underside.

For prawns:

- twist off the head

- working from the underside, pull the shell apart and away from the tail – sometimes the last piece of the tail shell is left attached (since this looks quite attractive)

- pull away the dirt tract lying along the tail.

Preparing oysters

Oysters should not be washed and prepared until the very last moment. Much of the pleasure in eating them is from their sea-fresh flavour and juices.

The oyster closes its shell as protection. To overcome this you need quite a lot of force and an oyster knife, with its short, very strong blade. Hold the oyster firmly in one hand with a cloth while you are prising the shell open. With the other hand:

- force the point of the knife blade between the two shells at the hinged end (the more pointed side)

- insert about 1 cm of the blade into the oyster

- twist the knife so that you prise the shells apart.

As you do this, keep the shell horizontal, with the deeper half at the bottom, so that the juices do not spill out. Then lift off the top (flatter) shell, pull away (you may have to cut the muscle to free it) and discard.

Still taking care not to allow the juices to spill, slip the knife blade under the oyster to free it from the shell.

When eaten raw, the oyster is left sitting in this shell, presented on a bed of crushed ice.

For cooked dishes, the oyster is taken out of the shell. Sometimes the juice from the shell is added to the cooking liquid.

Other ingredients

These are some of the other ingredients included in shellfish dishes, and the ways in which they are used:

- *dairy products* – cream and/or butter is sometimes used to enrich shellfish sauces. Just before serving scampi meunière, the shallow-fried scampi is coated with butter which has been cooked until nut-brown. After cooking mussels, the shell can be filled with parsley butter, the mussel placed on top, covered with some more of the butter, then baked briefly. Oysters can be cooked in a similar way, laid on a bed of spinach and covered with cheese sauce and grilled

- *eggs* – eggwash helps the breadcrumbs stick to deep-fried scampi. Egg yolks are used for the Japanese tempura batter (and sometimes egg whites). Sieved egg white and sieved egg yolk are used to decorate cold crab presented in its shell

- *fruit* – lemon juice is used in the marinade for mussels which are to be deep fried, and in some sauces for prawn, scampi and mussel dishes

- *vegetables* – chopped shallots or onions, sliced mushrooms and celery (along with wine and herbs) can be added to the cooking liquid for mussels. The accompanying sauce for different shellfish dishes may include chopped tomato flesh, chopped parsley, garlic, mushrooms, green and red peppers, fresh chillies, etc.

- *breadcrumbs* – one of the most popular ways of serving scampi is coated in flour, eggwash and breadcrumbs, and deep fried.

Types of shellfish

Crustaceans, e.g. crab and lobster, have tough outer shells which act like armour, and flexible joints which allow quick movement.

Molluscs fall into three sub-groups:

- with an external hinged double shell, e.g. scallops and mussels

- with a single spiral shell, e.g. winkles and whelks

- with soft bodies and an internal shell, e.g. squid and octopus.

Cooking shellfish

Shellfish takes a short time to cook – from one or two minutes for oysters to about 40 minutes for a large crab in its shell. Too much cooking and too long a delay between cooking and service of hot dishes cause the shellfish to become tough and rubbery.

Cooking and finishing shellfish dishes

There are four main methods for cooking basic shellfish dishes:

- *boiling* and *poaching* – these involve the use of water and/or other liquids such as wine, and sometimes chopped vegetables, herbs and lemon juice to give the cooking liquid more flavour. These are *wet cooking methods*
- *shallow frying* and *deep frying* – which use high temperatures and oil or fat to conduct the heat to the food. These are *dry cooking methods*.

To finish shellfish dishes, the methods include:

- *garnishing* – decorating so as to add to the appearance, e.g. with slices, segments or halves of lemon, or a sprinkling of chopped parsley
- *saucing* – blending in with, or pouring over, the accompanying sauce
- *dressing* – arranging the shellfish in the service dish, so that it looks attractive. Sometimes in a dish of prawns, a few will be cooked in their shells and used to decorate the finished dish.

Crab

Crab is boiled in its shell in salted water. Some chefs put the crab (sedated, see page 217) in cold, heavily salted water and bring to the boil for about 6 minutes for smaller crabs, 10 minutes for the larger ones.

For a cold dish (as a starter or main course, depending on the size of the crab), it can be presented in the (washed) shell, as dressed crab. Crack the claws open, remove the white meat, and shred or chop, taking care to remove any small pieces of shell. Open the body of the crab, remove inedible pieces (e.g. the gills and the sac from behind the eyes), and scrape the brown meat out. Mix this with breadcrumbs and mayonnaise to form a paste.

Place the white meat in the middle of the shell, with the brown on either side. Decorate the top with rows of sieved egg yolk, sieved egg white and chopped parsley (see photograph on page 221). You can also use anchovies, capers and slices of stuffed olives.

Crab meat is also used cold or hot to stuff mushrooms, avocado, etc., in shellfish and fish stews, and for complex dishes such as crab soufflé.

Scampi, prawns and shrimps

To boil scampi and prawns in their shells, a court-bouillon is often used: water which has been boiled for about 20 minutes with sliced onion, carrot, celery and leek, parsley stalks, bay leaf, thyme and wine vinegar. The shellfish is added, the liquid brought back to the boil and simmered gently for about 6 minutes.

There are many recipes which involve shallow frying scampi and prawns. If various chopped vegetables are part of the dish, the shellfish is added towards the end of cooking time, since between 3 and 6 minutes is long enough to cook it.

In some recipes the shellfish is fried first, removed and kept warm while the pan is used to make the accompanying sauce.

When deep frying shellfish, check what temperature the oil should be and the cooking time (around 180°C for about 2 minutes is typical). The oil should not previously have been used for cooking anything other than fish (see pages 115 and 226 for other advice).

Mussels

Mussels produce a lot of moisture as they cook, so you only need a small amount of liquid to cook them. They are usually boiled in a heavy pan over a high heat for just as long as it takes for their shells to open – around 4 minutes. Overcooked mussels tend to be rubbery.

In some recipes the mussels are served in the cooking liquid (flavoured with wine, vegetables, herbs, etc.). Or the mussels are removed once they have cooked, taken out of the shells and kept hot. Meanwhile the cooking liquid is reduced, and cream, etc. added. Finally, the mussels and sauce are combined and served.

For mussels coated in batter and deep fried, the mussels are boiled until the shells open, taken out of the shells, then marinaded (usually) before deep frying. For a more attractive presentation, some chefs pull off or trim the brown edge around the mussels, having removed them from the shells.

Oysters

Oysters (out of their shells) can be poached in their own juices. Use a small pan for the number of oysters you are cooking, so that the juice surrounds each oyster. Cover with a lid, bring to the boil and simmer for one or two minutes. Or you can remove the pan from the heat at once, and leave the oysters in the hot liquid for a few minutes.

The poached oysters can be returned to the shell, coated with mornay sauce, sprinkled with cheese and placed under a hot grill until the surface is brown.

Moules marinière

by Sea Fish Industry Authority

SERVES 4

2 litre	fresh mussels	4 pt
25 g	butter or margarine	1 oz
1	onion, chopped finely	1
1	clove garlic, crushed and peeled	1
300 ml	dry white wine, or fish stock	½ pt
30 ml	lemon juice	2 tbsp
3	bay leaves	3
45 ml	fresh parsley, chopped	3 tbsp
	seasoning to taste	

> Wash and scrub the mussels.

1 Melt the butter or margarine in a large saucepan and lightly fry the onions and garlic, until onions are soft and transparent.

2 Add the liquids, bay leaves and seasonings, and bring to the boil. Add the mussels all at once, cover and cook over a high heat, shaking the pan occasionally to ensure even cooking.

3 When all the mussels have opened (and discard any that have not) transfer to a heated serving dish, reserving the liquid.

4 Return the liquid to the heat and boil rapidly until reduced by half, stir in the parsley and season to taste.

5 Pour the sauce over the mussels, before serving.

From the operations manual of Toby Restaurants, this photographs shows the final presentation standard for breaded scampi. The scampi is fried from frozen, for 4 to 5 minutes at 175°C to 185°C, drained of excess oil (see photograph on right), and served immediately.

Moules à la bordelaise

by Sea Fish Industry Authority

SERVES 4

2 litre	fresh mussels washed and scrubbed	4 pt
125 ml	dry white wine	4 fl oz
25 g	butter	1 oz
1	medium onion, finely chopped	1
1	clove garlic, crushed and peeled	1
450 g	fresh tomatoes, peeled, deseeded and chopped	1 lb
45 ml	fresh parsley, chopped	3 tbsp
½	lemon, grated rind of	½
	seasoning to taste	
75 g	fresh brown breadcrumbs	3 oz
	melted butter	

1 Place the mussels and wine in a large pan, cover and boil vigorously until they have opened.

> This will only take a few minutes.

2 Strain the mussels and remove empty half shells. Reserve the cooking liquid.

3 Melt the butter and fry the garlic and onion for 2 minutes. Add the tomato, parsley, lemon and seasoning. Stir in the cooking liquid. Simmer until the tomato is cooked.

4 Arrange the mussels in a suitable heatproof dish (a gratiné dish, for example). Pour over the sauce (which should be quite thin), and sprinkle with breadcrumbs.

5 Dribble a little melted butter over the top and pop under a moderate grill until golden brown. Serve immediately.

Honey sesame prawns

by Dufrais

SERVES 4

15 ml	sesame oil	1 tbsp
6	spring onions, trimmed and finely chopped	6
5 ml	root ginger, grated	1 tsp
125 ml	water	4 fl oz
60 ml	light soy sauce	4 tbsp
15 ml	lemon juice	1 tbsp
60 ml	clear honey	4 tbsp
5 ml	sweet chilli sauce	1 tsp
45 ml	cornflour	3 tbsp
15 ml	water	1 tbsp
680 g	whole prawns	1½ lb
25 g	toasted sesame seeds	1 oz

1 Heat the sesame oil in a large pan and lightly fry the onions and ginger.

2 Add 125 ml water, soy sauce, lemon juice, honey and chilli sauce. Bring to the boil.

3 Mix together 10 ml cornflour and 15 ml water, add to the sauce, whisking continuously. Reduce heat.

4 Toss prawns in the remaining cornflour and deep fry at 177°C for a few minutes until golden. Drain on kitchen paper.

> Try not to get too much cornflour in the cooking oil: it will shorten the oil's cooking life.

5 Quickly mix the prawns with the hot sauce, add the sesame seeds and serve at once.

Deep fried scampi. The kitchen paper helps drain the excess cooking oil.

This recipe uses walnut oil, which gives its distinctive flavour to the dish. In the recipe for Honey prawns, sesame oil is used for a similar reason.

Nutty paella

by Dufrais

SERVES 2 to 3

30 ml	walnut oil	2 tbsp
1	medium onion, finely chopped	1
100 g	cleaned calamari, uncooked, sliced in rings	4 oz
5 ml	turmeric	1 tsp
175 g	risotto rice	6 oz
600 ml	fish stock	1 pt
100 g	shelled prawns	4 oz
100 g	frozen petits pois	4 oz
1 × 105 g	can smoked oysters, drained	1 × 3.7 oz
30 ml	garlic wine vinegar	2 tbp
75 g	cashew nuts, toasted	3 oz

1 Heat the oil in a large frying pan. Add onion, calamari, turmeric and rice, and fry for 1 to 2 minutes.

2 Add fish stock, cover and cook, stirring occasionally, for 15 minutes.

3 Add prawns, peas, smoked oysters and vinegar. Cook for a further 4 to 5 minutes.

4 Mix in cashew nuts and serve.

Stir fried crab

by Sea Fish Industry Authority

SERVES 4

450 g	white crabmeat (cooked)	1 lb
30 ml	sunflower oil	2 tbsp
	freshly ground black pepper to taste	
4	sticks celery, finely sliced	4
1	large red pepper, deseeded and sliced	1
50 g	mushrooms, sliced	2 oz
10–15 ml	soy sauce	2–3 tsp

1 Heat the oil in a large wok or large, deep frying pan.

2 Add all the vegetables, and stir fry for 2 to 3 minutes.

3 Add the crabmeat, soy sauce and black pepper, and cook for another 2 to 3 minutes until heated through.

Removing the flesh from a cooked crab

1 Holding the crab upside down, remove the claws one at a time. Twist sharply and pull, so that the claws become detached as close to the crab's body as possible.

2 Twist the smaller part of each claw back on itself, so it breaks off from the larger section (with the pincer).

Above: *removing the claws.*

3 Crack open the claw pieces by hitting sharply with the back of a heavy knife.

4 Remove the meat from each claw piece. The handle of a teaspoon comes in useful at this stage, especially for getting the meat out of the pincers. Alternatively, use the point of a skewer.

Above: *cracking open the claw pieces.*

5 Take care to free the meat of every bit of splintered shell. Place this, the *white meat*, aside in a clean dish.

Below: *pulling open the undershell.*

6 Holding the crab steady, grip the undershell firmly and pull open. If the mouth has not come away, press it down with your thumbs until it breaks cleanly with a click. (In the photograph the mouth has come away with the undershell: the chef demonstrator's thumb marks the position.)

7 Pull off and discard the gills (*dead man's fingers*). Scrape into a second bowl any *brown meat* clinging to this part of the crab. Cut the purse or *honeycomb* with a heavy knife and carefully pick out the white meat inside.

8 Remove the hard piece of sac behind the eyes and discard.

Above: *pulling off the gills.*

9 With a spoon (held in the usual way this time), scrape out all the soft yellowish-brown meat and any coral meat from inside the crab shell. Put this with other brown meat.

Below: *putting the finishing touches to the cold crab.*

10 Enlarge the opening of the shell: tap the false line surrounding it sharply with a mallet, then press down with your thumbs until the edges of the shell give way.

11 Wash the shell well and dry it out.

NVQ
SVQ

Skills check
Prepare and cook basic
shellfish dishes
Unit 2ND14

lev
2

For help to answer questions
relating to:

Health and safety

safe working practices

The hazards include sharp edges of
shellfish (on which you might cut
yourself), being caught in the claws
of live crab, injury from knives (e.g.
when opening an oyster), over-heated
oil in deep or shallow frying (see
page 14), splashes from boiling water
(e.g. as you drop in a large crab), and
handling large or awkward pots,
boxes of shellfish, etc.

Food hygiene

importance of good hygiene

Shellfish is a high-risk food, readily
contaminated with harmful bacteria.
Raw shellfish may carry slime, mud
and harmful bacteria.

importance of time and temperature

Bacteria increase rapidly in numbers
at the right temperature. You should
reject fresh shellfish which are dead
because you do not know how long
they have been dead. The greatest
care is needed while cooking
shellfish.

main contamination threats

Other food (e.g. fresh fish,
vegetables/fruit), food handlers, dirty
equipment/work area, harmful
cleaning substances, foreign bodies
(e.g. sand or grit).

products not for immediate use

So that it is the best eating quality,
shellfish should be alive until the
moment they are cooked, and there
should be no delay between cooking
and serving. Where this is not
possible, cold shellfish must be kept
below 5°C and hot shellfish dishes
above 63°C (but the quality will
quickly spoil).

Product knowledge

quality points for fresh shellfish

They should be alive and smell fresh.
See text (page 216) for specific points
for the different types.

quality points for cooked dishes

Remind yourself how the dish should
look (appearance, consistency), smell
(aroma), and taste (texture, flavour).

preparation methods

These are: trimming, shelling,
debearding, scraping/cleaning, and
coating.

cooking methods

These are: boiling, poaching, shallow
frying and deep frying.

identifying when dishes are cooked

Attention to recipe timings, the
appearance (e.g. firm texture,
outside of coating browned
attractively) and experience will tell
you. Shellfish is easily overcooked,
which spoils the eating quality.

Healthy catering practices

replacing high-fat ingredients

Because it is a luxury dish, and
shellfish has such a fine flavour,
many people enjoy it plainly cooked.
On the other hand, other people
associate fine food with rich sauces.
Offering a choice, and concentrating
on the recipes which use little or no
fat, may be the best option.

fats/oils for healthy eating

See page 110.

cooking methods, etc. to reduce fat

Boiling and poaching involve no fat,
but the sauce may include some.
Shallow and deep frying do involve
fat.

increasing fibre content of dishes

If the dish is served with brown rice,
this will increase the fibre content.

Self-check questions

1   Describe (or demonstrate) how you
hold the knife and the oyster to
prevent injury when opening an
oyster.

2   Give two reasons why a fresh shellfish
should be live until the moment it is
cooked.

3   State the quality points for fresh, live
crabs and one other shellfish of your
choice.

4   Describe where and the conditions in
which fresh shellfish should be stored
until use.

5   What should be done with a shellfish
that has died, or is dying? Why?

6   For each of the following, state the
cooking methods which can be used:
a) scampi, b) mussels, and c) crab.

7   Why is it important that the oil does
not get too hot when frying shellfish?

8   Describe some ways to garnish
shellfish dishes (use examples from
your workplace/a local restaurant
menu).

Element 1

Prepare basic shellfish dishes

Get your preparation areas and
equipment ready for use

PC

Select shellfish of the type,
quality and quantity required

PC

▲   Crab, prawns, shrimps, scampi, mussels, oyste

Identify and report problems with the
freshness or quality of ingredients

PC

Prepare shellfish and combine with
other ingredients

PC

▲   Preparation methods: trimming, shelling,
debearding, scraping/cleaning, coating
Other ingredients: dairy products, eggs, fruit,
vegetables, breadcrumbs

Correctly store shellfish dishes not for
immediate use

PC

Clean preparation areas and
equipment after use

PC

Prioritise and carry out your work in an
organised, efficient and safe manner

PC

Element 2

Cook basic shellfish dishes

Get your cooking areas and
equipment ready for use

PC

Cook shellfish dishes

PC

▲   Dry cooking methods: deep frying, shallow fryin
Wet cooking methods: boiling, poaching

Finish shellfish dishes

PC

▲   Finishing methods: garnishing, saucing, dressing

Correctly store shellfish dishes
not for immediate use

PC

Clean cooking areas and
equipment after use

PC

Identify and report problems with the
quality of shellfish dishes

PC

Prioritise and carry out your work in an
organised, efficient and safe manner

PC

Preparing and cooking battered
fish and
chipped potatoes

Preparing batter for frying

The thing customers notice and taste in a portion of fried fish is the batter. It should look an appetising golden brown. The light, crunchy taste should contrast pleasantly with the delicate flavour and soft texture of the fish.

Getting the right appearance and taste has a lot to do with how the batter is prepared. If it is too thin, it will not coat the fish sufficiently. If it is too thick, the fish may not be cooked sufficiently.

The main ingredients of batter are flour, egg, seasoning, water and/or milk. Many workplaces buy in batter as a dry mix. It requires no special storage, and can be made quickly and simply by adding water and, in some cases, salt.

Quality and storage points

Check the date stamp on the packaging of batter mixes and other dry ingredients. Provided you use the older stock first (rotate stock), there should not be a problem with stock that has exceeded its date.

Keep batter powder, salt, flour, etc. in an air-tight container, in a dry place. Keep milk and eggs chilled (these have a much shorter shelf-life).

Preparation methods and equipment

Batter can be made *manually*, using a *whisk* to blend the ingredients together. Do not over-whisk the batter, as too much air spoils its texture.

In large, busy workplaces, it is more common to use *mechanical methods*, making the batter with *automatic batter mixers*. These combine the ingredients very efficiently, and can be set to mix the batter for exactly the right length of time.

Whether you are making batter in the traditional way or from a convenience mix, you need to measure the ingredients accurately. The main items of *measuring equipment* are weighing scales and measuring cups or jugs.

After batter is made, it is kept in a *bucket* – stainless steel is the best type, as it is hard-wearing and can be cleaned effectively.

Testing and adjusting the consistency

If you have measured the quantities accurately, the consistency should be right. With a lot of experience, you can judge this by looking at how the batter runs when poured from a ladle or jug.

A much more reliable test, which many workplaces use every time batter is made, is the flow cup method. A special cup, with a hole in the bottom, is filled with batter. The time taken for the cup to empty (e.g. 1 minute 15 seconds) is timed with a stop watch.

If the batter is too thick, mix in a little more cold water.

Storing batter

Cover the buckets of batter, and place them in the refrigerator or cold room. Label each bucket – the time it was made and the date, or a batch number, or both (depending on the system in your workplace).

Batter which was made first should be used first. There will be a maximum time for keeping batter. Do not prepare too much too far in advance, or some will be wasted.

The batter will settle during storage. To re-mix it, pour into a clean bucket before using.

Guidelines on making batter

- Store batter powder in a dry, sealed container.
- Use cold water to make up batter.
- Before measuring out batter powder, shake storage container to ensure thorough mixing of all ingredients.
- Use correct measuring cup to measure salt and pepper.
- When making batter in advance, store in the chiller until needed.
- For batter mixes that have been standing for a long time, transfer to another bucket before use. This will allow ingredients that may settle during standing to become evenly mixed.
- If batter is unsuitable for use, record on a kitchen wastage report how much is thrown away.
- Monitor batter colour, texture and flavour of fried products when carrying out quality checks.

Quality points for finished batter

The batter will thicken on keeping, especially when it is at the fryers. This is why frequent checks are recommended, using an accurate method such as the flow cup.

Warning signs of a problem include:

- not coating the fish evenly
- crystals forming on the surface of the batter
- poor colour when the fish is cooked
- poor flavour and texture when the fish is cooked.

Getting the right appearance and taste has a lot to do with how the batter is prepared.

Element 2

Preparing and cooking battered fish

The preparation tasks depend on how the fish comes into your workplace. This reflects the space available, the location and your employer's marketing policy. For example:

- very limited space: all fish ready to cook
- good suppliers in the area: all fish is fresh
- reputation for selling only the best quality fresh fish, purchased daily: preparation and portioning done on the premises.

Hygiene standards must be very high at all times. Fish sometimes carries bacteria when it arrives. It is attractive to bacteria brought into your workplace on people, other foods, or in dirt and dust.

When you're working at the fryer, you represent the company and everyone who works for it. Customers will see what you do (or do not do) as a reflection of the hygiene standards of the whole business.

Equipment

The equipment in your workplace includes:

- *cutting boards* – for preparation tasks, e.g. skinning, trimming and portioning. These should be made of plastic material which will not crack, split or smell, and which can be effectively cleaned. To reduce the risk of cross contamination, use different chopping boards for each type of food
- *fish storage containers* – to store prepared fish in the refrigerator. These containers keep the fish covered and are easy to clean. There may be a system for labelling containers so that you know what type of fish is in each one, the portion size and the date of preparation
- *knives* – for preparation tasks (see Section 4). As with boards, there should be a different set of knives for each type of food, to prevent cross contamination

- *frying range* – purpose-made item of equipment, so that everything is to hand for those using it: the deep fat fryers, containers for the batter, scrap pans for collecting bits of batter and fish that have fallen off during cooking, heated display cabinet for holding the cooked fish, etc.
- *fish turners / slices* – for handling the fish during and after cooking
- *temperature monitoring devices* – to check the temperature of cooked fish waiting to be served (this must be above 63°C), and of the frying medium (as a safeguard against failure of the thermostat).

Fish types, quality points and preparation methods

Most restaurants which specialise in fried fish prefer to offer two or three varieties of the very best quality, rather than a big choice. Cod and haddock are favourites nationwide. Others include skate, plaice, halibut and hake. Often the choice varies from day to day, depending on what is available at local fish markets.

The fish is available in three main types:

- *frozen portions* – ready to cook after defrosting, and *frozen fillets* – which need defrosting, sometimes skinning and boning (to remove the very small bones left in the fillets of round fish), then portioning
- *fresh portions* – ready to cook, and *fresh fillets* – ready to prepare
- *whole fish* – to prepare as fillets (e.g. plaice) or to cook whole after trimming (e.g. plaice and sole).

The packaging of frozen fish should be in good condition, with no sign of thawing. The flesh should be of a good colour and feel firm when thawed.

Fillets of fresh fish should be of good colour and aroma, the flesh firm with no signs of bruising or blood clots. Whole fish should look, smell and feel fresh and bright (see also page 111).

Defrosting fish

Defrosting cannot be hurried. Large blocks of frozen fish take 24 hours or longer to defrost. This means forecasting the next day's sales, taking into account what's on in the area, the day of the week, etc. – usually a management decision.

Defrosting should be done in a room separate from the cooking area (which would be too hot, especially when the cooking equipment is on). But the main danger is that bacteria from uncooked fish will get on to cooked fish, leading to food poisoning.

Some workplaces use a defrosting cabinet. This provides controlled conditions, so the defrosting time can be worked out. The refrigerator is another option, provided there is no risk of water, etc. from the thawing fish getting on to other foods.

Big fish restaurants have a room set aside for defrosting (sometimes combined with the preparation room). This has suitable draining surfaces and is cool at all times of the year.

Before defrosting, remove the outer, cardboard packaging. If the fish is also wrapped in plastic, take this off after defrosting.

Never try to speed up the thawing process by putting the fish in water. This makes the fish soggy, difficult to cook and unappetising.

Once defrosted, fish must never be refrozen:

- the quality would be poor – when fish is commercially frozen, the process is completed very quickly using powerful freezers
- there is a hygiene risk – if bacteria have come into contact with the fish after thawing, they will multiply in numbers. When the fish is defrosted a second time, all these bacteria will come into life once more, multiplying to dangerous levels.

Skinning fish

Do not attempt to skin fish which has not fully thawed. Whether you are using a machine or doing the skinning by hand, it is difficult to remove the skin cleanly. You are also likely to cut yourself.

Boning fish

Fillets of round fish sometimes have very small bones remaining. You can feel these *pin bones* with your fingers, at the head-end of the fillet. Once you have located them, cut down either side of the pin bones into the flesh, but without penetrating the skin (if the skin is on). This is called a *V-cut*. Some people find it easier and less wasteful to pull the bones out with pliers.

Portioning

Get to know the different portion sizes (e.g. specials, children's) offered by your workplace. Look at the overall shape of the fillet, and weigh it. Then make a judgement about the best way to cut it, so that:

- each portion is a good shape, looking generous for its weight
- there are no pieces left over, too small to make a portion – you might achieve this by cutting some portions of the larger size, some of the smaller size.

Check the weight of each portion, and place it on the appropriate tray.

Storing fish before cooking

Cover the trays of portioned fish and place in the refrigerator. Only raw fish should be kept in these refrigerators. The recommended temperature is between 2°C and 4°C.

Label each tray, so you and work colleagues know what type of fish it is, the size of fillet and when it was prepared. Ideally, fish should be used on the day of preparation, and certainly by the following day – follow your workplace rules on maximum storage time.

Coating fish

When you are ready to fry the fish, coat it evenly (but completely) in the batter. With plaice and other, quite thin pieces of fish, it helps to wiggle the fish in the batter. Hold the fish over the batter for a few moments, so the excess batter can run off.

There are different views on where to hold the fillet: by the tail end (less effect on the appearance of the batter), by the wide end (better grip, and the fish less likely to break in two). Follow the preference in your workplace.

Looking after the batter during service

Do not leave the batter on top of the frying range, or elsewhere in the kitchen during quiet periods. It will spoil if it is kept too long at kitchen temperatures.

Before starting on a fresh batch of batter, check its thickness, e.g. by the flow cup method. You can thin it down by adding more water.

During frying, regularly check the batter thickness. During a slow period, it may get too thick to use. In this case, you must discard it, and collect a fresh supply.

Do not overfill the batter can (three-quarters full is best). From time to time during service, clean the batter can (or replace it with a clean one). This avoids a build-up of old batter, broken off pieces of fish, and any pieces of cooked batter which have fallen in.

Cooking fish

Set up everything before opening time, including:

- fryers filled with the freshly-filtered frying medium (fat or oil)

- extractor fans and fryers turned on

- utensils for handling fish

- batter ready to use and first tray(s) of fish to cook

- service plates and/or requirements for take-away service: wrapping paper, salt, vinegar, etc.

Once the fryer is up to the right temperature, the main points to pay attention to are:

- putting the coated fish into the fryer – lower the pieces in gently so the fat does not splash on your hand

- cooking the fish evenly – half-way through cooking, turn the pieces over

- cooking times – short (3 to 6 minutes, typically) but because the fat is very hot, a minute too long can spoil the fish

Fryers opening duties

- Switch on ventilation/extraction system.
- Switch on gas and electricity to equipment.
- Check and if necessary, change the frying medium. Always try to change fat at the start of the day. This will avoid loss of time and product later, when the priority is getting the orders out quickly.
- Make sure filter bag, filter tank and crumb filters are clean. Are baffles in correct way, with drainage holes facing downwards?
- Top up the frying medium to minimum of 25 mm above thermostat fat guard levels.
- Set fryers to 100°C. When reached, check that the thermostats are correct by using the probe thermometer.
- Collect frying utensils. Check that they are clean.
- Make batter to required standard.
- Check temperature of freezer and fish fridge. Is there enough fish ready for the day's business?
- 10 minutes before opening, turn all equipment to working temperature: fryers at 185°C and 170°C, top boxes (for cooked fish) at 65°C, chip boxes at 150°C.

- keeping pace with the flow of orders – so you do not keep customers waiting, but avoid keeping cooked fish hot for a long time (10 minutes is the maximum time in many workplaces)

- getting the best presentation – the side of the fish which was skinned does not look as good as the other side. Cook this side, the presentation side, first. Once the fish has been turned over in the fat, the presentation side always remains on the top: when it is taken out of the fat, while it is waiting to be served, and when it is on the customer's plate.

As the fish cooks, the bubbles around it become smaller. Small bubbles are a sign that the fish is cooked.

During frying, regularly empty the scrap pans. This looks tidier, and reduces the fire risk.

Looking after the frying medium

The cooking fat (some fish and chip restaurants use refined beef dripping) or oil, spoils with use. The process:

- starts the moment the fat is exposed to air – light and oxygen cause substances in the fat or oil to break down

- gets faster when the fat is hot

- gets faster still with cooking – this applies not just to pieces of fish, but even the tiniest piece of batter or fish, which has been left behind in the fat from cooking

- becomes very rapid when the fat is overheated – smoke coming off the surface of the fat and an unpleasant burning smell are danger signs – a few degrees higher and the fat will burst into flames.

To help keep the frying medium in good condition for longer:

- follow strictly your workplace routine for filtering, topping up and replacing fat/oil. Tell your manager when there is a problem

- do not fry too much food at once, the proportion of food to fat should be 1:6

- remove any loose pieces of fish and batter

- let excess batter run off the fish before frying

- season fish away from the fat

- turn down the temperature when fryers are not busy, and turn off fryers which are no longer required. Never heat three fryers when two will do

- cover the fryers when not in use.

Warning signs that the fat is spoiling include thickening, longer cooking times, and a strong smell of fat from the cooked fish. The fat is not suitable to use when any or all of these things happen:

- it turns dark brown
- a froth forms on the surface
- food cooked in it tastes and smells unpleasant
- excessive smoke is given off.

Fat and oil are very expensive – do not throw them away without your manager's approval. Your workplace will have an arrangement for waste fats and oils to be collected (see Section 6).

Quality points of cooked fish

The cooked fish should be:

- evenly coated with golden brown batter, well drained
- piping hot, crisp and good shape
- fish flesh moist and white colour.

To prevent quality problems, tell your manager immediately if the batter is becoming dark or thick, raw fish is the wrong colour (e.g. haddock grey, cod brown) or smelling strongly, or if the fat is smoking, even though the thermostat is set correctly.

Closing down after use

Turn off fryers as business quietens. Do not remove more fish or batter from the refrigerator than you expect to use.

Follow the closing down checklist at your workplace – if one is not available, ask your manager to help you make one. Pay particular attention to which equipment should be turned off, and which should be left on.

When you have completed everything, do one final check. Are all surfaces clean? Are fryers covered? Has everything been put away? Are refrigerators locked?

Quality and storage points for potatoes
- the variety ordered, e.g. Maris Piper
- an even size (otherwise chipping is difficult)
- dry, with no sprouting
- no excess soil or dirt
- no slug holes or frost damage
- no bruising or damage from harvesting/handling
- store in a cool, dark, dry, airy place, away from anything with a strong smell.

Preparing and cooking chipped potatoes

The other half of a good piece of fried fish is the chips. Some people even prefer the chips without the fish.

Most fish and chip restaurants make their own chips, rather than buy in frozen, chilled or freshly prepared varieties. The thicker, random shape of chips made on the premises gives them a home-made appeal. Each bite has a generous amount of potato, more of the taste of potato, and less of the fat it is cooked in.

Preparation methods and equipment

Potato peelers are also called *rumbling machines* because of the noise made by the potatoes tumbling around in the revolving drum. The movement of the machine tosses the potatoes against the drum's rough inner surface (like very coarse sandpaper). This rubs off the potato skin, which is carried away by cold water run through the machine while it is operating.

The starting sequence is: turn the machine on, then the water supply, then add the potatoes (gradually). The finishing sequence is: open the trap, let the peeled potatoes tumble out, turn off the machine, then the water.

Do not overfill the drum – the potatoes will not peel evenly. Do not run the machine for too long – this wastes potato. As a guide, 30 seconds for new crop potatoes and two minutes for old potatoes are sufficient.

Eyeing and final *peeling* is done by hand. Inspect each potato, and use a *knife, eyeing tool* or hand potato peeler to cut out any eyes, remove any remaining skin, and cut away damaged or bruised parts. Throw away any stones you find among the potatoes. If stones get into the chipping machine they will damage the blades.

Put the peeled potatoes in a sink with plenty of cold water running over them. If you are dealing with a large quantity, your workplace may have a holding tank or skip to keep the potatoes until they can be made into chips.

Chipping

Chipping machines are dangerous if misused. Follow the instructions carefully. Always turn the machine off at the mains switch before attempting to dislodge a blockage. Never remove, or try to bypass, safety guards.

Collect the cut chips in *buckets* or a skip (depending on the quantity being prepared).

Thoroughly rinse the chips in cold water, until the water runs clear.

In some workplaces, the next step is to soak the chips in a whitening agent. This means they can be left to drain thoroughly for an hour or so before frying, without risk of the potato going dark. Besides its convenience, this method reduces the risk of water getting into the frying medium. Water causes the fat to foam, which is very dangerous if the fryer overflows. Water also harms the quality of the fat.

Keep whitening agents well away from:

- cooked food – they will harm the taste and appearance
- frying medium – they will spoil the fat or oil.

Cooking equipment and methods

Chips are usually cooked at the *frying range*, alongside the fish, but in a different fryer. Using separate fryers helps the frying medium last longer. The fish and the chips both taste better.

The range will have one or more bins for keeping chips hot, and a scuttle for letting the fat drain from the chips before they go in the bin.

The range of utensils include *lifters* for getting chips out of the frying medium, and *scoops* for measuring the portions at service time.

To check that the thermostat on the fryer is operating accurately, and that chips are being served piping hot, there will be a *temperature monitoring device* (i.e. a temperature probe).

Cooking chips

The critical factors for good tasting chips are the temperature and quality of the frying medium, and not keeping the chips for too long after cooking. Your manager will give you specific guidance, and here are some general points:

- *frying temperature* – this mostly depends on the frying medium used, the size of the chips, and how customers like their chips. The variety of potatoes and whether they are new season or old can also make a difference. If chips are blanched (i.e. partly cooked), this is done at a lower temperature (e.g. 165°C), and the final cooking and browning in very hot fat (e.g. 190°C). For cooking straight through, the temperature is not quite as hot (e.g. 185°C)

- *quality of the frying medium* – the points made earlier about looking after the quality of the fat or oil (page 226) apply: filtering and topping up, turning down the temperature when fryers are not in use, etc. While frying, regularly skim off any scraps from the top of the fat, using a spider. After cooking each batch of chips, remove chip bits and particles with a long-handled, fine-mesh sieve: pull the sieve several times through the fat, so you catch as many bits as possible

- *keeping the chips hot* – chips do not keep well after frying, going soggy and greasy. Customers like to be served quickly, so the ideal is to keep a few minutes ahead of demand, but not to cook too much. To avoid quality problems, most fish and chip restaurants have a rule that chips not served within so many minutes are thrown away. Do not mix batches of chips cooked at different times, otherwise customers get some freshly cooked chips, and others that are soggy and greasy.

Some other points to help you cook good chips:

- do not overload the fryer – this makes the temperature drop sharply, so the chips take longer to cook and absorb more fat

- while the chips are cooking, stir occasionally – they cook more evenly, and do not stick together

- do not overcook the chips – when the chips start floating (less than five minutes, typically), this is a sign that they are cooked

- let the excess fat run off the chips before you place them in the chip box ready for service. If you do this in a chip scuttle, do not put drained fat back in the fryer – it will spoil the quality.

If you are blanching (part-cooking) chips, the timing has to be accurate. Too long, and the chips begin to cook through. Too short, and you lose the saving on final cooking time (when customers are likely to be waiting) which is the main purpose of blanching. Blanched chips should still be white, and feel firm when pinched between the fingers.

Portioning

Portion the chips accurately. Often this is done by using a certain size scoop. Another method is to put the chips into cones or upright cartons – these give the impression of a generous portion.

Safety when frying

Remember that frying is dangerous. Smoking fat can quickly turn into a fire. If you drop chips in the fryer carelessly, splashes of hot fat can get on to your hands and arms, causing severe burns.

Quality points

To test that the chips are cooked properly, allow a chip from the batch to cool slightly, then pinch it between the fingers. It should be soft all the way through, and crisp on the outside. The colour should be golden brown on the outside and pale in the centre.

Sometimes, if the sugar content of the potato is higher than usual, the chips go dark. Potatoes like this should not be used, as customers mistakenly complain that the poor colour is to do with the quality of the fat.

?

For help to answer questions relating to:

Health and safety

? safe working practices

The hazards include use of dangerous equipment (i.e. knives, mixing and chipping machines), deep frying (fat which overheats, smokes and bursts into flames, burns from contact with the hot oil or fat), and moving or lifting large, heavy or otherwise difficult-to-handle items (e.g. bags of potatoes, large trays of frozen fish).

Food hygiene

? importance of good hygiene

Fish is a high risk food. If it is badly stored or handled, bacteria can multiply to dangerous numbers. The main controls are also important for quality purposes, e.g. maximum time for keeping fish hot after cooking, and minimum temperature. Other points to pay attention to include: preventing cross contamination, keeping prepared fish, batter and chips at a safe temperature, and personal hygiene.

? main contamination threats

These include dirt, insects and chemicals which might be on potatoes when they are delivered, inadequate cleaning of the preparation and cooking area or equipment, cleaning agents and chip whitening agents stored or used the wrong way, and poor personal hygiene.

? importance of time and temperature

Bacteria increase rapidly in numbers at the right temperature. This is one reason why there are strict controls over how long and at what temperatures batter, fish and chips are kept before and after cooking. You may have to complete food production charts with these details.

? monitoring temperature of oil/fat

From a hygiene point of view, there is a risk of the fish or chips not reaching a safe temperature. The main reasons are for quality and safety. If the oil temperature is too low, the food will be soggy and absorb too much fat. Too high temperatures will result in burning on the outside and undercooking at the centre. High

temperatures cause the oil to spoil more quickly, and there is a fire risk if the flash point is reached.

? filtering and changing oil/fat

The oil/fat has a longer frying life when it is filtered regularly to remove pieces of fish, batter and chips which have broken off during cooking. But even with such care, the oil eventually starts to smoke at normal frying temperatures (which is dangerous), to thicken, and to leave the food with an unpleasant flavour and smell. Before this point is reached, the oil must be changed.

Product knowledge

? quality points

Batter should be well mixed, and have a good colour and appearance, the right consistency, and a golden brown colour, crisp texture when cooked.

Battered fish should be piping hot and look good. The flesh of the fish should be moist, white and covered in a golden brown, crisp batter.

Chips should be of good colour and flavour, soft all the way through.

? testing consistency of batter

If batter is too thin, it will not coat the fish. Too thick, and there is a risk the fish will be uncooked at the centre. In either situation, customers will be dissatisfied. As batter thickens after it has been made, you should test the consistency regularly.

? improving consistency of batter

A little water will thin the batter.

? resting batter before frying

This allows the flour particles to expand in the liquid and gives a tender, light result.

? testing when fish is cooked

The batter should be a golden brown colour, the flesh of the fish white. Pay attention to cooking times and you should not have a problem.

? testing when chips are cooked

The chip should be soft all the way through, and the colour a golden brown.

? use of coatings for deep fried food

Coatings give the food an attractive brown appearance and crisp texture, add flavour, help the food to hold its shape during cooking, reduce moisture loss and prevent the food absorbing too much oil.

Healthy catering practices

? temperature of the oil/fat

If the oil/fat is not hot enough, the food will absorb a lot of fat.

? fats/oils which contribute to healthy eating

See page 110.

? reducing salt

While many people like salt with their chips, others want to reduce the amount of salt they eat for health reasons. Where possible, give customers the choice.

Self-check questions

1 What safety points should you consider before attempting to lift a large container of oil?

2 State the routine which must be followed in your workplace in the event of a fire.

3 Why should batter be kept covered and chilled when it is prepared in advance?

4 Describe the method used in your workplace to test the consistency of batter. How can you thin the batter?

5 Why is it important to let the excess batter run off fish before frying?

6 State the frying temperatures in your workplace for a) fish and b) chips. What can go wrong if the temperature is too low?

7 State the maximum time in your workplace for keeping a) fish and b) chips hot before service. What temperature should each be held at?

8 Describe the quality points (or service standard) for a portion of fish and chips in your workplace.

Closing down checklist

- Turn off pilot and main gas controls.
- Turn off range electrics.
- Strip and clean range boxes, grids and glasses, chip boxes and grids, crackling boxes and grids. Empty oil drawers into pan.
- Turn off extraction system after 15–20 minutes.
- Dispose of batter and wash batter box.

- Wash all range tools.
- Transfer unused fish portions to chiller.
- Dispose of cooked chips and batter scraps.
- Remove cooked fish and throw away.
- Empty rubbish bins.
- Wash floors of frying area and preparation area.

Quiet trading times

- Turn all pans down to 150°C.
- Run down stocks of cooked fish and chips. Transfer cooked fish into one box. Turn off other boxes.
- Fry only to order. Most customers are happy to wait when they know their food will be freshly cooked.
- Empty and wash batter box.
- Clean range and frying area. Always clean as you go.

From the Training Manual for Fish Friers, *published by the Sea Fish Industry Authority.*

Using beef dripping

- When unwrapping fat, check that it is golden yellow, and free from surface moisture and strong odours.
- Ensure that stock is rotated. Store fat at 10°C or less, in a dry place, away from strong odours. Keep covered, preferably in original wrapping (light causes the fat to spoil).
- Fat levels in the fryer should be sufficient just to cover the product being fried and the thermostat.
- Rotate fat: first use for chips, second use for fish, then discard.

- Avoid contact with excessive batter powder, water, cleaning materials, vinegar, anything acidic, etc.
- When melting down fat, always do so at a low temperature, no higher than 130°C. The pan base should be covered with fat before igniting. Once the fat is melted, it can be heated to normal frying temperature.
- Never heat fat above 205°C, as this will cause a fire. To cool fat down, use a small number of chips after turning the heat off. Never use water.

- Do not bring pans up to heat too far in advance. Ideally, pans should be up to frying temperatures 10 minutes before service begins.
- Always turn pans off during quiet periods. If necessary, keep pans at a lower temperature and, where possible, turn pans off and work from one range rather than two.
- At least once a day, check that pan temperatures match the display on the range, using a temperature probe.
- Filter pans three times a day: first thing in the morning, mid-session, end of the day before close down.

NVQ SVQ

Skills check
Prepare and cook battered fish
and chipped potatoes
Unit 2ND20

level 2

Use this to check your progress against the performance criteria.

Element 1

Prepare batter for frying

Get your preparation and cooking areas and equipment ready for use ☐ PC1

Select ingredients of the type, quality and quantity required ☐ PC2

Identify and report problems with the quality of ingredients ☐ PC3

Prepare batter using manual and mechanical methods ☐ PC4

 Equipment: automatic batter mixers, buckets, whisks, measuring equipment

Correctly store batter not for immediate use ☐ PC5

Clean preparation and cooking areas and equipment after use ☐ PC6

Prioritise & carry out your work in an organised, efficient, safe manner ☐ PC7

Element 2

Prepare and cook battered fish

Get your preparation and cooking areas and equipment ready for use ☐ PC1

△ Equipment: cutting boards, fish storage containers, knives, frying range, fish turners/slices, temperature monitoring devices

Select fish of the type, quality and quantity required ☐ PC2

△ Fish: frozen fillets/portions, fresh fillets/portions, whole fish

Identify and report problems with the quality or quantity of ingredients ☐ PC3

Prepare fish for frying ☐ PC4

△ Preparation methods: skinning, boning, portioning, coating

Fry fish ☐ PC5

Look after frying oil/fat during use ☐ PC6

Keep cooked fish on display at correct temperature ☐ PC7

Close down frying range after service ☐ PC8

Clean preparation and cooking areas and equipment after use ☐ PC9

Prioritise & carry out your work in an organised, efficient, safe manner PC10

Element 3

Prepare and cook chipped potatoes

Get your preparation and cooking areas and equipment ready for use ☐ PC1

Select potatoes of the type, quality and quantity required ☐ PC2

Identify and report problems with the quality or quantity of potatoes ☐ PC3

Prepare potatoes for frying ☐ PC4

△ Preparation methods: peeling, eyeing, chipping Equipment: peeling/rumbling machines, chipping machines, buckets, eyeing tools/knives, frying range, chip lifters/scoops, temperature monitoring devices

Look after frying oil/fat during use ☐ PC5

Cook chipped potatoes ☐ PC6

Clean preparation and cooking areas and equipment after use ☐ PC7

Prioritise & carry out your work in an organised, efficient, safe manner ☐ PC8

Preparing pizza products

Pizza restaurants are favourite eating places for many people. They like the food, they enjoy the atmosphere, and they know they will get good value.

Another plus is that most restaurants offer a take-away service, and some a delivery service. Professionally prepared and cooked pizzas can be enjoyed at home, or anywhere customers want.

But pizza restaurants are up against strong competition – usually there are several other places nearby where people can eat, without spending a lot more. Standards have to be very high all the time, yet prices must be competitive. Profit depends on serving a large number of customers each day, quickly and efficiently.

This is made easier by a menu which focuses on a few items, offering choice through the range of fillings.

Contract caterers want their customers to eat on the premises, not go out to a competitor. Theme menus is one way of keeping customer interest and loyalty.

Preparation equipment

You will find that preparation tasks can be well planned, and good use made of the specialist equipment available, such as:

- *provers* – these provide the warmth (about 32°C) and moistness which the pizza dough needs to rise properly, and, because they are closed cabinets, protect the dough from dust and other contamination

- *retarders* – these cool the dough after it has proved to between 2°C and 5°C, thus holding back (i.e. retarding) the action of the yeast. Often the same machine is used for proving and retarding, and it can be programmed to switch automatically to retarding

- *food mixers* – for mixing the dough ingredients and some toppings

- *slicing and cutting equipment* – for preparing vegetable and meat toppings and the ingredients of salads

- *chilled preparation tables* – these keep the different toppings at a safe temperature during service, so they are ready to hand when the pizzas are assembled to match customers' orders

- *refrigerators* – to keep food chilled. There will usually be separate refrigerators for food waiting to be prepared, and food which has already been prepared. Cooked foods should always be kept apart from uncooked food

- *freezers* – for storage of frozen foods, including pizza dough which comes in as pre-prepared frozen discs

- *containers* – for storing toppings and other ingredients.

Ingredients and quality points

Ingredients fall into two groups:

- *pre-prepared and convenience foods* – canned foods (e.g. anchovies), pre-made toppings, and dough which is ready to be proved and baked. Some pizza restaurants get their dough supplied as frozen discs, others as portion-size balls of fresh dough ready to be shaped

- *fresh vegetables* – for making toppings.

Check the date stamp, and also the appearance. If these are not right, and/or there is an unpleasant smell, do not use the product. Inform your manager, so that the loss can be accounted for.

Use the older stock when you remove ingredients from refrigerators or stores (but no stock should be used if it has passed the date mark on the packaging). Rotating stock in this way cuts down wastage (see page 63).

Preparation methods

It is wasteful to prepare too much: unused food spoils in quality, and it may have to be thrown away. If you prepare too little, service will be delayed while you stop what you are doing to get more ready. When you are very busy, you won't have time, and customers will not understand why they cannot have their chosen dish.

But judging how much to prepare is never easy. Check with your manager, who will know about any advance bookings, and have some idea of business levels for the day of the week, etc.

Planning your work

Some pizza sauces require a few hours for the flavours to blend. Doughs need time to defrost and to prove. These are examples of processes that cannot be hurried.

Begin with the tasks which require most time between preparation and service. Then move down the priority order, tackling last those items which spoil most quickly after preparation.

Using hygienic preparation methods

Wash fresh vegetables thoroughly to remove all soil and dirt, bacteria and any traces of chemicals (used by the growers to protect the vegetables from insects).

Use a food preparation sink (check that it is clean). If you are adding a sanitiser to the washing water, measure the amount accurately.

Keep prepared vegetables separate from unprepared vegetables – or bacteria can spread to the vegetables you have just cleaned. For the same reason, do not use

In many pizza restaurants, customers have a full view of the cooking area.

Delicious pizzas are made from good quality ingredients, carefully prepared.

Preparation checklist: make-table

- switch on, allow to chill to between 2°C to 5°C before filling
- fill crocks only one hour before opening
- check that fans, seals, etc. are in place and working
- ensure cable is not a hazard
- set-up cups, scoops, rings for each ingredient, for correct sizes of pizza
- products must be defrosted and drained when set out
- use drainer inserts for wet ingredients
- check that specification charts are in place
- make a visual check of products
- clean all surfaces with sanitiser

the knives and chopping boards reserved for vegetables for any other preparation task. An example of a colour-coding system is:

- *green* – for salad vegetables and fruit
- *brown* – for vegetables which will be cooked
- *turnip coloured* – for cooked meats
- *white* – for cheese, other dairy products and bread
- *red* – for raw meat.

Each time you use the slicing machine, clean it carefully. If you do not, the flavour of the food can be spoilt, especially if the machine was last used for onions, peppers or chillies.

Cleaning helps prevent cross contamination. Bacteria can spread via an unwashed cutting blade, for example, from one food to another. This is particularly dangerous when the food is not going to be cooked – bacteria double in numbers every 20 to 30 minutes when conditions are right (as they are in a warm kitchen).

Put vegetables, toppings, etc. which you prepare in advance in a covered container. This will stop them drying out and being contaminated.

Before opening canned foods, clean the lid of the can. If you don't do this, dirt and dust gets on the cutting edge of the can opener, and from there into the food.

Once you have cut around the lid, make sure it does not fall into the food. Tip the contents of the can into a suitable container, cover, label with the contents and date, and put in the refrigerator until required.

Using safe preparation methods

Cutting machines – because of their sharp blades – are very dangerous if misused. By law, you must not operate any machine of this sort unless you are being instructed or supervised at the time, or you have already been trained.

Never use your fingers to hold food in the machine, or to push it against the blade.

Do not use glass bowls to store food in. They are meant for presenting salads, desserts, etc. to customers. If one does find its way into food preparation and cooking areas and smashes by accident, broken glass could get into the food or into equipment (damaging it).

Catering for vegetarians

Use a different set of spoons, knives, spatulas, etc. for dishes described on the menu as suitable for vegetarians. This reduces the risk of meat or fish accidentally getting into a vegetarian dish, e.g. if you cut the two types of pizza before service with the same knife.

Defrosting

Defrosting cannot be hurried. You spoil the quality of the food and there is a risk of food poisoning if food still frozen at the centre goes into the oven.

A safe, practical way of defrosting food is to put it in a refrigerator several hours or the day before you require it (exactly how long depends on the product). That means that the food, once defrosted, is kept well chilled.

Leaving food to defrost at room temperature saves time. But there is a danger, if you leave it out too long, of the food warming to temperatures at which bacteria multiply very rapidly.

Proving

This helps the dough expand in size through the action of the yeast (see page 200). The temperature, moistness and time allowed for proving have to be carefully controlled, which is why a prover is best.

After proving, the dough is chilled or retarded. This stops the yeast over-working.

If the dough has not risen – the pizza is much flatter than it should be – discard it. Tell your manager, so the reason can be investigated, and the loss recorded.

There will be a maximum time that pizza dough can be kept after retarding: follow your workplace rules.

Slicing

When slicing ingredients for toppings (e.g. vegetables or smoked meats), keep them at the same thickness and size. This gives the finished pizzas a consistent, balanced appearance. Customers will be appreciative, knowing that thought and effort has gone into making their food look and taste good.

Chilling

Toppings and other ingredients prepared in advance must be kept chilled. They keep better this way, and you much reduce the risk of bacteria multiplying.

Before placing toppings in the chilled preparation table, check that the temperature is between 2°C and 5°C. The machine has to be turned on two hours or so in advance.

Follow your workplace rules on the length of time toppings can be kept, and on what to do with those left over at the end of service.

Assembling and cooking pizza products

With practice, you will find it easier to keep track of lots of orders at the same time. What certainly helps is to have as much as possible ready before service starts.

Try to approach your various tasks logically. With a little thought, you can often get two things done in one journey, e.g. on your way to the refrigerator for extra toppings, taking empty food containers to the wash-up.

Equipment

As there are certain items of equipment you will definitely need during service, it makes sense to get them ready before the first customers arrive. Make your own checklist, or use the one provided in your workplace. Some of the items you might need are:

- spoons, scoops, etc. for toppings
- chopping boards and knives for final preparation
- spatulas and slices for removing pizzas from the baking tray
- tongs for handling garlic bread
- a second set of equipment for handling vegetarian dishes
- plates to serve the pizzas on
- cartons/boxes, bags, napkins, and other *packaging* used for take-away/delivery service.

Pizza *ovens* must be at their operating temperature at the start of service. Check how long in advance you should turn them on – if this is done too soon, you waste energy. There will probably be other equipment to turn on at the same time, e.g. the extractor fan.

Using equipment safely
- do not be distracted
- do not rush
- do not fool around
- be sensible, be safe.

Oven safety
- ensure the gas has ignited
- ensure the conveyor continues to run when the burner has been turned off, to prevent rapid contraction of the belt
- ensure the belt is the correct way on the frame
- beware of hot areas such as the top of the oven and the side entry doors
- do not put your hands into the cooking chamber while the oven is in operation
- take care when putting items on to the conveyor belt and through the access window
- use tongs to remove hot items from the conveyor belt
- stack hot empty pans safely – warn others that pans are hot
- do not attempt to clean the interior of the oven until it has cooled
- isolate power before cleaning oven
- always wear goggles, gloves and mask when cleaning the oven

Portioning and assembling pizza products

Shape the *pizza base* as required for the type of product. Then add the *sauces* and *toppings*.

Get to know what goes on the pizzas at your workplace:

- how much of each ingredient, e.g. 4 slices of tomato, 6 olives, a spoon (or cupful) of sweetcorn, 2 spoons of sauce
- any last minute preparation, e.g. stirring the sauce
- the order in which ingredients are placed on the pizza base, e.g. pepperoni followed by vegetables, and lastly the meat
- how best to place the topping ingredients, e.g. working from the outside in, to avoid overloading the centre
- the position of each ingredient, e.g. olives evenly placed around the outside.

In some restaurants, pizzas are brushed or sprayed with a glaze around the edge before they go in the oven. This helps the dough to brown and become crisp.

Do not oil pizza pans while they are still hot from cooking the last pizza. Doing so is dangerous: a colleague seeing the pan prepared with oil, might pick it up, not expecting it to be hot.

Garlic bread must be crispy when served, but not overcooked. To get the best product, some pizza restaurants use a special tray for baking garlic bread.

When adding *seasonings*, remember that some customers want to cut down on the amount of salt they eat. Many pizza toppings are highly flavoured, so you may not need to add salt at all.

Cooking pizza products

In a busy service period, when new orders are arriving in quick succession, it takes a lot of skill to keep control of the cooking. The challenge is to get the timing and oven temperature exactly right, so that each pizza is perfectly cooked.

Automatic pizza ovens, carrying the food on a conveyor belt through the oven, make your job a little easier. But remember to adjust the speed of the conveyor belt, and perhaps the temperature, for different sizes and types of pizza.

Finishing and presenting pizza products

Before you let the pizza go to the customer, check that it matches what was ordered, and the quality is up to standard:

- height, colour and texture of the dough
- arrangement, quantity and quality of the toppings.

It is easier to sort out problems before the pizza reaches the customer. And if there is a complaint about the wrong pizza being delivered, you know you got it right.

For restaurant and take-away/delivery service

Once the pizza is cooked, transfer it to the service plate, or the box for a take-away/delivery. Use a spatula or slice, not your hands (for hygiene reasons). Keep the pizza horizontal (otherwise the topping can run to the side that is lower).

In some workplaces, pizzas are cut into pieces – e.g. a small pizza into quarters – as part of the presentation:

- do this before you put the pizza on the plate or in the box – otherwise the knife will scratch the plate or cut through the box
- before cutting a pizza which has cheese as one of the toppings, let the pizza stand for 30 seconds – this allows the cheese to harden. If you cut the pizza too soon, the toppings tend to slide towards the centre.

Check the box for take-away and delivered pizzas has been assembled correctly, and use the right size box for the pizza. If the pizza slides around in a box which is too big, or gets squashed because the box support has been forgotten, it will not look very appetising.

Preparation checklist: cut-table

- stock all items, takeaway boxes, inserts, box supports, bags
- clean all surfaces with sanitiser
- set up cut boards for vegetarian/meat products
- set up rocker knives
- visual check of cooked items
- ensure sufficient supplies of plates, napkins and cork mats

---

Pizza topping ideas

Marguerita	Mozzarella cheese, tomato
Mushroom	Mushroom, Mozzarella, tomato
Seafood special	Tuna, calamari, mussels, prawns, anchovies, olives, tomato, Mozzarella
Giardinera	Tomato, Mozzarella, mushroom, onion, peppers, sweetcorn
American	Mozzarella, tomato, pepperoni, sausage
Mexican	Mozzarella, tomato, pepperoni, hot chilli, peppers
Sunnyside up	Ham, pepperoni, egg, capers, olives, Mozzarella, tomato
Quattro formaggio	Tomato, four cheeses
Chilli	Chilli con carne, Mozzarella, tomato
Hawaiian	Mozzarella, tomato, pineapple, ham, chicken
Tuna fish and banana	Tuna, banana, Mozzarella, tomato, oregano
Vegetarian	Tomato, green and red peppers, sweetcorn, mushrooms, onions, fresh herbs, Mozzarella
Jamaican hot	Pepperoni, chilli, spinach, tuna, tomato, Mozzarella
Toscana	Ham, olives, mushroom, Mozzarella, tomato, basil
Garlic inferno	Tomato, garlic, hot chilli peppers, onion, creamed garlic, Mozzarella

With thanks to McDougalls Catering Foods

NVQ SVQ

Skills check
Prepare, assemble and cook
pizza products
Unit 2ND21

leve 2

For help to answer questions
relating to:

Health and safety

safe working practices

Some of the equipment you use is
dangerous, e.g. cutting machines
(sharp blades) and ovens (hot
surfaces). Other hazards include:
using knives, and handling
equipment bulk packages of food,
waste bags, etc. which are difficult to
lift or move.

Food hygiene

importance of good hygiene

There are many ways in which
harmful bacteria can come into
contact with food, some of which you
may not have thought about before,
e.g. dust on a can lid gets on to the
blade of the opener, and from there
on to the food. Hygiene has to be a
priority in everything you do.

In some pizza restaurants, the
cooking area is open to the
restaurant. Customers will get a
good impression when they see high
standards of hygiene in operation,
clean uniforms, etc.

main contamination threats

These include dirt, insects and
chemicals which might be on
vegetables when they are delivered,
inadequate cleaning of the
preparation and cooking area or
equipment, cleaning agents stored or
used in the wrong way, pieces of
broken china getting into food, and
poor personal hygiene.

importance of time and temperature

Bacteria increase rapidly in numbers
at the right temperature. This is why
there are strict controls over how
long and at what temperatures each
of the food items you deal with are
kept. You may have to complete food
production charts with these details.

Product knowledge

proving time for pizza dough

The yeast in the dough needs time
(and the right temperature and
moistness) to do its work. Otherwise
the pizza will have an unpleasant
texture.

menu items for vegetarians

The menu will say what these are.
They may have the Vegetarian
Society's V-sign by them. When you
are making up a vegetarian pizza, do
not use any utensils or other
equipment which has been in contact
with meat or fish.

Sometimes it is not as obvious as you
might think which dishes are
suitable for vegetarians. For
example, the rennet used in some
cheese is of animal origin. Some
vegetarians will only eat free-range
eggs. (See page 144.)

quality points for pizza products

Remind yourself how the dish should
look (*appearance*), smell (*aroma*) and
taste (*texture, flavour*).

Healthy catering practices

replacing high fat ingredients

Pizzas are not high-fat foods,
although some toppings are (e.g.
with cheese). Most restaurants offer
customers a wide choice of menu
items, including dishes which are low
in fat.

**fats/oils which contribute to healthy
eating**

See page 110.

increasing fibre content of dishes

Pizzas made with brown flour will be
richer in fibre. Some topping
ingredients are good sources of fibre
(e.g. kidney beans).

reducing salt

The quite strong flavours of many of
the toppings mean that it is not
necessary to add much salt, or it is
possible to omit it altogether.

Self-check questions

1   What must you do if the dough is flat
after retarding?

2   How are toppings measured when
making pizzas?

3   Why should you not touch cooked
foods with your hands?

4   In stock rotation, what does first in,
first out (FIFO) mean?

5   What is the minimum temperature for
serving hot food?

6   How long can pre-topped pizzas be
kept?

7   Why should you have separate boards
and knives for vegetarian and meat
products?

8   Why is a visual check of the finished
product so important?

Questions with thanks to Pizza Hut

Use this to check your progress agains
the performance criteria.

Element 1

Prepare pizza products ready for cooking

Get your preparation areas and
equipment ready for use   PC

Select ingredients of the type,
quality and quantity required   PC

⚠ Ingredients: pre-prepared/convenience foods,
fresh vegetables

Identify and report problems with the
quality of ingredients   PC

Prepare ingredients   PC

⚠ Preparation methods: proving, chilling, slicing

Correctly store ingredients not for
immediate use   PC

Clean preparation areas and
equipment after use   PC

Prioritise and carry out your work in an
organised, efficient and safe manner   PC

Element 2

Assemble and cook pizza products

Get your preparation and cooking
areas and equipment ready for use   PC

Identify and report problems with the
quality of pizza products   PC

⚠ Pizza products: pizza bases, garlic bread,
prepared/convenience sauces and toppings,
seasoning

Portion and assemble pizza products   PC

Cook pizzas and pizza products   PC

Finish pizza products   PC

Package pizza products for take-away
or delivery   PC

Clean preparation and cooking areas
and equipment after use   PC

Prioritise and carry out your work in an
organised, efficient and safe manner   PC

Portioning, packing and blast-chilling food

Cook-chill is the name of a special catering system. The food is prepared and cooked in bulk at a central production unit, chilled very rapidly, then kept at low temperatures until required. At the time of service, dishes are quickly and easily reheated.

Because the food is prepared in bulk, there are economies of scale. Because it can be kept chilled for some days, and the reheating is straightforward, greater menu choice can be offered.

As required, the chilled food can be taken to service points spread over a wide area. These might be schools and hospitals, hotels, restaurants and pubs, aircraft and trains, staff catering facilities in offices and factories, or the homes of those relying on a meals-on-wheels type service.

Briefly, the system works like this:

- at a central unit, the food is prepared and cooked

- it is placed in suitable containers and chilled very quickly in a blast-chiller

- the food is stored at just above freezing point, between 0°C and 3°C

- the maximum time it can be kept chilled is five days, with day 1 being the day the food is cooked and chilled, and day 5 the day it is served and eaten

- immediately before service, the food is reheated to a temperature (at the centre) of 70°C to 75°C, for at least two minutes.

In some cases, the food is reheated at the production unit, and possibly taken to a number of different service units using heated trolleys. Alternatively, the food is transported in its chilled state, and reheated at the point of service.

Because most cook-chill operations are on a large scale, good teamwork is a key aspect of the work.

Why hygiene is so important

Bacteria which cause food poisoning grow at temperatures between 5°C and 63°C. Below 5°C they grow very slowly, or not at all. Above 63°C, the bacteria start to die.

When the food is cooked, it passes through this dangerous temperature range. As the high temperatures reached in cooking kills most bacteria, this is not a problem. The risks are greatest during the two subsequent stages in cook-chill, when the food again goes through the danger zone:

- *chilling after cooking* – any bacteria, or the poisons some of them make, which survive cooking will multiply

- *reheating before service* (sometimes called regenerating) – bacteria again have a chance to multiply: any which survived cooking and any introduced through poor hygiene practices during chilling, storage, transportation, or reheating.

Types of food and quality points

A lot of development work goes into deciding what dishes are suited to the cook-chill system, what changes are required to the recipes and production methods, and how they are packed for chilling and storage. The aim is that each dish should taste as good as it does when freshly prepared and cooked immediately before service.

Even if you are not yet working in a place where the cook-chill system is used, you will know from the wide range of cook-chill products on sale in large supermarkets many of the foods which are suitable:

- *meat and poultry dishes* – stews, casseroles, roasts, grills, burgers, pies, stir-fries, shallow or deep-fried meat

- *joints and whole chickens* – roast or boiled joints of beef, lamb, pork and roast chicken. Because large joints take too long to cool after cooking, the maximum weight before cooking of whole poultry and joints of meat should not be more than 2½ kg, and the thickness or height not greater than 10 cm

- *vegetables and fruit* – most types for hot vegetable dishes: boiled, steamed, fried, roasted. Those fruits which can be cooked and served hot or cold (e.g. baked apple and poached peaches), and fruits which do not require cooking and keep well chilled (e.g. a fruit salad with orange slices, apple, cherries and grapes). Some salad vegetables are not suitable (e.g. lettuce and watercress)

- *fish dishes* – most types poached, shallow and deep fried, or steamed. Grilled fish is not usually suitable (it will be too dry)

- *sauces and soups* – all those that can be kept hot or reheated without difficulty in conventional cooking. Those that use egg as the thickener (e.g. hollandaise) are unlikely to be used

- *egg dishes* – scrambled eggs and omelettes respond the best of the various egg dishes. The difficulty with poached and fried eggs is that the yolk will be very firm after reheating

- *desserts* – those that can be kept hot or reheated without difficulty in conventional cooking, e.g. fruit pies and tarts, sponge-based, pancakes, egg-based and rice-based. Many cold desserts are also suitable, e.g. jellies, mousses and trifles.

These dishes will have been prepared and cooked elsewhere in your workplace, and various checks made to ensure their quality is satisfactory. Nevertheless, you must keep alert and report anything unusual, e.g. food which has dried out or been burnt, sauces which contain lumps or a thick skin, and food which has broken up.

Working hygienically

Cook-chill central production units have very strict rules on hygienic work practices.

In many cases, different activities take place in different rooms, and staff are not allowed to move between areas. To make it easy to notice people in the wrong place, all staff in portioning and packing might wear green aprons, for example. All items of small equipment for each area might be colour-coded in the same way, so that the risk of cross-contamination between uncooked and cooked food – because the same equipment is used for both purposes – is kept to the minimum.

Having separate areas also means that the temperature in the portioning and packing area can be kept at 10°C or below. This would be very difficult if there was cooking going on in the same room.

Wear disposable gloves at all times. Change gloves regularly. Before putting on new gloves, thoroughly wash and dry your hands using the hand-cleaning agent and means of drying provided.

Portioning and packing

The rule is that food must be portioned, packed and ready to go in the blast-chiller within 30 minutes of being cooked. (Longer is allowed for joints of meat which are sliced or cut when cold, since they take 90 minutes or more to cool sufficiently.)

To complete your tasks within time, have everything ready before the food arrives from the cooking area:

- sufficient containers available, of the correct portion size

- containers of the type that are re-used (e.g. made from stainless steel) have been properly cleaned and sanitised

- single-use or disposable containers (e.g. made from aluminium foil) are undamaged, and have been hygienically stored

- lids for containers are to hand

- equipment for handling and portioning the food is available and clean

- labels are prepared (see below)

- temperature probe, sanitising wipes, temperature record forms, pen, etc. are available.

Check your instructions or ask a supervisor, so that you know:

- what portion sizes are required and how to measure them (e.g. using a certain size of spoon or ladle, or weighing each dish)

- how the food has to be packed in the container (see below).

Packing and covering

The safety of cook-chill dishes depends on very rapid chilling and reheating (so that the food spends the shortest possible time in the temperature range at which bacteria multiply). This is why powerful chilling and reheating equipment is required, and why careful attention is given to the sorts of container used and how the food is packed in them.

Spreading the food quite thinly (not more than 50 mm deep at any point) in a shallow container is the main way of ensuring that it chills and reheats quickly. The danger is that it dries out – this can happen at any of the stages – and burns during reheating. The problem is greatest when a large surface area of a food which should remain moist is in direct contact with the base of the container, e.g. a slice of roast meat.

You will get guidance on what to do, but here are some points to look for when packaging:

- *slices of meat* – how the first slice should be protected (e.g. placed on a layer of meat trimmings or vegetable garnish), and how the others should be overlapped

- *pieces of fish* – how they can be kept apart to prevent sticking together (battered fish may do this), or damaging each other (if they slide around the dish during handling)

- *poached fish* – whether it should be chilled in the poaching liquid or the sauce, when the sauce is added

- *gravies and sauces* – whether they should be added hot or cold, what to do if a skin forms, how much to use, whether some should be used to coat the base of the dish, and the thickness of the gravy or sauce

- *fatty foods* – how they can be well drained of their fat (e.g. sausages chilled, then transferred to a clean container)

- *pieces of food* – how they can be arranged to avoid too much surface contact with the base of the dish, or touching the underside of the lid

- *scrambled egg* – whether to place on fried bread/ buttered toast

- *creamed vegetables* – whether to pipe, or layer in dish and flute the surface (increasing the surface area reduces chilling time)

- *baked jacket potatoes* – how to avoid contact with lid (e.g. cutting in half), and whether to chill the filling separately

- *rice and pasta* – what depth to fill the dish (e.g. thin to prevent starchiness)

- *pastry* – how to prevent shrinkage (can happen if portioned when hot), keeping the pastry crisp (what to do with sauces), preventing the top of the pastry from touching the lid, reducing the risk of damage (e.g. as pies slide around the dish during handling).

Labelling

The label plays an essential information-giving and control role in the cook-chill system. The various people handling each container during storage, transportation, reheating and service need to know at the minimum:

- what the dish is

- number of portions

- when it must be used by.

The label can also provide other helpful information, such as:

- how to reheat the food – as a reminder to, or in place of, more detailed workplace instructions

- garnish and service suggestions

- if the dish is a vegetarian one

- special diets that the dish is suitable for, e.g. gluten-free, or not suitable for, e.g. contains nuts.

For control purposes, it is helpful to be able to trace back from the label information about the preparation of the dish. This might be the date and time it was packed, or, more usefully, a batch number. When linked with the production planning system and temperature records, this number can help identify:

- order and delivery details of each ingredient

- total number of portions of the dish prepared

- recipe used

- by whom the dish was cooked, portioned, packed and blast-chilled

- when each of these stages started and finished, and the temperatures

- where the dish was stored after blast-chilling.

The label should be placed where it can be easily read during handling and storage. Often a colour-coding system is used, for types of dishes, or particular diets, or day of packing.

Blast-chilling

Production schedules in your workplace will be planned so that:

- chilling starts within 30 minutes of the food being cooked (with roast joints and large chickens, a longer time may be allowed)
- the blast-chiller is ready for use at the time required
- the blast-chiller is filled with the same dishes (if possible)
- mixed loads consist of dishes which take the same length of time to reach the required temperature
- the food is chilled to between 0°C and 3°C within 90 minutes from start of chilling
- once chilling is complete, the food is transported without delay to the chill store.

Containers must be stacked so that the air can circulate around them. Many cook-chill units use purpose-built trolleys to ensure this and to reduce the amount of handling. After chilling, the trolley and its load of containers are wheeled into the chilled store where they remain until required.

There will be special instructions for those dishes which are chilled without being covered.

Monitoring and recording temperatures

Your responsibilities may include:

- checking the temperature of the food after chilling. Use a temperature probe which you have dipped in a sanitising solution, or wiped with a sanitising cloth
- recording the temperature and the time it has taken to chill the food. Be accurate and write neatly so there is no doubt over what you have written down. If your 8°C is mistaken for 5°C, managers might be unaware of a serious problem.

Opening the chiller door more than necessary increases chilling time and wastes energy. To avoid this, many blast-chillers have built-in probes which are placed in a sample of dishes. The probe is linked to an external display, so you can see what the temperature is at any time. There may also be an alarm system to indicate when the pre-set temperature has been reached, and an automatic system for recording temperatures.

The temperature reached at the end of blast-chilling and the time taken are critical control points. Inform your manager at once if you find variations, or encounter a problem.

Transporting to the storage area

Some cook-chill production units are designed so that trolleys of food can be pushed into the blast-chiller through one door, and when ready out the other door directly into the chill store.

If the design of your workplace is different from this, you will have further to push the trolley. Make the journey as quickly as you can, and allow nothing to interrupt it – unless your safety or that of your colleagues is at serious risk.

At central production unit

Cooking ← Preparation

Portioning

Blast chilling → Storage (up to 5 days) 3°C → Transport (chilled)

Service points

Reheated

Reheated

Reheated

Storing cook-chill food

Cook-chill foods must be kept within the range 0°C to 3°C. At lower temperatures the food freezes, harming the quality. At higher temperatures eating quality also suffers, and the risks of food poisoning become serious.

Cook-chill stores have external monitors so you can see what the temperature is at any time. There is usually a device which sounds an alarm if the temperature goes outside the range.

If there is no alarm system, or if you are unsure whether the alarm has been heard by a manager or supervisor, at once inform the person in charge.

The sooner the temperature can be restored to the right level, the better the chance of saving the contents of the cook-chill store. Small temperature variations, quickly corrected, may be acceptable – but this decision is for management to take, not you.

When trolleys are used for storing food (normally the same ones on which the food was blast-chilled), the space between each container allows good air circulation. When the containers are kept on shelves, or on trolleys which have not been purpose-built for the size of container used, you should stack them so that:

- cold air can circulate freely around each container
- containers are above floor level and away from the door, to keep them out of draughts which might cause temperature variation.

Cook-chill stores should not be used for any other food. The risk of cross contamination, e.g. from uncooked meat, is too great. Furthermore, keeping other food in the store would increase the number of times the door is opened and shut. This would cause unacceptable variation in the temperature of cook-chill foods.

Stock rotation

Food that has been stored longest should be used first.

You will be familiar with the rule *first-in, first-out* from earlier sections of this book. Not following it in a cook-chill system can be very costly because food not used within five days of being cooked must be destroyed.

Problems occur when people put trolleys or containers in the most convenient space every time (e.g. near the door). Or when people don't take the trouble to look at the labels of what is already in the store, so you end up with stocks of the same dish in several places.

To prevent this happening, follow a proper routine for labelling and/or positioning trolleys. It should be as clear as possible to the people issuing or collecting containers from the chill store, where stocks of each dish are kept and which ones to use first.

Keeping records

The efficient running of cook-chill systems depends on management knowing the pattern of stock usage. This helps to:

- decide what and how much food to purchase
- plan production
- cross-check quantity of food used with the numbers of meals served
- compare value of food purchased with income received/value of meals served.

So that this information is available and accurate, you will be expected to complete various forms and documents when you take food into the chill store, and on any occasion you remove food.

Monitoring temperature

There may be an automatic system for recording the temperature of the chill store, throughout the day and night and all the time the store is in use. The result is like an endless graph, with temperature on one axis, the day and time on the other.

Some equipment produces a printout of the temperature at certain intervals, e.g. every two hours.

If the recording is done manually, you will have a log book or temperature record sheet on which to write the temperature at particular times of the day (e.g. first thing in the morning, at mid-day, and in the late afternoon).

Security and cleanliness

The safety of cook-chill foods depends on the very highest standards of hygiene – in chilled storage, and in every other area where food is handled. There will be a cleaning schedule or rota in your workplace to ensure that the chill store is cleaned regularly and thoroughly.

Some aspects may be done by cleaning-operatives on a contract basis, e.g. cleaning the walls and fixed shelves. Others will be done by you or colleagues, using cleaning equipment and methods specially designed for a cook-chill operation.

Good security is essential because of the considerable value of food stocks. But there are two other reasons for controlling access to the stores:

- unauthorised personnel are unlikely to know, and may not have the incentive to follow, procedures regarding hygiene, recording stock movements, and stock rotation
- to reduce the risk of someone deliberately making food stocks unsafe – by a person with a grudge against your employer, or by a copycat of those who have sabotaged food sold through supermarkets.

NVQ
SVQ

Skills check
Cook-chill
food
Unit 2ND15

leve

2

For help to answer questions relating to:

Health and safety

safe working practices

The hazards will include handling large, heavy and/or awkward containers, possibly in difficult situations (e.g. very low temperatures), moving loaded trolleys, exposure to very low temperatures (e.g. working in the chill store), and using mechanical equipment for packing food.

hygienic clothing

High standards of personal hygiene are essential in a cook-chill system. To prevent cross contamination between uncooked and cooked food, there are usually rules – and distinctive colour uniforms – to discourage people moving from one area to another during working time.

Food hygiene

importance of good hygiene

Because cook-chill food passes through the dangerous temperature zone at three stages, hygiene standards have to be strict.

importance of time and temperature

The time the food spends in the danger zone must also be strictly controlled, e.g. 30 minutes to portion and pack the food, 90 minutes to reduce its temperature to under 3°C.

main contamination threats

It is important that there are none. This is why cook-chill food should be stored separately from any other food, why strict stock rotation is required, and why standards of cleanliness must be very high.

sealing and labelling containers

Sealing the containers protects the food from contamination and spoilage by contact with the air. The label says what the contents are, and when they must be used by.

monitoring and recording temperature

If the temperature gets higher than 3°C, or lower than 0°C, then the food may have to be destroyed. If there is a problem with the food quality, or it is found to be contaminated, management will wish to check each stage of the process and in particular the temperature records while the food was in storage.

Product knowledge

portion control

If too much is put in the container, you are likely to run short, and customers will be getting more than they should. There is a risk that the food will not chill quickly enough, or that it overfills the container with the result that it dries out.

Putting too little in the container means customers are cheated, chilling time will be too long, and the food may dry out because there is not enough for the container size.

quality points when portioning

Some allowance may have to be made because the food is not hot, the sauce will be added later, and there is no garnish. But in other respects, the appearance and smell of the food should be what you expect of the same dish, freshly prepared.

stock rotation

The efficiency of cook-chill systems depends on matching production with demand. If poor stock rotation results in food passing the 5-day limit and having to be destroyed, this could result in shortages. It is also wasteful and expensive.

security of the chill store

People not authorised to go into the chill store may not follow the procedures which safeguard hygiene and stock control. They may also have the intention to cause harm.

Self-check questions

1 Describe how you should push a loaded trolley to avoid back injury. (See page 60.)

2 What rules must you follow with regard to work clothing?

3 Describe how you should wash your hands before starting work. On what other occasions must you wash your hands?

4 For three of the dishes you portion and pack, say what equipment you use, and describe how the food is placed in the container.

5 For these same dishes, give examples of problems which would affect the quality.

6 Why is timing so important in a cook-chill system? What is the maximum time allowed for a) portioning and packing food, and b) blast-chilling?

7 Describe how cook-chill dishes should be positioned in the chill store to ensure proper stock rotation.

8 If you were asked to carry out a thorough inspection of the chill store, what would you check?

Use this to check your progress against the performance criteria.

Element 1

Portion, pack and blast-chill food

Get your preparation areas and equipment ready for use — PC

Select food of the type, quality and quantity required — PC

△ Meat/poultry dishes, joints/whole chickens, vegetables/fruits, fish dishes, sauces/soups, egg dishes, desserts

Identify/report problems with equipment and freshness or quantity of food — PC

Portion, pack and cover food — PC

Blast-chill, seal and label food — PC

Transport food containers to storage area — PC

Handle food containers correctly during transportation — PC

Accurately monitor and record food temperatures — PC

Prioritise and carry out your work in an organised, efficient and safe manner — PC

Element 2

Store cook-chill food

Store cook-chill items in hygienic conditions — PC1

Follow stock rotation procedures and use stocks in date order — PC2

Keep accurate records of stock movement — PC3

Handle correctly food items — PC4

Accurately monitor and record food temperatures — PC5

Keep storage areas clean, tidy and free from rubbish — PC6

Keep storage areas secure from unauthorised access — PC7

Identify and report problems with the storage of cook-chill items — PC8

Prioritise and carry out your work in an organised, efficient and safe manner — PC9

Portioning, packing, blast-freezing and storing **cook-freeze** food

Portioning, packing and blast-freezing food

Cook-freeze is a specialised food production and distribution system used by a few, very large catering operations. It means quite a range of dishes can be offered to several thousand or more customers in hospitals, schools, factories, etc., spread over a large geographical area.

All the preparation and cooking are done in bulk at a central site. Production can be planned around the times of the year when particular foods are readily available and lower in price. Efficient use can be made of large-scale equipment and skilled staff. Some cook-freeze units operate on a non-stop basis with shift working.

The food is rapidly frozen using special equipment and can be kept deep frozen for several weeks or longer without the quality suffering. As required, it is transported to the satellite kitchens or service points, and there quickly and easily reheated.

Comparison with cook-chill

Under similar operating conditions, the running costs of a cook-freeze system are higher than they are for cook-chill (see Section 25). This is because a lot of energy is required to:

- blast-freeze the food
- store the frozen food at very low temperatures
- transport the food in its frozen state to the points where it is required. This has to be done in vehicles which can keep the food deep-frozen. For short distances, special insulated containers can be used.

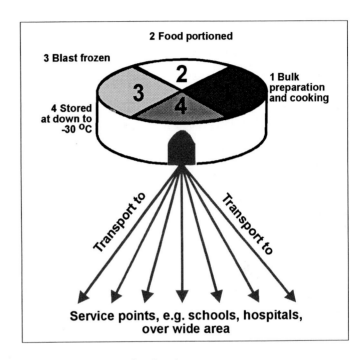

What happens to the food

If you put food in a freezer at home, it eventually freezes solid. But this may take several hours and large ice crystals form in the food. These damage the cell structure of the food, which harms its eating quality and nutritional value. You can get an idea of the damage caused from the pool of liquid which comes out of such food as it defrosts.

The equipment used to freeze food in a cook-freeze production unit is many times more powerful than domestic or commercial freezers (which are designed to keep food frozen). Blast-freezers, as they are known, take the temperature of the food down to $-5°C$ within 90 minutes, and then to $-18°C$. The freezers into which the food is transferred keep it at a temperature as low as $-30°C$.

Not all food is suited to this process. One problem is that flour-thickened sauces, soups, stews and gravies tend to break down (or separate). This can be overcome by using a special type of flour, and making changes to the recipe.

Another problem is that some foods spoil, even at these very low temperatures. Dishes made with pork, poultry and fish – which contain quite a lot of unsaturated fats – can develop a rancid taste after 2 or 3 months.

Vegetables and fruit with a fragile structure and high water content do not freeze well. Strawberries and tomatoes, for example, collapse into a mushy heap.

Types of food and quality points

Cook-freeze operations devote a lot of effort to developing dishes that freeze well. They want to offer a comprehensive, varied and nutritionally-balanced menu to their customers. A menu made up largely or entirely of frozen dishes that can be got ready for service with minimum effort.

This is not the same as a frozen food supplier specialising in a limited range, e.g. ethnic dishes, or one type of dish only, e.g. gâteaux.

But if you do not work in a cook-freeze operation at the moment, you will get a good idea of the dishes which freeze well by looking at the catalogues of different frozen food suppliers, and the range sold in supermarkets and frozen food centres.

Cook-freeze operations are likely to include:

- *meat and poultry dishes* – those which have a sauce or gravy, and which are made with good-quality, very lean meat. Stews and casseroles tend to be more successful than roast meats. Plain, grilled meats are not suitable

- *joints and whole chickens* – there has to be a limit on the weight and size of these, otherwise the freezing process would take too long: not more than 2½ kg and not more than 10 cm in thickness or height

- *vegetables and fruit* – the range is not as wide as you may think. This is because there is such a good choice of frozen vegetables that can be cooked in a few minutes, e.g. frozen peas (boiled or steamed) and frozen chips (deep fried or oven-baked). But some vegetable and fruit dishes are suited to the cook-freeze system, where they are regenerated (i.e. thawed and reheated in one step) in a sealed container in an oven, e.g. cauliflower in cheese sauce, vegetable bakes, puréed spinach and apple crumble

- *fish dishes* – those with sauces, in breadcrumbed or batter coating

- *sauces and soups* – most are suitable, but those which rely on eggs as a thickener, or which have a lot of butter or cream in them are better made fresh, or replaced by another type of sauce

- *egg dishes* – scrambled eggs and omelettes give reasonably satisfactory results

- *desserts* – those which can be served hot, e.g. pies and tarts, and cold dishes, e.g. trifles, fruit salads.

Working hygienically

The strictest standards of hygiene are necessary in cook-freeze systems. Harmful bacteria still present in the food after cooking, or introduced during the portioning and packing stage, will survive the freezing temperatures. And when the food is regenerated, these bacteria will multiply to dangerous levels given the opportunity (e.g. because of a delay in service).

Equipment and working areas must be regularly and thoroughly cleaned and sanitised.

Most cook-freeze operations insist that all staff, before entering the work area:

- thoroughly wash and scrub forearms, hands and finger nails with a suitable sanitising soap

- take a shower before changing into clean uniform

- wear colour-coded uniform according to the area of the kitchen they are working in, and special footwear

- after changing, wash forearms and hands again in a sanitising solution and walk through a disinfectant footbath.

Portioning and packing

The whole cook-freeze process will follow a detailed production plan. Delays create food safety risks and may increase energy costs (e.g. if equipment is lying idle). Before you start each task, check carefully that you:

- know what has to be done, and how the food is to be arranged in the container

- have the containers/packaging you need ready to hand – the right size and quantity, thoroughly cleaned (for re-usable ones), or removed from their outer packaging (for single-use ones)

- have the equipment required for portioning and handling the food

For hygiene reasons, you should:

- wear disposable gloves. Before beginning a new task, thoroughly wash and dry your hands and put on a fresh pair of gloves

- avoid touching the inside of the containers.

To protect the quality of the food:

- handle aluminium foil, paper and plastic containers carefully as they are not very rigid

- pack the food to an even depth, of not more than 50 mm at any point (35 mm if a microwave oven is being used to regenerate the food)

- keep the food away from the edges of the containers (as far as possible)

- cover the food, sealing the container if necessary.

Packing the food in a cook-freeze production unit. The sealed containers go straight on to the trolley (right of photo), and into the blast freezer.

Labelling

The label is the only practical way of telling people what is in a container, once you have packed it and put the lid on. The system will break down if labelling is not accurate, or if batches of food slip through without any label.

Besides identifying the contents, the label says:

- when it must be used by – beyond this date, it will not be safe to serve

- when the food was packed – usually the date and time, and a batch number. If there is a quality problem, then each stage of the dish's life can be investigated, including the raw ingredients used

- how many portions it will serve

- special dietary information, e.g. suitable for vegetarians

- instructions for regenerating, e.g. type of oven to be used, temperature, timing, lid on or off, stirring before service, special finishing touches, etc.

Attach the label firmly. There will usually be a particular place for it to go, e.g. bottom right-hand corner. This saves time for the other people handling the container (e.g. in storage, transport and service), as they know where to look.

Blast-freezing

The rule which cook-freeze operators work to, is that freezing starts within 30 minutes of the food being cooked. In 90 minutes the food must be frozen to –5°C or lower.

Blast-freezers do this by blowing very cold air over and around the food. In some types, the food goes through a sort of tunnel. The speed is controlled by the machine so that the food emerges at the end of the tunnel when it is sufficiently frozen.

Another type, which freezes the food in around half-an-hour, uses liquid nitrogen at a temperature of –196°C.

Because blast-freezers are very advanced pieces of equipment, the controls over how long the food is allowed to freeze and the temperatures reached are mostly automatic. You need to be familiar with how the controls work, and what to do should a problem occur.

Monitoring and recording temperatures

Cook-freeze operations have to follow very strict procedures to protect food safety. This is partly because of the way cook-freeze works – making possible a long delay between the time of cooking and the time of service. And partly because of the large scale of the operation – many people would become ill if something serious goes wrong.

You will have to play your part in these procedures, by recording temperatures reached at particular stages, and the time. Write neatly, and be accurate. If you become aware of a problem, something unusual or out of place, tell your manager or supervisor at once.

Transporting to the storage area

Immediately after blast-freezing, transfer the food to the deep-freeze storage.

In some operations, individual containers are put into larger boxes or cartons at this stage. Each carton takes a number of containers, making handling and storage easier. Another reason for packing in cartons is that aluminium-foil, and most other types of single-use container, are quite difficult to pick up.

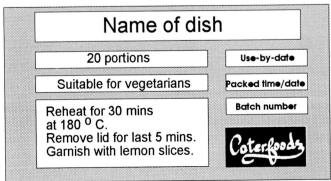

Information that might go on the label for a cook-freeze dish.

Storing cook-freeze food

You put yourself in great danger if you remain in the freezer store for more than a few minutes at a time. Wear the protective clothing supplied, and make sure that someone knows you have gone into the freezer. Then if there is an accident, help should not be long in coming.

Temperature

The temperature should be kept:

- in the range −20°C to −30°C so that the activity of food-spoilage organisms is kept to the minimum

- as constant as possible – an increase of even a few degrees will cause some of the ice crystals in the food to melt. As the temperature drops again this liquid re-freezes, forming bigger, more damaging crystals.

The packaging

If the packaging is damaged:

- serious moisture loss can occur. This leads to freezer burn, when the surface of the food discolours and gets a sort of dry, spongy texture

- frost (fine ice crystals) build up on the food. Cold air cannot hold as much moisture as warm air. If warm air enters the freezer, for example when the door is opened, the extra moisture turns into fine ice as the air cools again, and collects on exposed food and food packaging.

Stock rotation

One of the reasons operators use the cook-freeze system is to reduce food wastage. Dishes can be reheated as needed, in the quantity required.

This advantage can be easily lost through poor stock rotation. Suppose the most recent stock is taken from the freezer every time. The older stock is left untouched at the back of the freezer. Not only will the quality of this stock not be as good as it should be, but the time will come when it has to be destroyed. Frozen food which has passed the date indicated on the label cannot be used.

To avoid this sort of problem, the stock in the freezer must be kept in date order. Follow the system in your workplace so that you put new stocks in the right place.

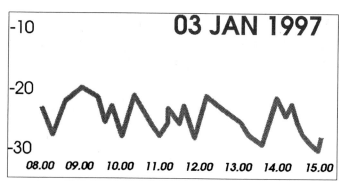

Print-out from the temperature monitoring equipment on a cook-freeze store.

Monitoring temperature and keeping records

The deep-freeze will have an alarm device to alert the attention of someone in charge if the temperature rises above the operating range. A display (usually near the door of the freezer) will indicate what the temperature is inside.

There will be a system for recording the temperature at intervals during the day and night. Management and the authorities responsible for enforcing food safety will look at these records on their regular inspections, and when a problem has occurred. They want to be satisfied that the temperature has been kept within the acceptable range.

Some types of equipment automatically record the temperature. If this is not the case, follow carefully the instructions on when you should note the temperature, and write neatly.

Security and cleanliness

The value of the stocks in the freezer is considerable. The other reason for strict security is that people not familiar with the procedures may:

- take the most recent stock – because they do not know about stock rotation

- wear inappropriate clothing – with the result they get frostbite

- cause a food safety problem – because they have not followed the hygiene rules.

You, and others who have access to the freezer, will be expected to keep it tidy:

- remove packaging which is no longer required

- if you drop something, clear it up quickly

- handle containers and packages so they do not get damaged

- position trolleys so they do not block access to other parts of the freezer

- move trolleys so they do not knock into other trolleys, the freezer walls or the doorway.

For help to answer questions relating to:

Use this to check your progress against the performance criteria.

Health and safety

safe working practices

The hazards include handling difficult loads, pushing trolleys and exposure to very low temperatures.

hygienic clothing

To prevent contamination of the food, there will be strict rules on work clothing, and probably which colour uniform to wear in the portioning and packing area.

Food hygiene

importance of good hygiene

Hygiene standards have to be very high in cook-freeze production because of the risks involved.

importance of time and temperature

Any bacteria which survive cooking will increase rapidly in numbers if too long is taken to portion and pack the food. Although they are inactive while the food is frozen, inadequate reheating or delays at service stage may lead to further growth in numbers of the bacteria and food poisoning.

main contamination threats

Other foreign objects which could get into the food (e.g. poor personal hygiene, dirty equipment/work area, harmful cleaning substances and pieces of packaging). Usually the portioning and packing area and the people who work in it are kept separate from preparation and cooking activities. This is to prevent cross-contamination from uncooked to cooked food.

sealing and labelling containers

Sealing protects the food from contamination, freezer burn and frosting. The label gives vital information on what the contents are, when they must be used by, how they should be regenerated, etc.

monitoring and recording temperature

Management and those responsible for enforcing food safety have to check that the requirements for cook-freeze operations are being met.

Product knowledge

portion control

The amount of food you are given will be carefully worked out so that the portion size is correct. A small variation on what you put in each container will soon become a problem when the food is meant to make, say, 250 portions.

stock rotation

Food which has passed the date by which it should be used has to be destroyed. This is unlikely to happen if proper stock rotation is followed.

security of storage areas

People not authorised to go into the freezer store may be unaware of, or decide to ignore the procedures which protect their personal safety and the safety of the food.

Self-check questions

1 Describe the safety precautions you should follow when working in the freezer store.

2 Describe the correct way to lift a large container of food from a low shelf to the top of a trolley. What should you consider before starting the task?

3 State the rules you should follow at work for a) personal hygiene, b) wearing uniform.

4 For four of the dishes you portion and pack, state how you measure the portion size accurately.

5 For the same dishes, give the points which require attention when you place the food in the container (e.g. overlapping slices of meat).

6 Why is it important that food goes into the blast-freezer on time? What should you do if for some reason this cannot happen?

7 Where in the freezer do you place new stocks of food? How are these kept separate from older stocks of the same food?

8 What temperature should the freezer in your workplace be operating at? How is it monitored and recorded?

Element 1

Portion, pack and blast-freeze food

Get your preparation areas and equipment ready for use — **PC1** ☐

Select food of the type, quality and quantity required — **PC2** ☐

⚠ Meat/poultry dishes, joints/whole chickens, vegetables/fruits, fish dishes, sauces/soups, egg dishes, desserts

Identify/report problems with equipment and freshness or quantity of food — **PC3** ☐

Portion, pack and cover food — **PC4** ☐

Blast-freeze, seal and label food — **PC5** ☐

Transport food containers to storage area — **PC6** ☐

Handle food containers correctly during transportation — **PC7** ☐

Accurately monitor and record food temperatures — **PC8** ☐

Prioritise and carry out your work in an organised, efficient and safe manner — **PC9** ☐

Element 2

Store cook-freeze food

Store cook-freeze items in hygienic conditions — **PC1** ☐

Follow stock rotation procedures and use stocks in date order — **PC2** ☐

Keep accurate records of stock movement — **PC3** ☐

Handle correctly food items — **PC4** ☐

Accurately monitor and record food temperatures — **PC5** ☐

Keep storage areas clean, tidy and free from rubbish — **PC6** ☐

Keep storage areas secure from unauthorised access — **PC7** ☐

Identify and report problems with the storage of cook-freeze items — **PC8** ☐

Prioritise and carry out your work in an organised, efficient and safe manner — **PC9** ☐

Index

Index

Index